AN INTRODUCTION TO
BUSINESS
ETHICS

AN INTRODUCTION TO
BUSINESS
ETHICS

Third Edition

Joseph DesJardins

College of St. Benedict/St. John's University

Boston   Burr Ridge, IL   Dubuque, IA   New York   San Francisco   St. Louis
Bangkok   Bogotá   Caracas   Kuala Lumpur   Lisbon   London   Madrid   Mexico City
Milan   Montreal   New Delhi   Santiago   Seoul   Singapore   Sydney   Taipei   Toronto

McGraw-Hill
Higher Education

A Division of The McGraw-Hill Companies

Published by McGraw-Hill, an imprint of The McGraw-Hill Companies, Inc., 1221 Avenue of the Americas, New York, NY 10020. Copyright © 2009, 2006, 2003. All rights reserved. No part of this publication may be reproduced or distributed in any form or by any means, or stored in a database or retrieval system, without the prior written consent of The McGraw-Hill Companies, Inc., including, but not limited to, in any network or other electronic storage or transmission, or broadcast for distance learning.

This book is printed on acid-free paper.

1 2 3 4 5 6 7 8 9 0 DOC/DOC 0 9 8

ISBN: 978-0-07-338658-4
MHID: 0-07-338658-8

Editor in Chief: *Mike Ryan*
Publisher: *Frank Mortimer*
Sponsoring Editor: *Mark Georgiev*
Marketing Manager: *Pamela Cooper*
Developmental Editor: *Marley Magaziner*
Project Editor: *Regina Ernst*
Manuscript Editor: *Leslie Ann Weber*
Text Designer: *Srdjan Savanovic*
Cover Designer: *Ashley Bedell*
Photo Research: *Nora Agbayani*
Production Supervisor: *Richard DeVitto*
Composition: *10/12 Palatino by Laserwords Private Limited*
Printing: *45# New Era Matte Plus, R. R. Donnelley & Sons*

Cover: ©Matthias Clamer/ Getty Images

Credits: *p. 1* Royalty-Free/Corbis, *17* Ryan McVay/Getty Images, *45* Royalty-Free/Corbis, *72* Stockbyte/Punchstock Images, *91* PhotoDisc/Getty Images, *113* Library of Congress Prints and Photographs Division [LC-DIG-ppmsca-03420], *140* Digital Vision, *168* The McGraw-Hill Companies, Inc./Photo by Eric Misko, *190* Elite Images Photography, *213* The McGraw-Hill Companies, Inc./John Flournoy, photographer, *232* D. Falconer/PhotoLink/Getty Images, *260* Keith Brofsky/Getty Images, Brand X Pictures

Library of Congress Cataloging-in-Publication Data
DesJardins, Joseph R.
    An introduction to business ethics / Joseph DesJardins.—3rd ed.
        p. cm.
    Includes index.
    ISBN-13: 978-0-07-338658-4 (alk. paper)
    ISBN 0-07-338658-8 (alk. paper)
    1. Business ethics. I. Title.
    HF5387.D392 2009
    174′.4—dc22

                                                        2008005187

The Internet addresses listed in the text were accurate at the time of publication. The inclusion of a Web site does not indicate an endorsement by the authors of McGraw-Hill, and McGraw-Hill does not guarantee the accuracy of the information presented at these sites.

www.mhhe.com

About the Author

J oe DesJardins is Associate Provost and Academic Dean, and Professor of Philosophy, at the College of St. Benedict and St. John's University in Minnesota. He also serves as the Executive Director of the Society for Business Ethics. He received his B.A. (1973) from Southern Connecticut State University, and his M.A. (1976) and Ph.D. (1980) from the University of Notre Dame. He previously taught for twelve years at Villanova University.

His books include *Environmental Ethics: An Introduction to Environmental Philosophy; Contemporary Issues in Business Ethics* (edited with John McCall); *Business Ethics: Decision Making for Personal Integrity and Social Justice*, with Laura Hartman (McGraw-Hill, 2007); and *Business, Ethics, and the Environment: Imagining a Sustainable Future.*

To Linda

Contents

Preface to the Third Edition

My overarching goal in the third edition of this text remains what it was for the first edition: "to provide a clear, concise, and reasonably comprehensive introductory survey of the ethical choices available to us in business." This book arose from the challenges encountered in my own teaching of business ethics. Over the years I have taught business ethics in many settings and with many formats. I have sometimes relied on an anthology of readings; other times I have emphasized case studies. I have taught business ethics as a lecture course and in a small seminar. Most recently, I have taught business ethics exclusively to undergraduates in a liberal arts setting. It is difficult to imagine another discipline that is as multidisciplinary, taught in as many formats and as many contexts, by faculty with as many different backgrounds and with as many different aims, as business ethics.

Yet, while the students, format, pedagogy, and teaching goals change, the basic philosophical and conceptual structure for the field remains relatively stable. There are a range of constituencies with whom business interacts: employees, customers, suppliers, governments, society. Each of these relationships creates ethical responsibilities and every adult unavoidably will interact with business in several of these roles. A course in business ethics, therefore, should ask students to examine this range of responsibilities from the perspective of employee, customer, and citizen as well as from the perspective of business manager or executive. Students should consider such issues in terms of both the type of lives they themselves wish to lead and the type of public policy for governing business that they are willing to support.

My hope was that this book could provide the basic framework for examining the range of ethical issues that arise in a business context. With this basic framework provided, individual instructors would then be free to develop their courses in various ways. I have been grateful to learn that this book is being used in a wide variety of settings. Many people have chosen to use it in a stand-alone course in business ethics as a supplement to the instructor's own lectures, an anthologized collection of readings, a series of case studies, or some combination of all three. Others have chosen to use this text to cover the ethics component of another course in such business-related disciplines as management, marketing, accounting, and human resources. The book also has been used to provide coverage of business-related topics in more general courses in applied or professional ethics. I take this variety of uses as evidence that the first edition was reasonably successful in achieving its goals.

A new edition offers an author the opportunity to correct the shortcomings and mistakes of the earlier editions. On one hand, it is gratifying to have the opportunity to correct one's mistakes. However, this opportunity also creates the temptation to write a much longer book. In this third edition, I have tried to correct mistakes, update cases and examples, clarify sections that were less than clear, and explicate some of the analyses that were less than fully developed. But I have also tried to do this without sacrificing the primary goal of providing a concise and clear introduction to business ethics.

Readers of the previous editions will find a familiar format. Each chapter begins with a discussion case developed from actual events. The intent of these cases is to raise questions and get students thinking and talking about the ethical issues that will be introduced in the chapter. The text of each chapter then tries to do three things: identify and explain the ethical issues involved, direct students to an examination of these issues from the points of view of various stakeholders, and lead students through some initial steps of a philosophical evaluation of these issues. The emphasis remains on encouraging student thinking, reasoning, and decision making rather than on providing answers or promoting a specific set of conclusions.

This third edition differs from previous editions in several ways. I have tried to update cases and examples throughout the book, relying more on actual events than on hypothetical cases. I have added an entirely new chapter (chapter 4) that covers topics of corporate culture, corporate governance, ethical leadership, and compliance. Chapter 7 (formerly chapter 6) now includes an expanded treatment of ethical responsibilities in accounting and finance.

This third edition continues to develop a theme that was introduced with the second edition. The years since the initial edition of this book have witnessed an increasing demand from accrediting agencies that business ethics be among the areas in which schools and teachers are able to demonstrate student learning. I began to address this requirement in the second edition by including various pedagogical supports that could help teachers create assessable learning goals for business ethics. This edition has refined opening goals and objectives for each chapter to focus more on student learning than on teaching or course goals. Once again, end of chapter reflection and review questions are targeted at reinforcing the learning goals established at the start of each chapter.

ACKNOWLEDGMENTS

As with the first edition, my greatest debt in writing this book is to those scholars engaged in the academic research of business ethics. I have tried to acknowledge their work wherever I have relied on it in this text, but in case I have missed anyone I hope this general acknowledgment can serve to repay my debt to the business ethics community. I again acknowledge two members of that community who deserve special mention and thanks. My own work in business ethics has, for over 20 years, benefited from the friendships of John McCall and Ron Duska. They will no doubt find much in this book that sounds familiar. Substantial portions of chapters 6 through 9 owe much to their thinking. Twenty years of friendship and collaboration tend to blur the lines of authorship, but it is fair to say that I have learned much more from John and Ron than they from me.

The first edition benefited from the advice of a number of people who read and commented on various chapters. An early version of chapter 10 appeared in Norman Bowie's *Blackwell's Guide to Business Ethics* and I benefited from Norm's advice and suggestions in writing that chapter. I've also learned a good deal about economics and sustainable development from my colleague Ernie Diedrich. Chapter 10 could not have been written without his help. The two chapters on marketing ethics were helped by the thoughtful comments of Patrick Murphy, whose own work was the initial prod to broaden my understanding of marketing ethics beyond the customary and narrow topic of advertising. The second edition benefited from conversations with Denis Arnold and Christopher Pynes at the University of Tennessee and Laura Hartman of DePaul.

The following teachers and scholars were gracious enough to review the initial manuscript for McGraw-Hill: Dr. Edwin A. Coolbaugh—Johnson & Wales University; Jill Dieterlie—Eastern Michigan University; Glenn Moots—Northwood University; Jane Hammang-Buhl—Marygrove College; Ilona Motsif—Trinity College; Bonnie Fremgen—University of Notre Dame; Sheila Bradford—Tulsa Community College; Donald Skubik—California Baptist University; Sandra Powell—Weber State University; Gerald Williams—Seton Hall University; Leslie Connell—University of Central Florida; Brad K. Wilburn—Santa Clara University; Carlo Filice—SUNY, Genesco.

The third edition benefited from the thorough and thoughtful reviews of

- Brian Barnes, University of Louisville
- Marvin Brown, University of San Francisco
- Patrice DiQuinzio, Muhlenberg College
- Julian Friedland, Leeds School of Business, University of Colorado at Boulder
- Derek S. Jeffreys, The University of Wisconsin, Green Bay
- Albert B. Maggio, Jr., bicoastal-law.com
- Andy Wible, Muskegon Community College

Joseph DesJardins

1 CHAPTER

Why Study Ethics?

L E A R N I N G   O B J E C T I V E S

After reading this chapter, you will be able to:

- Identify reasons why the study of ethics is important;
- Explain the nature and meaning of business ethics;
- Explain the difference between ethical values and other values;
- Clarify the difference between ethics and the law;
- Describe the distinction between ethics and ethos;
- Distinguish between personal morality, virtues, and social ethics;
- Identify ethical issues within a case description.

DISCUSSION CASE: Enron

On December 2, 2001, Enron Corporation, once listed as the seventh largest corporation among the Fortune 500, declared bankruptcy. (See the discussion case that opens chapter 6 for more detail.) In the months and years that followed, numerous other major corporations were found to have been guilty of similar accounting and financial frauds. A wave of scandals swept though the corporate world as fraudulent and dishonest practices were uncovered at such firms as WorldCom, Tyco, Aldelphia, Global Crossing, Qwest, Merrill Lynch, Citigroup Salomon Smith Barney, Marsh and McClennen, Credit Suisse First Boston, and even the New York Stock Exchange itself. But none of these captured the public's attention as did Enron.

Enron's collapse followed public disclosure of significant debts that had been concealed by complicated and fraudulent accounting practices. Not only were Enron's top executives deeply involved in this scheme, they personally received tens of millions of dollars from it. This massive ethical fraud was perpetrated with the support of Enron's accounting and auditing firm, Arthur Andersen, at the time one of the top five international accounting firms. Andersen played both ends of a conflict of interest by earning money both as Enron's auditor and as consultants in concealing these debts. To make matters worse, while the stock price was collapsing, senior executives sold hundreds of millions of dollars worth of stock to unwary investors, making personal fortunes from the collapse. During this same period, employees were prevented from selling their own stock that was held in their 401(k) retirement plans. Arthur Andersen's accountants, meanwhile, were busily shredding hundreds of documents that could have been used in criminal and civil legal cases. Enron's board of directors, and particularly their audit committee, twice waived internal rules of ethical conduct that prohibited the conflict of interest practices that enabled Enron executives to profit at the expense of shareholders.

DISCUSSION QUESTIONS

1. Identify any ethical issues involved in the Enron case.
2. Identify all the people who were harmed by Enron's collapse and explain the ways in which they were harmed.
3. Do you think that corporate scandals such as Enron are the result mostly of unethical individuals, or do you think that organizations can be responsible? Was this a failure of individuals, of organizational structure, or of government?
4. What would you change to try to prevent future Enrons?

1.1 WHY STUDY BUSINESS ETHICS?

Why should anyone study business ethics? As recently as the mid-1990s, articles in such major publications as the *Wall Street Journal*, the *Harvard Business Review*, and *U.S. News and World Report* questioned the legitimacy and value of teaching classes in business ethics. Few disciplines faced the amount of skepticism that commonly confronted courses in business ethics. Many students believed that, like "jumbo shrimp," business ethics was an oxymoron. Many also viewed ethics as a mixture of sentimentality and personal opinion that would interfere with the efficient functioning of business. After all, who's to say what's right or wrong?

Throughout the 1980s and 1990s, this skeptical attitude was as common among business practitioners as it was among students. But this simply is no longer the case in contemporary business. The questions today are less about *why* or *should* ethics be a part of business, than about *which* ethics should guide business decisions and *how* can ethics be integrated within business.[1] Students unfamiliar with ethical issues will find themselves as unprepared for careers in business as students who are unfamiliar with accounting and finance. Indeed, it is fair to say that students will not be fully prepared even within fields such as accounting, finance, human resource management, marketing, and management unless they are familiar with the ethical issues that arise specifically within those fields. You simply will not be prepared for a career in accounting, finance, or any area of business if you are unfamiliar with the ethical issues of these fields.

Why has this change come about? To answer this question, consider who was harmed by the collapse of Enron. Stockholders lost over a billion dollars in stock value. Thousands of employees lost their jobs, their retirement funds, and their health care benefits. Consumers in California suffered from energy shortages and blackouts that were caused by Enron's manipulation of the market. Hundreds of businesses that worked with Enron as suppliers suffered economic loss with the loss of a large client. Enron's accounting firm, Arthur Andersen, went out of business as a direct result. The wider Houston community was also hurt by the loss of a major employer and community benefactor. Families of employees, investors, and suppliers were also hurt. Many of the individuals directly involved will themselves suffer criminal and civil punishment, including jail sentences for some. Indeed, it is hard to imagine anyone who was even loosely affiliated with Enron who did not suffer harm as a result of the ethical failings at Enron. Multiply this harm by the dozens of other companies implicated in similar scandals and one gets an idea of why ethics is no longer dismissed as irrelevant. The consequences of unethical behavior and unethical business institutions are too serious to be ignored.

Today, business managers have many reasons to be concerned with the ethical standards of their organizations. Perhaps the most straightforward reason is that the law requires it. In 2002, the U.S. Congress passed the Sarbanes-Oxley Act to address the wave of corporate and accounting scandals. Section 406 of that law, "Code of Ethics for Senior Financial Officers," requires that corporations have a Code of Ethics "applicable to its principal financial officer and comptroller or principal accounting officer, or persons performing similar functions." The Code must include standards that promote

1. honest and ethical conduct, including the ethical handling of actual or apparent conflicts of interest between personal and professional relationships;
2. full, fair, accurate, timely, and understandable disclosure in the periodic reports required to be filed by the issuer; and
3. compliance with applicable governmental rules and regulations.

Beyond these specific legal requirements, contemporary business managers have many other reasons to be concerned with ethical issues. Unethical behavior not only creates legal risks for a business, it creates financial and marketing risks as well. Managing these risks requires managers and executives to remain vigilant about their company's ethics. It is now clearer than ever that a company can lose in the marketplace, it can go out of business, and its employees can go to jail if no one is paying attention to the ethical standards of the firm. Ethical behavior and an ethical reputation can provide a competitive advantage, or disadvantage, in the marketplace and with customers, suppliers, and employees. Consumer boycotts based on allegations of unethical conduct have targeted such well-known firms as Nike, McDonalds, Home Depot, Gap, Shell Oil, Levi-Strauss, Donna Karen, K-Mart, and Wal-Mart. Managing ethically can also pay significant dividends in organizational structure and efficiency. Trust, loyalty, commitment, creativity, and initiative are just some of the organizational benefits that are more likely to flourish within ethically stable and credible organizations.

In 2003, Deloitte polled 5,000 directors of the top 4,000 publicly traded companies and reported that 98 percent believed that an ethics and compliance program was an essential part of corporate governance. Over 80 percent had developed formal codes of ethics beyond those required by Sarbanes-Oxley, and over 90 percent included statements concerning the company's obligations to employees, shareholders, suppliers, customers, and the community at large in their corporate code of ethics.[2] In practice, if not yet in theory, corporate America has adopted the stakeholder model of corporate social responsibility. Contemporary business now takes seriously its ethical responsibilities to a variety of stakeholders other than its shareholders.

For business students, the need to study ethics should now be as clear as the need to study the other subfields of business education. Without this background, students will be unprepared for a career in contemporary business. But even for students not anticipating a career in business management or business administration, familiarity with business ethics is just as crucial. It was not, after all, only the managers at Enron who suffered because of their ethical lapses. Our lives as employees, as consumers, as citizens are affected by decisions made within business institutions, and therefore everyone has good reasons for being concerned with the ethics of those decision makers.

The case for ethics is by now clear and persuasive. Business must take ethics into account and integrate ethics into its organizational structure. Students need to study business ethics. But what does this mean? What is *ethics* and what is *business ethics*? To begin our investigation let us turn to a more general question: Is ethics good for business?

1.2 VALUES AND ETHICS: DOING GOOD AND DOING WELL

As described in their best-selling book, *Built to Last: Successful Habits of Visionary Companies,* authors James Collins and Jerry Porras researched dozens of very successful companies looking for common practices that might explain their success. These companies not only outperformed their competitors in financial terms, they also have outperformed their competition over the long term. On average, the companies they studied were founded in 1897. Among their key findings was the fact that the truly exceptional and enduring companies all placed great emphasis on a set of core values. These core values are described as the "essential and enduring tenets" that help define the company and are "not to be compromised for financial gain or short-term expediency."[3]

Collins and Porras cite numerous examples of core values being articulated and promoted by the founders and CEOs of such companies as IBM, Johnson & Johnson, Hewlett Packard, Procter and Gamble, Wal-Mart, Merck, Motorola, Sony, Walt Disney, General Electric, and Philip Morris. Some companies made a commitment to customers as their core value; others focused on employees, their products, innovation, or even risk-taking. The common theme was that core values and a clear corporate purpose, what together are described as the organization's core ideology, were essential elements of enduring and financially successful companies.

These examples suggest that there are many different type of values. In general, we can think of values as those beliefs or standards that incline us to act or to choose in one way rather than another. Thus, the value that I place on an education leads me to study rather than play video games. I choose to spend my money on groceries rather than on a vacation because I value food more than relaxation. A company's core values, then, are those beliefs and principles that provide the ultimate guide in its decision making. Understood in this way, we can recognize that there can be many different types of values. There are financial, religious, historical, nutritional, political, scientific, and aesthetic values. Individuals can have their own personal values and, importantly, institutions also have values. Talk of a corporation's "culture" is a way of saying that a corporation has a set of identifiable values. All the companies described by Collins and Porras, as well as Enron, have been described as having strong corporate cultures and clear sets of values.

At first glance, *Built to Last* seems to reach an extremely attractive conclusion. The most successful companies all share in common a commitment to core values. This would seem to provide very persuasive reasons for any business to make a strong commitment to ethics. Good ethics seem to be connected to good business. Unfortunately, things are not as they appear. Collins and Porras are explicit in pointing out that while having a set of core values was essential in long-term success, they discovered no *right* set of core values. Their conclusion was that it was important only that companies have values, not that they have any particular values. In fact, executives at one of their "visionary" companies, Philip Morris, were described as defiant and self-righteous in their prosmoking ideology. The authors quote a *Fortune* magazine description of Philip Morris CEO Michael Miles as "ruthless, focused . . . cold-blooded." Miles is also quoted as saying "I see nothing morally wrong with the [tobacco] business. . . . I see nothing wrong with selling people products they don't need."[4]

Collins and Porras make a strong case for the conclusion that having a set of strong core values is important for the long-term financial success of a business. But, if these values can include ruthless and cold-blooded promotion of smoking, much more needs to be said about *ethical* values. One way to distinguish these various types of values is in terms of the ends that they serve. Financial values serve monetary ends, religious values serve spiritual ends, aesthetic values serve the end of beauty, and so forth. So, how are ethical values to be distinguished from these other types of values? What ends are served by ethics?

Values, in general, were earlier described as those beliefs or standards that incline us to act or choose in one way rather than another. Different types of values were distinguished by the various ends served by those acts and choices. Consider again the harm attributed to the ethical failures at Enron. Thousands of innocent people were hurt by the decisions made by some individuals seeking their own financial and egotistical aggrandizement. This example reveals two important elements of ethical values. First, ethical values serve the ends of human well-being. Acts and choices that aim to promote human well-being are acts and choices based on ethical values. Controversy may arise when we try to specify more precisely what is involved in human well-being, but we can start with some general observations. Happiness certainly is a part of it, as is respect, integrity, and meaning. Freedom and autonomy surely seem a part of human well-being, as do companionship and health.

Second, the well-being promoted by ethical values is not a personal and selfish well-being. After all, the Enron scandal resulted from many individuals seeking to promote their own well-being. Ethics requires that the promotion of human well-being be done impartially. From the perspective of ethics, no one person's well-being counts as more worthy than any other's. Ethical acts and choices should be acceptable and reasonable from all relevant points of view. Thus, we can offer an initial characterization of ethics and ethical values. Ethical values are those beliefs and principles that seek to promote human well-being in an impartial way.

Chapter 2 will examine the nature of philosophical ethics in more detail. But we should acknowledge that there are disagreements about what ethics commits us to and what ends are served by ethical values. There are also cases in which ethical values conflict, and such ethical dilemmas are a significant part of business ethics. The prosmoking values of Philip Morris, for example, allegedly promoted the values of personal freedom and autonomy. Critics charge that these same values result in serious illness and death to many people. How do we decide if Philip Morris is an ethical company?

Simply, there are few if any unambiguous and absolute rules that can guide ethical decisions making. To evaluate the Philip Morris case we would begin by exploring the meaning and value of the freedom to choose relative to the value of health. We might also examine the motivation of Philip Morris executives to discover if they truly valued the personal freedom of their customers, or if their motivation was less impartial and more self-serving. Ethical controversy is only the starting point of philosophical ethics. Accordingly, one major goal of this text will be to emphasize reasoning and analytical skills as much as informational content.

Let us now return to the question with which this section began. Is ethics good for business? Consider Malden Mills, a well-known business case that made headlines some years ago.

During the early evening hours of December 11, 1995, a fire broke out in a textile mill in Lawrence, Massachusetts. By morning, the fire had destroyed most of Malden Mills, the manufacturer of Polartec fabric. The fire seemed a disaster to the company, its employees, its customers, and the surrounding communities. Malden Mills was a family-owned business, founded in 1906 and run by the founder's grandson Aaron Feuerstein. Polartec is a high-quality fabric well known for the outdoor apparel featured by such popular companies as L.L. Bean, Land's End, REI, J. Crew, and Eddie Bauer. As the major supplier of Polartec, the company had sales of $400 million in the year leading up to the fire. The disaster promised many headaches for Malden Mills, for its employees, for the numerous businesses that depend on its products, and for an entire community.

The towns surrounding the Malden Mills plant have long been home to textile manufacturing. The textile industry was born in the nineteenth century and thrived for one hundred years along the rivers in these New England towns. The textile industry effectively died during the middle decades of the twentieth century when outdated factories and increasing labor costs led many companies to abandon the area and relocate, first to the nonunionized south, and later to foreign countries such as Mexico and Taiwan. As happened in many northern manufacturing towns, the loss of major industries, along with their jobs and tax base, began a long period of economic decline from which many have never recovered. Malden Mills was the last major textile manufacturer in town and with 2,400 employees it supplied the economic lifeblood for the surrounding communities. Considering both its payroll and taxes, Malden Mills contributed approximately $100 million a year to the local economy. The fire was a disaster for many people and many businesses beyond those directly involved with Malden Mills.

As CEO and President, Aaron Feuerstein faced some major decisions, decisions that would be guided by his core values. He could have used the fire as an opportunity to follow his competitors and relocate to a more economically attractive area. He certainly could have found a location with lower taxes and cheaper labor and thus have maximized his earning potential. He could have simply taken the insurance money and decided not to reopen at all. Instead, as the fire was still smoldering, Feuerstein pledged to rebuild his plant at the same location and keep the jobs in the local community. But even more surprising, he promised to continue paying his employees and extend their medical coverage until they could be brought back to work. For this, Feuerstein became famous. Featured on television and in such magazines as *Fortune, Newsweek,* and *Time,* Mr. Feuerstein was honored by President Clinton and invited to attend the State of the Union address as the president's guest. He was praised by many as a model of ethical business behavior.

Initially, all went well. Malden Mills was able to rebuild its factory and reopen sections within a year. Employees came back to work and the community seemed to recover. Unfortunately, Malden Mills couldn't recover fully. Insurance covered only three-fourths of the $400 millions cost of rebuilding and by 2001 Malden Mills filed for bankruptcy protection. During the summer of 2004, Malden Mills emerged from bankruptcy but its board of directors was now controlled by its creditors, led by GE Commercial Finance Division. The new board replaced Aaron Feuerstein as CEO and Board Chairman, although he retained the right to buy back the controlling interest if he could raise sufficient financing. In October of 2004, the board rejected Feuerstein's offer to buy back the company. In response to the company's contract offer that included cuts in health care benefits, the union representing the remaining 1,000 workers at Malden Mills voted to authorize a strike in December 2004, the first in company history.

Are strong ethical values good for business? The only reasonable answer is that sometimes they are and sometimes they are not. Many of the companies examined by Collins and Porras seem to attain the ideal, high ethical standards and long-term financial success. Others, like Philip Morris, attained long-term success with values that would not indisputably be considered ethical. Some unethical companies, Enron perhaps most famously, failed as a business because of their ethical failures. Others, like Malden Mills, seem to suffer financially because of their high ethical standards. The record is mixed. The choice is yours.

1.3 THE NATURE AND GOALS OF BUSINESS ETHICS

How, then, might we define business ethics? In a descriptive sense, "business ethics" refers to those values, standards, and principles that operate within business. But "business ethics" also refers to an academic discipline that not only studies those standards, values, and principles, but also seeks to articulate and defend the ones that ought or should operate in business. In this way, business ethics includes normative as well as descriptive elements. This text is a contribution to that academic field of business ethics. Its aim is to describe, examine, and evaluate ethical issue that arise within business settings.

Unlike some business disciplines, there is no single set of answers in ethics, no single body of information, nor is there even a single framework for thinking about ethics. Business ethics is a truly multidisciplinary field, incorporating information from a variety of disciplines including philosophy, management, economics, law, marketing, and public policy.

Given this diversity, there is no single way—let alone single *right* way—to teach and learn business ethics. But this does not mean that there are not common goals, concepts, principles, and frameworks of business ethics. There is a growing body of scholarly literature in business ethics, and, in an academic setting at least, an important element of a course in business ethics is to become familiar with that scholarly literature. Just as there are Generally Accepted Accounting Principles (GAAP) for accountants, there are a set of principles, standards, concepts, and values common to business ethics. Chapter 2 will introduce some of the most common ethical theories and principles. But beyond this academic side, business ethics has a practical side in the sense that it aims at judgment, behavior, and actions. We all hope that books and classes in business ethics translate into more ethical behavior among business practitioners.

Unfortunately, things are not always that simple. First, there is the daunting gap between ethical judgment and ethical behavior. From at least the time of Plato and Aristotle, Western philosophy has acknowledged a real discontinuity between judging some act as right and following through and doing it. It is difficult enough knowing the difference between good and bad, right and wrong. But knowing is different from doing, and not everyone has the fortitude, strength of character, or motivation to act in ways that we know are best. While many observers expect an ethics class to teach ethical behavior, most ethicists have the more modest goal for their courses. It is not at all clear, for example, that an ethics course would have made any difference to the executives at Enron and Arthur Andersen.

A more modest and judicious goal for business ethics is to focus on the cognitive and intellectual (as opposed to behavioral) side of ethics. Business ethics as an academic discipline is more a matter of ethical reasoning and thinking than ethical behavior. But even here there is a major dilemma confronting ethics courses. On one hand, few would teach ethics in a way that aims to indoctrinate students. Few teachers would think that it is the role of an ethics course to *tell* students the right answers or *proclaim* what they ought to think and how they ought to live. The role of an ethics course should not be to convey information to a passive audience, but to treat students as active learners and engage them in an active process of thinking and questioning. Taking Socrates as the model, philosophical ethics rejects the view that blind obedience to authority or the simple acceptance of customary norms is an adequate ethical perspective. Teaching ethics must, on this view, involve students *thinking for themselves*. The unexamined life, Socrates claimed, is not worth living.

The problem, of course, is that when people think for themselves they don't always agree with each other, and they certainly don't always act in a way that others would judge as ethical. The other side of this dilemma is the specter of relativism and emotivism. If the ethics classroom does not teach students the right answers, many students will conclude that there are no right answers. If there are few teachers who use the classroom to preach ethical dogma, there are probably fewer still who believe that there are no right answers and that anything goes from an ethical point of view.

Thus a major challenge for business ethics is to find a middle ground between preaching the truth to passive listeners on one hand, and encouraging the relativistic conclusion that all opinions are equal on the other. A common goal for most courses in business ethics navigates this difficulty by emphasizing the *process* of ethical reasoning. Business ethics is concerned more with reasoning than answers. Responsible reasoning must begin with an accurate and fair account of the facts; one must listen to all sides with an open mind, one must become familiar with all the relevant issues at stake, and one must pursue the logical analysis of each issue fully and with intellectual rigor. Business ethics essentially involves this process of ethical analysis. Without it, one risks turning ethics into dogmatism; with it, one has gone as far as possible to deflate relativism. With this process, we are best prepared to avoid the dilemma of dogmatism and relativism.

This dilemma not only confronts business ethics in an academic setting, it is also true for ethics within business settings as well. Even if they could be successful in doing so, few business managers would want to approach ethical issues by making pronouncements of ethical dogma. Like good teachers, good business managers and leaders seek to empower their employees to make their own decisions. But responsible businesses also do not suggest that anything goes or that all values are equal. Value relativism in the workplace will likely lead only to power struggles and conflict.

1.4 BUSINESS ETHICS AND THE LAW

Some believe that the way out of this dilemma is to concentrate on legal compliance. For many business people, ethics is identified with the law. Business behaves ethically when it obeys the law. An ethical business, therefore, should have an ethics officer or an ethics department that monitors compliance with the legal and professional standards of conduct.

Unfortunately, compliance with the law alone will prove insufficient for ethically responsible business. It is common to think of the law as a set of rules that one can obey or violate in an unambiguous way. Traffic laws, for example, require stopping at a red light and prohibit speeds over a certain limit. But this is a very incomplete understanding of the law. Even when there are specific regulations requiring or prohibiting certain action, ambiguity is always possible in the application of those regulations.

For example, consider the following case. At a management training program I recently attended, two corporate attorneys outlined some of the legal responsibilities for managers under the Americans with Disabilities Act. This law requires business to make "reasonable accommodations" for workers with disabilities. This law goes on to specify some, but not all, of the conditions that would count as a disability. During the question period, one manager explained that she had an employee who suffered from asthma and she wondered if asthma was a disability. The two attorneys conferred for a moment and answered simply: "It depends." The law's definition of a disability involves, in part, how serious the impairment is, how much it limits the worker's life activities, and whether or not it is easily corrected by medication. Given this ambiguity, the manager must make a judgment about how to treat this worker. Imagine this manager is committed to doing the ethically correct thing, but believes that one's ethical responsibility is to obey the law. What should this manager do? In such a case, the decision is unavoidable, the law doesn't help, and the manager therefore is forced to make a judgment about what ought to be done.

More generally, much of the civil law governing business is based on the legal precedents of case law rather than specific statutes or regulations. Case law is fundamentally ambiguous in a way that statutory law is not. In a very real sense, many acts are not illegal until a court rules that they are. For example, both the attorneys and the auditors in the Enron case were expected to "push the envelope" of legality by Enron's aggressive management practices. Given that many of Enron's financial practices were quite literally unprecedented, their attorneys and accountants offered advice that they believed could be defended in court. Until and unless these acts were challenged in court there was a real sense in which they were perfectly legal. While admittedly "pushing the envelope" on accounting and tax regulations, what they did was not obviously illegal.

These facts demonstrate that one cannot always rely on the law to decide what is right or wrong. The manager whose employee suffers from asthma will need to make a decision and the law won't decide this for her. Sometimes, the law itself requires ethical analysis for many of its decisions. Legal decisions in the Enron case will not be based solely on legal precedent (since, by definition, "pushing the envelope" is to go into the gray area beyond what is obviously prohibited by precedent) but upon a judge and jury's determination that the acts were unfair and unethical. Because most business decisions never get to the point where a judge and jury are asked to make a determination, business managers will be faced with the unavoidable responsibility of looking beyond the law for guidance in making ethical decisions.

Expressed in these terms, perhaps the major reason to study ethics is because whether we *examine* ethical questions explicitly or not, they are *answered* by each and every one of us every day in the course of living our lives. Presumably, the executives at Enron did not wake up one morning and choose to defraud their stockholders and employees. The actions we take and the lives we lead give practical answers to these fundamental ethical questions. Our only real choice is whether we answer them deliberately or unconsciously. Thus, the philosophical answer to why you should study ethics was given by Socrates over 2,000 years ago. "The unexamined life is not worth living."

1.5 ETHICS AND ETHOS

Ethics is a vast field of study that really addresses only one question: How should we live our lives? The question of human well-being ultimately focuses on how we should live. But while this may seem a simple question, it is perhaps the most fundamental question any human can ask. We can begin to answer it by reflecting on the nature of philosophical ethics. Within the Western tradition philosophical ethics is often traced to the ancient Greek philosopher Socrates. There is perhaps no better characterization of ethics than Socrates' statement that it "deals with no small thing, but with how we ought to live." Like all cultures, the Greeks had a set of beliefs, attitudes, and values that guided their lives. The word *ethics* is derived from the Greek word *ethos,* meaning "customary" or "conventional." Most Greeks would have answered Socrates by claiming that we ought to live an ethical life. Like most people in other cultures, an ethical life for the Greeks would have been a life lived according to the beliefs, attitudes, and values that were customary in their own culture. Often, these customary values are connected to a culture's religious worldview. To be ethical, in the sense of *ethos,* is to conform to what is typically done, to obey the conventions and rules of one's society and religion. In this sense, *ethics* would be identical to *ethos.*

Taking its lead from Socrates, philosophical ethics is not content to accept this as an answer to the question of how we should live. We said earlier that each one of us answers ethical questions every day by how we choose to live our lives. For many people, this choice is made implicitly by conforming to the ethos and customs of their culture. Philosophical ethics denies that simple conformity and obedience are the best guides to how we should live. From the very beginning, philosophy rejects authority as the source of ethics and has, instead, defended the use of reason as the foundation of ethics. Philosophical ethics seeks a reasoned analysis of custom and a reasoned defense of how we ought to live.

Philosophical ethics distinguishes what people *do* value from what people *should* value. What people do in fact value is the domain of such social sciences as sociology, psychology, and anthropology. As a branch of *philosophy,* however, ethics asks us to step back and rationally evaluate the customary beliefs and values that people do hold. Philosophical ethics requires us to abstract ourselves from what is normally or typically done, and reflect upon whether or not what *is* done, *should* be done, and whether what *is* valued, *should* be valued. The difference between what *is* valued and what *ought* to be valued is the difference between ethos and ethics.

Perhaps this observation helps to explain some of the skepticism surrounding business ethics. Any philosophical focus on business ethics seems to suggest some dissatisfaction with, or misgivings about, what is normally or customarily done in business. Why step back from what is normally done unless you have reason to doubt that what is being done should be done? But while philosophical ethics is *critical* in the sense of demanding reasons for each decision, it need not be *critical* in the sense of rejecting or disagreeing with the customary norms and standards.

As a branch of philosophical ethics, business ethics asks us to step back from our daily decisions, step back from the ethos of business, to reflect upon how business decisions affect our lives. In what ways do the practices and decisions made within business promote or undermine human well-being? Raising these questions does not imply that what is normally being done is unethical. After examining ethical issues in business, we may end up defending the same values and making the same decisions that we would have originally. But what philosophical ethics does require is a conscious reflection and analysis of those beliefs and values upon which we act. Again, to rely on Socratic wisdom, philosophical ethics assumes that "the unexamined life is not worth living." As we proceed through an examination of business ethics, we are really doing little more than reflecting upon daily events and echoing Socrates' question: How ought we to live?

1.6 MORALITY, VIRTUES, AND SOCIAL ETHICS

How ought we to live? This fundamental question of ethics can be interpreted in two ways. "We" can mean each one of us individually, or it might mean all of us collectively. In this first individual sense, this is a question about how I should live my life, how I should act, what I should do, what kind of person I should be. This meaning of ethics is sometimes referred to as morality. Part of morality involves examining principles and rules that might help us decide how to act. Another important part of morality involves an examination of those character traits, or virtues, that would constitute a life worth living. This distinction is sometimes made in terms of deciding how we should *act,* and deciding the type of person we should *be.* In the collective sense, this is a question about how a society ought to be structured, about how we ought to live together. This area is sometimes referred to as social ethics and it raises questions of public policy, law, civic virtue, and political philosophy.

Business ethics addresses both kinds of questions. Questions of individual morality will be a major theme throughout this text. One of the most fundamental goals of business ethics is to provide opportunities for students to step back from the immediate concerns of day-to-day life and ask: "What kind of person should I be?" "What should I do?" "What kind of life will I live?" "What would I have done if I were in the position of an auditor at Enron?" Is the kind of greed, aggressiveness, and selfishness exhibited at Enron a model for my life?

No doubt most of us at most times of our lives are too concerned with more immediate issues such as completing an assigned task, paying our bills, and having fun, to consciously step back and ask about the meaning and value of what we do. But this is what philosophical ethics demands. Morality takes the larger perspective. Imagine late in your life looking back to reflect on the kind of life you have led and asking: "Has this life been worth living? Am I proud of my life? Am I proud or ashamed of the person I have been? Has this been a full and meaningful life?" These are among the fundamental questions of morality.

Business ethics also addresses issues of social ethics and public policy. Understanding this viewpoint can start with the recognition that business institutions are human creations. The fact that businesses are human institutions means that humans cannot avoid responsibility for them. As the Enron case indicates, business institutions have a tremendous influence on many lives. We depend on business for our jobs, our food, our health care, our homes, our livelihoods. The public policy perspective invites us to step back from the actual practice of business to ask: "How *should* business be structured?" If we had it all to do over again, how would we arrange business institutions in our society? In this sense, public policy questions ask us to take the point of view of the citizen who is deciding how society—and business institutions are a part of society—ought to be organized and conducted.

When we ask this question we can see that important ethical questions remain even when the particular decision facing an individual business manager appears clear-cut. As an executive at Enron, you are free to pursue energy trading business, but citizens get to decide whether or not to regulate energy and public utilities to control such trading. Should such important social goods as energy be left in the hands of unregulated private corporations?

1.7 ETHICAL PERSPECTIVES: MANAGERS AND OTHER STAKEHOLDERS

This focus on questions of morality and public policy also calls attention to the fact that a variety of perspectives can be taken when examining issues in business ethics. A major part of business ethics deals with questions of management. *Business* ethics often is interpreted to mean the ethics of those charged with acting on behalf of a business. What should a business *manager* do in various situations? In this sense, business ethics can be interpreted as managerial ethics.

But, a decision faced from the point of view of business management raises different issues than those faced from the point of view of employees or owners. Decisions made within Enron and Arthur Andersen were of monumental importance to employees, suppliers, and customers, as well as to the citizens of Houston and California. This is not to suggest that right or wrong depends on who is asking the question. But it does suggest that the types of questions asked and issues faced will vary from perspective to perspective. Because a reasoned evaluation of any ethical issue demands that all relevant concerns be addressed, this text will regularly ask you to shift perspectives and ask the moral questions from the point of view of management, employees, owners, consumers, suppliers, and citizens. Whether our future interaction with business occurs in the role of CEO or just plain consumer, we must examine business decisions from a variety of perspectives.

These observations suggest that all decisions faced by business managers, from finance and marketing to ethics and human resources, exist in a social and legal context. This context not only helped create the situation but also determines what alternatives are available. Whatever social arrangements exist, we need to recognize that each of us, in our roles as citizens, is responsible for them. A mature, responsible life requires us to step back and reflect upon the kind of society we choose to live in, as well as the particular decisions we choose to make.

We can summarize this introduction by saying that business ethics asks us to step back from what is usually and customarily done in the business world to ask the essential normative question of ethics: "How *should* we live? How should I live as an individual, and how should we live in community?" Throughout this text, indeed throughout your life, you should regularly step back to ask: "What kind of person am I choosing to be?" and "What kind of society ought we to create?" To return to our opening question, the study of ethics is relevant to business because it is essential to living a responsible and meaningful life.

REFLECTIONS ON THE CHAPTER DISCUSSION CASE

Several lessons can be drawn from this brief description of Enron. The Enron case demonstrates the wide range of people who can be adversely affected by the decisions made within contemporary business. Each and every day the lives and well-being of millions of people depend on decisions made by business managers from small family-run businesses to the world's largest corporations. Recognition of this fact has led many to argue that the social responsibility of business must recognize duties to a wide range of stakeholders beyond simply those people who own a company's stock.

The collapse of Enron and the widespread harm caused by that collapse surely can be traced to the ethical corruption of specific individuals working for the firm. Arrogant and greedy individuals willing to violate legal and ethical standards can be faulted for much of the problem. Unfortunately, such people are all too common. But we should also recognize the failure of the many "gatekeepers," those people and institutions whose role is to provide checks on such behavior. Auditors, accountants, attorneys, financial analysts, board members, and government regulators have roles to play within the economic system to insure the integrity of that system and to prevent fraud and abuse. Another lesson from Enron is that there was a systematic breakdown in this gatekeeping function.

Preventing future Enrons will require steps to be taken at each level: individual employees with higher ethical standards, internal structures within corporations to establish and enforce higher standards, legal requirements and other regulatory reforms to act as external checks upon corporate behavior.

REVIEW QUESTIONS

1. Describe several reasons why ethics is relevant to business. Can a "good business" be an unethical business?

2. What are values? What is the difference between ethical values and other types of values? What is the difference between *value* when used as a verb, and *value* when used as a noun?
3. What is the difference between *ethics* and *ethos?*
4. How is *descriptive* business ethics different from *normative* business ethics?
5. This chapter introduced a distinction between morality, virtues, and social ethics. How would you describe each?
6. How would you answer someone who asked: "Why should I study ethics if I want to be an accountant?"
7. Other than business managers and owners, which other constituencies might have a stake in business decisions?

ENDNOTES

[1] A persuasive case for why this shift has occurred can be found in *Value Shift* by Lynn Sharp Paine (New York: McGraw-Hill, 2003).

[2] "Business Ethics and Compliance in the Sarbanes-Oxley Era," A Survey by *Deloitte and Corporate Board Member Magazine,* July 2003 (www.deloitte. com/dtt/cda/doc/content/ethicsCompliance_f.pdf).

[3] *Built to Last: Successful Habits of Visionary Companies,* James Collins and Jerry Porras (New York: HarperCollins, 1994), p. 73.

[4] Ibid., p. 67. The Fortune article quoted is "How Philip Morris Diversified Right," *Fortune,* October 23, 1989.

2 CHAPTER

Ethical Theory and Business

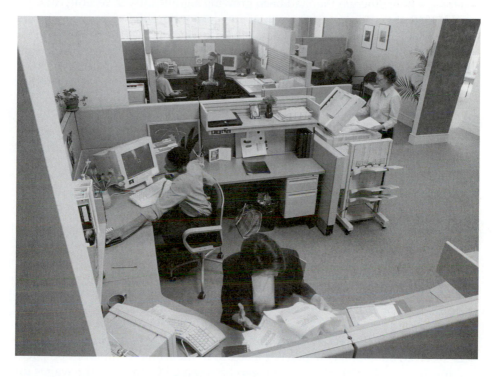

After reading this chapter, you will be able to:

- Understand the basic categories and concepts of ethical theory;
- Identify the errors of ethical relativism;
- Explain the ethical theory of utilitarianism;
- Explain how utilitarian ethics provides support for market economics and business policy;
- Clarify several major challenges to utilitarian ethics;
- Explain the rights- and duty-based ethics of deontology;
- Explain the basic concepts of virtue ethics.

DISCUSSION CASE: Executive Compensation

"Inside The Great CEO Pay Heist" exclaimed the cover story of the June 15, 2001, issue of *Fortune* magazine. This well-respected business magazine detailed how many top corporate executives now receive "gargantuan pay packages unlike any seen before." In the words of *Fortune*'s headline, "Executive compensation has become highway robbery—we all know that."[1] This story documented a phenomenon that had been growing significantly in recent years.

In 1960 the after-tax average pay for corporate chief executive officers (CEOs) was 12 times the average pay earned by factory workers. By 1974 that factor had risen to 35 times the average. In 1995 *BusinessWeek* estimated that the factor had risen to 135 times the average pay received by factory workers. A 1998 *Fortune* magazine article estimated the factor had risen to 182. Another estimate for 2000 had the multiple of CEO pay to average worker at 500! This means that if the average factory worker earned an annual salary of $30,000 (40 hour week × 52 weeks × $15.00 p/hr), the average CEO earned almost $15 million. Importantly, these numbers only address the *average* pay; the differences would be more dramatic if we compared the top salary for CEOs and minimum-wage workers. In two of the more well-publicized cases, Sandy Weill, the CEO of Travelers, received over $230 million in compensation for 1997 and Michael Eisner of Walt Disney received $589 million in 1998.

A 1998 *Forbes* magazine article reported that there was little correlation between CEO pay and performance. Comparing CEO compensation to stock performance over a five-year period, *Forbes* described 15 CEOs who earned over $15 million while their company's stock lagged well behind the market average of 23 percent. One CEO, Robert Elkins of Integrated Health Systems, received over $43 million during this five-year period while his company's stock value *declined* by 36 percent. Another report, based on data for 1996, showed that the top executives of firms that laid off more than 3,000 workers in the previous year received an average 67 percent increase in their total compensation package for the year. In 1996 the average gap between CEO pay and the wages for the lowest paid worker for the top 12 job-cutting companies was 178 to 1.

The 2001 *Fortune* story showed that these gaps continued to increase. For the decade ending in 2000, the U.S. minimum wage increased 36 percent, from $3.80 per hour to $5.15 per hour. The median household income in the United States increased 43 percent from $29,943 to $42,680. The average annual salary for a tenured New York City teacher increased 20 percent, from $41,000 to $49,030. During this same decade the total compensation for the Citicorp CEO increased 12,444 percent from $1.2 million to $150 million annually, and General Electric's CEO Jack Welch's salary increased 2,496 percent, from $4.8 million to $125 million.

Some predicted that the wave of corporate accounting scandals in 2001 and 2002 would provide an incentive for corporations to bring CEO pay under control. Early evidence indicates that this has not happened. *USA Today* reported that for 2002, the median income for the CEO of the 100 largest American corporations was $33.4 million, a 15 percent increase from the previous year, compared to a 3.2 percent increase for the average worker.

Among the highest paid CEOs in 2002 was Richard Kovacevich, CEO of Wells Fargo, who earned $8 million in salary and bonus and was granted an additional $64 million in stock options. Jeffrey Barbaklow of Tenet Healthcare earned $5.3 million in salary and bonus, and an additional $72 million in stock options. H. Lee Scott, CEO of Wal-Mart, earned $2.9 million in salary and bonus, and $50 million in stock options. (The average wage for Wal-Mart sales associates for 2001 was $8.23 per hour.) David Cote, CEO of Honeywell, earned $3.1 million in salary and bonus, but an additional $117 million in stock options. In September 2003 Richard Grasso resigned his position as chairman of the New York Stock Exchange amid criticism over his pay package. Mr. Grasso was paid $140 million, and was slated to receive an additional $48 million in deferred pay.

Many of these large pay packages are the result of stock options that corporate boards grant to their executives. The portion of CEO pay derived from stock options increased from 27 percent in 1992 to 60 percent in 2000. Stock options are the right to purchase the company's stock at a predetermined price any time within a set period, often a 5- or 10-year time frame. For example, an executive might be granted the right to purchase 100,000 shares at a price of $10 per share any time within 10 years. If the stock price rises, the executive is able to cash in these options and make a windfall profit. For example, if the stock price rises to $20 per share, the executive would be able to make $1 million by exercising these options. Many observers believe that such options were much to blame for the accounting scandals of recent years. Stock options create a strong incentive to executives to increase the company's share value by whatever means possible. In theory, this ties the executive's pay to increases in shareholder wealth, but in practice it often led to short-term, unsustainable increases in share value, as the Enron case demonstrated.

These figures address only income; the distribution of wealth in the United States also raises questions of equality. Twenty million households, accounting for approximately 20 percent of the U.S. population, are classified as "poor"— earning less than $15,000 annually and having little or no net worth. For comparison, an average Wal-Mart sales associate in 2001 earned $8.23 per hour for a 32-hour workweek, equal to a yearly income of $13,694. Approximately 30 percent of the population are classified as lower middle class and earn between $15,000 and $30,000 annually. These families have a net worth of less than $55,000, the U.S. median net worth. "Middle class" families comprise 34 percent of the population and earn between $35,000 and $75,000. Equity in homes and retirement accounts raises the net worth of these families to the $55,000 to $500,000 range. Approximately 85 percent of the U.S. population live in families earning less than $75,000 a year.

The 1999 net worth of Bill Gates was estimated at $85 billion. Paul Allen, cofounder of Microsoft with Gates, was estimated to be worth over $40 billion. Financier Warren Buffett was third-ranked for 1999 with a net worth of $31 billion. These three individuals had a combined net worth of $156 billion. The median family net worth within the United States for that same year was $55,000. Therefore, in 1999 Gates, Allen, and Buffett had a combined net worth equal to that of 3 million average American *families*. By 2003, with the stock market in decline, their relative worth had dropped to $46 billion for Gates, $36 billion for Buffett, and $22 billion for Allen. In that same year, Helen Walton, widow of Wal-Mart founder Sam Walton, and her four children ranked as five of the wealthiest eight people in the United States. Their combined wealth was estimated to be over $100 billion, more than twice the worth of Bill Gates.

Are such inequalities of income unjust? Defenders will argue that CEOs have earned such salaries and deserve to be paid accordingly. Critics argue that significant inequalities are increasing within our economic system and ought to be controlled. One proposal for controlling such inequalities has been introduced in the U.S. Congress by Representative Martin Sabo from Minnesota.

Sabo's Income Equity Act would place a limit on tax deductions that a corporation can claim for executive compensation. Sabo argues that the government is subsidizing such gross inequalities by allowing corporations to count up to $1 million per year per executive as a tax-deductible business expense. Sabo's proposal would set a tax deduction cap at 25 times the company's lowest full-time salary. So, for example, if the lowest paid employee earns $18,000, then any amount paid in executive salary over $450,000 would no longer be tax deductible. While corporations would still be allowed the freedom to pay their executives whatever they decide, the federal government would decline to subsidize what the bill refers to as "excessive compensation."[2]

DISCUSSION QUESTIONS

1. The United States has established a minimum-wage law. Should there be a maximum-wage law?
2. What standards should be used to establish a fair wage? Are the standards for executives different from those for hourly workers? What factors determine what someone deserves for pay?
3. Should salary be tied to results such that an executive whose company loses money should earn less than an executive whose company makes a profit?
4. Are large salaries more justified as *incentives* to produce beneficial consequences, or as *rewards* for past accomplishments? Are there available alternatives to money that might serve as incentives and rewards?
5. Can anyone ever make too much money for their own good?
6. Would you support Sabo's Income Equity Act?
7. Is there an ethical difference between the wealth owned by a company's founder (e.g., Bill Gates) and the income received by a hired CEO? Do founders and entrepreneurs deserve their wealth in ways that executives do not deserve their salaries?

2.1 INTRODUCTION

In the previous chapter I suggested that the language and concepts of ethics are as unavoidable in business as are the language and concepts of other areas within business education. The issue of executive compensation demonstrates how business activities raise fundamental questions of fairness, justice, desert, and rights. If it is true that the language of ethics is inextricably a part of business, then it is advisable to begin our examination of business ethics with a short introduction to some of the basics of philosophical ethics. Just as you need to have a familiarity with the language and concepts of economics and management to make responsible business decisions, so, too, you need a basic familiarity with ethics. This chapter will introduce some of the key theories and concepts of ethics and show how these are both relevant and necessary for any study of business.

As a first step, let us reflect upon the reasoning that is offered to support and criticize such high rates of executive compensation. How would you defend such pay packages? What, if anything, is ethically wrong with them?

Several factors are typically cited in defense of these pay packages. Some defenders cite the agreement made between the executive and the company, acting through the board of directors. In effect, the company made a promise and therefore has an obligation to make good on it. Another defense suggests that such pay is something that is deserved for work accomplished or for the risks taken by the CEO. Thus, high salary is something that has been earned. Yet other reasons cite the beneficial consequences that follow from high pay. Great rewards provide a strong incentive for executives to work hard on behalf of shareholders. Stock options especially are thought to operate in this way by connecting future CEO pay with performance.[3]

Criticisms also raise similar issues. Some critics argue that corporate boards are not independent of the executives and therefore the pay agreements are unfairly biased in favor of the executives. In such cases, boards fail to fulfill their duty to the shareholders. Other critics point out that stock options are often repriced if the stock value does not rise and therefore are undeserved by executives. Other critics claim that great inequalities of income and wealth are unjust and unfair. Still other critics argue that such income is motivated by unseemly greed and ego and therefore ought not to be allowed.

Many observers insist that a distinction be made between the wealth accumulated by people who create a business and the income taken by hired executives. Bill Gates, Paul Allen, and Sam Walton are thought to deserve the wealth derived from their property and entrepreneurial creativity. In effect, the wealth accumulated by such people results from the willingness of others (shareholders) to pay them in order to become joint owners.

We will examine these arguments in more depth later. For now, the crucial thing to recognize is the inescapability of the language of ethics. Debates surrounding CEO pay are fundamentally debates about ethics: What do people deserve? What produces beneficial overall consequences? What is one's duty? What is fair or unfair, just or unjust? What is wrong with greed?

The ethical theories and concepts introduced in this chapter provide frameworks for thinking about such claims and counterclaims. One major theory, utilitarianism, determines right and wrong in terms of the consequences. Thus, if the overall social consequences of high CEO pay are beneficial, that pay is ethically justified. If they are not, the pay is ethically unjustified. Deontological theories emphasize ethics as a matter of principle and offer ways to think about such ethical principles as desert, duty, promises, property, rights, justice, and fairness.

Before turning to these theories, let us consider a philosophical perspective that raised a significant challenge to the very legitimacy of reasoning about ethics. Ethical relativism is a view that believes that all ethical judgments are relative to the person or culture that makes them. It is a perspective that is commonly found in discussions of business ethics. Reasoning through an analysis of ethical relativism will help demonstrate how one can, in fact, reason about ethics.

2.2 ETHICAL RELATIVISM AND REASONING IN ETHICS

The day on which I am writing this began with a morning class in business ethics. After class, a student remained to ask some questions about a paper assignment that I had returned during the previous class meeting. This young woman wanted to know how I had graded her paper, particularly why she had received an unexpectedly low grade. When I pointed out that much of the paper offered little more than her opinions, she asked a question that is familiar to many ethics teachers. "How can you say that my opinions are wrong? Isn't everyone entitled to their own opinions?" I answered that while people may be entitled to hold any opinion they wished, not all opinions are equal. Some are right, some are wrong, some are reasonable and some are unreasonable, some are thoughtful and others are less thoughtful. "But this is ethics," she responded. "Who's to say what's right or wrong?"

I suggested that anyone who had *reasons* could say what was right or wrong and asked if she herself didn't have some reasons to support her opinions. Why did she believe what she had written? She responded that she didn't know, but that it was "just the way I feel."

I suspect that this skeptical reaction is familiar to many students. Ethics is not like math, science, or accounting. One cannot look up the right answer or calculate the answer with mathematical precision. One cannot prove the truth of an ethical judgment in the way that one can offer a proof in geometry. One cannot run an experiment that supports, or refutes, an ethical opinion. Unlike these other disciplines, ethics appears to rest on mere opinion. People differ about ethical judgments, and there seems no rational way to decide between competing conclusions. Ethical issues seem based in personal feelings and emotions. It is very likely that the example of executives earning hundreds of millions of dollars a year causes strong emotional reactions for many people. But is that all there is to this case? Is it just a matter of envy or jealousy? Is the criticism simply a claim that they are greedy? Or, are there *reasons* for thinking that there is something wrong here? Is there any way to prove your conclusion?

There is an important perspective within the philosophical study of ethics, called *ethical relativism,* which holds that ethical values and judgments are ultimately dependent upon, or relative to, one's culture, society, or personal feelings. In this sense, ethics truly is simply a matter of opinion, be it the opinion of one's self, culture, society, or religion. Ethical relativism presents a serious challenge to any consideration of ethics. Relativism denies that we can make rational or objective ethical judgments. There is no right or wrong, moral or immoral, except in terms of a particular culture or society.

The student who remained after class was implicitly assuming a version of ethical relativism. In her view, ethical judgments were a matter of opinion and if two people differed in their opinions, there was no legitimate way to decide between them. Each person is entitled to their own opinion, and no one opinion is more legitimate or more correct than another.

Relativism represents a serious challenge to ethics, including business ethics, because if it is correct there is no reason to continue our study of ethics. If all opinions are equally valid, then it makes little sense for us to attempt to evaluate ethical judgments in business. If it were ethically right for Aaron Feuerstein to rebuild his plant and pay his workers, it could be just as right for a different person from a different background to move operations to Taiwan or Mexico. If relativism is correct, then at best business ethics can help explicate the cultural or social values that underlie our ethical judgments, but it can do little to evaluate them. Philosophical ethics, from the relativist perspective, becomes little more than a process of values clarification in which we can clarify and elucidate our values but not justify them.

Relativism is especially important as we think about ethical issues involving international business. Consider the issues raised by child labor. Some Western businesses have been criticized for using suppliers who rely on child laborers working under harsh conditions for long hours and very low wages to produce expensive consumer goods like sneakers and designer clothing. A common response to such criticism points out that such working conditions are accepted in the host country and, therefore, Western critics have no justification for imposing their own cultural norms on others. This, in a nutshell, is ethical relativism.

Let us use another example from business ethics, a case of sexual harassment, and consider how my relativist student might scrutinize it. One form of sexual harassment occurs when submission to sexual favors is made a condition of employment. (This is called *quid pro quo* harassment.) Imagine a male manager telling a female job applicant that she would be hired only if she submitted to his sexual advances. Now imagine that our relativist concludes that the criticism of harassment is simply a matter of opinion, that all opinions are equally valid, and that while the women may *feel* that harassment is wrong, the manager may *feel* that it is right. (He might answer criticism as did my student, "it's just the way I feel.") From the relativist perspective, each opinion or feeling is equally valid. Is there any way to defend the claim that such harassment is unethical?

One might argue, among other things, that sexual harassment would subject a woman to unfair workplace discrimination. The inequality of power in this situation places the woman in the unacceptable position of having to choose between her livelihood and her own sexual integrity. Such a choice is fundamentally coercive and threatening. One might point out that the male manager would unlikely accept as a general rule the principle that employers are justified in using threats to coerce employees into submitting to such degrading acts. In developing such arguments, we seem to have moved the discussion from mere opinion to a more reasoned conclusion.

Of course, the relativist could argue that such values as equality, fairness, integrity, self-respect, and freedom from coercion and threats are all themselves a matter of personal or social opinion. From the relativist perspective, all that we have shown is that harassment is wrong as long as you assume that people deserve a workplace that is free from discrimination and threats. But who is to say that people do deserve such things? While we may have advanced the debate somewhat, we still haven't proven to the relativist that harassment is wrong.

Let us consider how the debate has been advanced. If, like my student, we start with mere opinions and feelings, then this discussion has moved beyond mere opinion by appealing to certain values and principles that justify and legitimize that opinion. This is no longer mere opinion, but opinion based on principle. In developing this argument we would point to certain facts, such as the disproportionate power relationship that exists between job applicant and employer. We would point out the crucial importance that jobs play in our lives and the harms that can occur from the loss of a job. We could explain the psychological good of self-respect, offer a conceptual analysis of integrity and its value to the self, and discuss the importance of personal autonomy. We could take a social perspective and consider the present status of women in the workplace, and the social harms that can result from discrimination. And very importantly, we would employ the careful and rigorous rules of logic throughout our reasoning. Conclusions reached after this process surely are more reasonable and justified than mere opinion.

In the face of such reasoning, the relativist could continue to insist on proof and this demand could go on indefinitely. (Although, as I would point out to my student, a paper that argues against harassment by reasoning along the lines suggested above would be more reasonable, and therefore receive a higher grade, than one which simply asserts the opinion that harassment is wrong because "that's just the way I feel.") But note that at this point the relativist would have to reject not only the original conclusion (sexual harassment is wrong) but also a wide variety of other beliefs and values (everyone should be treated with equal respect, people should be free from coercion and threats, self-respect is good, loss of dignity is harmful, and so forth). The costs of relativism—what you would need to give up to maintain it—just got much higher. If the relativist is determined enough, and if her standards of proof are high enough, then perhaps we could never satisfy the demand for proof.

We'll set more modest goals for this text. Throughout this book, I will assume that we can reason about ethical matters and that it is possible to rationally defend some views against others. I will assume that a conclusion defended by appeal to such values as equality, fairness, freedom from coercion, integrity, freedom from harm, and honesty (among others) is a conclusion that is more reasonable than one that is simply asserted as a matter of personal feelings or opinion. A conclusion that is reached through careful logical analysis and reasoning is rationally better than one that is simply asserted. An argument that goes on to elucidate such values as equality, fairness, and freedom from coercion is more rational still.

We may discover that the most interesting and challenging ethical controversies involve a clash between two or more of such values. I will also assume that it is exactly at such points that more, rather than less, rigorous and careful reasoning is required. For example, some might argue that as long as the woman was not physically prevented from walking away, her freedom was not violated by the threat of job loss. Others might argue that freedom is violated when such central human needs as a job are threatened as the means for getting someone to conform to the desires of a more powerful person. Disputes about the meaning and scope of such fundamental values provide a greater justification for the need of ethics.

Perhaps, then, we can learn from ethical relativism, and take it as a challenge to our own complacency and laziness. Whenever we are ready to give up and simply assume that our own opinions are adequate, let us call to mind the relativist question as a challenge: "Who is to say what's right?" It will be a challenge worth answering.

Providing answers to the relativist has long occupied philosophical ethics. The ethical theories that we examine in the following sections can be thought of as philosophical attempts to provide more fundamental answers to the relativist. But before we turn to these theories, and before we leave this consideration of ethical relativism, let me call your attention to several confusions that often lead students into the relativist trap. In my own teaching experience many students who do not avoid these traps end up reaching relativist conclusions by default.

The first trap has been mentioned already. We should be careful not to hold ethics to too high a standard of proof. If we start with the assumption that an ethical judgment must be proven as absolutely certain and beyond doubt, then ethics assuredly will fail to meet this standard. Mathematics and the more theoretical side of physics, engineering, and chemistry may meet this standard, but very few other intellectual fields would pass such a test. Reasoning in all of the humanities, the social sciences (including economics), the biological sciences, medicine, meteorology, and the applied sides of physics, chemistry, and engineering would fail to meet this standard in most of their conclusions. The business-related disciplines of management, marketing, finance, and accounting never establish their conclusions as certain beyond doubt. So, before rejecting ethics as little more than mere opinion, we should be careful that we are not using a standard that would commit us to similar conclusions about most other areas of human knowledge.

The second trap involves confusing the fact that there is wide disagreement about values, with the conclusion that no agreement is possible. The first view, often called *cultural relativism,* offers a factual description of different cultures and societies. People do not agree about ethical matters. As discussed in chapter 1, the *ethos* of various cultures differ widely. People hold a wide variety of ethical opinions. Some cultures may believe, in fact, that children are little more than slave labor. However, in itself, the fact of disagreement provides no reason for concluding that all of these diverse opinions are equally valid. To understand this point, consider the wide disagreement about scientific matters. We could find people, indeed perhaps entire cultures, that believe the Earth is flat, that the Earth is only a few thousand years old, that evolution has never occurred, that aliens visit regularly, that people can foresee the future by charting the course of the planets and stars. Of course, believing that the world is flat does not make it flat and believing that aliens exist does not mean that they do. So, too, with ethics. The fact that people hold different opinions does not, in itself, mean that each of these opinions is equally valid.

We should also be careful not to assume too quickly that there is a wide disagreement about fundamental ethical values. Certainly there is a wide variety of cultural beliefs, customs, values, and practices. But there is also wide agreement about many values as well. Child abuse, torture, genocide, and slavery are just some practices that are universally condemned on ethical grounds. No doubt, we can find cases where individuals and even societies engage in such atrocities, but we would find very few who would seriously defend these practices as justified or merely a matter of personal opinion. While it may appear that some cultures legitimize child labor, it is more likely the case that such circumstances are seen as an unfortunate but necessary alternative to starvation. Accepting a deplorable situation as the least harmful of the alternatives is not the same as accepting it as ethically valid.

A third trap involves confusing values such as respect, tolerance, and impartiality with relativism. Respect for other people is a fundamental ethical value. Part of what it means to respect someone is to listen to his or her opinions and to show tolerance for opinions that differ from our own. But tolerating diverse opinions and values is not the same as ethical relativism. Let us turn the relativist challenge back on to the value of tolerance. Is tolerance (and respect and impartiality) merely a matter of opinion? If it is, then intolerant people have no reason to change their views. Condemning intolerance is simply your opinion. If, on the other hand, tolerance is not merely a matter of opinion, if in other words, it is put forward as a legitimate social value, then we have at least one value—tolerance—that has escaped the relativist critique.

Let us now turn to two of the most prominent and influential approaches to ethics in contemporary society: utilitarianism and deontological ethics.

2.3 MODERN ETHICAL THEORY: UTILITARIAN ETHICS

Utilitarianism is the first ethical theory that we need to consider. Utilitarianism has had a significant impact on the modern world and has been especially influential in shaping politics, economics, and public policy. It therefore has had, and continues to have, an enormous influence on business. It will be helpful to start our consideration by locating utilitarianism within its historical context. Roots of utilitarian thinking can be found in Thomas Hobbes (1588–1679), David Hume (1711–1776), and Adam Smith (1723–1790), but the classic formulations are found in the works of Jeremy Bentham (1748–1832) and John Stuart Mill (1806–1873). Each of these social philosophers was writing against a background of the great democratic revolutions of the seventeenth and eighteenth centuries.

Utilitarianism tells us that we can determine the ethical significance of any action by looking to the consequences of that act. Utilitarianism is typically identified with the policy of "maximizing the overall good" or, in a slightly different version, of producing "the greatest good for the greatest number." Acts that accomplish this aim are good; those that do not are bad.

This emphasis on the overall good, and upon producing the greatest good for the greatest number, directly opposed authoritarian policies that aimed to benefit the political elite. Thus, utilitarianism provided strong support for democratic institutions and policies. Government and all social institutions exist for the well-being of all, not to further the interests of the monarch, the nobility, or some small minority. Likewise, the economy exists to provide this highest standard of living for the greatest number of people, not to create wealth for a privileged few.

Thus, utilitarianism is a *consequentialist* ethics. Good and bad acts are determined by their consequences. (How else might we judge acts? Well, sometimes we determine that we should or should not do something as a matter of principle, regardless of consequences. We'll look at this approach in more detail in the next section.) In this way, utilitarians tend to be pragmatic thinkers. No act is ever right or wrong in all cases in every situation. It will all depend on the consequences. For example, lying is neither right nor wrong in itself. There might be situations in which lying will produce greater overall good than telling the truth. In such a situation, it would be ethically right to tell a lie.

Consider as an example the case from the start of this chapter. Should the U.S. government pass a law that limits the amount of money corporate CEOs can be paid (or, at least, that can be credited as tax-deductible)? A utilitarian approach to this question will consider the likely consequences of either alternative. Limiting the amount of executive salary that can be deducted from taxes should provide a disincentive to corporations to pay such large salaries. In a world of finite resources, this should work to increase the average pay for other workers or lower costs to consumers. On the other hand, lower salaries might make it more difficult to attract highly qualified executives to U.S. firms and could result in less competitive U.S. companies. This would result in harm to everyone, including lower-paid workers and consumers. Either way, the ethical judgment made about the decision is a function of what happens after the fact.

By reasoning in this way, utilitarianism acknowledges two different types of value. Most value judgments are judgments of instrumental value; acts (e.g., telling the truth, allowing the manufacture of generic drugs) are valuable as a means (an instrument) to the end of producing some greater good. But there must be this other good, something valued for its own sake, which is the end for which other acts aim. If we judge our acts in terms of their consequences, then we must have some independent standard for deciding between good and bad consequences. There must be something of intrinsic value by which we can judge the consequences of our acts. All utilitarians agree that good and bad is a function of maximizing the overall good. They disagree, and therefore we find different versions of utilitarianism, over what is valued not for its consequences, but for itself.

In general, the utilitarian position is that happiness is the ultimate good. The only thing that is and can be valued for its own sake is happiness. (Does it sound absurd to you to claim that unhappiness is good and happiness is bad?) The goal of ethics, both individually and as a matter of public policy, should be to maximize the overall happiness. But, what exactly is happiness?

Jeremy Bentham argued that only pleasure, or at least the absence of pain, was intrinsically valuable. Happiness, according to Bentham, must be understood in terms of pleasure and the absence of pain; unhappiness is understood as pain, or the deprivation of pleasure. On Bentham's view, pleasure and pain are the two fundamental motivational factors of human nature. In his words,

> Nature has placed mankind under the governance of two sovereign masters, pain and pleasure. It is for them alone to point out what we ought to do, as well as to determine what we shall do. . . . They govern us in all we do, in all we say, in all we think.[4]

Consider, then, Bentham's utilitarian reasoning. Only pleasure and the absence of pain are valued for its own sake. Only pleasure and the absence of pain, therefore, are intrinsically, objectively, and indisputably good. If pleasure and the absence of pain are good, more pleasure (or less pain) is better and maximum pleasure (or minimum pain) is best. Therefore, maximizing pleasure (the utilitarian principle) is the fundamental, objective, and indisputable ethical principle.

While the imperative to maximize pleasure sounds egoistic, utilitarianism differs from *egoism* in important ways. Egoism, either psychological or ethical, focuses on the happiness of individuals. Utilitarian acts are judged by their consequences for the general and overall good. Consistent with their commitment to democratic equality, however, the general good includes the well-being of each individual affected by the action.

While agreeing with the general framework of Bentham's utilitarianism, John Stuart Mill defended a different understanding of happiness. Mill believed that there is a qualitative dimension to happiness that is missed by Bentham's focus on pleasure. Human happiness is not mere hedonism. According to Mill, humans are capable of enjoying a variety of experiences that produce happiness. Besides the pleasures of sensation that Bentham mentions, humans also experience social and intellectual pleasures that are qualitatively different from, and superior to, mere feelings. In a famous passage, Mill claims that "it is better to be a human being dissatisfied than a pig satisfied; better to be a Socrates dissatisfied than a fool satisfied."[5]

But the claim that there is a form of happiness that is qualitatively better than sensations of pleasure is controversial. How do we know, or how can we prove, that it is better to be Socrates dissatisfied than a fool satisfied? Mill's answer has significant ethical and social implications. To decide which pleasures and what type of happiness is better, according to Mill, we should consult with someone with the experience of both. Such experienced and competent judges are the best test for determining the highest happiness.

> Of two pleasures, if there be one to which all or almost all who have experience of both give a decided preference, . . . that is the more desirable pleasure.[6]

And if disagreement continues beyond this, Mill next suggests that

> From the verdict of the only competent judges, I apprehend there can be no appeal. On a question which is the best worth having of two pleasures . . . the judgment of those who are qualified by knowledge of both, of if they differ, that of the majority among them, must be admitted as final.[7]

Thus, Mill acknowledges that not all opinions are equal. Some people are more competent and more qualified than others in judging what is good. Mill's utilitarianism does not support an uncritical majority rule in which every opinion of what is good is treated as equally valid. However, we shouldn't abandon democracy because of this. The way to develop competent judges is through experience and education. People need to be educated and experienced in a variety of pleasures before they are competent to judge. Once they are experienced, then majority-rule democracy is the best way to make decisions.

Thus, in John Stuart Mill we find one of the classic defenses of liberal democracy and liberal education. The most fundamental ethical principle commits us to arranging society in such a way that we maximize the happiness for the greatest number of people. The best means for attaining this goal is an educated citizenry making decisions through a majority-rule democracy. The best method for securing an educated citizenry is to allow individuals the freedom of choice to pursue their own ends. Even when those choices are unwise, individuals are gaining the experience needed to distinguish between good and bad, higher and lower, pleasures.

These views have significant implications for business and economics. In classical free market economics, consumer demand is sovereign. Economic transactions occur when individuals seek their own happiness, understood as getting what they demand. If individuals make mistakes and buy products that fail to bring them satisfaction, they learn from their mistakes, no longer buy the product and, according to supply and demand, market forces eventually eliminate unsatisfactory products.

Perhaps utilitarianism's greatest contribution to social and political thought has come through its influence in economics. With roots in Adam Smith as well as in Bentham and Mill, the ethics of twentieth-century neoclassical economics—essentially what we think of as free market capitalism—is decidedly utilitarian. It is in this way that utilitarianism has had an overwhelming impact on business and business ethics.

Under free market economies, economic activity aims to satisfy consumer demand. The law of supply and demand tells us that economies should, and healthy economies do, produce (supply) those goods and services that consumers want (demand). Since scarcity and competition prevent everyone from getting all that they want, the goal of free market economics is to optimally satisfy wants. Free markets accomplish this goal by allowing individuals to decide for themselves what they most want and then bargain for these goods in a free and competitive marketplace. This process of allowing individuals to set their own preferences and bid for them in the marketplace will, over time and under the right conditions, guarantee the optimal satisfaction of wants.

This brief description suggests how free market economics fits the utilitarian framework. The end or goal of economic activity, what economists often refer to as utility or welfare, is the maximum satisfaction of consumer demand. We do the most good for the greatest number when we get as many people as possible as much of what they want as possible. The "good" is defined in terms of satisfying one's wants. But, since scarcity and competition prevent us from getting all that we want, individuals are left to rank-order their wants or, in other terms, to establish their own preferences. Thus, free market economics can be thought of as a version of preference utilitarianism, where the utilitarian goal is the maximum satisfaction of preferences.

Given this goal, free market economics advises us that the most efficient means to attain that goal is to structure our economy according to the principles of free market capitalism. We should allow individuals the freedom to bargain for themselves in an open, free, and competitive marketplace. Self-interested individuals (and mainstream economics assumes that this is at least a strong tendency among human motivations) will always be seeking ways to improve their own position. Agreements (contracts) will occur only in those situations where both parties believe that a transaction will improve their own position. In such a situation, the competition among rational and self-interested individuals will continuously work to promote the greatest overall good. Whenever a situation occurs in which one or more individuals can attain an improvement in their own happiness without a net loss in others' happiness, market forces will guarantee that this occurs. Thus, the market is seen as the most efficient means to the utilitarian end of maximizing happiness.

2.4 CHALLENGES TO UTILITARIANISM

We will examine the debates surrounding the free market version of utilitarianism in chapter 3. For now, let us consider some general challenges to the ethics of utilitarianism. We can classify these challenges into two groups. There are problems raised from within a utilitarian perspective that involve finding a defensible version of utilitarianism, and there are problems raised from outside that challenge the plausibility of the entire utilitarian project.

We will mention two challenges that are debated from within utilitarian perspectives. First, all utilitarians must find a defensible way to measure happiness. Phrases like "maximize the overall good" and the "greatest good for the greatest number" require some form of measurement and comparison (how else would you know that this situation rather than another has maximized the good?). Bentham went to great lengths to develop a "hedonistic calculus" to help quantify pleasures. Mill left it to the judgment of a majority of well-informed, competent judges. Economists substitute such measures as the Gross National Product for determining overall happiness. Bentham, Mill, and neo-classical economics all sought a scientific, measurable ethics. But there simply is no consensus among utilitarians on how to measure and determine the over-all good.

This problem is only compounded by the fact that utilitarians are commit-ted to considering all the consequences to all affected parties. Many business ethics issues highlight how difficult this could be. Consider the consequences of using nonrenewable energy sources and burning fossil fuels for energy. It is hard to see how a utilitarian could ever hope to calculate the consequences of a choice between investing in nonrenewables and continuing the present reliance on coal and oil. Yet this is exactly what is required by the utilitarian principle. (Attempts to shift focus, as economists often do, on to the "expected" utility of an act is to abandon utilitarianism. At that point we have adopted an ethics not of consequences but of intentions and that is no longer utilitarianism. We'll see this view developed in the following section.)

The second problem with the utilitarian perspective deals with differing versions of the good and the implications for human freedom. Historically, utilitarians are social and political liberals. That is, they all placed a very high value on individual freedom of choice. But there is a tension between objective accounts of the good and individual freedom. Simply put, free individuals do not always choose to do what is good for them. The more utilitarians empha-size freedom, the more likely they hold more relativistic accounts of the good. On this view, good is simply a matter of opinion, or individual desires, prefer-ences, and wants. However, this seems to abandon the entire project of ethics since, after all, people often desire what is trivial, immoral, and bad. On the other hand, the more utilitarians are willing to specify a content to the good life, the more the need to abandon the commitment to individual freedom. If we know what is truly good, then individuals ought to act in certain ways (to maximize the good) even if they don't want to. Finding a balance between indi-vidual freedom and the overall good is a challenge that confronts most versions of utilitarianism.

The final challenge is raised not from within the utilitarian perspective but goes directly to the core of utilitarianism. The essence of utilitarianism is its consequentialism. Good and bad acts are judged by their consequences. In short, the end justifies the means. But this seems to deny one of the earliest and most fundamental ethical principles that many of us have learned: The ends don't justify the means.

This challenge can be explained in terms of rules or principles. When we say that the ends don't justify the means what we are often saying is that there are certain rules or principles we should follow no matter what the conse-quences. Put another way, we have certain duties or obligations that we ought to obey even when doing so does not produce a net increase in overall happiness.

Examples of such duties are those required by such principles as justice, loyalty, and respect, as well as the duties that flow from our roles as parent, spouse, friend, and citizen. The approach to ethics, which emphasizes duties and obligations, is called *deontological ethics,* from the Greek word for duty. We will examine that ethical tradition in more detail in the next section.

Several examples can be used to explain this criticism. Since utilitarianism focuses on the overall consequences, utilitarianism seems willing to sacrifice the good of individuals for the greater overall good. So, for example, it might turn out that the overall happiness would be increased if we forced a small minority of the population into slave labor. Utilitarians could object to slavery, not as a matter of principle, but only if and to the degree that slavery detracts from the overall good. If it turns out that slavery increases the net overall happiness, utilitarianism would have to support slavery. In the judgment of many people, such a decision would violate the principles of justice, equality, and respect. As we will see developed in the following section, deontological ethics would appeal to the concept of ethical *rights* in criticizing utilitarianism. From that perspective, individuals possess certain basic rights that should not be violated even if doing so would increase the overall social happiness. Thus, critics of the Sabo Bill argue that businesses should be free to decide for themselves what to pay their executives. The income paid to executives belongs to the corporation, not to the government, and therefore such a law would violate their property rights. Rights function to protect certain central interests from being sacrificed for the greater overall happiness. Utilitarians can defend rights only to the degree that rights contribute to the overall good.

Another counterexample that can be raised against utilitarianism looks to specific relationships and commitments that we all make. For example, as a parent we love our children and have certain duties to them. Imagine a situation in which you have to choose between saving the life of your child and saving the life of a talented dedicated brain surgeon. Utilitarians are committed to determining the ethical decision by calculating the overall consequences of each choice and doing whatever will maximize the overall good. The example can be arranged in such a way that saving the brain surgeon clearly contributes to the overall good. But what ethical judgment should we make about the parent who even begins to make such calculations?

Utilitarians would seem to be committed to parental love and duty only to the degree that such love and duty contributes to the overall good. Parents should love their children because this contributes to the overall good of society. (And if it doesn't?) But surely this misrepresents (and insults) the nature of parental love. I do not love my children because of the consequences that this might have for society. Deontologists would argue that there are certain commitments that we make, certain duties that we have, which should not be violated even if doing so would increase the net overall happiness. Violating such commitments and duties would require individuals to sacrifice their own integrity for the common good. Thus, Aaron Feuerstein might claim that despite bad overall consequences, he had to remain loyal to his employees as a matter of principle. Or, critics of excessive executive compensation might claim that gross inequality in pay is unfair and unjust in principle. We will consider similar themes of professional commitments and duties when a later chapter examines the role of professional responsibilities within business institutions.

2.5 UTILITARIANISM AND BUSINESS POLICY

Before moving on to deontological ethics, it will be helpful to connect utilitarian ethics to some general concerns of business ethics. At its most basic, utilitarianism is a social philosophy, offering criteria by which the basic structure of social institutions, such as business and the economy, ought to be determined. Social institutions should be structured in whatever way will maximize the overall good.

As we have seen, critics of utilitarianism deny that this is an adequate or complete social ethics. But even among utilitarians there is disagreement about the best means for attaining the utilitarian goal. It will be useful to introduce two versions of utilitarian thinking at this point. In general, utilitarians are committed to whatever means attain the ends of maximum happiness. On this view, policy questions are really pragmatic questions that depend on the specific circumstances of time and place. Nevertheless, some general policy patterns can be identified.

One version of utilitarianism public policy holds that there are experts who can predict the outcome of various policies and carry out policies that will attain our ends. These experts, usually trained in social sciences such as economics, are familiar with the specifics of how society works and can therefore determine which policy will maximize the overall good.

This approach to public policy underlies one theory of the entire administrative and bureaucratic side of government. On this view, the legislative body (from Congress to local city councils) establishes the public goals, and the administrative side (presidents, governors, mayors) executes (administers) policies to fulfill these goals. The people working within the administration, the classic government bureaucrats, should know how the social and political system works and use this knowledge to carry out the mandate of the legislature. The government is filled with such people, typically trained in such fields as economics, law, social science, public policy, and political science. This approach, for example, would justify widespread government regulation of business on the grounds that such regulation will ensure that business activities do contribute to the overall good.

Consider how the Federal Reserve Board sets interest rates. There is an established goal, a public policy "good," that the Federal Reserve takes to be the greatest good for the country. (This goal is something like the highest sustainable rate of economic growth compatible with minimal inflation.) The Fed examines the relevant economic data and makes a judgment about the present and future state of the economy. If economic activity seems to be slowing down, the Fed might decide to lower interest rates as a means for stimulating economic growth. If the economy seems to be growing too fast and the inflation rate is increasing, they might choose to raise interest rates. Lowering or raising interest rates in itself is neither good nor bad; the rightness of the act depends on the consequences. The role of the public servant is to use his or her expertise to judge the likely consequences and make the decision that is most likely to produce the best result.

A second influential version of utilitarian policy invokes the tradition of Adam Smith and claims that competitive markets are the best means for attaining utilitarian goals. This version would promote policies that deregulate private industry, protect property rights, allow for free exchanges, and encourage competition. In such situations the self-interest of rational individuals will result, as if led by "an invisible hand" in Adam Smith's terms, to the maximum satisfaction of individual happiness.

The dispute between these two versions of utilitarian policy, what we might call the "expert" and the "market" versions, characterizes many disputes in business ethics. One clear example concerns regulation of unsafe workplaces. One side argues that questions of safety and risk should be determined by experts who then establish standards that business is required to meet. Government regulators (in this case, the Occupational Health and Safety Administration, or OSHA) are then charged with enforcing safety standards in the workplace. The other side argues that the best judges of acceptable risk and safety are workers themselves. A free and competitive labor market will ensure that people will get the level of safety that they want. Individuals calculate for themselves what risks they wish to take and what trade-offs they are willing to make in order to attain safety. Workers willing to take risks likely will be paid more than workers who demand safe work environments. Thus, a market-based solution will prove best at optimally satisfying these various and competing interests.

There is no question that utilitarian reasoning dominates among policy makers and policy administrators. Policy experts at all levels are focused on results and on getting things done. This makes the utilitarian emphasis on consequences particularly attractive to fields such as economics, business, and government. It seems obvious that policy questions should be judged by results and consequences. The utilitarian emphasis on measuring, comparing, and quantifying also re-enforces the view that policy makers should be neutral administrators. The standard view is that policy goals should be left to the democratic decisions of the people. The people decide what they want and what makes them happy; the job of social policy is simply to help them attain those goals in as efficient a manner as possible. Efficiency is simply another word for maximizing happiness.

Finally, like utilitarians, policy experts are concerned with the well-being of the whole community. Their focus is on the collective or aggregate good. By their very nature, policy makers take a broad social perspective. This, too, is consistent with the utilitarian emphasis on the overall good.

Despite these close connections between utilitarianism and public policy, serious ethical challenges remain. We turn now to a major alternative to utilitarian ethics: deontological ethics.

2.6 DEONTOLOGICAL ETHICS

Deontology and deontological ethics refer to a concept that is quite familiar to most of us. This approach to ethics, both in matters of individual morality and of public policy, emphasizes the fact that sometimes the correct path is determined not by its consequences but by certain duties. More familiar synonyms for *duty* include obligations, commitments, and responsibilities. The deontological approach faults utilitarianism for thinking that our acts should always be judged by their consequences to the overall good. Deontology denies the utilitarian belief that the ends do justify the means. It holds that there are some things that we should, or should not, do regardless of the consequences.

To understand why the ends don't justify the means we need to emphasize that utilitarian ends are focused on the collective or aggregate good. Utilitarianism is concerned with the well-being of the whole. (This was one of the things that makes utilitarianism attractive to public policy makers.) But many of us have a deep commitment to the dignity of individuals. We believe that individuals should not be used as a mere means to the greater overall good. A prominent way of explaining this is to say that individuals have rights that should not be sacrificed simply to produce a net increase in the collective good.

Consider the debate mentioned previously concerning child labor in the developing world. Some policy makers in impoverished countries believe that the best means for raising the standard of living within their country is to increase exports. This brings in hard currency with which the country can pay for food, medicine, and education (and repay debts!). Increasing exports will raise the standard of living for all citizens and thereby meet the utilitarian goal of improving the collective good. However, to increase exports a country must be capable of selling their goods at costs below that of competing countries. Since labor is a major production costs, keeping labor costs low helps the country as a whole. Unfortunately, one means for maintaining low labor costs is to employ young children. (Cases of child labor in the manufacture of sneakers and clothing are only the most well-publicized instances of an all too common phenomena.)

Is it ethical to use young children in such circumstances? Defenders of this practice argue, typically on good utilitarian grounds, that the children are better off with the jobs than without them, that they contribute to their own family's income, and that they contribute to the overall welfare of their society. Critics claim, on deontological grounds, that it is unethical to treat young children this way even if there are beneficial results. On this view, child labor is ethically equivalent to child abuse and slavery. It is something wrong on principle.

Within one tradition of deontology, our ethical duty is explained in terms of a principle that the German philosopher Immanual Kant called the categorical imperative. (An imperative is a command or duty; *categorical* means that it is without exception.) Our primary duty is, according to Kant, to act only in those ways in which the maxim of our acts could be made a universal law. This is a very abstract way of saying something that is fairly intuitive. The "maxim" of our acts can be thought of as the intention behind our acts. The maxim answers the question: What am I doing?

Kant tells us that we should act only according to those maxims that could be universally accepted and acted on. (Consider how Kant might respond to the egoist view that all human behavior is intended for one's own self-interest.) For example, Kant believed that truth telling could, but lying could not, be made a universal law. If everyone lied whenever it suited them, rational communication would be impossible. Thus lying is unethical. This condition of universality, not unlike the Golden Rule, prohibits us from giving our own personal point of view privileged status over the points of view of others. It is a strong requirement of impartiality and equality for ethics.

Kant also provided two other versions of this categorical imperative that are less abstract. He claimed that ethics requires us to treat all people as ends and never only as means. In yet another formulation, we are required to treat people as subjects, not as objects. These formulations restate the commitment to treat people as capable of thinking and choosing for themselves. Humans are subjects (they perform the act rather than being acted upon, to use the familiar subject/object categories from grammar). They have their own ends and purposes and therefore should not be treated simply as a means to the ends of others. In chapter 3, we will examine a view on corporate social responsibility that concludes, on Kantian grounds, that business managers have direct ethical responsibilities to all parties (stakeholders) who are affected by business activities.

Thus, on this Kantian theory our fundamental ethical duty is to treat people with respect, to treat them as equally capable of living an autonomous life. But since each person has this same fundamental duty towards others, each of us can be said to have the right to be treated with respect, the right to be treated as an end and never as a means only. I have the right to pursue my own autonomously chosen ends as long as I do not in turn treat other people as means to my ends.

This points to a common way of understanding rights and duties. Philosophers will sometimes claim that rights and duties are correlative. This is to say that my rights establish your duties and my duties correspond to the rights of others. The deontological tradition focuses on duties, which can be thought of as establishing the ethical limits of my behavior. From my perspective, duties are what I owe to others. Other people have certain claims upon my behavior; they have, in other words, certain rights against me.

Thus, to return to the earlier example, the Kantian would object to child labor because such practices violate our duty to treat children with respect. We violate the rights of children when we treat them as mere means to the ends of production and economic growth. We are treating them merely as means because, as children, they are incapable of rationally and freely choosing their own ends.

From this beginning, the deontological, or rights-based, approach to ethics gets more complex. A complete theory must specify what rights we have and how they are justified, the range and scope of rights, and some process for prioritizing rights and resolving conflicts between different rights. As preparation for evaluating many of the debates to follow, we will pursue these questions briefly.

One way to understand rights is to think of them as protecting interests. We often make a distinction between a person's wants and interests. Wants (or desires) are psychological states of an individual. They are what, as a matter of fact, people will pursue. Wants are subjectively known, in the sense that individuals enjoy a privileged status for knowing what they want. (Imagine disagreeing with a person's claim that they want something.) Interests work for a person's benefit and are objectively connected to what is good for that person. People don't always want what it is in their interest to have.

For example, if given the choice my children would want to eat sugar-coated breakfast cereal each morning. Their parents deny them this on the grounds that it is not in their interests to eat such food. In this case, wants and interests conflict. Likewise, many college students want to skip class, but it is not in their interest to do so. On the other hand, wants and interests can coincide. You want a good education and good health, both of which are in your interests to have.

As we have seen, some versions of utilitarianism take happiness, understood as the satisfaction of wants, as the final goal of ethics. This version would either deny the distinction between wants and interests (interests being simply strong wants) or argue that the best way to decide what is in someone's interest is to let them decide for themselves (i.e., let them pursue their own wants). Either way, utilitarians believe that all wants/interests equally deserve to be satisfied to the degree that they equally produce happiness. If your desire for protection against an unsafe workplace is equal to my desire for high wages, each equally deserves satisfaction. Given this equality, the utilitarian commitment to satisfy as many wants as possible seems a reasonable strategy. But deontologists argue that wants and interests are not equal. They argue that at least some interests are so important to the well-being of an individual that they should not be sacrificed simply for a net increase in the overall happiness. Rights serve to protect these interests from being sacrificed.

Consider the case of downloading and sharing music and movie files over the Internet. A plausible case could be made that we would promote greater overall happiness by adopting a public policy that allowed unlimited and unrestricted downloads. Only a relatively small minority of people, mostly performing artists and producers, would be unhappy. On utilitarian grounds, it would seem that we would best serve the public interest by allowing unregulated downloads. However, the artists and producers would claim that they have property rights that should prohibit such a policy. The interests that the public might have in listening to free music or watching free videos is not on a par with the interests that individuals have in controlling their own property. Rights are sometimes described as "trumps" that override the collective will. They function in this way because they protect certain interests that are more important and central to human well-being than the mere happiness of others. The connection between rights and interests is important because it provides a way for determining which rights we have. By identifying central important interests, and distinguishing them from mere wants, we can determine the range of human rights.

So what rights do we have? The challenge is to develop an account that creates neither too many nor too few rights. Here is another example from my local community. City planners have a blueprint for road construction throughout the area. One of the planned roads would cut through and destroy a rare oak woodland within the city. When the plan was announced, local residents objected to the road on a variety of environmental grounds. The director of the regional planning group answered protesters by claiming that local citizens "have a right to uncongested roads." Surely this theory of rights is too extensive. The connection between rights and duties that we mentioned previously is a good test for this. If rights imply duties, and if people have a right to uncongested roads, then it would seem that someone (local government?) has the duty to provide enough roads to prevent people from ever having to sit in a traffic jam. It is difficult to see how this could be done without wreaking havoc on the well-being of many people by raising taxes, destroying neighborhoods, taking away property, and so on.

This suggests that we do not get "rights" simply by wanting something very badly. (Critics charge that this is a problem with rights-based ethics. It encourages people towards self-centered individualism, trying to privilege their own selfish wants by calling them rights. Anything that someone wants eventually gets called a right and thereby people come to expect society to provide this for them.) But we also don't want to have too narrow a view of rights. Too weak an account, or too few rights, collapses the entire theory towards utilitarianism.

We can at least sketch a general account of rights by returning to the original idea of respect and the elements of autonomy and dignity on which it is based. What human characteristic justifies the assumption that humans possess a special dignity? Why would it be wrong to treat humans as mere means or objects, rather than as ends or subjects?

The most common answer offered through the Western ethical tradition is that the human capacity to make rational choices is the distinctive human characteristic. Humans do not act only out of instinct and conditioning, they make free choices about how they live their lives, about their own ends. In this sense, humans are said to have autonomy. Humans are subjects in the sense that they originate action, they choose, they act for their own ends. To treat someone as a means or as an object is to deny to them this distinctive and essential human characteristic; it would be to deny to them their very humanity.

From this we can see how two related rights have emerged as fundamental within philosophical ethics. If autonomy, or self-rule, is a fundamental characteristic of human nature, then the freedom to make our own choices deserves special protection as a basic right. But since all humans possess this fundamental characteristic, equal treatment (or equal consideration) is also a fundamental right.

In summary, we can say that rights offer protection of certain central human interests, prohibiting the sacrifice of these interests merely to provide a net increase in the overall happiness. But interests, as opposed to desires, are connected to human well-being in an objective manner. Human nature, characterized as the capacity for free and autonomous choice, provides the grounds for distinguishing central interests from mere wants.

2.7 VIRTUE ETHICS

For the most part, utilitarian and deontological approaches to ethics focus on rules and principles that we might follow in deciding what we, both as individuals and as citizens, should do. Chapter 1 pointed out, however, that ethics also involves questions about the type of person one should become. Virtue ethics is a tradition within philosophical ethics that seeks a full and detailed description of those character traits, or virtues, that would constitute a good and full human life. Before concluding this chapter, it will be worthwhile to consider some of the virtues, and corresponding vices, that might be relevant to business ethics.

To understand how virtue ethics differs from utilitarian and deontological approaches, return to the discussion of psychological egoism. The biggest challenge posed by egoism, and according to some the biggest challenge to ethics, is the apparent gap between self-regarding and other-regarding motivation. Ethics requires us, at least at times, to act for the well-being of others. The degree to which we are capable of doing this seems to depend on a variety of factors such as our interests, our desires, our beliefs, our dispositions, our values; in short, on our character or the type of person we are. If a person is caring, empathetic, charitable, and sympathetic, then the challenge of egoism is simply not a factor in their decision making. One senses that, given the type of person he is, Aaron Feuerstein never really considered the possibility of moving his manufacturing plant to a foreign country. Such a self-centered decision was not really an option for someone with his values and character.

As another example, consider the case of excessive CEO pay. It is important to remember that not every CEO demands an exorbitant salary. The language of virtues and vices would seem very relevant as we think about the motivations involved. Why do some people demand hundreds of millions of dollars a year while others are happy with much less? Virtues such as modesty, moderation, self-control, unselfishness, and humility come to mind when we think about a CEO who could, but does not, take an excessive salary. Self-indulgence, greed, callousness, competitiveness, and selfishness come to mind about the others. To a person with moderate and constrained desires, an exorbitant salary is simply not an option. It would be out of character.

Whereas Kantian ethics especially, and utilitarian ethics to a lesser degree, requires us to disregard personal emotions and feelings, virtue ethics gives the more affective side of our character equal standing. Virtue ethics recognizes that our motivations—our interests, wants, desires—are not the sorts of things that each one of us chooses anew each morning. Instead, human beings act in and from character. These character traits are, typically by adulthood, deeply ingrained and conditioned within us. Given that our character plays such a deciding role in our behavior, and given the realization that our character can be shaped by factors that are controllable (by conscious individual decisions, by how we are raised, by the social institutions in which we live, work, and learn), virtue ethics seeks to understand how those traits are formed and which traits bolster and which undermine a meaningful, worthwhile, and satisfying human life.

Virtue ethics can offer us a more fully textured understanding of life within business. Rather than simply describing people as good or bad, right or wrong, an ethics of virtue encourages a fuller description. For example, we might describe Aaron Feuerstein as heroic and courageous. He is a man of integrity, who sympathizes with employees and cares about their well-being. Other executives might be described as greedy or ruthless, proud or competitive. Faced with a difficult dilemma, we might ask what would a person with integrity do? What would an honest person say? Do I have the courage of my convictions?

But virtue ethics seeks more than a detailed description of business life. Like all ethical theories, virtue ethics is also prescriptive in offering advice on how we should live. Virtue ethics calls on us to reflect on two deeper questions. Given a more detailed and textured description of moral behavior, which set of virtues are more likely to embody a full, satisfying, meaningful, enriched, and worthy human life? Business provides many opportunities for behavior that is generous or greedy, ruthless or compassionate, fair or manipulative. Given these opportunities, each one of us must ask which character traits are likely to help us live a good life and which are likely to frustrate this. What type of person are we to be?

Besides connecting the virtues to a conception of a fuller human life, virtue ethics also reminds us to examine how character traits are formed and conditioned. By the time we are adults, much of our character is formed by such factors as our parents, schools, church, friends, and society. But powerful social institutions such as business and especially our own places of employment and our particular social roles within them (e.g., manager, professional, trainee) have a profound influence on shaping our character. An accounting firm that hires a group of trainees fully expecting that fewer than half will be retained and only a very small group will make partner encourages motivations and behavior very different from a firm that hires fewer people but gives them all a greater chance at long-term success. A company that sets unrealistic sales goals will find it creates a different sales force than one that understands sales more as customer service. Virtue ethics reminds us to look to the actual practices we find in the business world and ask what type of people are being created by these practices. Many individual moral dilemmas that arise within business ethics can best be understood as arising from a tension between the type of person we seek to be and the type of person business expects us to be.

Consider an example described to me by someone who is conducting empirical studies of the values found within marketing firms and advertising agencies. This person reported that on several occasions advertising agents told her that they would never allow their own children to watch the very television shows and advertisements that their own firm was producing. By their own admission the ads for such shows aim to manipulate children into buying, or getting their parents to buy, products that had little or no real value. In some cases the ads promoted beer drinking and the advertisers themselves admitted, as their "dirty little secret," that they were targeted for the teenage market. Further, their own research showed them how successful their ads were in increasing sales.

Independent of the ethical questions we might ask about advertising aimed at children, a virtue ethics approach would look at the type of person who is so able to disassociate oneself and one's own values from one's work, and the social institutions and practices that encourage it. What kind of person is willing to subject children to marketing practices that they are unwilling to accept for their own children? Such a person seems to lack even the most elementary form of personal integrity. What kind of institution encourages people to treat children in ways that they willingly admit are indecent? What kind of person does one become working in such an institution?

2.8 SUMMARY AND REVIEW

No doubt this survey of philosophical ethics might appear very abstract and far removed from the business world. Despite such appearances, these are fundamental categories for thinking about ethical issues. But we should resist the temptation to treat these theories as some external rules that should be applied to situations in a way that produces specific decisions. It is better to think of these theories as attempts to extract and articulate the basic principles already present in common ways of thinking. Once such principles are clearly described, the philosopher's role is to draw out their implications and offer justifications of them. Then the principles can be brought back to bear on practical decision making. Understood in this way, ethical theories are not as abstract and nebulous as they might at first appear. They have emerged from common ways of thinking as much as they are intended to guide our ways of thinking.

Consider utilitarianism. The fundamental insight of utilitarian thinking is that we should consider the consequences, all the consequences, of our actions before deciding what to do. A reasonable principle is that we should consider not only the consequences that our acts might have for ourselves, but also the consequences of our acts for all parties affected by them. The ethical theory of utilitarianism tries to work out the implications of this insight. In doing so, this theory has presented a powerful approach to answer the fundamental ethical question: How should we live our lives?

It would not be an overstatement to suggest that most economic decisions are implicitly justified on utilitarian grounds. Understanding utilitarianism, both its strengths and weaknesses, is necessary for developing a reasoned perspective on many economic matters. From the original rationale for market-based economies found in Adam Smith, to the original legal rationale for creating limited-liability corporations, to much public policy and law-governing finance, employment, consumerism, and world trade, utilitarian considerations have played a prominent, if not deciding, role.

Likewise, deontological approaches to ethics capture another insight that is recognized in such common observations as "the ends don't justify the means." If utilitarian ethics make judgments in terms of consequences, deontological approaches demand that something should, or should not, be done regardless of the consequences. Some acts are right or wrong as a matter of principle, and it is our duty to act accordingly even if beneficial consequences would suggest otherwise. Respecting individual rights and fulfilling our ethical obligations can set limits on decisions aimed at producing good consequences.

The language of rights and obligations will play a major role in all the discussions that follow. One need only reflect on such phrases as "human resource management" and "labor as a factor of production" to see that Kantian ethics will have much to contribute to discussions about how employees ought to be treated. Treating employees as mere means to the end of productivity, while perhaps useful in terms of beneficial consequences, is something that deontological ethics rejects. Likewise, the professional duties associated with the gatekeeping roles as accountants, auditors, lawyers, financial analysts, and boards of directors also function as ethical limitations on business activities.

Finally, virtue ethics encourages us to step back from specific decisions and actions to ask the very profound and personal questions: Who am I? What type of person am I to be? Throughout the course of our lives, each one of us develops a personal character that is reflected in what we believe, what we value, what we desire, and how we act. This character is manifested in our habits, dispositions, personality. The ethics of virtue seeks to articulate which of those habits and character traits are likely to be part of a meaningful and happy human life. Whether reflected in the ordinary language of such virtues as honesty, integrity, modesty, and trustworthiness, or such vices as greed, materialism, belligerence, and rudeness, virtue ethics plays an important role in ordinary business life.

The basic approaches to ethics outlined in this chapter will provide essential tools for understanding business ethics, and for making responsible ethical decisions in business.

REFLECTIONS ON THE CHAPTER DISCUSSION CASE

Consider two very different responses to the enormous pay packages described in the opening discussion case. One response might be to shrug one's shoulders and claim that this is just the way it is. One could simply acknowledge that some people have power over vast amounts of corporate wealth and they use that power to reap huge financial benefits for themselves and their friends. In fact, few observers either within or outside of corporate business have taken this approach. Without exception, the public response to these pay packages has been normative or evaluative. That is, everyone takes a stand either to criticize or to defend these decisions. It would be difficult to have an opinion about executive compensation that did not involve ethical concepts and categories.

Reflecting on these stands, one can discover patterns in the way that most people think about such normative issues. Many people judge the ethics of executive compensation in terms of consequences, either beneficial for defenders or harmful according to critics. Deciding between these views would involve, at least in part, investigating the real world consequences that result from such pay packages. Ethical analysis will sometimes require such empirical investigation: Is high executive compensation, in fact, highly correlated with performance? Do stock options, in fact, encourage short-term thinking or earnings manipulation? Determining the facts will often play an important role in ethical analysis, and this would be a helpful first step to take in the process of analysis.

This case also raises ethical issues of principles and standards that do not involve empirical consequences. Ownership rights and fiduciary duties are two such factors that establish ethical constraints on consequentialist thinking. For example, many argue that board members have a fiduciary duty to stockholders that should trump their desire to benefit corporate executives. A helpful step in the process of identifying principles and duties is to ask who might be benefited and who might be harmed by alternative decisions. Once such stakeholders have been identified, one should then ask if there are any individuals or institutions that have a duty to provide the benefit or prevent the harm.

Finally, this case also raises questions about personal virtues and vices. At first glance, this is a descriptive activity: Describe someone who so desires money that he would manipulate an earnings report; describe someone for whom a salary of several hundred thousands of dollars each year is not enough. But within these descriptions are normative and evaluative components. A person described as greedy has a real character flaw; a person of integrity is to be praised and honored. One challenge to such descriptions, of course, is to answer the "so what?" question. So what if I am greedy? Why should I care if I lack integrity? These questions go to the heart of ethical motivation. Business ethics seeks not only to justify good and right behavior, it also seeks to motivate people to act accordingly. This is among the foremost ethical challenges facing contemporary business managers.

REVIEW QUESTIONS

1. Describe ethical relativism and at least three philosophical challenges to this position.
2. Distinguish between psychological egoism as an empirical claim and as a conceptual claim. What is the most serious challenge to each version?
3. Distinguish between utilitarian, deontological, and virtue-based approaches to ethics. What are the strengths and weaknesses of each?
4. How are utilitarian ethics relevant to business? Explain at least three major challenges to utilitarian ethics.
5. How does deontological ethics establish a connection between individual rights and the nature of human beings?
6. Develop a list of virtues and vices. As a helpful way to begin, think about the pledge offered by Boy Scouts and Girls Scouts that begins: "A scout is trustworthy, loyal, helpful. . . ." Are these various virtues unified in any way?

ENDNOTES

[1]*Fortune,* June 25, 2001. This special report included the following articles: "The Great
CEO Pay Heist" by Geoffrey Colvin (p. 64), "This Stuff Is Wrong" by Carol Loomis
(p. 73), and "The Amazing Stock Option Sleight of Hand" by Justin Fox (p. 86).

[2]The following sources were used in developing this case: Herman Daly, *Beyond Growth*
(Boston, Beacon Press, 1996); Bethany McLean, "Where's the Loot Coming From?"
Fortune (Sept. 7, 1998), 128–130; John Byrne, "The Flap over Executive Pay,"
BusinessWeek (May 6, 1994); Anne Fisher, "Readers on CEO Pay: Many Are Angry,
a Few Really Think the Big Guy Is Worth It," *Fortune* (June 8,1998); Edward Wolff,
Top Heavy: A Study of the Increasing Inequality of Wealth in America (New York:
Twentieth Century Fund Press, 1995); *Forbes* (May 18, 1998, and May 17, 1999);
"Executive Summary;" *Executive Compensation Report,* United for a Fair Economy
(Boston: 1996); Congressional Record, February 11, 1999; and Representative Mar-
tin Sabo's webpage: www.house.gov/sabo.

[3]For a persuasive analysis of the ethics of executive compensation, see Jeffrey Moriarty,
"How to (Try to) Justify CEO Pay," Bill Shaw, "Justice, Incentives, and Executive
Compensation," and Jared Harris, "How Much Is Too Much: A Theoretical
Analysis of Executive Compensation from the Standpoint of Distributive Justice"
in *The Ethics of Executive Compensation,* Robert Kold, editor (Boulder, CO: Japha
Volume in Business Ethics, Blackwell Publishing, 2005).

[4]Jeremy Bentham, *An Introduction to the Principles of Morals and Legislation* (Oxford:
Clarendon Press, 1907), p. 1.

[5]John Stuart Mill, *Utilitarianism,* ed. George Sher (Indianapolis: Hackett Publishing Co.,
1979), p. 10.

[6]Ibid., p. 8.

[7]Ibid., p. 11.

3 CHAPTER

Corporate Social Responsibility

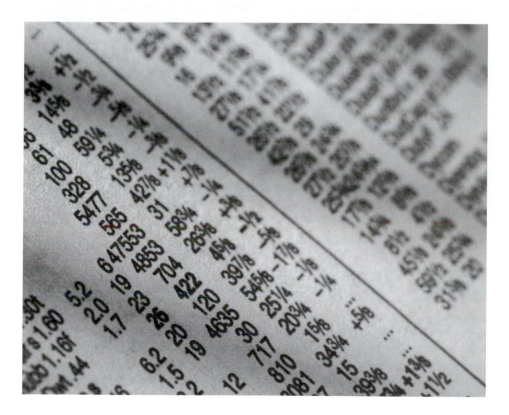

After reading this chapter, you will be able to:

- Explain and review the utilitarian and rights-based justifications for the classical model of corporate social responsibility;

- Explain how the classical model is extended and developed through a moral minimum;

- Describe the stakeholder model of corporate social responsibility;
- Explain the ethical foundations of the stakeholder model.

DISCUSSION CASE: Wal-Mart

In October 2005, the *New York Times* published a story detailing a Wal-Mart internal memo that outlined various proposals for reducing health care costs paid for Wal-Mart employees. The memo recommended two major areas for action: increase reliance on part-time workers who do not qualify for health care benefits, and seek ways to encourage healthier and discourage unhealthy job applicants and employees. The memo also acknowledged long-standing criticisms of Wal-Mart's treatment of its employees and offered suggestions for a public relations strategy that would deflect criticism of these proposed changes.

The memo was written by M. Susan Chambers, Wal-Mart's executive vice president for employee benefits. The memo pointed out that Wal-Mart employees "are getting sicker than the national population, particularly in obesity-related diseases," including diabetes and coronary artery disease. In one passage, Chambers recommended that Wal-Mart would arrange for "all jobs to include some physical activity (e.g., all cashiers do some cart-gathering)" as a means to deter unhealthy employees and job applicants. "It will be far easier to attract and retain a healthier workforce than it will be to change behavior in an existing one," the memo said. "These moves would also dissuade unhealthy people from coming to work at Wal-Mart."

Recognizing that young workers are paid less and require fewer health benefits than older workers and are equally productive, the memo recommended strategies, including reducing 401(k) retirement contributions and offering education benefits, for attracting younger employees and discouraging older employees. The memo stated: "The cost of an associate with seven years of tenure is almost 55 percent more than the cost of an associate with one year of tenure, yet there is no difference in his or her productivity. Moreover, because we pay an associate more in salary and benefits as his or her tenure increases, we are pricing that associate out of the labor market, increasing the likelihood that he or she will stay with Wal-Mart."

The memo pointed out that 46 percent of the children of Wal-Mart's 1.33 million U.S. employees were uninsured or on Medicaid. "Wal-Mart's critics can easily exploit some aspects of our benefits offering to make their case; in other words, our critics are correct in some of their observations. Specifically, our coverage is expensive for low-income families, and Wal-Mart has a significant percentage of associates and their children on public assistance."

As this memo acknowledged, Wal-Mart has had a mixed record on social responsibility. By most accounts Wal-Mart is among the most successful companies in the world. Its revenues for 2004 were $259 billion, more than three times larger than the next largest retailer. For comparison, in the same year

Saudi Arabia was ranked as the thirtieth largest economy in the world with an estimated GDP of $287 billion and Switzerland was ranked thirty-fifth largest with a GDP of $240 billion. Wal-Mart operates almost 5,000 stores, and over 3,000 of them are in the United States. It is estimated that 138 million people shop at Wal-Mart each week. Worldwide, Wal-Mart employs 1.4 million people. It is the largest private employer in the United States and the single largest employer in 25 separate U.S. states.

Wal-Mart's financial performance has been remarkable. Wal-Mart stock was first publicly traded in 1970 when 300,000 shares were offered at $16.50 per share. In 1999 Wal-Mart stock experienced its eleventh 2 for 1 split. One hundred shares bought in 1970 would be equal to 204,800 shares valued at $53 a share at the end of 2004. An initial $1,650 investment would be worth $10.8 million. In 2003 Helen Walton, widow of Wal-Mart founder Sam Walton, and her four children ranked as five of the wealthiest eight people in the United States. Their combined wealth was estimated to be over $100 billion, more than twice the worth of Microsoft founder Bill Gates.

Wal-Mart was founded in the early 1960s by Sam Walton in Rogers, Arkansas. Walton's original marketing strategy was to emphasize low prices and this strategy continues today as reflected in its marketing campaign of "Everyday low prices." Wal-Mart is able to achieve low retail prices by leveraging its buying power as the world's largest retailer and by controlling labor costs. Wal-Mart sells more socks, toothpaste, dog food, sporting goods, guns, diamonds, and groceries than any other business in the world. Alone, they account for 30 percent of all household goods (laundry detergent, soap, paper towels), 15 percent of all CDs as well as 28 percent of Dial soap's total sales, 24 percent of Del Monte Foods, 23 percent of Clorox, and 23 percent of Revlon.[1] Wal-Mart is the single largest importer from China, accounting for almost 10 percent of all Chinese imports to the United States, worth an estimated $12 billion in 2002. In 2003 Wal-Mart was named *Fortune* magazine's "Most Admired" retail company.

At first glance, there are many values promoted by Wal-Mart's success. Stockholders have received significant financial benefits from Wal-Mart. Consumers also receive financial benefits in the form of low prices, employees benefit from having jobs, many businesses benefit from supplying Wal-Mart with goods and services, and communities benefit from tax-paying corporate citizens.

Wal-Mart cites several other values that it promotes in its own self-description. Wal-Mart describes itself as a business that "was built upon a foundation of honesty, respect, fairness and integrity." What is described as the "Wal-Mart culture" is based on three "basic beliefs" attributed to founder Sam Walton: respect for individuals, service to customers, and striving for excellence.

Despite this, not everyone agrees that Wal-Mart lives up to high ethical standards. In contrast to *Fortune* magazine's claim, critics portray Wal-Mart as among the least admired corporations in the world. Ethical criticisms have been raised against Wal-Mart on behalf of every major constituency—customers, employees, suppliers, competitors, communities—with whom Wal-Mart interacts. For example, some critics charge that Wal-Mart's low-priced goods, and even their placement within stores, are a ploy to entice customers to purchase more and higher-priced goods. Such critics would charge Wal-Mart with deceptive and manipulative pricing and marketing.

Perhaps the greatest ethical criticisms of Wal-Mart have involved treatment of workers. Wal-Mart is well-known for its aggressive practices aimed at controlling labor costs. Wal-Mart argues that this is part of their strategy to offer the lowest possible prices to consumers. By controlling labor costs through wages, minimum work hours, and high productivity, and by keeping unions away, Wal-Mart is able to offer consumers the lowest everyday prices.

Among the criticisms of Wal-Mart's labor practices are claims that Wal-Mart pays its workers poverty-level wages. The average annual salary for a Wal-Mart sales associate in 2001 was $13,861, and the average hourly wage was $8.23. For the same year, the U.S. federal poverty level for a family of three was $14,630. Wal-Mart offers health care benefits to full-time workers, but, relative to other employers, Wal-Mart employees pay a disproportionately high percentage of the costs. According to critics, these low wages and benefits result in many Wal-Mart employees qualifying for government assistance programs such as food stamps and health care, effectively creating a government subsidy for Wal-Mart's low wages.

Wal-Mart has also been accused of illegally requiring employees to work overtime without pay and to work off-the-clock. Employees in Wisconsin, Michigan, Missouri, Kansas, Ohio, Washington, Illinois, West Virginia, and Iowa have filed lawsuits alleging such illegal labor practices. Wal-Mart has also been accused of obstructing employees' attempt to organize unions. The National Labor Relations Board filed suit against Wal-Mart stores in Pennsylvania and Texas charging illegal antiunion activities. Maine's Department of Labor fined Wal-Mart for violating child labor laws, finding 1,436 child labor law infractions in some 20 different Wal-Mart stores. Wal-Mart has also been sued in Missouri, California, Arkansas, and Arizona for violating the Americans with Disabilities Act.

Lawsuits and other legal investigations, of course, do not prove guilt. Every business faces lawsuits and regulatory investigations and, for the world's largest business, being sued and investigated is a daily fact of life. But two recent events have attracted more widespread attention. In June 2001 current and former employees from California, Illinois, Ohio, Texas, and Florida filed a class action lawsuit against Wal-Mart alleging sex discrimination against women employees. The suit claimed that women were denied equal opportunity in the workplace and were relegated to low-paying jobs with little opportunity for promotion.

Wal-Mart employs more women than any other private employer in the United States. Women comprise over 70 percent of Wal-Mart's sales associates, but men hold 90 percent of the store manager positions. Less than one-third of all managerial positions are held by women, significantly lower than the 56 percent among Wal-Mart competitors Target and K-Mart. Only one of the top 20 positions at Wal-Mart is held by a woman.

In June 2004, a federal judge in California ruled that the suit could proceed as a class action lawsuit on behalf of all female employees of Wal-Mart. This case thereby became the largest-ever civil rights class action lawsuit. In his decision, Judge Martin Jenkins noted that "plaintiffs present largely uncontested descriptive statistics which show that women working at Wal-Mart stores are paid less than men in every region, that pay disparities exist in most job categories, that the salary gap widens over time, that women take longer to enter management positions, and that the higher one looks in the organization the lower the percentage of women."

A second case stems from federal raids on 60 Wal-Mart stores in 20 states in October 2003. The raids resulted in arrests of over 250 illegal aliens who were working as janitors in Wal-Mart stores. All of the workers were employed by third party subcontractors that Wal-Mart had hired for overnight janitorial services. A lawsuit was filed on behalf of several of these workers claiming that Wal-Mart knowingly employed illegal workers as part of a scheme to pay below minimum wages, deny overtime pay, and otherwise exploit their illegal status.

Late in 2003, federal prosecutors in Pennsylvania announced that Wal-Mart was being investigated by a grand jury regarding these illegal workers. Wal-Mart faces a federal fine of up to $10,000 for each illegal immigrant if it is proven that company officials knowingly were involved in employing illegal workers. Wal-Mart denied all charges, claiming that the company was ignorant of the illegal activities of their subcontractors. Lawyers representing the illegal workers countered with evidence and affidavits, including some from competing janitorial companies who lost business to the subcontractors who employ illegal workers, which seemed to show that Wal-Mart executives had known about the practice.

Critics point out that when the largest national employer establishes low workplace standards for wages, benefits, and labor practices, other employers have both the incentive and opportunity to follow. As the competing janitorial service companies learned, competing fairly and legally can result in the loss of business.

Many local communities also criticize Wal-Mart as a major factor in the demise of small towns and local businesses. Small retail businesses find it difficult to compete with Wal-Mart's pricing and marketing strategies and local communities suffer when Wal-Mart builds giant stores in suburban and rural locations. This not only encourages sprawl and places additional burdens on roads and transportation, it can undermine the local tax base. Further, the loss of local business has a trickle-down effect when local suppliers and professionals, such as accountants, lawyers, and banks, suffer the loss of local business to Wal-Mart's national and international suppliers. The problem is compounded when Wal-Mart receives tax subsidies and tax breaks offered by local governments hoping to attract a Wal-Mart store.

Wal-Mart's aggressive strategy to lower costs also is criticized for the harms it can cause suppliers both nationally and internationally. Wal-Mart has been known to force suppliers to bid against each other in a type of "reverse auction" in which suppliers compete to see who can offer their products at the lowest costs. Because Wal-Mart controls such a large market segment, many suppliers cannot survive if Wal-Mart declines to carry their product. This practice has caused some businesses to go out of business, and many others to find ways to send production off-shore. One result is that Wal-Mart, which promoted a "Buy American" marketing campaign in the 1980s, is responsible for the loss of uncounted American jobs as American businesses have been forced to out-source their production as the only means available to meet Wal-Mart's price targets. Finally, the labor practices of Wal-Mart suppliers in China, Central America, and Saipan have all been accused of producing sweatshop conditions in factories manufacturing clothing produced for Wal-Mart.[2]

DISCUSSION QUESTIONS

1. How would you describe the managerial philosophy of Wal-Mart? What principles are involved? What are the overriding aims, values, and goals of Wal-Mart?
2. Evaluate the management philosophy of Wal-Mart from the point of view of stockholders, employees, customers, the local community, and suppliers.
3. Should business management always seek the lowest prices for its customers and the highest rate of return on investment? What reasons might there be for seeking something less for customers and stockholders?
4. Economists define costs in terms of opportunities forgone. What opportunities are forgone by Wal-Mart's "everyday low price" marketing strategy? Who pays the costs of Wal-Mart's low prices?
5. Wal-Mart's wages are above the legally required minimum wage, and health benefits are not legally mandated. Are there reasons for a business to take actions not required by law but which might reduce profits?
6. Does Wal-Mart have any responsibilities to its suppliers other than those specified in their contracts?

3.1 INTRODUCTION

Like the Enron and Malden Mills cases discussed in chapter 1, this Wal-Mart case describes the range of socially significant decisions that business management often faces. As we've discussed, philosophical ethics is not concerned merely with *describing* the facts of managerial practice. Business ethics is essentially normative: What is the *proper* role of business management in making such decisions? What is the proper role of business in society? Should business managers take Aaron Feuerstein as their model, or do the executives at Enron or Wal-Mart provide a better model? Do business managers have an overriding ethical responsibility to serve the interests of stockholders before acting for society's interests? Do business managers serve society's interests *by* serving the interests of stockholders? Do business managers have ethical responsibilities to employees, suppliers, and customers beyond the responsibilities mandated by law? Do the interests of stockholders override the interests of such other stakeholders as employees, customers, suppliers, and the wider community? This chapter will examine such questions by considering the major theories of corporate social responsibility.

3.2 THE CLASSICAL MODEL OF CORPORATE SOCIAL RESPONSIBILITY

What we shall call the classical model of corporate social responsibility has its roots in free market, or neoclassical, economic theory. This perspective is perhaps the most influential theory of corporate responsibility of the past century. On this view, the role of business management is to maximize profits within the law. This management role flows from the function assigned to business institutions within free market economies. In turn, as its ethical foundation, this economic theory can appeal to two distinct traditions in ethics: utilitarianism and individual rights to freedom and property.

Perhaps the best-known defender of the classical model of corporate social responsibility is the Nobel Prize–winning economist Milton Friedman. In his book, *Capitalism and Freedom,* Friedman offers this clear statement of the classical model:

> The view has been gaining widespread acceptance that corporate officials . . . have a social responsibility that goes beyond serving the interests of their stockholders. . . . This view shows a fundamental misconception of the character and nature of a free economy. In such an economy, there is one and only one social responsibility of business—to use its resources and engage in activities designed to increase its profits so long as it stays within the rules of the game, which is to say, engages in open and free competition, without deception or fraud. . . . Few trends could so thoroughly undermine the very foundations of our free society as the acceptance by corporate officials of a social responsibility other than to make as much money for their stockholders as possible.[3]

This can appear as a narrowly selfish understanding of business to some critics. On closer analysis, however, we can see the ethical roots of this view within Friedman's quote. (It would also be useful to review the skepticism about business ethics examined in chapter 1 in light of this quotation.) The social responsibility of managers is "to make as much money for their stockholders as possible." This responsibility follows from the "character and nature of a free economy." Thus, a particular economic theory, what for simplicity sake we shall call the *free market theory,* provides the rationale for this managerial role. But why should we accept this economic theory? Friedman offers hints for how he might respond to this decidedly ethical question. By disregarding the role assigned management by the free market theory we would likely "undermine the very foundations of our free society." Managers are ethically obliged to maximize profits in order to avoid this serious ethical wrong.

This short passage only hints at the variety of social, political, ethical, and economic issues that are embedded in the market approach to business ethics. Indeed, it would be fair to describe "the market" as one of the most influential public policy philosophies in modern history. For issues ranging from environmental protection to the allocation of health care, and certainly for virtually every controversy in business ethics, we can commonly find a recommendation to "let the market decide." In this text alone, we shall examine market-based recommendations for such diverse issues as employee health and safety, deceptive advertising, product safety, employee rights and responsibilities, and environmental protection. It will be worthwhile to examine this view in depth.

Let us examine the Wal-Mart case from the perspective of this classical model of corporate social responsibility. Wal-Mart's tremendous financial accomplishment is good evidence that management's strategy of offering "everyday low prices" has been successful in the marketplace. Wal-Mart has been able to attain such low prices by following a variety of managerial strategies. They have pursued several aggressive policies to keep labor costs down. They have used their purchasing power to bargain forcefully with suppliers to keep prices down and, as a result, have encouraged suppliers to outsource their production to China and other countries with lower labor and supply costs. They have outsourced their janitorial services to independent firms and negotiated with these suppliers for the lowest possible price. Wal-Mart has entered new markets where their efficiencies have been able to defeat competitors, and has bargained with local municipalities to attain favorable tax and financial incentives. Despite lawsuits and regulatory infractions, we can assume that as a matter of corporate policy, Wal-Mart has always been committed to obeying the law. In short, Wal-Mart's managers have sought to maximize stockholder profit within the law.

How would "the market" evaluate this corporate strategy? Wal-Mart seems to be exactly the type of socially responsible corporation envisioned by Friedman's model. Wal-Mart's return on investment over the last 35 years has been extraordinary. Assuming that the retail industry has been free and open, and assuming that Wal-Mart has not engaged in fraud, deception, or illegal activities, Wal-Mart's corporate strategy has, on the market view, attained several significant ethical objectives. Perhaps most importantly, Wal-Mart's low prices have meant that more consumers have been able to purchase more of what they want. Society benefits when efficient companies sell more products at lower prices. By pursuing the lowest possible labor and supply costs, Wal-Mart is able to hire more workers and buy more products for the same costs. This strategy provides an incentive to move the production of everything from janitorial services to soap and electronics to their most efficient supplier. Greater efficiency means that more beneficial consequences result from each spending decision. In turn, this efficiency attracts more investors whose resources can then be used to increase business. Overall, society benefits from Wal-Mart's pursuit of profit.

This justification of the free market clearly is based on the utilitarian ethical principle that one should act so as to maximize the overall good. But besides utilitarianism, there is another ethical defense of the free market. Rather than appealing to the good consequences of the market, this approach appeals instead to the right of private property.

Again, Milton Friedman offers us a succinct statement of this principle:

> In a free-enterprise, private property system a corporate executive is an employee of the owners of the business. He has direct responsibility to his employers. That responsibility is to conduct the business in accordance with their desires, which generally will be to make as much money as possible while conforming to the basic rules of society, both those embodied in law and those embodied in ethical custom. . . . The key point is that, in his capacity as a corporate executive, the manager is the agent of the individuals who own the corporation . . . and his primary responsibility is to them.[4]

From this perspective, a business is understood as private property, and like any private property, the owners get to decide what to do with it. If Aaron Feuerstein, as the owner of Malden Mills, chose to use his property to benefit the workers and community, fine. That is his free choice. But if the managers of Wal-Mart chose to use their stockholders' property to serve the interests of employees and the local community, they are acting irresponsibly. Pursuing any social objective other than the maximization of profit is spending someone else's money for your own purposes. According to defenders of the classical model, this is ethically equivalent to theft.

Accordingly, the classical model of corporate social responsibility directs business management to pursue maximum profits. This is the primary ethical responsibility of business management and is defended on both utilitarian and individual rights grounds. These same ethical considerations also direct government to adopt a laissez-faire approach to business. Business ought to be free from government regulation and control, allowing the market to function most efficiently.

3.3 CRITICAL ASSESSMENT OF THE CLASSICAL MODEL: THE UTILITARIAN DEFENSE

The classical model of corporate social responsibility has been seriously challenged on a variety of grounds.[5] For our purposes, we can focus on the ethical challenges and examine, in turn, those challenges directed at the utilitarian defense and then those directed at the private property defense.

The utilitarian defense of the classical model returns us to the discussion of utilitarianism found in chapter 2. Utilitarian ethics can be thought of in terms of means and ends, of acts and consequences. Managers are assigned a certain role within a free market economy because, by filling this role, they contribute to the production of beneficial consequences. Seen in this way, we can raise two general types of challenges: those that focus on the adequacy of free markets as means to the ends of maximally satisfying consumer demand, and those that focus on the appropriateness of these ends as legitimate ethical goals. More simply, is the free market an adequate means to our ends, and are the ends ethically appropriate?

Economists are familiar with a variety of situations in which the pursuit of profit will not result in a net increase in consumer satisfaction. In fact, such situations are called *market failures* precisely because in these cases markets fail to do what they were designed to do. We can mention three general cases of market failures that are familiar examples from economics.

Externalities such as pollution and resource depletion are perhaps the best-known examples of market failures. Externalities provide examples of efficiently functioning markets failing to achieve optimal results. Common examples of externalities would be such things as air pollution, groundwater contamination and depletion, soil erosion, and nuclear waste disposal. The costs of such problems are borne by parties (e.g., people downwind, neighbors, future generations) who are not a part of the exchange between seller and buyer. Such parties are said to be external to the economic exchange. Since the "costs" of these problems are borne by external parties, the exchange price does not represent an equilibrium between true costs and benefits. Such external costs (or benefits) mean that market exchanges will not achieve the optimal distribution of costs and benefits that is represented by that equilibrium. In short, markets fail to achieve their intended result. If we wish to attain that optimal distribution, the market will need to be regulated and controlled so as to internalize these externalities.

A second example of market failure occurs in the case of public goods. There are many social goods—clean air, groundwater, ocean fisheries, scenic views, friendly and supportive neighborhoods and communities, or safe streets for example—for which no pricing mechanisms exist. Without an economic price, no means are provided for markets to ensure that these goods get allocated to those who most value them. Thus, there is no guarantee that markets result in the optimal satisfaction of the public interest in regards to public goods. If we wish to preserve and protect such goods, something other than economic markets will be needed as our policy mechanism.

A third type of market failure occurs in situations in which individual pursuit of rational self-interest—the sort of behavior required by competitive markets—results in a worse outcome than what would have occurred had the parties' behavior been coordinated, either through cooperation or regulation. So-called *prisoners' dilemma* cases are examples of situations in which cooperation has a more optimal outcome than competition.[6] But perhaps more common are situations in which individual rationality results in public harms.

Important ethical and policy questions can be missed if we leave policy decisions solely to the outcome of individual decisions. This problem arises for many issues in business ethics, particularly for health risks involved in such things as exposure to workplace chemicals, consuming food treated with pesticides or food additives, drinking water that contains nitrates and chemical residues, or pollution that results from the individual choices of numerous consumers. As a particular example, consider the decision involved in choosing to drive a low-mileage sports utility vehicle.

Driving such vehicles increases the amount of airborne pollutants discharged per mile driven. A 13-mpg SUV will discharge 134 tons of CO_2 over its 124,000 mile lifetime. A 36-mpg compact car will discharge 48 tons over the same distance. If I act as the rationally self-interested individual presupposed by free market economics, I would calculate the benefits of driving an SUV and weigh them against the increased costs and health risks that I face from pollution. Since the increased risks to me (or to any individual facing such a choice) of *my* driving an SUV rather than a compact are infinitesimally small, my self-interested choice to drive an SUV is reasonable according to market conceptions of individual rationality.

Consider these same facts not from an individual point of view but from the point of view of the population of, say, Los Angeles. Since, as our individual calculation indicated, it can be rational for any individual to choose an SUV, the individualistic approach implicit in market solutions would accept the Los Angeles pollution rate as a rational policy. The overall social result of such individual calculations might be significant increases in pollution and such pollution-related diseases as asthma and allergies. There are a number of alternative policies (e.g., restricting SUV sales, increasing taxes on gasoline, treating SUVs as cars instead of light trucks in calculating corporate automobile fuel efficiency standards) that could address pollution and pollution-related disease. However, these alternatives would only be considered if we examine this question from a social rather than an individualistic perspective. Because these are important ethical questions, and because they remain unasked from within market transactions, we must conclude that markets are incomplete (at best) as a means to attaining the overall social good. In other words, what is good and rational for a collection of individuals is not necessarily what is good and rational for a society. Once again, if society wishes to address these concerns it will need to reply on public and not private (i.e., the market) decision-making mechanisms.

The upshot of these challenges is that economic markets are so complex that it is extremely unlikely that a single and simple directive such as maximize profits will produce the greater overall good in all cases and in every situation. As we have seen in chapter 2, utilitarianism is a very pragmatic theory. Ethical judgments about particular acts are always contingent upon what happens after the act. Utilitarians are committed to specific principles only when, and only to the degree that, they produce the desired results. Because we can never know the future in a complex and ever-changing world, utilitarians always remain ready to revise their principles in light of changing consequences. An unconditioned ethical directive, such as the one that the classical model of corporate social responsibility demands of business management, is inappropriate for a utilitarian theory. A more precise formulation of a utilitarian-based market principle for management would be: Maximize profit whenever doing so produces the greatest overall good for the greatest number of people. This principle, in turn, will require management to consider the impact that a decision will have in many ways other than merely financial.

Of course, defenders of market solutions have ready responses to these challenges. Even free market defenders could support regulation that would require business to internalize externalities. Presumably they would support legislation to create shadow prices for unpriced social goods or for exempting such goods from the market, as when national parks and wilderness areas are set aside as public lands. The law is also the appropriate mechanism for addressing social goods that are unattainable through individual choice. In short, the law is the obvious remedy for social harms resulting from market failures. Once again, as Friedman says, as long as business obeys the law it meets its social responsibility by responding to consumer demand in the marketplace.

But there are good reasons for thinking that such ad hoc attempts to repair market failures are socially inadequate. First is what I call the *first-generation problem.* Markets can work to prevent harm only through information supplied by the existence of market failures. Only when fish populations in the North Atlantic collapsed did we learn that free and open competition among the world's fishing industry for unowned public goods failed to prevent the decimation of cod, swordfish, Atlantic salmon, and lobster populations. Only when workers died from exposure to such workplace pollutants as asbestos and coal dust, and only when consumers died from exploding fuel tanks and contaminated food products, did society learn about the dangers of these situations. That is, we learn about market failures and thereby prevent harms in the future only by sacrificing the first generation as a means for gaining this information. When public policy involves irreplaceable public goods such as public health and safety, such a reactionary strategy is ill-advised.

But even if we allow government regulation to establish social standards for business, we are still faced with the ability of business to influence both government regulation and consumer demand. The classical model of corporate social responsibility limits business's responsibility to obeying the law and responding to consumer demand. On this model, it is government's responsibility to prevent and compensate for market failures. Once market failures are adequately addressed, business need only obey the law and respond to the market. But this assumes that business cannot or does not inappropriately influence the law. "Inappropriate" influence, on this model, is influence aimed not at optimizing the overall good (the goal, after all, of markets) but at protecting the interests of business. An obvious example is the automobile industry's successful lobbying effort to have SUVs treated as trucks rather than as passenger vehicles so that manufacturers can meet corporate automobile fuel efficiency (CAFE) standards for passenger vehicles established by law.

But just as we must recognize the ability of business to influence government policy, we must also recognize its ability to influence consumers. To conclude that business fulfills its social responsibility when it responds to the demands of consumers is to underestimate the role that business can play in shaping public opinion. (We will examine this issue in more depth in chapter 8.) Advertising is a $200 billion a year industry in the United States alone. It is surely disingenuous to claim that business passively responds to consumer desires and that consumers are unaffected by the messages that business conveys. Assuming that business is not going to stop advertising its products or lobbying government, the market-based approach that is implicit within the classical model of corporate social responsibility is inadequate.

The second challenge to this utilitarian defense of the classical model claims that the ends attained even by an efficiently functioning market are unsatisfactory on ethical grounds. Throughout this chapter we have been referring to the ends or goals of the market variously as "maximize overall happiness," "optimal satisfaction of consumer demand," "greatest overall good," "greatest good for the greatest number," "maximally satisfying wants," and "the satisfaction of consumer preference." Let us return to a discussion from chapter 2 and become more precise in analyzing the ends of an efficiently functioning market.

Utilitarian ethics directs us to maximize happiness. How would a market serve this goal? At first glance, it seems that people are happy whenever they get what they want and markets function to satisfy consumer wants. But, more precisely, markets only address those wants that get expressed within markets. We might better call such wants consumer demand or consumer preferences. Now, of course, what people demand as consumers and what makes them happy, are not always identical. Friendship, psychological health, and love are important elements of happy lives, but you can find none of these sold on the open market. Drugs, pornography, and cigarettes are some things demanded by consumers that do not, in the ethical sense, make people happy. In fact, there is some evidence, both anecdotal and social scientific, that suggests that people who get a lot of consumer goods are often not as happy as those with fewer such goods. Put another way, even if people received all the goods and services that they desired as consumers, there is no guarantee that they would be happy.[7]

A defender of free markets might claim that even if consumer satisfaction does not tell the entire story of human happiness, it at least tells a part. Even if some good things cannot be bought, getting more rather than less of what can be bought still contributes to human happiness.

Let us step back here to recognize the significance of this issue. Market economies, and many of the political institutions that surround them, assume (often uncritically) the value of economic productivity and economic growth. The language of economic growth is simply a shorthand way of saying that more people are getting more of what they want. Specifically, it would be satisfying more of those wants that can be expressed in the marketplace. But is it true that getting more of what you seek in the market is good? Is it always ethically better to satisfy rather than frustrate consumer preferences? Is economic growth always good?

But surely the answer to this question is that economic growth itself is not always an ethically good thing. Economic growth measures only the quantity of what consumers spend, it does not assess the quality of what they are purchasing with that spending. From a strict market perspective, there is no difference between $10,000 spent on medical bills produced by an automobile accident and $10,000 spent on improved safety equipment that might have prevented the accident. Yet, ethically, there seems to be a major difference between the good accomplished by, and the reasons that lead to, these two different consumer choices.

Economic growth means only that consumers are getting more of what they want, as determined by what they spend in the marketplace. But some things that consumers want, such as nutritious food, education, health care, are good and worthwhile. Some of what people want is silly, vacuous, trivial; some is shameful or immoral. Some examples can help make this point. There is, unfortunately, a market for buying and selling infants, but buying and selling infants is ethically wrong. There is a market for child pornography and child prostitution, but these are grievous moral wrongs. There are also economic markets for drugs, nuclear weapons, chemical weapons, and military secrets. In short, markets provide no substantive ethical basis for evaluating the ethical content or quality of consumer choice. Efficient markets, which even in theory can accomplish nothing other than optimally satisfying consumer choice, offer no guarantee that an ethically worthy outcome has been achieved.

Of course, even Milton Friedman recognized that there are limits to the pursuit of profits. Management should pursue profits only "so long as it stays within the rules of the game, which is to say, engages in open and free competition, without deception or fraud," and only "while conforming to the basic rules of society, both those embodied in law and those embodied in ethical custom." These quotes are an admission that there are and should be ethical restrictions upon the pursuit of profit. Defenders of the classical model, however, would argue that these restrictions are very minimal. How extensive the ethical restrictions are is, in effect, the question for the remainder of this book. But the philosophical point should not be lost in this admission. The economic consequences of free market economics do not provide sufficient justification, in themselves, for the classical model of corporate social responsibility.

Thus, there are reasons to doubt the utilitarian rationale for the classical model. The well-established existence of various market failures shows that there is no guarantee that markets attain the utilitarian goals at which they aim. A close consideration of the consequences of even an efficiently functioning market suggests that these consequences cannot provide a conclusive ethical rationale for the market and, therefore, for the managerial role that follows from it.

3.4 CRITICAL ASSESSMENT OF THE CLASSICAL MODEL: THE PRIVATE PROPERTY DEFENSE

The second ethical defense of the classical model appeals to the rights of private owners rather than to the alleged beneficial consequences of markets. On this view, managers have an overriding obligation to maximize profits because that is what their employers, the owners of the corporation, want done with corporate resources. Any alternative constitutes an illegitimate restriction on the property rights of those owners. If a Wal-Mart manager, for example, decided to pay higher health care benefits to employees than was necessary to attract workers in the local labor market, they would be misallocating corporate funds. They would, in effect, be stealing from the owners of the business.

Again, let us return to some themes introduced in chapter 2 where we examined the nature of property rights within the context of a general examination of ethical theory. We can indicate two significant challenges to this defense of the classical model.

First, we need to recognize that property rights are not absolute. Minimally, one's right to use property is constrained by the rights of others. I cannot use my gun to shoot you, for an obvious example. Property rights are also restricted in much less dramatic ways. Zoning laws provide examples where property rights are restricted for the common good. In consideration of the interests of my neighbors, I cannot use my home as a business, for example, because the residential zoning in my neighborhood prohibits such commercial uses. I cannot rent my home as a residence to more than four unrelated local college students. I cannot use my backyard as storage for junk cars or for other trash. Because of a covenant entered into by the original residents of my neighborhood, I cannot even replace the natural wood siding on my house with vinyl or steel siding. There seems widespread acceptance of such limitations on private property throughout liberal democratic societies.

Of course, defenders of the classical model could acknowledge that such limitations exist, but argue that they are wrong. But, defenders would need to argue that the use of private property in pursuit of profits will always override other competing goods and other rights if they are to successfully defend the principle that business managers ought always pursue profits for stockholders. Again, given the qualifications he mentions, it seems even Milton Friedman does not wish to make this extreme claim. Even Friedman restricts property rights when they conflict with the basic rules of society as embodied in "law and ethical custom."

The second challenge questions the understanding of stockholders implied by this defense. We need to recognize that, historically, corporate property rights differ from personal property. Stockholder rights and responsibilities were legal creations with particular social goals in mind. Stockholders are granted limited legal liability for the acts of their corporate property. This protects stockholders from losing their personal property in judgments against their corporation. In return for this protection, society gained a beneficial economic tool: an efficient means for raising large amounts of capital to finance major economic activities. This suggests that corporate ownership may not include all of the rights and privileges that are included with ownership of personal property. Specifically, the connection between ownership and control that exists for personal property does not legally exist for corporate property.

This challenge can be understood by distinguishing between *owners* and *investors*. In some corporations, a few individuals privately own the stock. Malden Mills, for example, was owned by Aaron Feuerstein and his family. But stock ownership in publicly traded corporations, such as Enron and Wal-Mart, might be divided among millions of shares of stock. Stockholders in these corporations are better understood as investors rather than owners. Investors buy their stocks, as Friedman suggests, with the hope of maximizing the return on their investment. But from the perspective of management, investors are less owners than they are customers. A corporation needs the capital supplied by investors, just as it needs the labor supplied by employees, material provided by suppliers, advice and resources supplied by financial institutions, accountants, and lawyers, and the market supplied by consumers. Market pressures require management to provide a high enough return on investment so that investors will keep their capital in the company's stock. Likewise, market pressure requires management to pay a high enough salary and benefit package to keep qualified employees with the firm. Just as there is a labor market, there is a capital market. Investors are owed a competitive rate of return on their investment and employees are owed a competitive wage and benefit package. If investors disagree with managerial decisions, they are free to move their capital elsewhere. If employees disagree with managerial decisions, they also are free to take their labor elsewhere. If enough do either, managers will be directed by market forces to adjust their policies accordingly.

This is not to say that management can do just anything they want with corporate resources. We shall examine the ethical limits to managerial prerogative throughout this book. But these ethical limits come not only from the interests of stockholders; they can come from the interests of employees, consumers, and society at large, or so critics of the classical model claim. The classical model of corporate social responsibility treats stockholder interests as overriding all else.

A final theme in Friedman's essay that deserves consideration is the suggestion that obeying the law is the only legitimate constraint on the pursuit of profit. This philosophical conclusion is reflected in the practice of many corporations that have established ethics programs and ethics officers. Much good work gets done by ethics officers, but it is fair to say that much of their work focuses on issues of legal compliance. That is, in practice, much of corporate ethics is identified with obedience to the law. But, as was described in chapter 1, compliance with the law is not enough to ensure ethical behavior.

On a practical level, telling business that its ethical responsibilities end with obedience to the law is just inviting more and more legal regulation. It was the failure of personal ethics among such companies as Enron and World-Com, after all, that led to the creation of the Sarbanes-Oxley Act and many other legal reforms. If business restricts its ethical responsibilities to obedience to the law, it should not be surprised to find a new wave of government regulations that require what were formerly voluntary actions.

More importantly, the perspective that compliance is sufficient for ethical responsibility relies on a misleading understanding of law. This perspective suggests that laws are clear-cut, unambiguous rules that can be easily applied. As chapter 1 argued, this rule model of law is very common, but not very accurate. If the law was clear and unambiguous, there wouldn't be much of a role for lawyers and courts.

It is worth remembering several points made in chapter 1. Many of the people involved in the wave of recent corporate scandals were lawyers. In the Enron case, for example, corporate attorneys and accountants were encouraged to "push the envelope" of what was legal. Especially in civil law where much is established by past precedent, there is always room for ambiguity in applying the law. After all, every new case is different in some way from the past. Further, in civil law there is a real sense in which one has not done anything illegal unless and until a court decides that one has, and this means that if no one files a lawsuit to challenge some action, it was legal.

If a corporate manager is told, as Friedman suggests, that she has a social responsibility to maximize profits within the law, then responsible managers will go to their corporate attorneys and accountants to ask what the law allows. A competent attorney or accountant will advise on how far one can reasonably go before they would do something that is obviously illegal. In this situation, it would seem a manager has a responsibility to "push the envelope" of legality in pursuit of profits. In Friedman's view, whatever is not obviously illegal is the socially responsible action. Most of the corporate scandals in recent years involved attorneys and accountants advising their clients that what they were doing could be defended in court. The off-book partnerships that were at the heart of the collapse of Enron and Arthur Andersen were designed with the advice of attorneys who thought that, if challenged, they had at least a reasonable chance of winning in court. At this point, the decision to "push the envelope" becomes more a matter of risk assessment and cost-benefit analysis than a matter of ethics. On this model, there is a strong incentive to assess the likelihood of being challenged in court, the likelihood of losing the case, the likelihood of settling for financial damages and comparing those costs against the financial benefits of taking the action.

Because the law is ambiguous, because in many cases it simply is not clear what the law requires, business managers will often face decisions that will reply on their ethical judgments. To suggest otherwise is simply to hold a false picture of corporate reality. Thus, the fundamental ethical questions will confront even the business person who is committed to obeying the law. What should I do? How should I live?

3.5 MODIFIED VERSION OF THE CLASSICAL MODEL: THE MORAL MINIMUM

In theory, the classical model remains an attractive ideal. It is an elegant theory that appeals to such important ethical norms as utilitarianism, freedom, and private property. It carries strong rhetorical force by its connection to the free enterprise system, free markets, and capitalism. But the fact of the matter is that even its staunchest defenders acknowledge its limitations. The imperative to maximize profits is always conditioned by such phrases as "within the law," "without deception or fraud," "while conforming to the basic rules of society, both those embodied in law and those embodied in ethical custom." These restrictions simply acknowledge the legitimacy of placing ethical limitations beyond merely obeying the law on the pursuit of profit. In many ways, the only debate remaining is the debate over where those limits are to be set.

It was perhaps considerations such as this that, in 1991, led philosopher Norman Bowie to claim that "something of a consensus has emerged in the past

10 years regarding the social responsibility of business." Bowie labels this consensus the *neoclassical* model of corporate social responsibility. On this model, the pursuit of profit is constrained by an obligation to obey a moral minimum. Business managers must first meet certain moral obligations which, once met, open the door to the pursuit of profit.[8]

To explain this notion of a moral minimum, Bowie appeals to a framework for distinguishing duties that is fairly standard in some traditional ethical theories. In fact, Bowie identifies his approach as a Kantian theory of business ethics. In simple terms, this framework distinguishes between ethical imperatives to cause no harm, to prevent harm, and to do good. People have a strong ethical duty to cause no harm, and only a *prima facie* duty to prevent harm or to do good. Doing good is something that people should be encouraged to do and praised for doing. But it is not something that people are ethically obligated to do, since such an obligation would impose unreasonable burdens and limitations on people. The obligation to cause no harm, on Bowie's view, overrides other ethical considerations. The pursuit of profit legitimately can be constrained by this ethical duty. On the other hand, Bowie accepts the classical model's view that managers are the agents of stockholder-owners and thus they have a duty (derived from the contract between them) to further the interests of stockholders. Thus, while it is ethically good for managers to prevent harm or to do some good, their duty to stockholders overrides these concerns. As long as managers comply with the moral minimum and cause no harm, they have a responsibility to maximize profits. In this way, the neoclassical model is a revised version of the classical model of corporate social responsibility.

While the distinction among causing harm, preventing harm, and doing good might be clear initially, distinguishing among these cases on a consistent basis presents a major challenge. The difference between causing and preventing harms may not be as significant ethically as one might think. Distinguishing between harm and good, also, is not always clear and easy. How significantly the neoclassical model differs from the classical model is a function of how one interprets these distinctions. If we interpret the imperative to "cause no harm" narrowly, the range of duties faced by management under the neoclassical model is not much different from the classical model. If we do not make a hard and fast distinction between causing and preventing, and between harm and good, then the range of managerial duties increases and the differences between these two models changes accordingly. Let us consider an example from liability law to investigate this issue further.

The distinction between causing harm and failing to prevent it from occurring has been a major question for courts to untangle when they have considered liability claims against businesses. *Palsgraf v. Long Island Railroad* is a classic legal case that examines this issue in detail. Mrs. Palsgraf was standing on a train platform waiting for the arrival of her train as an earlier train began to leave the station. As that train pulled away, a late arriving passenger ran to jump aboard and was helped by the train conductors. This passenger was bumped and as a result dropped a package under the train. Unbeknownst to the conductors, the package contained fireworks that exploded when crushed by the train. The explosion set off a chain reaction that led, eventually, to an injury to Mrs. Palsgraf. In deciding if the railroad should be held liable for her injuries, the court addressed the question of causality. Did the action of railroad employees *cause* Mrs. Palsgraf's injuries?

An initially plausible account of causality holds that the cause of some harm is that, without which, the harm would not have occurred. The cause is the *sine qua non* (that without which) of the harm. But understood in this way, there are an indefinite number of causes: the late-arriving passenger, the fireworks, the train wheels, the conductor's actions, the scale location, Mrs. Palsgraf's decision to take the train, etc. Interestingly, even things that did not occur can be understood as the cause of her injury. The railroad failed to prevent late-arriving passengers from running to catch moving trains, they failed to keep people away from moving trains, they failed to close the train doors before leaving the station or block access to the platform, they failed to prohibit explosives from being carried on board, etc.

The point is that the distinction between acts that cause and acts that prevent harm may depend more on our descriptions of the act than on any intrinsic character of the act itself. (This same question is central to debates concerning euthanasia: Is the decision to remove a mechanical respirator actively causing the patient's death or is it merely passively allowing the patient to die by failing to take steps to prevent the death?)

A similar challenge can be raised to the distinction between doing good and preventing harm. Consider the case of an automobile manufacturer that invests in a hybrid-electric or fuel cell-powered vehicle. Is this decision an ethical "good" that is praiseworthy but not required, or is it an ethically required obligation not to harm others through pollution and resource depletion?

The point of these examples is not to suggest that there is no distinction between harms and good or between causing harms and not causing harms. Rather, as a theory of corporate social responsibility, the modified version of the classical model cannot escape confronting the specific limits of corporate social responsibility head-on. The modified theory would need to offer a reasoned explanation for why any particular case is a matter of causing harm, and therefore is something ethically prohibited, or of doing good, and therefore something more akin to charity. Upon reflection, this suggests that we must abandon an in-principle determination of the extent of corporate social responsibility and decide this on a case-by-case basis. The implication of this is that for every case in which stockholder interests appears to conflict with the interests of employees, consumers, suppliers, or society, business management must carefully analyze the situation to determine its ethical responsibility.

The significance of the moral minimum approach lies in its recognition that compliance with the law is insufficient for being an ethically responsible business. An adequate theory of corporate social responsibility must extend beyond the law to acknowledge ethical duties. Business managers and executives must understand that hiring a compliance officer is only a first step in the process of integrating ethics into a business. However, in recognizing that ethical duties do bind business managers and create a constraint on the pursuit of

profit, the moral minimum approach has opened the door to a broader understanding of ethical responsibilities. We turn now to the stakeholder theory of
corporate social responsibility, an approach that carries the moral minimum to
its logical conclusion.

3.6 THE STAKEHOLDER THEORY

The stakeholder theory of corporate social responsibility begins with the insight
that every business decision affects a wide variety of people, benefiting some
and imposing costs on others. As we have seen in such cases as Enron and Wal-
Mart, decisions made by business managers produce far-ranging consequences
throughout society. Indeed, as economists have long recognized, every business
decision involves the imposition of costs in the sense that every decision forgoes
other opportunities. Any theory of corporate social responsibility that claims an
ethical basis must defend its answers to the question: Who should benefit, and
who should pay the costs, for each business decision? Both the classical model
and the moral minimum give stockholders a privileged position in the answer
to this question. Once minimal legal and/or moral constraints are met, stockholders ought to be the primary beneficiaries of business decisions.

The stakeholder theory rejects this privileged position for stockholders.
Stockholders do have an ethical claim upon managerial decisions and this claim
does establish a duty towards them. But, like all other constituencies who also
have a stake in the decisions of business managers, the ethical claims of stockholders must be balanced against any comparable ethical claims of anyone else
affected by managerial decisions. The logic of these previous theories acknowledges that managerial decisions should be constrained by ethically legitimate
claims of others. The stakeholder theory accepts this logic, but rejects the conclusion that only stockholders have ethically legitimate claims upon managers.
Logic would require that if the ethical claims of other parties are comparable to
those advanced by stockholders, then managers have a duty to these other parties. The stakeholder theory argues that many such ethically legitimate claims
do exist.

Let us return to the Wal-Mart case with which we opened this chapter.
The classical model of corporate social responsibility would direct Wal-Mart
executives and managers to make decisions (as allowed by law) that benefit
stockholders at the expense of employees, suppliers, customers, and local communities. The ethical rationale for this is the beliefs that such an approach has
more beneficial overall social consequences and that as owners the stockholders have a right to such benefits. However, as previous sections of this chapter
have argued, neither of these rationales is persuasive. Thus, we are left with
the more basic ethical assumption that the interests of every party affected by
a decision deserve equal consideration in that decision. From the stakeholder
perspective, when we consider the interests of other parties, we recognize a
broad range of managerial responsibilities. Stakeholder theory would argue that
Wal-Mart's executives have ethical responsibilities to employees, suppliers,

customers, and local communities that are ethically equal to their responsibilities to shareholders.

William Evan and R. Edward Freeman have offered a defense of the stakeholder model in their essay "A Stakeholder Theory of the Modern Corporation: Kantian Capitalism." Evan and Freeman describe both a narrow and a wider understanding of the concept of a stakeholder. In a narrow sense, a stakeholder includes "any group who are vital to the survival and success of the corporation." More widely, a stakeholder could be "any group or individual who can affect or be affected by the corporation."[9] While they focus on the narrow conception in their own writing, we can keep both interpretations in mind as we examine this view.

Evan and Freeman argue that the classical model fails as both an accurate descriptive and as a reasonable normative account of business management. As a descriptive account of business, the classical model ignores over a century of legal precedent arising from both case law and legislative enactments. While it might have been true over a century ago that management had an overriding obligation to stockholders, the law now recognizes a wide range of managerial obligations to such stakeholders as consumers, employees, competitors, the environment, and the disabled. Thus, as a matter of law, it is simply false to claim that management can ignore duties to everyone but stockholders.

We also need to recognize that these legal precedents did not simply fall from the sky. It is the considered judgment of the most fundamental institutions of a democratic society, the courts and legislatures, that corporate management must limit their fiduciary duty to stockholders in the name of the rights and interests of various constituencies affected by corporate decisions.

Economic considerations also diminish the plausibility of the classical model. The wide variety of market failures well-established in economics show that, even when managers pursue profits, there are no guarantees that they will serve the interests of either stockholders or the public. When markets fail to attain their goals, society has no reason to sanction the primacy of the fiduciary obligation to stockholders.

But perhaps the most important argument in favor of the stakeholder theory rests in ethical considerations. As we have seen, the classical model appeals to two fundamental ethical norms for its justification: utilitarian considerations of social well-being and individual rights. On each of these normative accounts, however, due consideration must be given to all affected parties. Essential to any utilitarian theory is the commitment to balance the interests of all concerned and to give to each equal consideration. The stakeholder theory simply acknowledges this fact by requiring management to balance the ethical interests of all affected parties. Sometimes, as the classical model would hold, that balancing will require management to maximize stockholder interests. But sometimes not. Utilitarianism requires management to consider the consequences of its decisions for the well-being of all affected groups. Stakeholder theory requires the same.

Likewise, any theory of moral rights is committed to equal rights for all. In its Kantian formulation, this ethical theory argues that the overriding moral imperative is to treat all people as ends and never as means only. Corporate managers who fail to give due consideration to the rights of employees and other concerned groups in the pursuit of profit are treating these groups as means to the ends of stockholders. This, in the Kantian tradition, is unjust. (Of course, ignoring the interests of stockholders is equally unjust.)

Thus, the stakeholder theory argues that on the very same grounds that are used to justify the classical model, a wider stakeholder theory of corporate social responsibility is proven ethically superior. Evan and Freeman argue that "the stakeholder theory does not give primacy to one stakeholder group over another, though there will be times when one group will benefit at the expense of others. In general, however, management must keep the relationships among stakeholders in balance."[10]

Two general types of challenges can be raised against the stakeholder theory. The first engage the debate on substantive grounds and argue for the primacy of stockholders' interests. The second argue that the stakeholder theory is so general and vague that it can offer little practical guidance to management.

To defeat the stakeholder theory on substantive grounds the defender of the classical model must argue that the responsibilities to stockholders always override the ethical responsibilities to other affected parties. On utilitarian grounds, this argument must claim that the net social consequences of profit maximization will always outweigh the net social consequences of decisions that constrain profit by consideration of the interests of others. On libertarian/ property rights grounds, this argument would have to establish the primacy of property over other individual rights. As we have seen, either argument faces significant philosophical challenges.

Practical challenges to the stakeholder theory are of two types: problems with identifying stakeholders and their interests, and problems deciding what course of action follows from the imperative to balance stakeholder interests. If we interpret the meaning of stakeholder widely as any affected party, we seem to place managers under an impossible burden of determining who might be affected by every decision. The narrow interpretation seems to offer a more practical option, but it might do so at the cost of ignoring ethically relevant parties. Even if we could identify all relevant parties and their affected interests, the stakeholder theory seems to offer little in the way of practical advice to managers. How, exactly, should a manager go about balancing the diverse and competing claims of all affected parties? The inability of stakeholder theory to answer this question is, in the views of some critics, a telling defect of the theory.

Nonetheless, perhaps these critics are asking too much of the stakeholder theory. It is tempting to think that a normative theory of managerial responsibility should provide specific practical guidance. Such a theory should make a difference in how corporations are managed. But we shouldn't make the mistake of concluding that the practical guidance offered by such a theory needs to provide univocal and specific advice in every potential situation.

Compare the two general normative principles that derive from the classical and stakeholder theories of corporate social responsibility. The classical model mandates that managers should maximize profits while the stakeholder theory requires managers to balance the competing claims of stakeholders. Which offers the more practical and specific advice? Even the classical model leaves business managers with significant latitude in making decisions. The imperative to maximize profits offers a general guideline, but it does not offer exact practical guidance. After all, managerial authority is justified within this theory by appeal to the expertise that managers bring to their fiduciary relationship with stockholders. This expert role for managers only makes sense when we assume significant discretion for managerial decision making. In all but the simplest business decisions—that is, for any decision that relies on the expert judgment of managers—it is unlikely that we could ever know in advance which course would, in fact, maximize profits. To prove, after the fact, that any particular decision did maximize profits would require that we prove a counterfactual: *If* the manager had made an alternative decision, then profits *would have been* lower. Except, again, in the simplest cases, it is difficult to know how this could be established. In practice, managerial effectiveness at profit maximization is measured by one thing: Do stockholders choose to keep their money invested in this firm?

Similar conclusions must be reached about the practical guidance offered by the stakeholder theory. It is difficult, if not impossible, to determine in advance what particular decision would appropriately balance stakeholder interests. It may well be that the best way to measure this is by asking a similar question: Do the various stakeholders choose to continue their relationship with management? Disgruntled employees, disaffected customers, and falling stock prices are good evidence that management is failing to balance stakeholder interests. Likewise, as demonstrated by countless successful corporations, there is good evidence that management can appropriately balance these competing interests.

Of course, this response has not refuted the criticism that the stakeholder theory is ineffective in its ability to guide managerial decision making. But it does suggest that the stakeholder theory is not peculiar in this respect. Like the classical model, it offers practical advice by ruling out some alternatives and, like the classical model, it can be tested in the marketplace. Perhaps it is practical enough.

3.7 SUMMARY AND REVIEW

This chapter has introduced some of the basic theories for understanding the ethical responsibilities of business. These theories provide normative models for understanding how business should operate. Since they are normative models, they should not be judged solely by how accurately they describe contemporary business. Nonetheless, there is much evidence that contemporary business has moved in the direction of a more explicit incorporation of ethical concerns into its daily operation.

One can think of these competing models of corporate social responsibility along a continuum of expanding ethical constraints upon the general goal of increasing profits by responding to consumer demand. At one extreme we find the very narrow view of corporate social responsibility associated with Milton Friedman and neoclassical economics. Business's social responsibility is to maximize profit by meeting consumer demand. The only constraint upon the pursuit of profit is obedience to the law. At its most libertarian extreme, of course, this view would also argue that the only appropriate laws are those that protect property and prohibit fraud and coercion.

Theories of corporate social responsibility become more moderate by expanding the range of constraints upon the pursuit of profit. Thus Norman Bowie, for example, argues on Kantian grounds that beyond obedience to the law business has an ethical duty to cause no harm. At its most extreme, the only harms recognized as ethically legitimate would be those that violate the rights of other people, but a broader understanding of harms would lead to a broader conception of business responsibility. Stakeholder theories essentially develop this notion by identifying ethically legitimate stakeholders other than investors and by articulating the specific duties that are owed to them.

We can thus characterize these theories as variations on the theme of balancing utilitarian and deontological ethics. The pursuit of profit is the mechanism by which business is thought to serve the utilitarian goal of satisfying consumer demand and thereby maximizing the overall good. But this utilitarian goal is itself to be constrained by the duties that one has to persons affected by these activities. Depending on the theory of rights and duties which one adopts, those constraints range from the minimal duty of obeying the law, to more extensive accounts of duties associated with the stakeholder theory.

As a final reflection, we might consider the implications that the stakeholder model has for our understanding the nature and purpose of business. When stockholders are given a privileged position in management's ethical responsibilities, it is common to conceptualize business on the model of private property being managed for the sake of its owners. But, when the interests of stockholders are given equal ethical standing with the interests of all other constituencies affected by managerial decisions, the model of business as private property is less compelling. If managers have the responsibility to balance the ethical interest of all stakeholders, then we can begin to understand the firm as an independent entity.

The claim, reflected so clearly in Milton Friedman, that the purpose of a business is to maximize profits makes sense only when stockholders—the beneficiaries of profit—are given a distinctive ethical status. But what would the purpose of business be if not to maximize profits? What goal should guide the management as they seek to balance the demands of various, and often competing, stakeholders?

A plausible alternative was suggested decades ago by Theodore Levitt, longtime professor of marketing at the Harvard Business School. Levitt's quote can provide a thought-provoking end to this chapter.

> The purpose of business is to create and keep a customer. To do that you have to produce and deliver goods and services that people want and value at prices and under conditions that are reasonably attractive. . . . It was not so long ago

that a lot of companies assumed something quite different about the purpose of business. They said quite simply that the purpose of business is to make money. But that proved as vacuous as saying that the purpose of life is to eat. . . . To say that profit is a purpose of business is, simply, morally shallow. . . . if no greater purpose can be discerned or justified, business cannot, morally, justify its existence. It is a repugnant idea, an idea whose time has gone. . . . Finally, it's an empty idea. Profits can be made in lots of devious and transient ways. . . . To say that they should attract and hold customers forces facing the necessity of figuring out what people really want and value, and then catering to those wants and values. It provides specific guidance and has moral merit.[11]

REFLECTIONS ON THE CHAPTER DISCUSSION CASE

It is perhaps not surprising that, as the world's largest retailer, Wal-Mart has been the target of widespread ethical criticism. Wal-Mart's presence throughout the world makes it a tempting target. Yet, Wal-Mart clearly serves a market segment by selling a wide range of consumer goods at low prices. Wal-Mart has also proven to be an exceptionally valuable investment for stockholders. In many ways, society would seem to benefit from Wal-Mart's success.

A plausible case can be made that Wal-Mart is the prime example of a business that has followed the classical model of corporate social responsibility. Wal-Mart has aggressively sought profits within the law. The many legal challenges to Wal-Mart suggest that where the law has been ambiguous, Wal-Mart has not shied away from pushing the limits of legal compliance. Wal-Mart has seldom gone beyond legal minimums in dealing with employees, local communities, and suppliers. The strategy has proven itself in the marketplace.

It would be worth considering how things might change if Wal-Mart took the advice of some of its critics. How would the world change if Wal-Mart offered employees higher salaries and better health care benefits? What might change if suppliers were not subjected to such aggressive price pressures and if Wal-Mart relied on more domestic suppliers? The economic assumption would be that such decisions engender costs and that these costs would have to be allocated somewhere: lower profits, higher prices, less growth.

The classical model of corporate social responsibility would argue that the market itself is an adequate mechanism for distributing these costs. Market forces eventually will determine the correct balance of wages, prices, and profits. Of course, the market requires certain preconditions to function efficiently: competition, available alternatives, freedom, and information. Yet one can question if suppliers are truly free when Wal-Mart accounts for 20 to 30 percent of their business. One wonders how free low-skilled employees are to bargain when there is no union to bargain collectively on their behalf.

Finally, it is worth reflecting on Wal-Mart's managerial philosophy from various perspectives. How do you evaluate Wal-Mart as a consumer? Do you, would you, shop at Wal-Mart? Why or why not? As a potential employee, would Wal-Mart be a place that you would work? Would you seek a Wal-Mart managerial position? Why or why not? If you lived in a neighborhood in which Wal-Mart planned to build a superstore, would you support or oppose the construction? If you were on the local city council, would you encourage and help Wal-Mart locate in your community? If you had a product to sell, would you try to get Wal-Mart to carry your product?

REVIEW QUESTIONS

1. Explain the connection between the classical model of corporate social responsibility and the free market (or neoclassical) economic theory.
2. What are the two ethical justifications for the classical model of corporate social responsibility? What are the most significant ethical challenges facing those justifications?
3. In what ways does the moral minimum model advance the classical model of corporate social responsibility? .
4. What is the purpose of business? Can this question be answered historically? What should the purpose of business be? What difference does it make if you answered these questions differently?
5. What are the ethical foundations of the stakeholder model of corporate social responsibility? How does the stakeholder model differ from the moral minimum?

ENDNOTES

[1] "Is Wal-Mart Too Powerful?" *BusinessWeek*, October 6, 2003.
[2] Besides *BusinessWeek*, sources used in this description of Wal-Mart include the Wal-Mart corporate website (http://www.walmartstores.com/wmstore/wmstores/ HomePage.jsp); National Public Radio broadcasts *Morning Edition*, June 2–5, 2003 (available at: http://www.npr.org/news/specials/walmart/); PBS, *Now with Bill Moyers*, broadcast December 12, 2003; "Wal-Mart: Sex Discrimination by the Numbers," *Forbes* June 6, 2004; "Should We Admire Wal-Mart?" by Jerry Useem, *Fortune*, February 23, 2004; Frontline, "Is Wal-Mart Good for America?" November 16, 2004 (available at: http://www.pbs.org/wgbh/pages/frontline/shows/walmart/); CNBC, *The Age of Wal-Mart*: originally aired November 10, 2004 (transcript and video: http://cnbc.burrelles.com/product.asp?ProductID=439911); *Wal-Mart Said to Be in Talks to Settle Illegal-Immigrant Case*, by Steven Greenhouse, *New York Times*, August 5, 2004; Judge Jenkins' quote is from *Duke v. Wal-Mart Stores, Inc. (N.D. Cal. No C-01-2252)*; "Wal-Mart Memo Suggests Ways to Cut Employee Benefit Costs," by Steven Greenhouse and Michael Barbaro, *New York Times*, October 26, 2005.
[3] Milton Friedman, *Capitalism and Freedom* (Chicago: University of Chicago Press, 1962), p. 133.
[4] Milton Friedman, "The Social Responsibility of Business Is to Increase Its Profits," *The New York Times Magazine* (September 13, 1970), reprinted in *Contemporary Issues in Business Ethics*, 4e., edited by Joseph R. DesJardins and John McCall (Belmont, CA: Wadsworth Publishing, 2000), p. 9.

[5]For example, in an article analyzing the Enron and Arthur Andersen cases, *Fortune* magazine called such a view the "cult of the shareholder" and attributed much of the blame for several corporate bankruptcies and financial falls to the "God-awful" accounting games played by executives seeking only to increase their company's stock price. The criticisms of the Friedman view considered in this chapter are ethical. *Fortune*'s criticisms are that this view adopts an unrealistic and inadvisable model of corporate control and ownership. See "Dirty Numbers" by Andy Serwer, *Fortune* (February 18, 2002), pp. 75–84.

[6]This classic case is represented by a grid in which two prisoners who are accused of a crime are offered two options by the police, confess or not. If one prisoner confesses while her partner does not, she is set free and her partner gets a 10-year prison sentence. If both confess, they each get a five-year sentence. If neither confesses, they each get six months in jail. What would rational, self-interested individuals do in such a situation? If I am prisoner A, then I look at my options: whichever choice my partner makes, it will be better for me to confess. If she confesses and I don't, I get 10 years in jail. So, if she confesses it is preferable for me to confess as well. If she doesn't confess and I confess, then I go free. Either way, it is rational for me to confess. But, since exactly the same reasoning will lead prisoner B to reach the same conclusion, the "rational" choice for two self-interested noncooperating individuals results in a suboptimal outcome for both. On the other hand, if the two prisoners cooperated, trusted each other, and kept their word, the reasonable thing to do would be for both not to confess and settle for a six-month sentence. But, this suggests that the ideal market situation should be abandoned in favor of a more cooperative, or at least coordinated, relationship.

[7]Many useful discussions of happiness and consumption, by social scientists as well as philosophers, can be found in *The Ethics of Consumption*, edited by David Crocker and Toby Linden (Lanham, MD: Rowman & Littlefield, 1998). An entertaining and informative video presentation of these issues is found in *Affluenza*. "Affluenza" is the contagious disease that accompanies affluence.

[8]Norman Bowie, "New Directions in Corporate Social Responsibility," in *Business Horizons*, July–August 1991, 56. Bowie's views are developed further in his *Business Ethics: A Kantian Perspective* (Oxford: Blackwell, 1999).

[9]"A Stakeholder Theory of the Modern Corporation: Kantian Capitalism," by William Evan and R. Edward Freeman, in *Contemporary Issues in Business Ethics*, 4e., edited by Joseph R. DesJardins and John McCall (Belmont, CA: Wadsworth Publishing, 2005), p. 80. Freeman's views are developed more fully in R. Edward Freeman, *Strategic Management: A Stakeholder Approach* (Marshfield, Mass.: Pitman, 1984).

[10]Ibid., p. 89.

[11]This quote is taken from "Marketing and the Corporate Purpose: The Purpose Is to Create and Keep a Customer," by Theodore Levitt, a speech delivered at New York University, March 2, 1977, available from *Vital Speeches of the Day*. Similar claims can be found in chapter 1, "Marketing and the Corporate Purpose," of *The Marketing Imagination*, by Theodore Levitt (New York: Free Press, 1983), pp. 5 and 7. I thank Lyla Hamilton for first calling my attention to this quotation.

4 CHAPTER

Corporate Culture, Governance, and Ethical Leadership

After reading this chapter, you will be able to:

- Define corporate culture;
- Explain how corporate culture impacts ethical decision making;

- Discuss the role of corporate leadership in establishing the culture;
- Explain the difference between effective leaders and ethical leaders;
- Discuss the role of mission statements and codes in creating an ethical corporate culture;
- Explain how various reporting mechanisms such as ethics hotlines and ombudsman can help;
- Integrate ethics within a firm;
- Discuss the role of assessment, monitoring, and auditing of the culture and ethics program;
- Explain how culture can be enforced via governmental regulation.

DISCUSSION CASE: Our Credo

We believe our first responsibility is to the doctors, nurses and patients,
to mothers and fathers and all others who use our products and services.
In meeting their needs everything we do must be of high quality.
We must constantly strive to reduce our costs
in order to maintain reasonable prices.
Customers' orders must be serviced promptly and accurately.
Our suppliers and distributors must have an opportunity
to make a fair profit.

We are responsible to our employees,
the men and women who work with us throughout the world.
Everyone must be considered as an individual.
We must respect their dignity and recognize their merit.
They must have a sense of security in their jobs.
Compensation must be fair and adequate,
and working conditions clean, orderly and safe.
We must be mindful of ways to help our employees fulfill
their family responsibilities.
Employees must feel free to make suggestions and complaints.
There must be equal opportunity for employment, development
and advancement for those qualified.
We must provide competent management,
and their actions must be just and ethical.

We are responsible to the communities in which we live and work
and to the world community as well.
We must be good citizens—support good works and charities
and bear our fair share of taxes.

We must encourage civic improvements and better health and education.
We must maintain in good order
the property we are privileged to use,
protecting the environment and natural resources.

Our final responsibility is to our stockholders.

Business must make a sound profit.

We must experiment with new ideas.

Research must be carried on, innovative programs developed
and mistakes paid for.

New equipment must be purchased, new facilities provided
and new products launched.

Reserves must be created to provide for adverse times.

When we operate according to these principles,
the stockholders should realize a fair return.

Johnson & Johnson has long been among the most admired firms in the world. Their principled and timely response to incidents of tainted Tylenol® in both 1982 and 1986 was consistent with their reputation as a company that puts integrity and safety ahead of profits. Nevertheless, Johnson & Johnson has been hugely profitable as well. J&J had sales in 2001 of $33 billion, almost triple those of the previous decade and representing its 69th year of consecutive sales increases. They have had 17 consecutive years of double-digit earnings increases and 39 consecutive years of dividend increases. Its market value ended in 2001 at more than $180 billion, up from $38 billion in 1991, evidence that a firm that lives according to its strong values and a culture that supports those values not only can survive but sustains profit over the long term. CEO Ralph Larsen credits these successes directly to the J&J credo: "It's the glue that holds our decentralized company together. . . . For us, the credo is our expression of managing the multiple bottom lines of products, people, planet and profits. It's the way we conceptualize our total impact on society."[1]

J&J's own description of the history of its credo provides insight into corporate culture, leadership, and the role of values in corporate governance.

J&J CREDO HISTORY

General Robert Wood Johnson, who guided Johnson & Johnson from a small, family-owned business to a worldwide enterprise, had a very perceptive view of a corporation's responsibilities beyond the manufacturing and marketing of products.

As early as 1935, in a pamphlet titled *Try Reality*, he urged his fellow industrialists to embrace what he termed "a new industrial philosophy." Johnson defined this as the corporation's responsibility to customers, employees, the community, and stockholders.

But it was not until eight years later, in 1943, that Johnson wrote and first published the Johnson & Johnson credo, a one-page document outlining these responsibilities in greater detail. Johnson saw to it that the credo was embraced by his company, and he urged his management to apply it as part of their every-day business philosophy.

The credo, seen by business leaders and the media as being farsighted, received wide public attention and acclaim. Putting customers first, and stock-holders last, was a refreshing approach to the management of a business. But it should be noted that Johnson was a practical-minded businessman. He believed that by putting the customer first the business would be well served, and it was.

The corporation has drawn heavily on the strength of the credo for guid-ance through the years, and at no time was this more evident than during the Tylenol® crises of 1982 and 1986, when the McNeil Consumer & Specialty Pharmaceuticals product was adulterated with cyanide and used as a murder weapon. With Johnson & Johnson's good name and reputation at stake, com-pany managers and employees made countless decisions that were inspired by the philosophy embodied in the credo. The company's reputation was pre-served and the Tylenol® acetaminophen business was regained.

Today the credo lives on in Johnson & Johnson stronger than ever. Com-pany employees now participate in a periodic survey and evaluation of just how well the company performs its credo responsibilities. These assessments are then fed back to the senior management, and where there are shortcomings, corrective action is promptly taken.

Over the years, some of the language of the credo has been updated and new areas recognizing the environment and the balance between work and family have been added. But the spirit of the document remains the same today as when it was first written.

When Robert Wood Johnson wrote and then institutionalized the credo within Johnson & Johnson, he never suggested that it guaranteed perfection. But its principles have become a constant goal, as well as a source of inspira-tion, for all who are part of the Johnson & Johnson family of companies.

More than 60 years after it was first introduced, the credo continues to guide the destiny of the world's largest and most diversified health care company.

Reprinted with permission from Johnson & Johnson,
http://www.jnj.com/our_company/our_credo_history/index.htm and
http://www.jnj.com/our_company/our_credo/index.htm

4.1 INTRODUCTION

Many of the issues examined in chapter 3 concern business as a social institu-tion and, in that sense, treat business from an external perspective. As citizens we ask and debate whether business has any social responsibility beyond the economic responsibilities of providing goods and services, jobs, and profits.

This chapter examines the ethical responsibilities of business from an internal perspective. How should businesses be governed and managed in order to bring about ethical behavior and ethical decision making within the firm? What is the appropriate role for various organizational actors—boards, executives, managers—in fostering and promoting ethical behavior? Does the responsibility rest with individuals, or with institutional structures? When things go wrong, who should be accountable?

The classical model of corporate social responsibility described in chapter 3 treats social and ethical considerations as external constraints being placed on business. It is as if business requires a strong external reason for acting in ways that are socially responsible. But as the Johnson & Johnson credo demonstrates, many businesses take social responsibility as an inherent, if not preeminent, element of their business model. This shouldn't be surprising; after all, the individuals who work in business are no less ethical than anyone else. Assuming then that a business seeks to operate in socially responsible and ethical ways, this chapter explores strategies for creating and maintaining ethically responsible businesses.

In particular, this chapter will consider ways in which corporations might develop ethical cultures, cultures in which individuals are encouraged and supported in making ethically responsible decisions. In ordinary thinking about ethics, it is easy to emphasize the responsibility of individuals for the decisions they make in business. These decisions impact one's own personal integrity and also have consequences for many stakeholders with whom business organizations interact.

But personal decision making and ethical behavior do not exist in a vacuum. Decision making within a firm will be influenced, limited, shaped, and in some cases virtually determined by the corporate culture of the firm. Individuals can be hindered or helped in making the right, or the wrong, decision by the expectations, values, and structure of the organization in which they live and work. This chapter surveys some of the major issues surrounding the development, influence, and management of a corporate culture and the role of business leaders in creating and preserving ethical cultures.

4.2 WHAT IS CORPORATE CULTURE?

So, what do we mean by "corporate culture"? Every organization has a culture, fashioned by a shared pattern of beliefs, expectations, and meanings that influence and guide the thinking and behaviors of the members of that organization. Organizational culture shapes the people who are members of the organization. Consider how your own company, organization, or school (or dormitory or fraternity or sorority) differs from a similar one. Is there a "type" of person stereotypical of your organization, dormitory, fraternity or sorority? Are there unspoken but still influential standards and expectations that shape students at your school? How would you be different if you had chosen a different institution, or had joined a different fraternity or sorority, or had participated in a different organization?

Businesses also have unspoken yet influential standards and expectations. IBM was once famous for a culture in which highly starched white shirts and ties (for it was a predominantly male culture) were part of the required dress code. Compare that with many software and technology companies today that have reputations for a culture of informality and playfulness. Some companies have a straight 9 to 5 work schedule; others expect employees to work long hours and weekends. A person with a 9 to 5 attitude who enters such a firm, intending to leave as the clock strikes 5, will have a difficult time fitting in and succeeding. The same holds true for a firm's values. If you join a firm with a culture that supports other values than those with which you are comfortable, there will be values conflicts—for better or worse.

No culture, in business or elsewhere, is static. Cultures change; but modifying culture or having any impact on it at all is a bit like moving an iceberg. The iceberg is always moving and, if you ignore it, it will continue to float with whatever currents hold sway at the moment. One person cannot alter its course alone, but strong leaders can have a significant impact on a culture, and a strong business leader can certainly have a significant impact on a corporate culture.

A firm's culture can be its sustaining value—that which offers it direction and stability during challenging times. It can, however, also serve to constrain an organization to the common ways of managing issues—"that's how things have always been done here," "that's our prevailing climate." The stability that can be a benefit at one time can be a barrier to success in another.

Does a corporate culture matter? As described in their best-selling book *Built to Last: Successful Habits of Visionary Companies,* authors James Collins and Jerry Porras researched dozens of successful companies looking for common practices that might explain their success. These companies not only outperformed their competitors in financial terms, but also have outperformed their competition over the long term. On average, the companies they studied were founded in 1897. Among their key findings was the fact that the truly exceptional and enduring companies all placed great emphasis on a set of core values. These core values are described as the "essential and enduring tenets" that help define the company and are "not to be compromised for financial gain or short-term expediency."[2]

Collins and Porras cite numerous examples of core values being articulated and promoted by the founders and CEOs of such companies as IBM, Johnson & Johnson, Hewlett Packard, Procter and Gamble, Wal-Mart, Merck, Motorola, Sony, Walt Disney, General Electric, and Philip Morris. Some companies made a commitment to customers as their core value; others focused on employees, their products, innovation, or even risk-taking. The common theme was that core values and a clear corporate purpose, what together are described as the organization's core ideology, were essential elements of enduring and financially successful companies.

When we talk about a corporation's "culture" we are saying that a corporation has a set of identifiable values. All the companies discussed by Collins and Porras have been described as having strong corporate cultures and a clear set of values. Of course, as the opening discussion case suggests, corporate values themselves might be open to ethical criticism.

4.3 CULTURE AND ETHICS

How, exactly, does the notion of culture connect with ethics? More specifically, what role does corporate culture play in business ethics? We can answer these questions by reflecting on several topics introduced previously.

Chapter 1 considered the relationship between law and ethics and concluded that compliance with the law is insufficient to guarantee ethical conduct. For example, the Americans with Disabilities Act requires businesses to make reasonable accommodations for employees with disabilities. But the law can be ambiguous in determining if a business should make a reasonable accommodation for an employee with allergies, depression, dyslexia, arthritis, hearing loss, or high blood pressure. In situations where the law is an incomplete guide for ethical decision making, the business culture is likely to be the determining factor in what gets decided. Ethical businesses must find ways to encourage, to shape, and to allow ethically responsible decisions. We can understand a corporate culture as the sum total of all the corporate practices that encourage, shape, or allow some types of decisions and discourage others.

An ethical culture therefore would be one in which employees are empowered and expected to act in ethically responsible ways even when the law does not require it. A corporate culture sets the expectations and norms that will determine which decisions get made. Later in this chapter we will examine types of cultures and various ways in which a corporation can create a culture that encourages ethical action. But to understand that cultures can encourage some types of behaviors and discourage others, consider as an example two organizational approaches to the relief efforts following hurricane Katrina in September 2005.

On one hand, the Federal Emergency Management Agency (FEMA) was charged with overall responsibility for the government's response to the hurricane. FEMA was created in 1979 when several governmental agencies, ranging from fire prevention and insurance to civil defense, were merged into one larger agency. FEMA itself was later subsumed into the federal department of Homeland Security. By all accounts at the time of the hurricane, FEMA was a bureaucratic, hierarchical organization. Established rules and procedures were to be followed in making decisions. Many decisions required approval from people in authority. At one point, emergency personnel were delayed in reaching the hurricane area for days because FEMA required that they first attend mandatory training sessions on preventing sexual harassment in the workplace.

Despite years of preparation and planning, the magnitude of the hurricane and resultant flooding overwhelmed FEMA's ability to respond. When the situation did not fit plans and the rules no longer applied, FEMA's bureaucracy seemed incapable of acting. Temporary homes and supplies, despite being stored nearby, were not moved into the area for months after the storm because those in authority had not yet given approval. Decisions were made, then retracted. Emergency housing, food, and medical supplies sat unused for weeks and months after the flood while people were homeless, hungry, and sick. Days after television news reports showed thousands of people stranded at the New

Orleans convention center, FEMA Director Michael Brown claimed that he had only learned of these survivors from a reporter's question. Apparently no one had told the director of FEMA, therefore he couldn't make a decision, therefore thousands of people went without help. The organization seemed unable to move information up to decision makers, and lower-level managers lacked authority to decide for themselves.

On the other hand, the United States Coast Guard is another organization with similar responsibilities for search and rescue during emergency situations. FEMA Director Brown was eventually removed from his position and replaced by a Coast Guard admiral. The Coast Guard has a reputation for being a less bureaucratic organization. Their unofficial motto is to "rescue first, and get permission later." The Coast Guard empowers front-line individuals to solve problems without waiting for superiors to make decisions or give directions. Imagine how the same person working in either of these organizations would approach a decision and you will have some idea of the importance of organizational culture.

It is fair to say that FEMA and the Coast Guard are two similar organizations with similar missions, rules, and legal regulations, but with very different cultures. The decisions made throughout both organizations reflect the culture of each. The attitudes, expectations, and habits encouraged and reinforced in the two agencies reflect the differences of culture.

The notion of expectations and habits suggests another previous topic that is relevant for our discussion of corporate culture. Chapter 2 introduced the ethics of virtue and described virtues as character traits and habits. The cultivation of one's habits, including the cultivation of ethical virtue, is greatly shaped by the culture in which one lives.

When we talk about ethical decision making and behavior, it is easy to think in terms of a rational, deliberative process in which a person consciously deliberates about and weighs each alternative before acting. But the virtue ethics tradition reminds us that our decisions and our actions are often less deliberate than that. We are as likely to act out of habit and based on character than we are to act after careful deliberations. So the question of where we get our habits and character is all-important.

Part of the answer surely is that we can choose to develop some habits rather than others. But it is also clear that our habits are shaped and formed by education and training—by culture. This education takes place in every social environment, ranging from families and religions to entire societies and cultures. It also takes place in the workplace, where individuals quickly learn appropriate and expected behaviors. Intentionally or not, business institutions provide an environment in which habits are formed and virtues, or vices, are created. To talk of such an environment is to talk of an ethical corporate culture.

Besides these more abstract considerations, an ethical culture can also have a direct and practical impact on the bottom line. If attended to and supported, a strong ethical culture can serve as a deterrent to stakeholder damage and improve bottom-line sustainability. If ignored, the culture could instead reinforce a perception that "anything goes," and "any way to a better bottom line is acceptable," which in the long term destroys sustainability. Responsibility for creating and sustaining such ethical corporate cultures rests in business leaders.

When reading Collins and Porras's book *Built to Last: Successful Habits of Visionary Companies,* one cannot help but be struck by the power of a corporate culture to shape the individuals who work within it. While it may be true that individuals can shape an organization, and perhaps charismatic leaders can do this especially well, it is equally true, if not more so, that organizations shape individuals. Imagine spending a 20-, 30-, or even 40-year career in the same organization. Imagine, for example, how the author of the Wal-Mart memo described in the opening discussion case might have addressed similar challenges if she were vice president of employee benefits at Johnson & Johnson. The corporate environment at Johnson & Johnson is very different from that at Wal-Mart. The person that you become—your attitudes, values, expectations, mind-set, and habits—will all be significantly determined by the culture of the organization in which you work.

4.4 ETHICAL LEADERSHIP AND CORPORATE CULTURE

If the goal of corporate culture is to cultivate values, expectations, beliefs, and patterns of behavior that best and most effectively support ethical decision making, it becomes the primary responsibility of corporate leadership to steward this effort. Leaders are charged with this duty in part because stakeholders throughout the organization are guided to a large extent by the "tone at the top."

Merck's CEO, Raymond Gilmartin, explains: "In thought, word, and deed, a company's leaders must clearly and unambiguously both advocate and model ethical behavior."[3] If a leader is perceived to be shirking her or his duties, misusing corporate assets, misrepresenting the firm's capabilities, or engaging in other inappropriate behavior, stakeholders receive the message that this type of behavior is not only acceptable, but perhaps expected and certainly the way to get ahead in that organization. Instead, if a leader is clearly placing her or his own ethical behavior above any other consideration, stakeholders are guided to follow that role model and to emulate that priority scheme.

Beyond personal behavior, leadership sets the tone through other mechanisms such as the dedication of resources. Ethical business leaders not only talk about ethics and act ethically on a personal level, but also allocate corporate resources to support and promote ethical behavior. There is a long-standing credo of management: "Budgeting is all about values." More common versions are "Put your money where your mouth is," and "Walk the talk."

For example, when ethics officers were first introduced to the corporate structure in the early 1990s, a clear indication of their relevance and influence within the organization was reflected in the extent to which they were supported financially. It was clear that ethics was not a priority if the general counsel served as the ethics officer "in their spare time" and no additional resources were allocated to that activity. To the contrary, ethics may hold a different position in the firm if a highly skilled individual is hired into an exclusive position as ethics officer and is given a staff and a budget to support the work required. Similarly, if a firm mandates ethical decision making from its workers through the implementation of a code of conduct, extending the same standard for its vendors, suppliers, and other contractors is a symbol of how seriously the code is taken.

One study of the nature of ethical leadership emphasized the importance of being perceived as a leader with a people-orientation, as well as the importance of leaders engaging in visible ethical action.[4] Traits that were also important included receptivity, listening, and openness, in addition to the more tradition-ally considered traits of integrity, honesty, and trustworthiness. Finally, being perceived as having a broad ethical awareness and concern for multiple stake-holders, and using ethical decision processes are also important. Those per-ceived as ethical leaders do many of the things "traditional leaders" do (e.g., reinforce the conduct they are looking for and create standards for behavior), but they do that within the context of an ethics agenda. People perceive that the ethical leader's goal is not simply job performance, but performance that is consistent with a set of ethical values and principles. Finally, ethical lead-ers demonstrate caring for people (employees and external stakeholders) in the process.

However, as previously mentioned, all of these traits and behaviors must be visible. If an executive is "quietly ethical" within the confines of the top management team, but employees down the line are unaware of it, she or he is not likely to be perceived as an ethical leader. Traits and behaviors must be socially visible and understood in order to be noticed and influence percep-tions. People notice when an executive walks the talk and acts on concerns for the common good, for society as a whole, and for the long term. Because execu-tives are expected to be focused on the financial bottom line and the short-term demands of stock analysts, when they focus on these broader and longer term concerns, people notice. Finally, making courageous decisions in tough situ-ations represents another way ethical leaders get noticed. Ethical leaders are "courageous enough to say 'no' to conduct that would be inconsistent with [their] values."[5]

4.5 EFFECTIVE LEADERSHIP AND ETHICAL LEADERSHIP

Being perceived as a leader plays an important role in a leader's ability to cre-ate and transform an ethical corporate culture. Key executives have the capa-bility of transforming a business culture for better or worse. If the corporate culture has significant impact on ethical decision making within the firm, then leaders have the responsibility for shaping that environment so that ethical decision making might flourish. But what does it mean to be a "leader" and, more important, what do we mean by an "ethical" leader? It is important to make a distinction between good leaders and ethical leaders. A good leader is simply anyone who does well what leaders do. Since leaders guide, direct, and escort others toward a destination, a good leader is someone who does this successfully and, presumably, efficiently. Good leaders are effective at getting followers to their common destination. But not every good leader is an ethical leader.

In the corporate context, Enron's Ken Lay and Jeffrey Skilling were good and effective business leaders. They were able to transform Enron from a small oil and gas pipeline company into one of the largest corporations in the world. By many accounts, they were inspirational, imaginative, and creative leaders who could motivate their staff to attain high levels of success. They were also unethical leaders. So, what is the difference between effective leaders and ethical leaders?

One key difference lies with the means used to motivate others and achieve one's goals. Skilling was said to be a very difficult boss. Effective leaders might be able to achieve their goals through threats, intimidation, harassment, and coercion. One can also lead using more attractive means such as modeling ethical behavior, persuasion, or simply by dint of one's institutional role.

Some of the discussions in the literature on leadership often suggest that ethical leadership is determined solely by the methods used in leading. Promoters of certain styles of leadership want to suggest that their style is superior to others. Consequently, they tend to identify a method of leading with "true" leadership in an ethical sense. On this line, for example, Robert Greenleaf's book *Servant Leadership* suggests that the best leaders are nonhierarchical individuals who lead by the example of serving others. Other discussions similarly suggest that "transformative" or "transactional" leaders employ methods that empower subordinates to take the initiative and solve problems for themselves, and that this constitutes the best ethical leadership style.

Certainly ethically appropriate methods of leadership are central to becoming an ethical leader. Creating a corporate culture in which employees are empowered and expected to make ethically responsible decisions is a necessary part of being an ethical business leader. But while some means may be ethically better than others (e.g., persuasion rather than coercion), it is not the method alone that establishes a leader as ethical. While perhaps necessary, ethical means of leading others are not sufficient for establishing ethical leadership. The other element of ethical leadership involves the end or goal toward which the leader leads.

One cannot be a leader, and there cannot be followers, unless there is a direction or goal toward which one is heading. In the business context, productivity, efficiency, and profitability are minimal goals. A business executive who leads a firm into bankruptcy is unlikely to qualify as an effective or good leader. An executive who transforms a business into a productive, efficient, and profitable business will be judged as an effective business leader. One who does this in a way that respects subordinates, or empowers them to become creative and successful, is (at least at first glance) both an effective and ethical leader. But, is profitability and efficiency done through ethical means alone enough to make a business leader an ethical leader?

Imagine a business leader who empowers his subordinates, respects their autonomy by consulting and listening, but who leads a business that publishes child pornography, or pollutes the environment, or sells weapons to radical organizations. Would the method alone determine the ethical standing of such a leader? Beyond the goal of profitability, other socially responsible goals might be necessary before we conclude that the leader is fully ethical.

In many ways, the remaining chapters of this book examine other goals that might be a part of the vision for an ethical business leader. Goals that address such topics as employee rights, consumer safety, ethical marketing, diversity, and environmental responsibilities are likely elements of the mission and goals of a fully ethical, and not merely effective, corporate leader.

4.6 BUILDING A VALUES-BASED CORPORATE CULTURE

Similar to the iceberg metaphor described previously, each individual in an organization has an impact on the corporate culture; though, except for perhaps the key leadership, no one individual can build or change the culture alone. Culture derives from leadership, integration, and assessment/monitoring. A variety of managerial strategies and methods can be used to create and maintain an ethical culture.

Mission Statements, Codes of Conduct, and Statements of Values

One of the key manifestations of ethical leadership is the articulation of values for the organization. Of course, this articulation may evolve after an inclusive process of values identification: it need not simply mimic the particular values of one chief executive. However, it is that leader's responsibility to ensure that the firm is guided by some set of organizing principles that can guide employees in their decision-making processes.

Before impacting the culture through a code of conduct or statement of values, a firm must first determine its mission. In the absence of other values, the only value is profit—at any cost. Therefore, without additional guidance from the top, a firm is sending a clear message that a worker should do whatever it takes to reap profits. The Johnson & Johnson credo described in this chapter's opening case discussion is an excellent example of a clearly articulated ethical mission statement. A code of conduct then may more specifically delineate this foundation both for internal stakeholders such as employees, as well as for external stakeholders such as customers. The code has the potential to therefore both enhance corporate reputation and also provide concrete guidance for internal decision making, thus creating a built-in risk management system.

When David Packard passed away, Bill Hewlett, his business partner in creating HP, commented, "As far as the company is concerned, the greatest thing he left behind him was a code of ethics known as 'the HP Way.'"[6] The vision can be inspiring—*should be* inspiring. Jim Collins, author of *Built to Last* and *Good to Great*, explains: "Contrary to business school doctrine, we did not find 'maximizing shareholder wealth' or 'profit maximization' as the dominant driving force or primary objective through the history of most of the visionary companies. They have tended to produce a cluster of objectives, of which money is only one—and not necessarily the primary one."[7] By establishing (especially through a participatory process) the core tenets on which a company is built, corporate leadership is effectively laying down the law with regard to the basis and objectives for all future decisions.

The 1990s brought a proliferation of corporate codes of conduct and mission statements as part of the corporate response to the Federal Sentencing Guidelines—and a 2002 survey found that 75 percent of these mention the word "ethics."[8] How successful these codes are depends in large part on the process by which they are conceived and written, as well as their implementation. As with the construction of a personal code or mission, it is critical to first ask yourself what you stand for or what the company stands for. Why does the firm exist, what are its purposes, and how will it implement these objectives? Once you make these determinations, how will you share them and encourage a commitment to them among your colleagues and subordinates? Again, the Johnson & Johnson credo provides an excellent example.

The second step in the development of guiding principles for the firm is the articulation of a clear vision regarding the firm's direction. Why have a code? Bobby Kipp, PricewaterhouseCoopers' Global Ethics Leader, explains that "we felt it was important for all our clients, our people and other stakeholders to understand exactly what we stand for and how they can expect us to conduct ourselves. . . . The code doesn't change the basic nature of the business we undertake, but instead it articulates the way we strive to conduct ourselves. The code shows how we apply our values to our daily business practices."[9]

The third step in this process is to identify how this cultural shift will occur. Referring to Enron's prominent Code of Ethics, Ethics Resource Center President Stuart Gilman advises that you can't simply "print, post and pray." Follow-through and implementation are crucial.

Finally, to have an effective code that will successfully impact culture, there must be a belief throughout the organization that this culture is actually possible, achievable. If conflicts remain that will prevent certain components from being realized, or if key leadership is not on board, no one will have faith in the changes articulated.

Ethics Hotlines, Ombudsman, and Integrating Ethical Culture

Recalling Gilman's warning not to "print, post and pray," business firms must have mechanisms in place that allow employees to come forward with questions, concerns, and information about unethical behavior. Integrating an ethical cultural throughout a firm and providing means for enforcement is vitally critical both to the success of any cultural shift and to the impact on all stakeholders. Integration can take a number of different forms, depending on the organizational culture and the ultimate goals of the process.

One of the most determinative elements of integration is communication, since without it, there is no clarity of purpose, priorities, or process. Communication of culture must be incorporated into the firm's vocabulary, habits, and attitudes to become an essential element in the corporate life, decision making, and determination of success. In the end, the Ethics & Policy Integration Centre contends that communication patterns describe the organization far better than organization charts!

To explore the effectiveness of a corporation's integration process, consider whether incentives are in the right place to encourage ethical decision making and whether ethical behavior is evaluated during a worker's performance review. It is difficult to reward people for doing the right thing, such as correctly filing an expense report, but incentives such as appropriate honors and positive appraisals are possible. But how does communication about ethical issues occur? The fact of the matter is that reporting ethically suspect behavior is a difficult thing to do. Childhood memories of "tattletales" or "snitches," and a general social prohibition against informing on others, create barriers to reporting unethical behavior. More ominously, individuals often pay a real cost when they report unethical behavior, especially if the people involved are workplace superiors.

"Whistleblowing" is a common topic in business ethics and will be examined in more depth in chapter 7. Whistleblowing involves the disclosure of unethical or illegal activities to someone who is in the position to take action to prevent or punish the wrongdoing. Whistleblowing can expose and end unethical activities, but it can also seem disloyal, it can harm the business, and it can extract significant costs on the whistleblower.

Whistleblowing can occur internally, as when Sherron Watkins reported her concerns to Enron president Ken Lay (see pp. 143). It can occur externally to the press, as when Jeffrey Weigand (as portrayed in the movie *The Insider*) reported to *60 Minutes* about Brown & Willamson's activities in not only concealing and knowingly misleading the public about the harmful effects of cigarettes, but also using additives that increased the potential for harm. Whistleblowing can also occur externally when employees report wrongdoing to legal authorities, as when rocket engineer Roger Boisjoly reported the activities of his employer Morton Thiokol and NASA prior to the launch of the space shuttle *Challenger*.

Because whistleblowing to external groups such as the press and the legal authorities can be so harmful to both the whistleblower and the firm itself, internal mechanisms for reporting wrongdoing are preferable. But the internal mechanisms must be effective, they must allow anonymity, and they also must protect the rights of the accused party. In addition to, or as part of the responsibilities of ethics officers and compliance officers, many firms have created ethics ombudsman and ethics hotlines. These mechanisms allow employees to report wrongdoing and create procedures for follow-up and enforcement.

Assessing and Monitoring the Corporate Culture: Audits

Unfortunately, if one cannot measure something, it often declines in importance. Such is the result with regard to culture. If we cannot measure, assess, and monitor culture, it is difficult to encourage others throughout the organization to pay attention to it. Yet, monitoring and an ongoing ethics audit allow organizations to uncover silent vulnerabilities that could pose challenges later to the firm, thus serving as a vital element in risk assessment and prevention. By engaging in an ongoing assessment, organizations are better able to spot these areas before other stakeholders (both internal and external) spot them. But how do you detect a potentially damaging or ethically challenged corporate culture—sometimes referred to as a "toxic" culture? The first clear sign would be a lack of any generally accepted base values for the organization, as previously discussed. In addition, there are warning signs in the various component areas of the organization. How does the firm treat its customers, suppliers, clients, workers? The management of its internal and external relationships is critical evidence of its values. How does the firm manage its finances? Of course, a firm can be in a state of financial disaster without engaging in even one unethical act (and vice verse), but the manner in which it manages and communicates its financial environment is telling.

4.7 MANDATING AND ENFORCING CULTURE: THE FEDERAL SENTENCING GUIDELINES

When internal mechanisms for creating ethical corporate cultures prove inadequate, the business community can expect governmental regulation to fill the void. The United States Sentencing Commission (USSC), an independent agency in the United States Judiciary, was created in 1984 to regulate sentencing policy in the federal court system. Prior to that time, disparity in sentencing, arbitrary punishments, and crime control had been significant congressional issues. In mandating sentencing procedures, Congress through the USSC has been able to incorporate the original purposes of sentencing in their procedures, bringing some of these challenges under control.

Beginning in 1987, the USSC prescribed mandatory Federal Sentencing Guidelines that apply to individual and organizational defendants in the federal system, bringing some amount of uniformity and fairness to the system. These prescriptions, based on the severity of the offense, assign most federal crimes to one of 43 "offense levels." Each offender also is placed into a criminal history category based upon the extent and recency of past misconduct. The court then inputs this information into a sentencing grid and determines the offender's guideline range (ranges are either in 6-month intervals or 25 percent, whichever is greater), subject to adjustments. In its October 2004 decision in U.S. v. Booker,[10] however, the Supreme Court severed the "mandatory" element of the guidelines from their advisory role, holding that their mandatory nature violated the Sixth Amendment right to a jury trial. Accordingly, though no longer mandatory, a sentencing court is still required to consider guideline ranges, but is also permitted to tailor a sentence in light of other statutory concerns. This modification has not come without confusion. "Judges are still generally following the guidelines with new cases. But figuring out what to do with all the cases that have been sentenced under the old guidelines is the closest thing to chaos you can describe," says Douglas Berman, a law professor.[11]

What is the relevance of these guidelines to our exploration of ethics and, in particular, to our discussion of the corporate proactive efforts to create an ethical workplace? The USSC strived in its guidelines to create both a legal and an ethical corporate culture through these adjustments. The Sarbanes-Oxley legislation instructed the USSC to consider and review its guidelines for fraud relating to securities and accounting as well as for obstruction of justice, and specifically asked for severe and aggressive deterrents. In recognition of the enormous impact of corporate culture on ethical decision making, the USSC updated the guidelines in 2004 to include references not only to compliance programs but to "ethics and compliance" programs. In addition, the criterion for an effective program, which used to be outlined in the Guidelines' commentary, is now a separate guideline itself.

The guidelines seek to reward corporations that create an effective ethics and compliance system so that they are not penalized (or the penalty is reduced) if they have an effective program but they find themselves in court as a result of a bad apple or two. On the other hand, firms that did not have effective ethics and compliance systems would be sentenced additionally to a term of probation and ordered to develop a program during that time.

The USSC notes that

> [d]ue diligence and the promotion of desired organizational culture are indicated by the fulfillment of eight minimum requirements, which are the hallmarks of an effective program that encourages compliance with the law and ethical conduct.

The guidelines identify those specific acts of an organization that can serve as due diligence in preventing crime and the minimal requirements for an effective compliance and ethics program. These include:

1. Establish compliance standards and procedures (reasonably designed, implemented, and enforced so that they will generally be effective in preventing and detecting violations of law).[12]
2. Establish a governing body (board), which has a duty to act prudently, to be knowledgeable about the content and operation of the compliance and ethics program, and must undergo ongoing and consistent training.
3. Assign specific high-level person to oversee compliance and to be responsible for the day-to-day operations of the program. This individual shall report directly to the board or other governing authority and shall have sufficient resources.
4. Use due care not to delegate important responsibilities to known high-risk persons.
5. Communicate the program effectively to all employees and agents. In addition to the board, training must be conducted throughout the organizational leadership, employees, and (where appropriate) its agents.
6. Monitor and audit program operation for effectiveness and to detect criminal activity, and establish a retribution-free, anonymous, or confidential means for employees and agents to report possible violations to management or to seek guidance.

7. Create an incentive and disincentive structure to encourage performance in accordance with the program, including consistent discipline for employee violations.
8. Respond promptly and appropriately to any offenses and remedy any program deficiencies.[13]

Though these steps are likely to lead to an effective program "[such a program] is more than checking off the items on a list. This concept of 'due diligence' is a restless standard, as flexible as changing events reflected in the day's headlines and as creative as the minds of potential wrongdoers."[14] For instance, the guidelines require an investigation in response to a report of wrongdoing, but they also seem to require more than that. A firm must learn from its mistakes and take steps to prevent recurrences such as follow-up investigation and program enhancements. The USSC also mandates consideration of the size of the organization, the number and nature of its business risks, and the prior history of the organization; mitigating factors such as self-reporting of violations, cooperation with authorities, acceptance of responsibility; as well as aggravating factors such as its involvement in or tolerance of criminal activity, a violation of a prior order, or its obstruction of justice. These standards are to be judged against applicable industry standards; however, this requires that each firm benchmark against comparable companies.

In a 1997 survey of members of the Ethics Officers Association, 47 percent of ethics officers reported that the guidelines were an influential determinant of their firm's commitment to ethics,[15] and another commission study showed that the guidelines influenced 44.5 percent of these officers to enhance their existing compliance programs.[16]

REFLECTIONS ON THE CHAPTER DISCUSSION CASE

When discussing topics in business ethics it is often easy to focus on the wrongdoers and concentrate on examples of fraud, corruption, and malfeasance. But it is just as important to consider cases of "best practice" so that we recognize that ethical business can be both possible and profitable. Johnson & Johnson is a helpful example for this approach.

Like the human beings who work in them, corporations are imperfect and even the most well-intentioned can act irresponsibly. Nevertheless, every corporation—like every person—faces a choice: should we strive for the highest ethical standards and work hard to maintain them, or are we satisfied with the bare minimum and willing to cut corners when it suits our purpose?

Those corporations that do strive for the highest ethical standards aim to create an ethical culture in which responsible behavior and decision making is encouraged, supported, and expected. The Johnson & Johnson experience, and the prominent role that their credo plays in creating that culture, provides a model of one way to advance these goals.

REVIEW QUESTIONS

1. To help understand an organizational culture, think about some organization to which you belong. Does your company or school or fraternity/sorority have its own culture? How would you describe it? How does it influence individual decision making and action? Would you be a different person had you attended a different school or joined a different fraternity or sorority? How would you go about changing your organization's culture?

2. Consider how you evaluate whether a firm is "one of the good guys" or not. What are some of the factors that you use to make this determination? Do you actually know the facts behind each of those elements, or has your judgment been shaped by the firm's reputation? Identify one firm that you believe to be decent or ethical and make a note of the bases for that conclusion. Next identify a second firm that you do not believe to be ethical or with questionable values and write down the bases for that conclusion. Now, using the Internet and other relevant sources, explore the firms' cultures and decisions, checking the results of your research against your original impressions of the firms. Try to evaluate the cultures and decisions of each firm as if you had no idea whether they were ethical. Were you accurate in your impressions or do they need to be modified slightly?

3. Changing a corporate culture is very difficult. Imagine that you are asked by your chief executive to help move your firm toward the use of a triple-bottom-line accounting model in which environmental and social factors are given equal weight to financial indicators. Assume that this would represent a major transformation of the firm. How would you begin to set the stage for this transition? What reasons would you use to support the change? How would you change attitudes and values?

4. Now that you have an understanding of corporate culture and the variables that impact it, how would you characterize an ethically effective culture, the one that would effectively lead to a profitable and valuable long-term sustainability for the firm?

5. One element that surely impacts a firm's culture is its employee population. While a corporate culture can shape an employee's attitudes and habits, this will be more easily done if people with those attitudes and habits already developed are hired in the first place. How would you develop a recruitment and selection process that would most successfully allow you to hire the best workers for your particular culture? How would you, and should you, get rid of employees who do not share the corporate culture?

6. What are some of the greatest benefits and deleterious costs of compliance-based cultures?

7. You are aware of inappropriate behavior and violations of your firm's code of conduct throughout your operation. In an effort to support a collegial and positive atmosphere, however, you do not encourage co-workers to report on their peers. Unfortunately, you believe that you must make

a shift in that area and need to institute a mandatory reporting structure. How would you design the structure and how would you implement the new program in such a way that the collegiality that exists is not destroyed?

8. Put yourself in the position of someone who is establishing an organization from the ground up. What type of leader would you want to be? How would you create that image or perception? Do you create a mission statement for the firm, a code of conduct? What process would you use to do so? Would you create an ethics and/or compliance program and how would you then integrate the mission statement and program throughout your organization? What do you anticipate might be your successes and challenges?

ENDNOTES

[1] Ralph Larsen, "Leadership in a Values-Based Organization," Sears Lectureship in Business Ethics, Bentley College (2/7/02).

[2] James Collins, Jerry Porras, *Built to Last: Successful Habits of Visionary Companies*, (New York: HarperCollins, 1994), p. 73.

[3] Raymond Gilmartin, "Ethics and the Corporate Culture," *Raytheon Lectureship in Business Ethics* (November 10, 2003).

[4] L. Trevino, M. Brown, L. Hartman, "A Qualitative Investigation of Perceived Executive Ethical Leadership: Perceptions from Inside and Outside the Executive Suite," *Human Relations*, v.56, no. 1 (January 2003), pp. 5–37.

[5] Ibid.

[6] James Collins, Jerry Porras, "Building Your Company's Vision," *Harvard Business Review* (September–October 1996).

[7] Mark Satin, "We Need to Alter the Culture at Places Like Enron—Not Just Pass More Laws," *Radical Middle Newsletter* (March/April 2002), http://www.radicalmiddle/com.

[8] American Management Association Report, *2002 Corporate Values Survey* (2002).

[9] PricewaterhouseCoopers, "Why Have a Code?" http://www.pwc.com/extweb/newcoatwork.nsf/docid/BCC554487E1C3BC680256C2B003115D5

[10] *U.S. v. Booker*, 543 U.S. 220 (2005) (*slip opinion*).

[11] Kris Axtman, "Cases Test New Flexibility of Sentencing Guidelines," *Christian Science Monitor* (February 18, 2005).

[12] USSC, *Guidelines Manual*, sec. 8A1.2, comment (n. 3(k)) (2000).

[13] USSC, *Guidelines Manual*, sec. 8A1.2, comment (n. 3(k)) (2000).

[14] Joseph Murphy, "Lost Words of the Sentencing Guidelines," *Ethikos* (November–December 2002), p. 5.

[15] Ethics Officer Association, 1997 Member Survey (2000), p. 9.

[16] USSC, Corporate Crime in America: Strengthening the "Good Citizen" Corporation, 123–91 (1995).

5 CHAPTER

The Meaning and Value of Work

After reading this chapter, you will be able to:

- Examine the goals and values of your own career and workplace decisions;
- Explain the variety of meanings and values attributed to work;
- Explain business's responsibility for providing employees with meaningful work;
- Describe a framework for evaluating business's ethical responsibilities to employees;
- Describe a framework for evaluating the rights and responsibilities of employees.

DISCUSSION CASE: Great Jobs and Meaningful Jobs

In the opinion of many people, Pat Tillman had a fantastic job. As a star safety for the Arizona Cardinals of the National Football League, Tillman had the money, fame, and influence that many believe are characteristics of a perfect job. Drafted out of college in 1998 by the Cardinals, Tillman turned down a five-year, $9 million contract offer from the St. Louis Rams in 2001 to re-sign a three-year, $3.6 million contract with the Cardinals. It was reported at the time that his motivation for accepting the smaller contract was loyalty to the Cardinals' organization. One year later, Tillman voluntarily quit the Cardinals' team to enlist in the U.S. Army. Tillman never spoke publicly about that decision, but friends explained that he felt a sense of duty to support his country after the terrorist attacks of September 11, 2001. On April 22, 2004, Tillman was killed during a battle in Afghanistan.

Pat Tillman undoubtedly was an exceptional individual. Few people would walk away from such a job to enlist in the military and risk their own life. Yet, Tillman's story is similar to those of people who continue working at unglamorous jobs when they no longer need to do so. One reads of lottery winners who remain working at ordinary jobs even when they could afford to retire, or of retirees who accept low-paying and seemingly lackluster jobs. Many other individuals leave lucrative jobs in business to become teachers or to take other social service positions. Rather than pursuing high-paying jobs in business, many college students volunteer to work in social service positions upon graduation. Clearly, people have many reasons for pursuing the type of work and the specific job they do choose. Yet, the common assumption is that most people work because they need to earn money to survive.

During the early decades of the twentieth century economists and other social scientists debated an issue that might seem quaint today. With the growing productivity of the industrial revolution moving many societies from the age of scarcity to an age of abundance, the question among social scientists was what would happen when workers reached the point where they obtained life's basic necessities? The fear of many economists was that people would stop working as much and that this would lead to a decline in productivity which, in turn, could lead to an economic downturn. The assumption was that once necessities and a few luxuries were obtained, workers would seek to reduce time spent at work. This same debate surfaced again in mid-century when technological advances and increased automation once again suggested that increased productivity might lead to an abundance of leisure time.

The facts, of course, are that nothing at all like this happened. The evidence suggests that consumer demand is unlimited and does not distinguish between necessities and luxuries. Contrary to some early theories, it appears that workers increased their commitment to work in order to keep up with an increasing demand for goods and services. Rather than decreasing the amount of time spent working, it seems most workers continue or increase work time in order to obtain what previously would have been considered luxuries.

Some observers think we are facing similar questions today. Economist Juliet Schor's 1991 book *The Overworked American* claimed that Americans are working more but enjoying it less. Schor's thesis was that the never-ending cycle of consumerism in which happiness is defined as satisfying consumer wants and in which the economy required an expanding pool of unfulfilled wants (how else would the economy continue to grow?) means that people are working more but enjoying life less.

Schor's conclusions about the amount of time Americans are working were challenged by several observers. The empirical data seemed ambiguous, depending in part on how one defines work (wage-earning labor only, or housework and other necessary activities). Yet there is more agreement on her conclusions about happiness. Americans report that they *feel* as if they are working more (even if in fact they are not) and report that they are less happy than their parents were.[1]

As we enter the first years of the twenty-first century it has become commonplace to hear talk once again about a "new economy," "greater productivity," and the "changing nature of work." This new economy was heralded by an unprecedented period of economic growth and prosperity fueled, in part, by increased worker productivity and technological advancements. The changing nature of work refers to movements away from an industrial model of long-term employment toward an economy with a smaller workforce and greater job volatility and mobility. The movement is stereotypically captured in such images as a middle-aged assembly line factory worker being replaced by a young webpage designer. Of course, it is easy to over-generalize such claims. While true for many people in, and parts of, Western developed economies, neither economic prosperity nor job mobility is true for all workers in these societies. It certainly is not true for most workers throughout the world for whom agricultural work remains the primary type of work done.

Nevertheless, it is still fair to say that the model of work that dominated economic thinking throughout most of the twentieth century is giving way to a broader understanding. "Work," perhaps especially in the decades after World War II, was understood primarily based on what we might call the industrial model. As an activity, work existed as a long-term relationship within a single firm. Employees received steady and stable employment, secure wages and benefits, and opportunities for promotion within the firm. Employers received the benefits of increased productivity created by a stable and competent workforce. This model of work thus served the purposes of both employees and employers reasonably well.

In such a workplace, the activities of work tend to be highly structured and routinized. The workplace can be highly bureaucratic with rules and expectations well-developed and spelled out. Such determinate rules characterized both the daily activities of work and the requirements for promotion and advancement within the firm.

In the last decades of the twentieth century attention was paid to a type of work that came to be called *contingent work*. This phrase referred to a wide variety of jobs and workers who didn't fit the more traditional industrial model. These jobs were more temporary, often part-time, and often filled by more entrepreneurial and freelance workers. The category of contingent work includes temporary workers (often supplied by temporary employment agencies), independent contractors and consultants, day laborers, and regular part-time or on-call workers. By 1995, such workers comprised almost 30 percent of the entire U.S. workforce and included almost 35 percent of all women workers.

In addition to such contingent work, the massive layoffs and corporate downsizing that occurred in the 1990s were an indication of further changes in the contemporary workplace. No longer could long-term employees assume that there would always be a job available for them as long as they performed their jobs adequately. This seemed to come as a particular shock to hundreds of thousands of middle-aged, white-collar workers who lost their jobs as a result of corporate downsizing. Similar issues have arisen more recently when an increasingly global economy has resulted in jobs being outsourced to lower-paid foreign workers. The rules and expectations of the workplace are clearly changing.

DISCUSSION QUESTIONS

1. Could you ever envision a point in your own life before retirement where you would be willing to trade wages and income for more leisure time? Besides taking time away from work to raise a family, what other reasons might lead you to consider such a decision? Do you know anyone who has done this?
2. What factors other than wages would influence you to change jobs? To take a job? To quit a job? Other than wages, what are the three most important aspects of any job you would seek?
3. If not for wages, why work? If you were granted extra time in each day would you choose to spend any of it at work?

5.1 INTRODUCTION

As described in chapter 1, philosophy asks us to step back from our everyday lives to reflect on and examine our decisions. Why do we do the things we do? Chapter 1 began with the very self-reflective question: Why study business ethics? But such questioning can be extended further. Why are you taking the courses that you do? Why are you enrolled in school? To answer such questions, many students would reason as follows. I am taking this course because it is required for my major. I am enrolled in this major because I hope to get a good job when I graduate. I want a good job so I can make a lot of money. I want to make a lot of money so that I can be happy.

Most, if not all, of our everyday thinking fits this means-ends reasoning pattern. We do something (enroll in a course, major in a certain subject, accept a particular job) as a means to some other end (a college degree, a job, money, happiness). Our own thinking about work typically fits this model as well. We work as a means to an end. But can work itself ever be an end, rather than only a means? What is, and what ought to be, the nature of work, and what values are served by working? What are the responsibilities for business as a place of work?

Previous chapters have considered "business" in a very general sense. Beginning with this chapter, we will look more closely at the ethical responsibilities of specific operations of business institutions. Perhaps most importantly for most of us, businesses are the places where we work. Along with producing goods and services, providing employment is the most important social function of business. In chapters 5, 6, and 7, we will examine a wide range of ethical issues that arise within the workplace.

We are all familiar with stories about people who win multimillion dollar lottery prizes and then claim that they intend to continue working at their present job. Most of us find these stories fascinating because such an attitude goes against the common wisdom that we work only to get paid. This more common attitude was captured some years ago by the *Chicago Tribune* columnist Mike Royko:

> Why do you think the lottery is so popular? Do you think anybody would play if the super payoff was a job on the night shift in a meat packing plant? People play it so if they win they can be rich and idle . . . like I told you years ago—if work is so good, how come they have to pay us to do it?[2]

Many people think of work with this type of ambivalence. Work is a very important part of our lives and it is not something that we easily would, or could, abandon. Yet, the very idea of work seems to suggest drudgery and toil, something to be avoided whenever possible. Work seems a necessary evil.

From the earliest times one can trace a continual human fascination with the nature of work. This fascination is often divided between glory and contempt. Work can be exalting, uplifting, fulfilling and degrading, tedious, troublesome. In *Genesis*, work was seen as a curse and punishment for original sin, yet humans were also called forth to work the land, to subdue the earth, to till and keep the garden.[3] The Greek philosopher Aristotle recognized work as necessary for the good life, yet he also disparaged work because of this very necessary, and therefore "slavish," nature.[4] Martin Luther, John Calvin, and Benjamin Franklin all acknowledged the drudgery of work, yet each emphasized how this very toilsome nature can be put to work for a higher cause.[5] Jean-Jacques Rousseau's romantic view of the self-reliant craftsman developing human creativity was tempered by a recognition that within society mankind is "everywhere in chains." For Karl Marx, labor had the potential to express our very humanity but, in modern capitalist societies at least, labor is alienated from this end.[6]

The two sides of this ambivalence raise distinct questions for business ethics. Work can provide opportunities for valuable, meaningful, and uplifting human activity, and work can be dehumanizing, degrading, and oppressive. To the degree that work can be uplifting, business ethics is challenged to articulate the vision of good work and the good workplace. To the degree that work is a burden that we all must endure, business ethics is challenged to articulate and defend the conditions under which work can be made fair, just, and humane.

This present chapter will examine a variety of theories about the meaning and value of work. How we conceptualize work has a significant impact on how we structure and organize the workplace. In the following chapter, we will examine a variety of workplace rights. Employee rights would offer protection of important human interests within the context of a situation in which those interests are jeopardized by the necessity of work.

5.2 THE MEANINGS OF WORK

Our understanding of the nature of work can have a significant impact on ourselves as individuals and on the institution of the workplace. Psychologically, the very attitude with which we face each day can be greatly influenced by our understanding of work in general, and of our own work in particular. For employees, the meaning and value found in work can contribute significantly to self-esteem as well as physical and mental health. For managers, how employees think about work will influence everything from performance and productivity to employee turnover, and from wages and benefits to absenteeism. As testimony to the importance of such questions, one need only look at the prevalent discussion of topics such as job satisfaction and worker morale in the field of business management.

So, what does *work* mean? At first glance, we should recognize that we use "work" with a variety of meanings, both as a verb and as a noun. As a verb, work refers to activities that involves perseverance, discipline, toil, usually performed with a degree of seriousness and concentration. The verb *to work* is contrasted with being idle, relaxing, playing. Sitting here at my computer, I might be working on a book, or I might simply be playing on the Internet. This afternoon, I may go out to play a round of golf, or I might go to the practice range to work on my game.

As a noun, work can refer to particular accomplishments (e.g., a work of art), any general undertaking or task (e.g., homework), or a job or employment. Our focus in this textbook on business ethics will be on work done in exchange for wages, "work" in the sense of a job or employment.

But even with this focus, it is important not to ignore the variety of work. People work as executives in large corporate institutions, on assembly lines in a factory, temporary or full-time jobs, and they work several jobs. People work for government agencies, as artists and craftsmen, in construction or teaching. Some work for corporations, others are self-employed, most work for small businesses; some commute or travel continuously, others work at home. Particularly when we are considering the value and significance of work, it is crucial that we not operate with too narrow of a focus.

For example, social programs such as Social Security and unemployment insurance, and many public policies concerned with marriage and divorce, have systematically undervalued or ignored the value of housework and child care. Since the women who typically filled such roles were not engaged in work for wages, their status under Social Security and tax law was dependent upon their husband's employment. Women who were engaged full-time with child care and homemaking were described, and often disparaged, as not working. Alternately, when women are employed in the workforce, social expectations can hold them responsible for the "work" of child care and household duties. Women, but not men, are expected to be the "super mom" who works a full-time job and still manages a household.

Even when we use "work" to refer only to those activities performed in exchange of wages and compensation, we find an assorted and distinct range of meanings. "Work" can suggest a job, profession, career, trade, labor, occupation, vocation, or a calling. In an important study of American culture and values, sociologist Robert Bellah and his co-authors of *Habits of the Heart* offer some insightful observations concerning various meanings of work and their relations. The authors distinguish between a job, a career, and a calling.[7] Each is distinguished by the degree to which the identity of the person filling the role is determined by the role itself.

What does it mean to say that one's identity is determined by work? Consider that "What do you do?" is a very common first question we ask when introduced to someone. People identify themselves to others by their work. "I am an accountant." "I manage a small business." "I am a college professor." "I work for the state social service department." What we do determines who we are. When you tell me that you are a computer programmer, you have identified yourself in terms of your work. We come to know others by knowing what they do. But we also come to think about ourselves, we develop our own self-image, in terms of our work. Sometimes our work can contribute to a strong positive self-image as when someone introduces herself as "I am vice president for marketing at a large international corporation." Sometimes our work, or lack thereof, contributes to a low self-image. "I'm unemployed" or "I work the night shift at the meat packing plant."

In *Habits of the Heart*, a *job* is described as work in which self-identity is independent of the activity. A job is simply a role that one steps into and out of as a means for earning money. "I just happen to work a job at this fast-food restaurant, but tomorrow I may change jobs and take a job working construction." Jobs have no meaning other than the instrumental value as a means for earning wages.

A career involves a developing relationship between the self and the activity. One might say that "after graduation I intend to begin my career in public relations" or "I am pursuing a career in real estate." A career suggests an ongoing activity that is defined in terms of wider social institutions that establish standards of achievement and advancement. One develops throughout a career, not in the sense of moving from one job to another, but in the sense of

mastering various stages and advancing to new levels. This sense of development means that careers involve social status and self-esteem in ways that jobs
do not. With careers, we hear echoes of the traditional crafts system in which
one progresses from apprentice to master and with this progression one gains
in status and self-esteem.

A calling also returns to an earlier tradition of work in which a person's
identity and activities were "morally inseparable." Who you are was determined fully by what you do. Traditionally, the professions, artisans, and farming were understood this way. "I am a minister," "I am a musician," "I am a
farmer" tells us a great deal about both the person and their work. Perhaps
less common today than in years past, individuals thought of themselves as
"called" to a life of medicine, military service, or teaching.

This categorization is not intended as absolute or exhaustive, but rather as
a helpful way to understand the complexity of work. Work has the potential to
be intimately connected to our deepest values, for better or for worse. When
the time comes to reflect back upon your entire life and judge its worth, what
work you did and how you did it will play a significant role in deciding how
worthwhile your life has been. The meaning and value of work, both actual
and potential, will therefore have important implications for the structure and
operation of the workplace.

5.3 THE VALUE OF WORK

Before reviewing various theories of work it will prove useful to consider some
of the values that work can hold. "Why work?" and "What is work good for?"
may seem obvious or trivial questions to some, but upon slight reflection we
can discover a wide variety of values associated with work.

Clearly work has significant value as the means for attaining an income
and, through that income, many other ends that we need and desire. One works
in order to buy food, pay the mortgage, buy clothing, pay for a child's education. I am fortunate to have a job that also provides health and life insurance,
educational benefits, and a retirement program. Work has high instrumental
value; by working one is able to attain many other goods. Because it is necessary for obtaining so many other goods, work can be said to have an exceptionally important instrumental value.

The extent of the instrumental value of work can be understood when we
ask if we would continue working if we attained all the other goods. If more
efficient substitutes can be found for some activity with only instrumental
value, we have no reason to continue the activity. For example, if I work only to
make money and I inherit a fortune, I would stop working.

To determine if there are other values in working, I often ask my students
what they would do if they won a multimillion dollar lottery. During one class,
a student answered that he would spend all his time playing golf. I asked if
he would simply *play* or if he would *work* on his game to improve. He admitted that he would likely get bored if he continued shooting high scores and

never improved his game. He readily acknowledged that he would be willing to work on his game with the goal of eventually shooting par. He would work on his golf game, but he would not continue to work for a living.

I then asked students to think about why someone such as Bill Gates continues to work. The day I write this, *Fortune* announced its 1999 estimate of Gates's fortune at more than $90 billion. Surely this is enough wealth to do whatever he wants, yet he continues to work full-time for Microsoft. Why? To the cynic who suggests that Gates works only to continually increase his wealth, I point out that Gates (as virtually all people of enormous wealth do) gives away significant amounts of money. If financial greed was his only motivation for working, he could stop giving his money away and work less.

Clearly there is more to work than simply earning money. As the golfing example suggests, people will work to attain many ends including, but not limited to, the feelings of satisfaction that come from achieving challenging goals. When employment can provide these others goods, people will continue working even if they no longer need the income. Thus, the instrumental value of work involves many goods other than wages and benefits. Think about why people do the work required to run a marathon, to teach a child with learning disabilities, to care for a dying patient, to run their own business, to be a police officer.

What goods, other than wages and benefits, come from working? While we cannot hope to be exhaustive, we can offer a general categorization of some goods. First, work is a means to attain goods other than income. Many of these goods have value that cannot be priced and therefore cannot be achieved solely through the money earned by working. There are what we might call various *psychic* goods associated with work. These include feelings of personal satisfaction and self-worth, of achievement, self-esteem, happiness. Work also can be an expression of a person's deepest attitudes and character. Many work because, simply, that's the type of person they are; for many people, their character is made manifest through work. People are industrious, motivated, earnest, active, and creative. A creative and industrious person not working is as unlikely as a lethargic and lazy person enthusiastically heading off to work.

Work can also have social meaning for many people. With work comes social status, honor, respect, companionship, and camaraderie. Aristotle described humans as social beings, and work can be a major activity through which our social nature is expressed. Consider the many reasons why someone might choose to be a teacher rather than an accountant, or a social worker rather than work in sales. Sometimes work can be associated with an entire lifestyle such as work in farming and in the military.

A personal story illustrates one way in which work can have deep social meaning and value. My wife is the fourth generation of her family to own and operate a small business. She had been successful at a previous job in a large corporation. She seemed well poised to advance up the corporate ladder when her father reached retirement age and sought to sell the business. The business had been started by her great-grandfather and had been open for nearly one hundred years. Rather than allowing the business to close or be sold to a stranger, she chose to leave her corporate career and purchase the family business.

In terms of mere instrumental value, this work decision had many costs: a lower salary (alas), much longer hours, more headaches and stress, and greater responsibilities. But this work also provides other important values, not the least of which is the fact that she is carrying on a legacy begun by her great-grandfather. This is what we might mean by the "social value" that work can have. Bill Gates's dedication to the company he founded likewise can explain why he continues to work when he has no financial need to do so.

Finally, some work is more valuable and worthwhile to society than others. Many people choose to work as nurses, day-care providers, social workers, police, or military personnel because these are positions in which they can make an important contribution to their community. These are important jobs that any stable community must fill. For many people, this alone is reason enough to pursue such work. Other work, such as the performance of artists and musicians or work in crafts or agriculture, is valuable either in its own right or for the product that results. Much of this work is valuable not only for the product, but for the quality of the product.

For example, I have a friend who is a potter. His work is extraordinarily dirty (he works with wet clay all day) and sweaty (as he stokes a roaring fire within his kiln). The hours are very long and the pay very modest. Yet, he produces some of the most beautiful and exquisite pottery imaginable. He also produces it in an environmentally sensitive and sustainable way. His work has significant value because of what is produced and how it is produced. This work is a significant part of his identity. These values far transcend the income he receives from this work.

In a classical essay, Douglas McGregor defended a management theory (what he called Theory Y) that recognized the many diverse values attained through work. Among these, McGregor mentioned survival, security, acceptance by others, association with others, friendship, self-esteem, status, respect, creativity, and self-development.[8]

Perhaps this is a good point at which to reiterate an earlier distinction. Work can refer both to an *activity* performed with diligence and perseverance and it can refer to *employment*. While there are values involved in any diligent activity that we might call "work," the values described above are also attainable through, and sometimes only through, employment. But if this is so, if work can be so valuable, why, as Mike Royko asks, "do they have to pay us to do it?"

We might venture a preliminary answer. Some jobs can hold so much value that people would do them for little or no pay. Some jobs provide their holders with significant meaning and worth. Others can be made valuable depending upon their circumstances. Working conditions such as the structure of the job, salary and benefits, its privileges and responsibilities, job security, its institutional setting, and its social status can add to or detract from a job's value. But for many people, work is necessary to make a living, and because it is necessary, the possibility of attaining other values often gets lost in the pursuit of income.

So what might be the goal of an ethical workplace? If work is so important for so many reasons, should every person have a moral and legal right to a job? Is it possible to provide all workers with meaningful, worthwhile, and highly valued jobs? If not, are there steps to be taken to make work more rather than less meaningful? Does business have a responsibility to provide employees with meaningful work, or is business's responsibility complete when it pays a fair wage for a fair day's work?

These questions take on added significance when we recognize three common aspects of the contemporary work scene. First, few workers have significant choices and alternatives open to them in the workplace. Given the significant instrumental value that work has as the means of making one's livelihood, few people are in the position where they put their job in jeopardy. This means that people may be put in situations where they must accept less than ideal working conditions.

Two further points concern what seem to be emerging trends in the contemporary economy. People today seem more likely to work many jobs over their lifetimes than they were in the past. Job mobility is more a fact of work-life today than it was for our parents and grandparents. Sometimes this is a matter of choice, but often it is the result of factors over which employees have no control. This suggests that at least some of work's values, income stability and self-esteem among others, may be at greater risk today than in times past. A second trend is the growth in what is sometimes called *contingent work.* More jobs today are temporary, part-time, or subcontracted out to third parties. In some cases this can be a value-added component to work, as when an individual is able to work part-time while also going to school or providing child care. But just as often this can mean that the values and benefits of work are more conditional and uncertain. Many of the social values of work, such as camaraderie and social status, can be lost or unavailable to part-time and temporary workers.

Before we turn to business's responsibilities in this regard, let us consider some major theories of work.

5.4 CONVENTIONAL VIEWS OF WORK

Journalist and social observer Studs Terkel's 1974 book *Working* chronicled the state of blue-collar work in America. The book opens with a statement that captures what we shall identify as the conventional view of work.

> This book, being about work is, by its nature, about violence—to the spirit as well as to the body. It is about ulcers as well as accidents, about shouting matches as well as fights, about nervous breakdowns as well as kicking the dog around. It is above all (or beneath all) about daily humiliations. To survive the day is triumph enough for the walking wounded among the great many of us.[9]

Work is seen as something that must be endured. It is difficult, arduous, laborious. The very words *work* and *labor* carry this negative connotation in ordinary language. Certainly this conventional view accurately characterizes work for many people. The essence of this conventional view is that work is something to be avoided whenever possible and endured when we must.

We can distinguish two trends within this conventional viewpoint. One perspective, with roots traceable to classical Greek thought, holds that there are higher and more meaningful human activities than work. Work is to be avoided so that one can pursue these more valuable and refined goods. The good life for humans would be a life of contemplation and a life spent enjoying the higher pleasures of art, politics, and culture. Perhaps a view such as this was implicit in the assumptions of those social scientists studying leisure and affluence mentioned in the discussion case at the start of this chapter. Once workers attained sufficient affluence to fill all their needs, they would reduce the amount of time spent working so that they could pursue more valuable and refined cultural goods.

This *classical interpretation of work* conceives of humans as intellectual beings, yet work is physical. Humans are free beings, work is a necessity. Work thus involves a constant diminishing of human nature and human potential. In the classical world, work was left to slaves. Cultured and civilized people avoided work as undignified.

The Roman philosopher Plutarch portrays this classical view in the following quotation:

> Gentlemen enjoy the contemplation of the sculptor's masterpieces, but he would never himself use hammer and chisel and get covered with sweat and dust.[10]

Twentieth-century philosopher Yves Simon echoes Plutarch's sentiments on the relative value of work:

> The rise of the working class in modern history has led to the glorification of work and the reduction of virtually all human activity to a species of work, while leisure becomes identified with idelness . . . . give work its due but recognize that true culture thrives on immanent activities of contemplation and joy that transcends both social utility and time.[11]

Another twentieth-century philosopher, Hannah Arendt, opens her influential book, *The Human Condition,* with similar sentiments.

> In the modern age . . . laborers are about to be freed from the fetters of labor, and this society no longer knows these higher and more meaningful activities for the sake of which this freedom would deserve to be won.[12]

The second version of the conventional model is much more common in the contemporary world. What we'll call the *hedonistic interpretation* understands work as a necessary means for obtaining life's pleasures. One works so that one can buy those things that will make you happy. Work is the price we have to pay in order to get both the necessities of life and the many other things that make life enjoyable and pleasurable. Whereas the classical interpretation defends a very specific content for human happiness, the hedonistic interpretation allows individuals to choose whatever ends they desire. Happiness for the classical model is the enjoyment of various cultural activities. Happiness for the hedonistic model is simply getting whatever one wants. While the classical model would see the hedonistic version as disreputable, they both agree that the drudgery of work prevents humans from obtaining happiness.

The hedonistic model's emphasis on happiness as want-satisfaction makes this view quite compatible with the assumptions of neoclassical economics. Individuals are free to choose their own preferences and the goal of economic activity is to satisfy preferences. Individuals exchange their labor in the market as a means for obtaining satisfaction. Work, for the most part, is simply a means to obtain our ends. Perhaps it is not surprising, therefore, that in a world greatly influenced by neoclassical economics, the most common view of work shares its assumption about human happiness. It is also perhaps not surprising that a workplace structured and administered according to the principles of neoclassical economics—a workplace in which employees work simply to earn wages and employers treat them simply as means to productive ends—is a workplace that gives rise to feelings of resentment and disaffection. From that perspective, work has no value in its own right; it is simply a necessary price that must be tolerated to achieve other ends.

5.5 THE HUMAN FULFILLMENT MODEL

The second approach we shall call the *human fulfillment* school. From this perspective, work is the primary activity through which people develop their full potential as human beings. In some ways, this is the opposite of the classical model. Both perspectives would agree that the good life involves the development and flourishing of the human potential. But while the classical model views work as hindering the development of human potential, the human fulfillment school views work as a primary means for this development.

Thus the philosophical roots of this school also lie with the classical Greek philosophers who argued that humans had a natural potential, or *telos,* and that the good life was a life spent developing or fulfilling that *telos.* This general approach is called a *teleological ethics,* and it is a tradition that was carried on through the great Christian philosophers of the medieval period. The contemporary slogan of the U.S. Army to "Be all that you can be" reflects the same ethical attitude. Humans have a potential that they don't always fulfill; the good life is a life in which this potential is actualized. The human fulfillment school believes that work can be the process through which this potential is fulfilled.

But what is this "potential" that can be fulfilled through work? Again, let us return to the distinction between work as any general activity requiring perseverance, diligence, and concentration (work as opposed to play) and work as employment. Let us also come at this question by asking what is lost if we do not work. First, let's consider what type of person we would become if we never engaged in activities requiring perseverance, diligence, and concentration. We can then turn to the question of what happens to individuals when they become unemployed.

Consider the student golfer example mentioned earlier. What happens to a person who plays at golf but never works to improve his game? While some people might continue to play and enjoy the game, this student admitted that he would get bored, frustrated and eventually lose interest. The golfer becomes apathetic, passive, lethargic, and the game of golf would lose its value. Generalizing from this example, we might say that diligence, perseverance, and concentration improve whatever talents and abilities to which we apply them. Our intellectual skills are improved when we focus our attention, think through what is required for performing a task. Diligence, perseverance, concentration are character traits, what philosophers would call virtues, that contribute to the improvement of human well-being. You are improved as a person when you have the ability to approach tasks with such a temperament. Conversely, people who do not work at any task risk becoming lazy, careless, and apathetic. Developing good work habits contributes to a character that is capable, competent, effective, and skillful. Parents, for example, seek to instill such good work habits in children to provide them with important lifelong skills. One study by psychologists George and Caroline Valliant concluded that "the willingness and capacity to work in childhood is the most important forerunner—more important than native intelligence, social class, or family situation—of mental health."[13]

But what about work as employment? Certainly unemployment has costs far beyond the loss of income. The psychic costs of unemployment are well-documented. Loss of self-esteem and self-respect, stress, anxiety, depression, isolation, and apathy are common consequences. The social costs of unemployment are also high. Employment has largely disappeared from the poorest neighborhoods in most large cities. The results of chronic unemployment can literally destroy a community.[14]

Conversely, work can provide the worker with the opportunity for such psychological goods as high self-esteem and self-respect as well as both stable mental and physical health. Work can also provide workers with social goods such as friendships, companionship, a sense of belonging, and a sense of purpose.

The human fulfillment model suggests that these psychological and social benefits are more than merely subjective and personal preferences. These are not simply goods that an individual chooses to value. The character traits developed and the ends achieved through work are connected to living a fulfilled and meaningful human life. They are connected to attaining the human *telos*.

The human fulfillment model acknowledges that not every job contributes to the development of human potential. However, the proper kind of work and the right kind of workplace can contribute to this development. This model also claims that individuals and work exist in a reciprocal relationship. Individuals exercise control over their jobs, but jobs also influence and shape individuals. Thus, under this model, the challenge for business ethics is to articulate the type of work that can foster the full development of human potential.

Contrast this with the hedonistic model of work. From that perspective, work is simply a means to further human ends. Work's value is merely instrumental and a worker's guiding question is "What will this work do *for* me?" The human fulfillment model challenges us to ask further questions: "What will this work do *to* me? What kind of person will I become through this work?" Even work that does good things *for* me (by providing an income) may do bad things *to* me (e.g., by lowering my self-esteem, harming my mental and physical health, etc.).[15]

   In developing this point, economist E. F. Schumacher details how work can do bad things to workers and hints at what the corresponding good work would be. Bad work is "mechanical, artificial, divorced from nature, utilizing only the smallest part of man's potential capabilities; it sentences the great majority of workers to spending their working lives in a way which contains no worthy challenge, no stimulus to self perfection, no chance of development, no element of Beauty, Truth, or Goodness. . . ."[16]

   The idea that there exists a human potential (or *telos*, in the language of classical philosophy) that can be either drawn out or repressed by work has its roots in Karl Marx's concept of alienation. In general terms, alienation is the result of work that prevents the full development of human potential. In such situations, humans are separated, or alienated, from their true selves (their potential). Part of Marx's critique of capitalism was based on the claim that under capitalist systems of production, workers inevitably faced a life of alienation. Marx suggested that workers face several types of alienation that occur within capitalist systems: from the products of their work, from the creative process of work itself, and from their very essence as social creatures.[17]

   In his early writings especially, Marx understands humans as social beings who both create and express themselves through their labor. Through work, humans create not just products, but also the very social world in which they live. Work is essentially a social activity and, as social beings, humans have the opportunity to express this humanity through work. Because these social structures also shape and influence human attitudes, beliefs, and values (what work does *to* people), work also serves to create our own character. According to Marx, in capitalist economic systems—particularly in the division of labor, assembly line production characteristic of industrial capitalism—workers are alienated from the products of their labor, from the activity of work, and from their fellow humans. Workers (or *human resources* in the contemporary phrase) and the products of their labor are treated as mere means to the end of profit. Workers are separated from what they produce, they lack control over both the products and the productive activity itself, and they exist as mere cogs in a machine.

   A similar view of work was presented in 1981 by Pope John Paul II in his Encyclical Letter, *Laborem Exercens*.[18] Integrating some themes found in Marx with more traditional Catholic theology, the Pope claims that "work is one of the characteristics that distinguish humans from the rest of creatures. . . . Only humans are capable of work, and only humans work." Citing the *Genesis* story in which humans are created "in the image and likeness of God" and in which humans are called forth "to subdue the earth," the Pope argues that work is an essential part of human nature. These Biblical passages suggest that humans are meant to be co-creators (made in the image of God the creator) in shaping the earth and using it to maintain their life on earth.[19]

   Once again, this perspective emphasizes the fact that humans and their work exist in a reciprocal, dialectical relationship with each side influencing and shaping the other. Humans create work in order to attain their needs and wants; but work also shapes humans. In the words of commentator Gregory Baum, "It is through labor that people create their world, and it is through the same labor that

in a certain sense they also create themselves."[20] Humans "must transform a portion of nature through labor to have food and shelter. In order to improve the conditions of survival, people must invent a division of labor, a social organization,
and a system of authority. Labor creates society." But in doing so, humans are creating the social and cultural world that socializes them, creates their conscious-
ness, attitudes, beliefs, values, and interests. In this sense, through labor humans
are creating themselves by determining what kind of person they become.[21]

In summary, then, what are the human potentials that work can help fulfill?
From this brief discussion, we can mention four. Through work we exercise our
freedom and autonomy in making choices and directing our lives. Work also
provides the occasion for developing our talents and exercising our creativity.
Through work, humans create their own society and culture and thereby create their own identities. Finally, work is an expression of our nature as social
beings; it prevents us from falling into a solipsistic and egocentric life.[22]

Philosopher Al Gini offers this summary of the human fulfillment model:

> Descartes was wrong. It isn't *Cogito ergo sum*, but, rather, *Laboro ergo sum*. We
> need work, and as adults we find identity and are identified by the work we
> do. If this is true then we must be very careful about what we choose to do
> for a living, for what we do is what we'll become. To paraphrase the words of
> Winston Churchill—first we choose and shape our work, then it shapes us.[23]

5.6 THE LIBERAL MODEL OF WORK

What we will call the *liberal* model of work can be thought of as occupying a middle ground between the conventional model and the human fulfillment school.
Like the conventional model, liberals hold that individual workers should be
free to choose the ends of their work. People choose to work for many reasons
and may willingly accept undesirable jobs simply as a means to earn money.
Liberals deny that there is some single human end that all work should serve.
Nevertheless, like the human fulfillment school liberals recognize that humans
can be significantly influenced by their work and argue that we should make
ethical assessments of work on the basis of how work affects workers. Liberals
part company with the fulfillment school when they specify the grounds on
which that assessment is made. The human fulfillment school makes that judgment on the basis of some vision of what makes a good, meaningful human life.
Liberals make that judgment in terms of how work affects a worker's ability to
make free and autonomous decisions about their own life.

Philosopher Norman Bowie provides a good example of a liberal theory of
work. Bowie explains his own Kantian theory of meaningful work as a middle
ground between those who think the value of work is to be left to the whim of
workers and those who defend an "objective normative definition" of meaningful work.[24]

> I have always believed that one of the moral obligations of the firm is to pro-
> vide meaningful work for employees. However, just what constitutes meaning-
> ful work has been a contentious matter. Is "meaningful work" to be defined

as nothing more than what the employees say it is? Or would the term "mean-ingful work" be given an objective normative definition which would permit managers to provide it even if the employees do not agree? A standard problem with the [former] approach is that it is subjective and individualistic. . . . Why should management have a duty to provide each employee meaningful work as he or she defines it? On the other hand, a standard problem with the objec-tive approach is that it has been difficult to find a justification for any objective normative definition that can be given.[25]

Let us consider Bowie's arguments. If we conclude that the meaning and value of work is whatever the worker determines it to be, as at least the hedo-nistic version of the conventional model would hold, then we cannot say that workers have any right to, nor management any duty to provide, meaningful work. Such an open-ended conception of worker rights would render the con-cept meaningless by failing to distinguish rights from mere desires. It also would imply a range of management duties that would be impossible to fulfill.

Of course defenders of this hedonistic model, especially those sympathetic to the more libertarian versions of free markets, would conclude that this means only that workers have no right to meaningful work. Bowie's belief that busi-ness has a moral obligation to provide meaningful work is, from that perspec-tive, simply mistaken. The meaning and value of work, like all the conditions of work, should be left to the free choices that emerge from individual bargaining between employee and employer.

Liberal approaches to work, such as Bowie's Kantian theory, reject this view as too impoverished an understanding of human freedom. Individuals may well choose to work tedious, difficult, depressing, low paying, even dan-gerous jobs. But if there are few alternatives available, we shouldn't honor this as a "free" choice. Bowie would argue that the more people are compelled to work, the greater the responsibility to ensure that workplace conditions are as humane as possible. In such cases, the very necessity of work obligates us to investigate what work does *to* workers. What kind of people are being created in the workplace?

Unlike the human fulfillment model, however, liberals do not believe that there is some substantive, objective norm to determine the kind of person every-one should be. Even if there were, Bowie asks, would managers be permitted—or required—to "create" such people even if employee do not agree? Should we design workplaces that force people to be creative, or sociable, or that force them to fully develop their talents and abilities? Who would decide such matters?

This conclusion mirrors the reluctance that liberal political philosophy has always had about concepts such as the human *telos* or common good. Liberal theories of justice argue that individual freedom is a fundamental and neces-sary element of social justice. Liberals have always rejected classical political theories that specify some common, specific, and particular way that all people should live. Even if we could specify what that life should be, it would seem that the only way to achieve it would be by forcing individuals to live lives other than the ones they choose. On the other hand, most liberals also reject the subjective and relativistic implication of more libertarian versions. It is not

good for humans to do just anything they want. Some ways of living are morally better than others.

Liberals resolve this tension by reference to such general characteristics and
goods as autonomy, rationality, and physical and mental health. Sometimes
called *primary goods,* these are goods that are necessary in order to achieve whatever other goods an individual chooses to pursue. Consistent with the assumptions of the conventional model, work may simply be valued as a means for
attaining whatever ends an individual chooses. However, if in the process of
work these primary goods are destroyed or undermined, individuals have little
chance of attaining their other ends. Thus, the liberal model argues that individuals have certain rights in the workplace and that these rights function to
protect certain central and primary goods.

What are these goods to be protected by worker rights? Philosopher Adina
Schwartz defends a classical liberal answer when she argues that highly routinized jobs in which workers passively and blindly fill roles determined by others
fail to respect the autonomy of individuals. Failing to recognize such jobs as
unjust

> . . . is fundamentally at odds with the widely held view that a just society
> respects all its members as autonomous agents. If we care about the free devel-
> opment of all members of society . . . we must demand that no one be employed
> at the sorts of jobs that have just been described. We must also advocate a cer-
> tain alternative to the current arrangement of industrial employment and must
> ask for government measures to effect this rearrangement.[26]

5.7 BUSINESS'S RESPONSIBILITY FOR MEANINGFUL WORK

This brief overview of differing theories concerning the nature and value of
work can now provide us with a helpful way to conceptualize the ethical
responsibilities that business has to make work meaningful. The classical model
would argue that, to the degree that work is necessary and physical, work cannot be made meaningful and therefore employers have little responsibility to
make it so. To the degree that work can be intellectual, leisurely, and free, work
can be meaningful; but it would be unlikely that employment and wage labor
can ever attain these conditions.

The hedonistic approach argues that work is meaningful when it is used to
attain the goals of the worker. Following Bowie's critique, however, it would
be difficult to hold a business responsible for such an open-ended goal. Surely
workers might desire many things that a business cannot—perhaps should
not—provide. At best, the hedonistic theory would encourage employees and
employers to bargain over workplace conditions, wages, and benefits. This
contract model might provide workers with the best chance for attaining workplace happiness but, presumably, business's only responsibilities would be
those freely accepted within the contract.

The boundary between the human fulfillment school and the liberal model
offers more fruitful directions for thinking about the responsibility to provide

meaningful work. In effect, liberals argue that business has a range of responsibilities derived from such primary goods as autonomy, rationality, and physical and mental health. The range of employee rights and responsibilities that we will survey in chapters 6 and 7 is an admittedly liberal conception of employee rights and employer responsibilities. This list might include such rights as participation (voting), due process, healthy and safe working conditions, fair wages and benefits, training and education, and privacy. Such goods might be said to be primary in the sense that they are necessary for any realistic opportunity to exercise autonomous, rational, and free choice.

Remember that Bowie argues that anything more substantive than this minimal list might involve employers forcing employees to accept conditions that they choose not to. Bowie argues that employers cannot have the responsibility to make employees better people, particularly against the wishes of the employees themselves.

But now consider the example offered by Adina Schwartz. Imagine that workers preferred to work highly routinized, unchallenging, and boring jobs. Do employers have a responsibility to eliminate such jobs, even if there are some employees who would be willing to fill them? Two options are open for liberals at this point. They could argue that as long as no one is forcing employees to work such jobs, as long as they are free from external constraint, employers have no responsibility to eliminate such jobs. This answer would reduce the liberal position to a narrower libertarian understanding of freedom in the workplace. But it also would accept the ethical legitimacy of employment conditions that tend to frustrate the very fundamental values—autonomous and free choice—that liberals hold dear. Social conditions of routinized, unchallenging, boring jobs tend to suppress the human faculties of rational and autonomous choice. On the other hand, if liberals argue that employers do have a responsibility to eliminate such jobs, then they acknowledge that employee choice alone is not the final factor for determining what constitutes an ethical workplace. This is to acknowledge that the conditions that create an ethical workplace are those that tend to encourage and advance the human good, at least as understood in minimal terms of the ability to make reasoned and autonomous choices. This conclusion opens the door to a wider discussion of those conditions necessary or conducive to the good of employees. Such conditions can be identified as a liberal theory of employee rights and employer responsibilities. Chapter 6 considers several of these potential rights.

This chapter has examined various models for understanding the nature and value of work. These models provide a framework for evaluating business's responsibilities to employees, as well as the rights and responsibilities that employees owe to the businesses that provide jobs. The nature and value of work also has implications for what we, as citizens in a democratic society, can expect of both private business and government regulation of the workplace. Work provides individuals with the means for satisfying their basic needs and desires. Work can provide good things, or bad things, *for* us. But work can also do good things, or bad things, *to* us. How the workplace gets structured, how we understand the rights and responsibilities of both employers and employees, will determine the ethical status of what work does both for, and to, us. In chapters 6 and 7 we will look in more detail at the ethical rights and responsibilities that exist in the workplace.

REFLECTIONS ON THE CHAPTER DISCUSSION CASE

It might seem unreasonable to draw any conclusions from the example of Pat Tillman. This is a very unusual case. After all, very few people ever become professional football players, and of those few only one quit to join the army. Nevertheless, this case does remind us that there can be more to one's career than money and fame. The case is also interesting for a little noticed aspect. Tillman turned down a higher-paying job with another business out of a felt loyalty to his present employer. While the decisions to join the army and accept a lower-paying job are understandable, it would be worth asking if they were reasonable. Why would a rational person do such things?

More generally, this case raises questions about great jobs and meaningful jobs. From all appearances, Tillman had a great job that he left for one he found more meaningful. These concepts are worth pursuing. What are some "great" jobs? Would being a star in the NFL be a great job? Can you list some other jobs you would consider great? Are there any similarities? What makes a job "great"? What are some jobs that you would describe as "meaningful"? Why might serving in the military be meaningful? What makes a job "meaningful"?

This is also a good opportunity to reflect on your own career choices. What job do you see yourself working in five years? In ten years? In forty years? Were there any overlaps between your list of great jobs, meaningful jobs, and jobs that you are likely to hold? If not, why not?[27]

REVIEW QUESTIONS

1. Explain at least three different meanings of the word *work*. Do any of these meanings include some value component?
2. How would you distinguish a *job* from a *career* from a *calling*?
3. What are the two different trends within the conventional view of work?
4. How does the Greek philosophical notion of a *telos* relate to the human fulfillment theory of work?
5. How can work become meaningful under the liberal model of work?
6. How might a defender of the liberal model criticize the human fulfillment model of work?

ENDNOTES

[1]This case was based on several sources. See Juliet Schor, *The Overworked American* (New York: Basic Books, 1991); Benjamin Hunnicutt, *Work Without End: Abandoning Shorter Hours for the Right to Work* (Philadelphia: Temple University Press, 1988);

Stanley Lebergott, *Pursuing Happiness: American Consumers in the Twentieth Century* (Princeton: Princeton University Press, 1993); and the classic David Riesman, *The Lonely Crowd* (New Haven, CT: Yale University Press, 1969).

[2]Mike Royko, "Silver Spoon Fits, Why Not Wear It?" *Chicago Tribune* (November 11, 1985), sec. 1, p. 3. Quoted in *It Comes with the Territory*, A.R. Gini and T. J. Sullivan, eds. (New York: Random House, 1989).

[3]*Genesis*, 1, 28; 2, 15; 3, 17–19.

[4]Aristotle, *Politics* 1256 a 30, 1253 b 25.

[5]An interesting and helpful overview essay on work is "Work: The Process and the Person" by Gini and Sullivan, chapter 1 of *It Comes with the Territory*, op. cit., pp. 1–36. For a more in-depth treatment of the ethical and philosophical issues concerning the nature and value of work, see Al Gini, *My Job, My Self: Work and the Creation of the Modern Individual* (New York: Routledge, 2000) and Joanne Ciulla, *The Working Life: The Promise and Betrayal of Modern Work* (New York: Times Books, 2000). These insightful books provide excellent resources for further thinking about work.

[6]For Rousseau, see especially *Emile*. For Marx, compare "Estranged Labor" in *The Economic and Philosophic Manuscripts of 1844*, translated by Martin Milligan (New York: International Publishers, 1964), and "The German Ideology," edited and translated by Loyd Easten and Kurt Guddat, in *Writing of the Young Marx on Philosophy and Society* (New York: Doubleday, 1967).

[7]*Habits of the Heart: Individualism and Commitment in American Life*, by Robert Bellah, Richard Madsen, William Sullivan, Ann Swidler, Steven Tipton (New York: Harper & Row, 1985), pp. 65–66.

[8]Douglas McGregor, "The Human Side of Enterprise," originally published in *The Management Review* 46, 11, 1957, reprinted in *Leadership and Motivation: Essays of Douglas McGregor* (Cambridge, MA: MIT Press, 1966).

[9]Studs Terkel, *Working* (New York: Pantheon Book, 1974), p. xi.

[10]Plutarch, *Lives* (New York: Modern Library, 1932), p. 132.

[11]Yves Simon, *Work Society, Culture*, edited by Vukan Kuic (New York: Fordham University Press, 1971), p. 78.

[12]Hannah Arendt, *The Human Condition* (Chicago: University of Chicago Press, 1958), p. 5.

[13]George E. Valliant and Caroline O. Valliant, "Natural History of Male Psychological Health: Work as a Predictor of Positive Mental Health," *American Journal of Psychiatry* 138, 1981, 433–440, as quoted in Robert Lane, *The Market Experience* (Cambridge: Cambridge University Press, 1992), p. 247.

[14]The downward spiral of unemployment, poverty, and crime characteristic of many cities is forcefully portrayed in William Julius Wilson, *When Work Disappears* (New York: Alfred Knopf, 1997).

[15]For two insightful discussions that rely on the distinction between what work does *for* and *to* individuals, see E. F. Schumacher, *Good Work* (New York: Harper Colophon Books, 1980), and the American Catholic Bishops' pastoral letter, *Economic Justice for All* (Washington: National Conference of Catholic Bishops, 1986).

[16]Schumacher, *Good Work*, p. 27.

[17]Karl Marx, *The Economic and Philosophical Manuscripts of 1844*, edited with an introduction by Dirk J. Struik. Translated by Martin Milligan (New York: International Publishers, 1964).

[18]*Laborem exercens*, reprinted in Gregory Baum, *The Priority of Labor* (Ramsey, NJ: Paulist Press, 1982). I rely on Baum's excellent and extensive interpretive commentary for much of this section.

[19]*Laborem exercens*, in Baum, pp. 95–102.

[20]Baum, p. 65.

[21]Baum, pp. 68–72.

[22]See Schumacher, *Good Work,* pp. 3–4 and Al Gini, "Work, Identity and Self: How We Are Formed by the Work We Do," *Journal of Business Ethics* 17, 1998, pp. 707–714.

[23]Gini, p. 714.

[24]Norman Bowie "A Kantian Theory of Meaningful Work," *Journal of Business Ethics* 17, 1998, 1083–1092. As will become clear, I take Bowie's "Kantian" theory, based on an overriding commitment to individual autonomy, as a clear example of a "liberal" approach.

[25]Bowie, p. 1083. Bowie's characterization of the first alternative as subjective and individualistic reasonably captures the more libertarian versions of the conventional model of work. His reference to an "objective normative definition" captures the essence of the human fulfillment model's understanding of a single human good, or *telos.*

[26]Adina Schwartz "Meaningful Work," *Ethics* 92, July 1982, pp. 634–646.

[27]I wish to thank Christopher Pynes from the University of Tennessee for these questions. His advice on using these questions in the classroom has benefited my own students on many occasions.

6 CHAPTER

Moral Rights in the Workplace

After reading this chapter, you will be able to:

- Distinguish moral rights from legal and contractual rights;
- Explain and examine various meanings of a right to work;
- Analyze arguments supporting an employee right to due process, participation, health and safety, and privacy;
- Distinguish due process from the legal doctrine of employment at will;
- Analyze arguments supporting an employee right to participation.

DISCUSSION CASES: Employee Rights and Wrongs

How much latitude ought employers have in determining the conditions and nature of the workplace? Consider the following examples, all taken from actual legal cases that courts have been asked to decide in recent years.[1]

A salesman is fired from his job soon before payment of a sale's commission is due to him. As a result, the commission is paid to his supervisor, the very person who fired him.

An employee is fired when a mandatory urinalysis test detected nicotine in her urine. Her company prohibits smoking by all employees. The company argues that increasing health care costs brought about by smoking justifies the action.

An employee is fired when her employer learns that she is pregnant and contemplating an abortion. Many of her co-workers who oppose abortion argue with her at work and create an uproar when they learn of her thinking. The employer fires her to prevent further workplace conflicts.

An employee is denied health care coverage offered to all other employees when his employer switches to health care providers who require medical examination before offering coverage. The employee is diagnosed as HIV positive during the examination. Rising health care costs from the previous provider, attributed to a large extent to costs associated with this employee, was the reason for the switch in providers.

An employee is fired when his employer reads his e-mail and discovers that e-mails highly critical of management have been sent to other employees.

As part of a pre-employment psychological test administered to applicants for security guard positions, a major department store asked potential employees to respond to the following statements: "I feel very strongly attracted to members of my own sex. . . . I have never indulged in any unusual sex practices. . . . I feel sure that there is only one true religion. . . . I go to church almost every week. . . . I wish that I was not bothered by thoughts about sex. . . . I have had no difficulty starting or holding my urine. . . . I believe that my sins are unpardonable."

Female employees were excluded from jobs they had previously held when it becomes clear that they were being exposed to chemicals that could be hazardous to the health of fetuses. Female employees who agreed to be sterilized were allowed to continue working in these jobs, others were transferred to other available jobs, and those for whom other jobs could not be found were fired.

DISCUSSION QUESTIONS

1. Do you think of a job as the private property of employers who are free to do with it as they choose? Why or why not?
2. If you were a judge and these cases were brought to your court, how would you decide each of the above cases? Explain and defend your decisions.

3. Put yourself in the position of the employer in each case and defend your actions.
4. If you were a member of a state legislature, would you consider drafting a law to prevent any of the above actions?

6.1 INTRODUCTION: EMPLOYEE RIGHTS

Chapter 5 reviewed some of the many meanings and values that work holds for people. Even for those who disparage it, work is valued as a necessary means to other crucial goals. Simply put, work is one of the most important and highly valued human activities in large part because it is necessary for so many other central human goods.

But just as work is inescapable for most people, it is just as likely to be something controlled by others. Few of us control our own working lives. This fact highlights a real vulnerability: While the overwhelming majority of people need to work, other people typically determine most aspects of our work, including whether we work at all. As we saw in chapter 2, the idea of moral *rights* is relevant in just those circumstances when central human interests are jeopardized by the actions of others. The more important these interests are to human well-being, the more likely we are to recognize that they should be protected by rights that impose duties on others to respect these interests. This present chapter will examine a range of potential moral rights in the workplace.

As an initial step, let us clarify the meaning of moral rights in the workplace, or employee rights, that we will be using in this chapter. Three senses of employee rights are common in business. First, there are those *legal* rights granted to employees on the basis of legislation or judicial rulings. Thus, employees have a right to a minimum wage, equal opportunity, to bargain collectively as part of a union, and so forth. Second, employee rights might refer to those goods that employees are entitled to on the basis of contractual agreements with employers. In this sense, a particular employee might have a right to a specific health care package, paid holidays, pension funds, and the like. Finally, employee rights might refer to those entitlements to which employees have a claim independent of any particular legal or contractual factors. Such rights would originate with the respect owed to them as human beings. While both legal and contractual rights will be relevant for our discussions in this chapter, our primary focus will be on the understanding of employee rights as moral entitlements that are independent of both legal and contractual acknowledgment.

To expand on this understanding, consider how legal and contractual rights interact. In general, both parties to an employment agreement bargain over the terms and conditions of work. Employers offer certain wages, benefits, and working conditions and in return seek worker productivity. Employees offer skills and abilities and seek wages and benefits in return. However, certain goods are legally exempt from such negotiation. An employer cannot make a willingness to submit to sexual harassment or acceptance of a wage below the minimum established by law a part of the employment agreement. In effect, legal rights remove certain goods from the employment contract. Such legal rights set the basic legal framework in which business operates. They are, in this sense, part of the price of doing business.

Employee rights as understood in this chapter, like minimum wage and protection against sexual harassment, lie outside of the bargaining that occurs between employers and employees. Unlike minimum wage, moral rights are justified by moral, rather than legal, considerations. We will understand employee rights as those general moral entitlements that employees have to certain goods (or to protection from certain harms) within the workplace. They establish the basic moral framework for employer–employee relations. To the degree that there are such rights, employees cannot be asked to forgo these goods to get a job or to gain an increase in employment benefits. Employee rights function to prevent employees from being placed in what would be a fundamentally coercive position of having to choose between these basic moral goods and their job.[2]

Thus the moral rights examined in this chapter fit within the liberal model of work introduced in chapter 5. While many conditions of work are open to negotiation between employers and employees (thus respecting the liberty of each), some fundamental constraints on that negotiation are necessary to ensure that the bargaining is fully free and equal. The goods protected by such constraints fall within a traditional liberal understanding of freedom, equality, and autonomy.

6.2 THE RIGHT TO WORK

If work is necessary to secure such central primary goods as food, clothing, and shelter, a right to work might seem an obvious candidate for being a moral right. There are indeed many who do argue that all people should have a right to work, including most of the human fulfillment school who see work as an essential part of human well-being. As a first step in evaluating this potential right, let us consider various understandings of the *right to work.*

In many contemporary legal contexts, the right to work refers to a right to work without being required to join a local union. As part of many collective bargaining agreements, unions will stipulate that all employees must join the union upon being hired. This requirement is seen as an essential means to protect the viability of the union by prohibiting "free riders," who reap the benefits of union membership without sharing the burdens. This also protects the entire collective bargaining system by preventing employers from hiring only those workers who promise not to join the union. Several states have passed legislation that prohibits such a requirement. This legislation is often referred to as a *right-to-work law.*

While this sense of a right to work is not our primary focus here (it is more a legal question than a philosophical one), we can consider the soundness of this reasoning. Should new employees be required to join a union when they enter a unionized workplace? The "free rider" argument is to be based on a reasonable understanding of fairness. If one receives benefits from a process that entails costs, it seems only fair that you share the costs. Especially if there is evidence that workers would receive lower wages and benefits without the union, mandatory union membership allocates the benefits and burdens of union membership in a fair and equal manner.

The second argument cites the traditional rationale for collective bargaining. Defenders of right-to-work laws argue that wages and benefits are more appropriately determined through a process of individual bargaining between employee and employer. In response, the traditional rationale for collective bargaining argues that bargaining is fair only when the parties are equal. Fair bargaining requires an equal incentive to compromise in the give and take of negotiation. In this context, *equality* means equally free to accept or reject the employment conditions. Only in this case is an agreement guaranteed to be mutually beneficial and optimally satisfactory. However, the two sides of this bargaining are a single employer and a collection of employees, and the bargaining will only be equal if all of the employees bargain collectively. Without collective bargaining, employers have little or no incentive to compromise with any single employee when they can continue to negotiate with all other employees individually. This suggests that there are good reasons for denying that in industries in which collective bargaining exists, individual employees do not have a "right to work" in this sense.

A more interesting meaning of right to work implies that employees have a right to a job. This position has had many defenders, ranging from the tradition of Catholic social philosophy to the U.N. Declaration on Human Rights.[3] There are two primary rationales for this claim, corresponding to two primary accounts of the significant value of work. Given the important instrumental value of work—that work is a primary means to such ends as food, shelter, clothing, and health care—some argue that we should recognize a human right to a job. Others, reflecting the human fulfillment school, argue that because work is part of the expression of a meaningful human life, each individual has a right to work. The type of work implied by these approaches might be different. In the first case, one would have a right to any work that supplies a living wage no matter how tedious or unchallenging. The latter would require the type of work that is capable of elevating and humanizing workers.

In response, critics cite the distinction between rights and merely desirable states of affairs. Not everything that is valuable and highly desired can be claimed as a right. The key point here seems to be that rights imply some responsibility on the part of others to provide what is claimed by the right. If every human has a right to a job, someone or some institution must have the responsibility to supply that job. By the same token, whoever is said to have the responsibility to provide a job must be in the position to be able to do so. A reasonable and standard philosophical observation is that "ought implies can." We can reasonably be said to have a responsibility only for those things that we can accomplish. But who should and who could supply jobs to every person?

Placing this responsibility on the shoulders of private employers surely is too burdensome in both an economic and ethical sense. Without significant limitations, such a right claimed against private employers would result in economic chaos. Would private employers be obligated to hire just anyone who applied for work? Would qualifications be relevant? Would this right depend on an employer's profit status? Providing any and all people with jobs is simply not something that a private employer can do and remain economically viable. An unprofitable business cannot continue to provide jobs to any employees. Further, the rights of employers also provide counterarguments to this view. Such considerations as employers' property rights (which, admittedly, are not absolute), freedom, and their own right to work would clearly limit significantly any responsibilities that an employer could be said to have for providing jobs to others.

Defenders of a right to a job might respond by placing the responsibility in the hands of government rather than private employers. Government could provide jobs either through incentives and subsidies to private employers (as many governments already do in the case of former welfare recipients) or by providing direct employment. This, for example, was the part of the proposed Federal right- to-work legislation offered by Senator Hubert Humphrey during the 1970s.

No doubt government is better situated to fulfill this responsibility than is private business. This proposal would not, after all, threaten the rights of "owners" as it would in the case of private employers. Governments have direct responsibilities to their citizens in ways that private employers do not. However, this approach can face many of the same challenges faced by the private employment option. Directly providing jobs to any citizen who desired one could lead to inefficiencies in government as easily as it could in private business. Although economic efficiency is clearly not the primary criteria by which we judge governments, too much inefficiency can create both economic and political turmoil. Simply put, government could not provide every citizen with a job. Since rights claimed against the government should (at least within a democracy) be held equally by all citizens, and since not every citizen could be employed by government, citizens cannot claim a right to a job from the government.

Of course, no defender of a right to a job is likely to claim that governments should supply every citizen with a job. A modified version would claim that government has the responsibility to provide jobs compatible with qualifications to those who are able to work but unable to find jobs in the private sector. Government would be the employer of last resort. Something like this seems to have been operating at least implicitly in many industrialized democracies through the latter half of the twentieth century. Something similar to this was also used by the U.S. federal government as a response to the Great Depression of the 1930s.

This modified version is on better ethical and economic grounds. It is difficult to imagine goods more worthy of government protection than those associated with work. The economic challenges to this version are more a matter of degree than principle. At one extreme, government would supply jobs to so many people that government spending drains money out of private markets, which leads to an economic downturn, which leads to more unemployment, which leads to more government employment, which continues to down-ward cycle further. At the other extreme, government provides no economic help for the unemployed. Even among those who would argue on economic grounds against government directly supplying jobs to the unemployed, there is a strong consensus that government has a responsibility to provide a social "safety net" of economic support. The remaining question seems to be, is this support better provided in the form of jobs, incentives to the private sector to hire the unemployed, or in the form of such payments as unemployment insur-ance, food stamps, and health insurance?

Something of a consensus, in theory if not always in practice, seems to be emerging within Western democracies (at least) in this regard. Governments have a responsibility to encourage, through such things as fiscal and monetary policy and tax incentives, private sector employment for all its citizens. As a last resort, and especially for hard-core unemployed, government has a respon-sibility to provide jobs for its citizens. In this restricted sense, then, it can be reasonable to claim that people have a right to a job.

Unfortunately, while this approach may address the instrumental value of work by providing opportunities to obtain wages with which to purchase food, clothing, shelter, and health care, it does little to address the intrinsic value of work associated with the human fulfillment school. To consider this issue we need to focus more directly on the types of work and working conditions available to workers. This, in turn, is to consider a third meaning of a "right to work."

Perhaps the most significant ethical objection to claiming a right to a pri-vate sector job is the burden that this would place upon private employers. We could not require private employers to employ just any and all people without imposing grave and serious restriction on that employer's freedom and prop-erty rights. We certainly can and should require that private sector employers provide an equal opportunity to work for all, but it is unreasonable to expect them to provide jobs for all. This, essentially, would be the position defended by the liberal theory of work.

But there is another sense to a *right to work* that can be claimed against private employers. This interpretation holds the right to work is not a right to a job, but the right, once hired, to hold that job with some degree of security. Once one has a job, this would be the right to keep that job or, in other terms, the right not to be fired without just and sufficient cause. On a parallel with legal restrictions on the authority of government, we will identify this as a *right to due process*. Before considering this right in more detail, let us think about this in the context of meaningful work.

As we saw in the previous chapter, liberals disagree with the human fulfill-ment school by denying that there is one human goal towards which all work should aim. They argue that there is no objective standard valid for every indi-vidual by which we could distinguish fulfilling from unfulfilling work. If one understands *meaningful work* to mean only work that fulfills the human *telos,* then liberals deny that work can be meaningful in that sense. Nevertheless, certain types of work and working conditions can harm individuals in ethically significant ways. Individuals may not have a right to a job, but they do possess ethical rights that protect them from being mistreated once they do have a job. In this sense, meaningful work would be work that is structured in ways that respect the rights of workers.

For example, Norman Bowie claims that he has "always believed that one of the moral obligations of the firm is to provide meaningful work for employees."[4] Note that this does not claim that a firm has an obligation to provide work, only that it has an obligation to its employees—that is, those already working—to structure the workplace in ways that protect their rights. Thus, while Bowie might claim that employees have a right to meaningful work, the emphasis is on the word *meaningful,* not *work.* Individuals have no prior existing right to work but, once employed, they have a right to a certain type of work. Further, an ethically structured workplace provides "meaningful" work not in the sense that the work is fulfilling or elevating of human potential, but in the sense that it is work that "allows the worker to exercise her autonomy and independence."[5]

The remainder of this chapter examines what a workplace might look like if it respected the ethical rights of employees. To provide a context for this examination, we will begin by reviewing an important legal doctrine that effectively denies the validity of employee rights. That doctrine is known as employment at will.

6.3 EMPLOYMENT AT WILL

Much employment law within the United States has developed against a background of nineteenth century, laissez-faire legal perspective on economic transactions. In general, courts were reluctant to recognize any obligations other than those explicitly agreed to by the parties concerned. Thus, unless there was an explicit employment contract that specified the length and conditions of employment (a very unusual event even today), all employees were employed "at will." An "at will" contract is one that exists only so long as both parties consent or, conversely, can be broken at the discretion of either party. Employment at will means that employees are free to quit their job at any time for any reason and employers are free to terminate an employee at any time and for any reason. In the words of an early court decision establishing this precedent, "all may dismiss their employee(s) at will, be they many or few, for good cause, for no cause, or even for cause morally wrong."[6]

If employment at will governs the workplace, if employees can be dismissed for morally wrong reasons without violating the law, then the concept of employee rights is, at least in the legal sense, meaningless. An employee right would be a legitimate claim to certain goods (or to protection against certain harms) in the workplace. To say that employees have a legitimate claim implies that they ethically cannot be placed in the position of having to choose between these goods and their job. If, for example, an employee has the right to be protected against sexual harassment in the workplace, then an employer cannot force an employee to choose between her job and accepting harassment. The interests that are protected by rights are, in effect, exempted from the bargaining between employers and employees that establishes the conditions of work. Yet, if employment at will holds sway, then no interests are protected in this way.

But even within the United States the legal doctrine of employment at will was limited from the very beginning. Over the last century, a growing consensus in both law and business practice has recognized the ethical deficiency of this doctrine. A brief review of the erosion of employment at will as a legal doctrine will set the stage for our examination of the ethical rights of employees.

From the very start, employment at will only applied to private sector, noncontractual employees. Federal and state constitutions grant government employees numerous rights against the government, which in this case is the employer. Union employees, protected as they are by union contract and federal and state legislation, are also exempt from the at-will rule.

Over the past century, a number of federal and state laws restrict the ability of employers to dismiss their employees. Civil rights laws protect employees from being fired on the basis of race and sex, for example. Employers are also prevented from firing employees because of union support, health or safety complaints, or disability by the Wagner Act, the Occupational Safety and Health Act, and the Americans with Disabilities Act. Federal and state laws also protect employees who blow the whistle on certain illegal or unethical acts committed by their employer.

Besides these legislative restrictions state and federal courts have created a wide range of judicial exemptions to employment at will. Many courts have recognized a "public policy" exemption that protects an employee's job when the dismissal would violate an important public policy. For example, some jurisdictions protect employees from being fired for serving on a jury, for reporting a crime, or for refusing to participate in a fraudulent business practice. Some courts have also recognized an "implied contract exemption" and provide employees with protections that are implied in such employer documents as employee handbooks, job descriptions, and job advertisements. Finally, some courts have created a more general "implied covenant of good faith" exemption which is a more open-ended protection against employment practices that violate a "good faith" condition. Thus, for example, firing an employee as a means for avoiding payment of an earned annual bonus was judged an illegal violation of an implied covenant of good faith.

Despite this legislative and judicial erosion, the employment-at-will rule remains as the background legal doctrine. The legal burden of proof rests with employees who believe that they have been unjustly fired. The employees must prove that they have been fired for an illegal reason and absent such proof, employers are free to dismiss employees at will. The ethical concept of due process, to which we now turn, seeks to reverse this burden of proof. Due process would require that employees can be dismissed only for just cause and the burden for establishing this cause rests with the employer. This, then, returns us to the third meaning of a right to work described in the previous section. Once hired, employees have a right to keep their job and can be fired only for good reasons.

6.4 DUE PROCESS IN THE WORKPLACE

The legal principle of due process can be traced to the Magna Carta's doctrine of *per legem terrae* ("by the law of the land"), which established limitations of the authority of the king. The essential idea was that while the barons recognized the legitimate authority of the king, they demanded that his authority be limited. Due process can be defined as limitations that offer protection against arbitrary uses of authority. This concept is seen in such modern legal guarantees as the right to a trial by jury, legal representation, the Miranda rights to remain silent, and so forth. The philosophical idea that underlies this legal concept is that even legitimate authority cannot be used in just any manner. While courts, legislatures, and police have legitimate authority over citizens, that authority can only be exercised in certain sorts of ways. Courts cannot decide guilt by flipping a coin, a legislature cannot pass legislation without voting, and the police cannot obtain confessions by torture or coercion.

Due process in the workplace would mean that employees have a right to be protected from the arbitrary use of managerial authority. Due process would mean that while employees can be dismissed for "good cause," they cannot be dismissed "for no cause, or even for cause morally wrong." Due process right would establish the procedures (the "process") that an employer must go through to ensure that the dismissal is not arbitrary.

What might such procedures involve? One approach would be to specify the acceptable reasons for dismissal. Such factors as incompetent job performance, intoxication, inordinate absenteeism, theft, fraud, and economic necessity would be obvious candidates. This approach seeks to establish *just cause* conditions for dismissal. However, specifying every possible acceptable reason and distinguishing them from unacceptable reasons beforehand might well be impossible. As a result typical due process policies outline a procedure through which employers must go before they can dismiss an employee. (The Miranda rights in law developed in just such circumstances. The Supreme Court concluded that it could not and would not attempt to specify every type of illegitimate police tactic. Instead, it required police to follow a particular process—reading the Miranda rights—and concluded that this process was sufficient to protect citizens against unjust police authority.)

This more procedural account of due process might include such things as prior warning, documentation, written performance standards, probationary periods, a process by which decisions can be appealed, an opportunity to respond to allegations, and prior determination of punishment that is proportionate to the infraction. Thus, an employee should know what is expected of her, know the consequences of failing to meet those expectations, be given a warning when any problem is first recognized, have an opportunity to change and respond to the warning, and have a right to appeal any decision to an impartial judge.

The strongest defense of an employee's right to due process appeals to the fundamental ethical concepts of respect and fairness. To understand this defense, consider a distinction, essential to political theory, between authority and power. Power might be defined simply as the ability to impose one's will on another. Authority exists when that power is justified or legitimate. A gunman has the power to take your money; the Internal Revenue Service has the authority to do so. Imposing one's will on another without justification is ethically wrong since it is to treat that other as a mere means to one's own ends. It violates the autonomy of that individual, and it denies him or her the respect that each is due as an autonomous person. Institutions, such as the criminal justice system or the workplace, that allow people to impose their will upon others without justification are fundamentally unfair and unjust. Due process demands nothing more than that the exercise of power be justified. A business manager has the ability to impose her will on employees. That is, she has power. Society should sanction that ability, should allow this authority, only to the extent that the manager can provide a justification. Due process rights in the workplace establish the criteria for that justification either by outlining just cause conditions ("an employee can be fired for reasons *a, b,* or *c*") or by creating procedural safeguards ("before terminating an employee, employers must *do a, b, and c*"). Without due process in the workplace, society is sanctioning an institution that allows individuals to exercise the power they have over others without restraint.

There are four major counterarguments to the right of due process: freedom, fairness, property rights, and efficiency. The first claims that due process involves an illegitimate restriction on the freedom of individuals to establish the conditions of their own work. The second argues that if employees are free to quit their job for any reason, it is only fair that employers be free to fire employees for any reason. The third claims that due process is an illegitimate restriction on the property rights of business owners. The fourth argues that without the fear of dismissal as motivation, the workers will likely become inefficient and unproductive. Against due process, these counterarguments would defend the employment-at-will rule. These arguments would most likely be proposed by free market defenders.

The first argument is familiar from our previous examination of the free market approach. It claims that employers and employees should be left alone to bargain individually over the conditions of work. Employees who desire due process protection should be free to bargain for it and should be willing to give up something, presumably wages, in return. Employees who prefer higher wages should be free to forgo the job security that due process provides. A competitive labor market will eventually find an equilibrium point where each employee gets as much job security and wages as he or she decides.

The second argument also begins with an appeal to freedom. It claims that restricting the freedom of an employee to quit at any time for any reason would border on slavery. Since employees are given the freedom to quit without just cause, fairness demands that employers have the equal freedom to fire without just cause.

Philosopher Patricia Werhane responds to these two arguments by pointing out a significant inequality between employees and employers.[7] Except in very unusual circumstances, employees are harmed more by the loss of their job than employers are harmed when they lose an employee. (In those unusual circumstances when this is not the case, employers typically have such key employees under contract.) A fired employee is further harmed by having future employment jeopardized by having been previously fired. An employer's ability to hire new employees is seldom harmed by the fact that former employees have quit. This inequality between employees and employers puts employees at a disadvantage in their bargaining with employers since the threat of being fired is more coercive than is the threat to quit. This inequality also means that it is not unfair to limit an employer's freedom more than an employee's.

Werhane also responds to the third counterargument to due process. She points out that property rights in the workplace do not include ownership of employees. While employers may have rights over material possessions, they do not have similar rights over employees. Humans are not resources that one can dispose of at will. Further, property rights are not absolute and can be legitimately restricted by other ethical considerations. Due process is the simple requirement that due consideration be given to such factors by articulating the ethical restrictions on the use of one's property.

The final counterargument to due process claims that employment at will would be a more efficient arrangement of the workplace. Due process requirements will interfere with the efficient functioning of business, will prevent both employers and employees from getting what they most prefer, and will only function to protect unqualified and unproductive workers.

Three responses to this are worth making. First, we should recognize that this is a utilitarian argument which, even if valid, would not justify the violation of employee rights. For example, it might turn out that a system of slavery or child labor is more efficient economically than the alternatives. But it would be unethical to adopt such a system nonetheless. So, too, with rights to due process. If the cost of economic efficiency would be the violation of employee rights to respect, autonomy, and fairness, then we must conclude that efficiency be sacrificed.

Second, lack of productivity and qualifications are exactly the types of reasons that would provide a just cause for dismissing an employee. Due process does not grant any and all workers an unqualified right to a job. It requires only that good reasons be given before an employee loses a job. In fact, due process might contribute to efficiency by preventing managers from terminating qualified and competent employees.

Finally, efficiency is an empirical claim that needs to be verified by the facts of worker productivity. This debate calls to mind the debate within management theory between the hierarchical scientific management theory of Frederick Taylor and the Theory Y view of management associated with Douglas McGregor. For present purposes, we need only recognize that there is significant evidence that workers who are provided with job security and due process can be more productive than those without. Decent and ethical treatment can be a more effective management tool than threats and control.

In summary, a strong ethical case can be made for recognizing due process rights in the workplace. Without such protections there is no guarantee that employees will not suffer unfair harms by the exercise of managerial power.

6.5 PARTICIPATION RIGHTS

If, like political authority, managerial authority ought to be constrained by due process rights, we should ask if it makes sense to extend the analogy further. Let us return to the distinction between power and authority to consider the question of managerial authority. Our discussion of due process assumed the legitimacy of managerial authority and focused on the limitations of that authority. In this section we ask perhaps a more fundamental question: What gives business owners and managers authority, rather than mere power, over employees?

Within democratic societies, the criterion for justifying political power is consent of the governed. Just political institutions are committed to equal respect for each individual as an autonomous agent. If the analogy is valid, we should conclude that managerial authority also ultimately rests upon the consent of employees. But is the analogy between politics and business valid? Is workplace democracy justifiable?

Both business and government are major social institutions in which select people have the power to coerce others to do as they say. This coercive power derives from the ability of the institution to grant or deny very important goods. Institutional roles decide who has and who lacks power. In either case, social justice demands that this coercive power be justified. In societies in which individuals are respected as autonomous and free decision makers, justification of authority is derived from the consent of the governed.

John McCall has argued that managerial authority must also be derived from the consent of the governed, in this case the employees. McCall offers five arguments to defend his claim that employees should have a right to participate in managerial decision making. Two arguments, based on respect and fairness, imply a strong managerial duty to allow employee participation. Three arguments anticipate beneficial consequences that would follow from participatory management.[8]

McCall argues that the fundamental right to be treated with respect implies that individuals be treated as autonomous decision makers, free from coercive interference by others. Human dignity is tied to the ability of humans to guide their own life and control their own activities. Any other option risks treating individuals as mere objects and means, rather than subjects and ends in themselves. Within the workplace, respect for this dignity prohibits workers from being treated merely as replaceable resources in the production process. Instead, employees should have rights to co-determine any policy that has a significant impact on their work lives.

The second argument cites "the fundamental objective of any morality— the impartial promotion of human welfare."[9] Every individual has a fundamental right to impartial and fair treatment. When decisions are made, the interests of every party affected by that decision must be given due consideration. The most effective means to guarantee that each affected party is represented is to allow each party to represent their own interests by participating in the decision.

McCall also argues that employee participation is likely to have several beneficial consequences. First, participatory management will create conditions of self-respect for employees. Institutions that encourage and honor employee participation will foster the important psychological goods of self-worth and self-respect among employees. Second, McCall believes that employees who participate in and contribute to decision making are less likely to suffer the mental and physical harms of alienation and burnout. Employee participation can be an effective means for bringing meaning and value into one's work life and this can counter both physical and psychological harms. Finally, McCall cites the political danger of voter apathy and indifference. In the United States, for example, fewer than 50 percent of the eligible voters turn out for most elections. This means that 25 percent of eligible voters can determine elections and 30 percent can constitute a landslide victory. McCall believes that one effective means to counter this political apathy is to create social institutions that encourage rather than discourage individual participation. Since the workplace occupies half of our waking lives, democratic workplaces will likely foster an environment in which political participation becomes the norm rather than the exception.

We can consider three major objections to proposals for employee rights to participate in business decision making. Employer property rights, managerial expertise, and considerations of efficiency are values that can all be raised against workplace democracy.

To respond to the challenge based on property rights it is helpful to distinguish those businesses that are privately owned from publicly traded incorporated businesses. A private business owner does have property rights that include rights to manage and direct the business. However, as we have seen several times previously, property rights are not absolute and can be legitimately restricted by the rights of others. I surely cannot manage my property in ways that cause significant harm to others. For example, while I own my own home, zoning laws prohibit me from using it as a business location or as a boarding house, and regulate such things as the size, shape, and location of my house. Likewise, I cannot claim the right to manage my business property in ways that harm my employees. If arguments for workplace democracy such as those offered by McCall are valid, then ownership rights alone are not sufficient to overcome employee rights not to be treated as mere human resources to be managed for the economic benefit of owners.

Corporate ownership raises different issues. In general, owners of corporate business do not have a legitimate claim on directing and managing the day-to-day operation of the business. In corporate settings, the owners have already surrendered to management their claim to control corporate property. Thus, objections to worker participation coming from stockholders must be based on some right other than an alleged right to control and manage one's property. Presumably, that claim would be the owner's interest in profiting from the business. Only if employee participation threatens a stockholder's investment would stockholder rights raise a relevant objection. Indeed, if workplace democracy increased corporate profits, then these very same owner interests would demand the surrender of managerial authority to workers. This, then, leads us to consider objections based on managerial expertise and efficiency.

The second objection to employee participation claims that workers lack the expertise and knowledge to manage a business competently. But this is an empirical claim that may not be supported by the facts.[10] We also need to distinguish different forms of employee participation. In some cases, employees may have exactly the expertise needed to improve decision making. But even in cases where employees may lack the relevant expertise (detailed issues of finance and corporate strategy come to mind here), nothing prevents employee representatives who do possess the expertise from participating. Just as managers come to rely on the expertise of financial, accounting, and legal advisors, so, too, could employee interests be represented by experts.

For example, when Chrysler Corporation faced a financial crisis and sought economic concessions from its union, the corporation agreed to give its union representation on its board of directors. Through this act Chrysler granted its union employees a right to participate at the highest levels of corporate decision making. The union representative, UAW President Douglas Frasier, could knowledgeably represent the interests of employees. If he lacked needed expertise, he had the ability to consult with his own financial and legal experts.

A third objection argues that employee decision making will be inefficient. In one sense widespread consultation and participation could hinder and delay decision making, thus leading to higher costs. Employee participation is also inefficient in the sense that employees will tend to make decisions for their own benefit rather than for the benefit of the firm. But again, employee participation need not involve direct democracy in which every employee must be consulted on every decision. A democratic business could adopt a more hierarchical pyramid management structure, as long as the decision makers represented employees. Further, while conflicts can exist between the interests of the firm and the interests of employees, this is a valid objection to employee participation only if such conflicts are more likely to occur than similar conflicts between the interests of managers and the interests of the firm. Conflicts of interests can occur under any decision-making structure, but evidence suggests that employees are no more likely to run a business into the ground than are traditional managers. After all, employees only hurt themselves by jeopardizing their jobs if they sacrifice the welfare of the business for their own short-term interests.

6.6 EMPLOYEE HEALTH AND SAFETY

Protecting employee health and safety is certainly one of the business's major ethical responsibilities. At first glance, there seems a wide consensus that employees have a right to a safe and healthy workplace. But this issue gets quite complicated upon closer examination. Not only is the very meaning of workplace health and safety in dispute, there is also significant disagreement concerning the best policies for protecting health and safety.

Like work itself, health and safety are goods that are valued both as a means for attaining other valuable ends and as end in themselves. When we are healthy and safe, we are much more likely to be able to attain whatever other goods we desire. Health and safety have a very high instrumental value. Yet health and safety are also valuable in and of themselves. They have intrinsic as well as instrumental value.

But what does it mean to be healthy? When is a workplace safe? When is it unsafe? If *healthy* is taken to mean a state of flawless physical and psychological well-being, no one is perfectly healthy. If *safe* means completely free from risk, no workplace is perfectly safe. If health and safety are interpreted as such impossible to realize ideals, then it would be unreasonable to claim that employees have a right to a healthy and safe workplace. Employers cannot be responsible for providing an ideally safe and healthy workplace. Instead, many discussions about employee health and safety will tend to focus on the relative risks faced by workers and the level of acceptable workplace risk. From this perspective, a workplace is safe if the risks are acceptable.

But we should note a subtle yet important shift that occurs when we focus on acceptable risks rather than on health and safety. *Risks* can be defined as the probability of harm, and *relative risks* would entail comparing the probabilities of harm involved in various activities. Thus, both risks and relative risks are things that can be determined by scientists who compile and measure data. It is an easy step from this to certain conclusions about acceptable risks. If it can be determined that the probability of harm involved in a specific activity is equal to or less than the probability of harm of some more common activity, then it would be easy to conclude that this activity faces an acceptable level of risk. In turn, this suggests that determining an activity as safe (in the sense of involving an acceptable level of risk) is something that can be determined by experts rather than the individuals involved in facing the risks.

Consider an example offered by philosopher Mark Sagoff. Sagoff attended a conference addressing potential health hazards faced by neighbors of a toxic waste dump. Citizens had learned of a high rate of leukemia among area residents. Government and corporate officials responded that these fears were irrational because the relative risks involved in living near this waste site were much lower than those faced by smokers. Because people commonly accept the risks involved with smoking, and because experts could show that risks of living near the waste site were lower than those, the government and corporate experts could assure the citizens that they faced an acceptable level of risk.[11]

Imagine if we generalize this and set all workplace health and safety standards in this manner. Such an approach would place the responsibility for workplace safety solely on management. Business would hire safety engineers and other experts to determine the risks faced within their workplace. These experts would know the risk levels that are otherwise accepted throughout the society. These might involve the risks involved in driving a car, in eating high-fat food, in smoking, in jogging, and so forth. Comparing these to the risks faced in the workplace, safety experts could perform a risk assessment and determine the relative risks of work. If the workplace was less risky than other common activities, management could conclude that they have fulfilled their responsibility to provide a healthy and safe workplace.

But there are several problems with such an approach to workplace health and safety issues. First, this approach treats employees disrespectfully by ignoring their input. Such paternalistic decision making effectively treats employees like children and makes crucial decisions for them. Second, in making this decision, the approach assumes that health and safety are mere preferences that can be traded-off against competing values. Third, it assumes an equivalence between workplace risks and other types of risks when there are significant differences between them. Unlike many daily risks, the risks faced in the workplace may not be freely chosen, nor are the risks faced in the workplace within the control of workers. Perhaps most importantly, unlike daily risks the risks faced at work can be controlled by others and particularly by others who may stand to benefit by not reducing them. Relative to the risks I face by smoking, living next to a toxic waste site may not be very risky. In the former case, I choose to take the risk and I can take steps to minimize or eliminate them. In the latter case, I cannot avoid the risks if I want to keep my job, and very often someone else can minimize or eliminate them but this other party has a financial incentive not to do that. Surely we need another approach to workplace health and safety.

Individual bargaining between employers and employees would be the approach to workplace health and safety favored by defenders of the free market and the classical model of corporate social responsibility. On this account employees would be free to choose the risks that they are willing to face by bargaining with employers. Employees set their own risk versus wage preferences and decide how much risk they are willing to face for various wages. Those who demand maximum safety presumably would have to settle for lower wages; those willing to take higher risks presumably would demand higher wages. In a competitive and free labor market, such individual bargaining would result in the optimal distribution of safety and income. Of course, the market approach can also sanction compensatory payments to injured workers when it can be shown that employers were negligently liable for causing the harms. The threat of compensatory payments also acts as an incentive for employers to maintain a reasonably safe and healthy workplace.

But as we have also seen previously, there are a number of serious problems with this free market approach. First, labor markets are not perfectly competitive and free. Employees do not have the kinds of free choices that the free market theory would require in order to attain optimal satisfactions. For example, risky jobs are often also the lowest-paying jobs held by people with the fewest employment choices rather than the higher paying, freely chosen jobs that the market would suggest. Second, employees seldom if ever possess the kind of perfect information required by markets. If employees do not know the risks involved in a job, they will not be in a position to freely bargain for appropriate wages. This is a particular concern when we recognize that many risks faced in the workplace are in no sense obvious. An employee may understand the dangers of heavy machinery or a blast furnace, but few employees can know the toxicity or exposure levels of workplace chemicals or airborne contaminants.

Such market failures can have deadly consequences when they involve workplace health and safety issues. Of course, market defenders argue that markets will, over time, compensate for such failures. Over time, employers will find it difficult to attract workers to dangerous jobs and, over time, employees will learn about the risks of every workplace. But this raises what we have previously described as the *first generation* problem. The means by which the market gathers information is by observing the harms done to the first generation exposed to imperfect market transactions. Thus, workers learn that exposure to lead is dangerous when women workers exposed to lead suffer miscarriages and their children are born with serious birth defects. We learn that workplace exposure to asbestos or cotton dust is dangerous when workers die from lung disease. In effect, markets sacrifice the first generation in order to gain information about safety and health risks.

The final problem with individual bargaining has also been discussed previously. Important questions of social justice and public policy are ignored if we approach questions solely from the point of view of an individual. For example, suppose the risk of lung cancer for the general population is 7 in 100,000 per year. Suppose that the risk faced by workers exposed to various workplace chemicals increases to 20 in 100,000. Consider the questions that would be asked solely from the point of view of an individual bargaining with an employer. While the increased risk is tripled, it still remains quite low and the increased risk over the background rate of lung cancer is only 13 in 100,000. Given the benefits of work and given the relatively low marginal increase in risk, it might well be reasonable for an individual to choose to work that job. However, imagine that there are 100,000 workers industrywide facing the same decision. In this situation, we can be statistically certain of an additional 13 cases of lung cancer each year. Are these 13 cancers a price worth paying for the freedom of 100,000 individuals to choose? They may be, but the point is that this question would never be asked if public policy relied exclusively on the individual perspective. Might there be standards such as maximum exposure levels that would reduce the number of cancers? Might some public policies such as tax incentives to safe businesses reduce cancer rates? These questions of public policy, questions that after all will affect human lives, would never even be asked by an individual facing the choice of working at a risky job. To the degree that these are important questions that ought to be asked, individual bargaining will fail as an ethical public policy approach to worker health and safety.

In response to such concerns, government regulation of workplace health and safety appears more appropriate ethically. Mandatory government standards address most of the problems raised against market strategies. Standards can be set according to the best available scientific knowledge and thus overcome market failures that result from insufficient information. Standards prevent employees from having to face the fundamentally coercive choice between job and safety. Standards also address the first generation problem by focusing on prevention rather than compensation after the fact. Finally, standards are fundamentally a social approach that can address public policy questions ignored by markets.

In 1970 the U.S. Congress established the Occupational Safety and Health Administration (OSHA) and charged it with establishing workplace health and safety standards. Since that time, the major debates concerning workplace health and safety have focused on how such public standards ought to be set. The dominant question has concerned the appropriateness of using cost-benefit analysis to set health and safety standards.

When OSHA was first established, regulations were aimed to achieve the safest feasible standards. Let us consider how this "feasibility analysis" would operate in setting standards for exposure to workplace chemicals. The first step would involve a determination by scientists and medical experts of the toxicity of the specific chemical. Specifically, these experts would determine the exposure level at which impairment of some physical function occurs. OSHA then determines if it would be technologically and economically feasible, on an industrywide basis, to attain this level. *Technologically feasible* means that the technology exists to meet the standards. *Economically feasible* means that the standards could be met without putting the entire industry out of business. If the answer is yes, then OSHA establishes the standard at this point. If the answer is no, OSHA then establishes the standard at the lowest level at which it is technologically and economically feasible. If an individual firm is unable to meet the standards that are attainable within the industry, the standard still applies. In effect, the standard becomes part of the costs of doing business and uncompetitive firms suffer in the market.

This feasibility approach allows OSHA to make trade-offs between health and economics, but it is prejudiced in favor of health and safety by placing the burden of proof on industry to show that high standards are economically unfeasible. Health and safety standards are not required come what may; but an industry is required to meet the highest standards attainable within technological and economic reasons.

Some critics charge that this approach does not go far enough and unjustly sacrifices employee health and safety. From that perspective, industries that cannot operate without harming the health and safety of their employees should be closed. But the more influential criticism has argued that these standards go too far. Critics in both industry and government have argued that OSHA should be required to use cost-benefit analysis in establishing such standards. From this perspective, even if a standard is technologically and economically feasible, it would still be unreasonable and unfair if the benefits did not outweigh the costs. These critics argue that OSHA should aim to achieve the optimal, rather than highest feasible, level of safety.

Using cost-benefit analysis to set standards, in effect, returns us to the goals of the market-based, individual bargaining approach. Like the market approach, this use of cost-benefit faces serious ethical challenges. We should note, however, that rejecting cost-benefit analysis in setting standards is not the same as rejecting cost-effective strategies in implementing those standards. A commitment to cost effectiveness would require that, once the standards are set, we adopt the least-expensive and most efficient means available for achieving those standards. Cost-benefit, in contrast, uses economic criteria in setting the standards in the first place. It is cost-benefit, not cost-effective, analysis that is ethically problematic.

The use of cost-benefit analysis in setting workplace health and safety standards commits us to treating worker health and safety as just another commodity, another individual preference, to be traded off against competing commodities. It treats health and safety merely as an instrumental value and denies its intrinsic value. Cost-benefit requires that an economic value be placed on one's life and bodily integrity. Typically, this would follow the model used by the insurance industry (where it is used in wrongful death settlements, for example) in which one's life is valued in terms of one's earning potential. Perhaps the most offensive aspect of this approach is the fact that since, in feasibility analysis, health and safety is already traded off against the economic viability of the industry, a shift to cost-benefit entails that health and safety is traded off against profit margin. Since feasibility analysis is willing to compromise standards to ensure the viability of the industry, and since profitability is a necessary condition for viability, cost-benefit aims only to improve the profit margin. In effect, critics of feasibility are arguing that employee health and safety should be sacrificed to increase profits in an already (as guaranteed by the economically feasible criteria) profitable industry.

The policies that have emerged by consensus within the United States seem to be most defensible. Employees have a legitimate ethical claim on mandatory health and safety standards within the workplace. To say that employees have a right to workplace health and safety implies that they should not be expected to make trade-offs between health and safety standards and job security or wages. Further, recognizing that most mandatory standards reduce rather than eliminate risks, employees should also have the right to be informed about workplace risks. If the risks have been reduced to the lowest feasible level and employees are fully aware of them, then a society that respects its citizens as autonomous decision makers has done its duty.

6.7 PRIVACY IN THE WORKPLACE

Privacy is a surprisingly obscure and disputed value in contemporary society. With the tremendous increase in computer technology, calls for greater protection of privacy have increased in recent decades. Yet there is widespread disagreement concerning the nature, extent, and value of privacy. Few Western countries, for example, acknowledge a legal right to privacy as recognized within the United States. Even within the United States, there is significant disagreement about privacy. The U.S. Constitution, for example, makes no mention of a right to privacy and the major Supreme Court decisions that have relied on a fundamental right to privacy, *Griswold v. Connecticut* and *Roe v. Wade*, remain highly contentious and controversial.[12]

Two general understandings of privacy can be found in the legal and philosophical literature on this topic: (1) privacy as a right to be "let alone" within a personal zone of solitude and (2) privacy as the right to control information about oneself. Each interpretation is problematic, but each has important implications for business.

The right to be "let alone" with some personal "zone of privacy" has had the longest history within the U.S. legal system. This understanding of privacy is traced to an 1890 *Harvard Law Review* article by Samuel Warren and Louis Brandeis. Warren and Brandeis argued that increasing population and technological advances (e.g., photojournalism) were increasing the threat to the solitude of individual citizens. In their view, the law should recognize a right to "be let alone." Seventy-five years later in *Griswold v. Connecticut* the U.S. Supreme Court relied on a similar understanding in recognizing a Constitutionally guaranteed right to privacy. This case invalidated a Connecticut law that prohibited the use, sale, and prescription of contraception.

Critics have claimed that this understanding of privacy seems to involve something closer to a general right to liberty and, as a result, is too broad. Surely no one living in a social setting can expect to be let alone in any full sense. In a fundamentally social and cooperative activity like work, privacy in this meaning certainly would make little sense. But a closer look at the major legal cases shows that courts have not claimed that individuals should not be let alone to make just any decision. Rather, courts have concluded that only certain very personal decisions, involving family, reproduction, sexuality, home life, and decisions regarding life-sustaining medical treatment are rightfully private. A reasonable interpretation of these judicial decisions suggests that certain decisions are so fundamental to establishing our own identity as an individual, that they ought to be protected as rightfully private.

Concerns that privacy as the right to be let alone is too broad have led some to conclude that a better understanding of privacy focuses on privacy as involving the control of personal information. From this perspective, the clearest case of an invasion of privacy occurs when others come to know personal information about us—as when a stranger reads your e-mail or eavesdrops on a personal conversation. But, again, this might be too broad an understanding if we are to claim a *right* of privacy. Surely there are many occasions when others, particularly within an employment context, can legitimately know even personal information about us.

Philosopher George Brenkert has argued that the informational sense of privacy involves a relationship between two parties, A and B, and personal information X about A. Privacy is violated only when B comes to know X and no relationship exists between A and B that would justify B knowing X. Thus, whether my privacy is violated or not by a disclosure of personal information depends on my relationship with the person or persons who come to know that information. My relationship with my mortgage company, for example, would justify that company coming to know my credit rating while my relationship with my students would not justify them getting that information. Limiting access of personal information only to those with whom one has a personal relationship is an important way to preserve one's own personal integrity and individuality. This will prove important when we turn to the employment context and consider the relationship between employer and employee.

But first it would be worth thinking about the connection between these two senses of privacy. Certain decisions that we make about how we live our lives, as well as the control of personal information, play a crucial role in defining our own personal identity. Privacy is important because it serves to establish the boundary between individuals and thereby serves to define one's individuality. The right to control certain very personal decisions and information helps determine the kind of person we are and the person we become. To the degree that we value individuality and treating each person as an individual, we ought to recognize that certain personal decisions and information are rightfully the exclusive domain of the individual.

What are the implications of this for the workplace? Answering this question requires us to think about the relationship between employer and employee. The nature of that relationship will help determine the appropriate boundary between employers and employees and therefore the decisions and information that ought to remain rightfully private within the workplace. On one hand, if employees work totally "at will" and are fully subject to the demands of employers, then it might well be that employees have no legitimate expectation of privacy within the workplace. Likewise, if employers and employees are closely bound in a joint project of mutual support and loyalty, as members of a family for example, then privacy might also be less important. But neither model of the employment relationship seems appropriate. On the other hand, if we adopt something more like a contractual model of employment, where the conditions and terms of employment are subject to the mutual and informed consent of both parties, then legitimately private decisions and information should be exempt from employer concern.

We might summarize this by saying that employee privacy is violated whenever (1) employers infringe upon personal decisions that are irrelevant to the employment contract (implied or explicit) or whenever (2) personal information that is irrelevant to that contract is collected, stored, or used without the informed consent of the employee. Further, since consent plays a pivotal role in this understanding, the burden of proof rests with the employer to establish the relevancy of personal decisions and information at issue.

For example, consider two of the cases mentioned at the start of this chapter. In one case, an employee is fired for smoking and in the other she is fired for having an abortion. Are the decisions to smoke or to have an abortion job-relevant? Further, should we assume that they are (i.e., that the employer is justified until shown otherwise), or should the burden of proof rest with the employer to first establish their relevancy? If consent is necessary for establishing a valid contract and if we are to take consent seriously, then we must conclude that the burden rests on the employer to prove the relevance of these actions.

In the smoking case, perhaps the employer can show a just cause for dismissal. Assuming that insurance rates are markedly higher for smokers, one could argue that the costs of providing health insurance for employees makes the decision to smoke, even outside of the workplace, a job-relevant factor. It may well cost business more to employ a smoker than it would to employ an equally qualified nonsmoker. On the other hand, it is difficult to see how the choice to have an abortion would prove to be job-relevant (the woman worked in a hair salon). Thus, privacy would seem to protect an employee against dismissal for having an abortion.

We could again rely on the ethical conditions for valid contracts to establish the limits of informational privacy within the workplace. In general, we can say that a valid contract must be voluntary, informed, and consensual. The parties must freely enter into it, they must understand it, and they must agree to its conditions. The informational sense of privacy is violated, therefore, whenever personal information is collected or used without the informed and voluntary consent of the employee. Using this framework, we can offer an initial account of what information can be known, who ought to have access to it, how it can be used, and what methods for collecting personal employee information are appropriate.

Information required to make an initial job offer—for example, concerning the employee's past work experience, education, and abilities—is surely job-relevant. So, too, is information required by law (e.g., Social Security number), or necessary for employee benefits such as health care and insurance. Information about marital status, family plans, religion, and other personal issues seems irrelevant. Returning to one of the cases mentioned at the start of this chapter, information about a potential employee's sexual life or religious beliefs would be irrelevant and inappropriate job-interview requests. Further, given the central role of consent, employees ought to have access to inspect, challenge, and be informed about any information that employers possess or gather about them. Employers ought not to use personal information for any purposes for which employees have not given their consent. So, for example, employers ought not sell employee information or use it for any marketing or economic purposes.

Finally, perhaps the most interesting aspect of employee privacy concerns the methods by which employers might gather information about employees. In recent years polygraph and drug testing, surveillance, third-party background checks, and psychological testing have all been used as means to gain information about employees. More recently, electronic monitoring and surveillance has raised privacy issues in the workplace. Typically, but not always, such techniques are used to investigate misconduct such as employee theft. In addition, genetic screening of potential and present employees suggests that this new technology will keep employee privacy concerns in the public eye for many years to come.

A useful exercise would involve examining each of these information-gathering techniques and deciding what conditions, if any, should be placed upon their use in order to protect employee rights. First, we should require that the information sought through such techniques itself be job-relevant and legitimately knowable by the employer. For example, genetic screening to gather medical information that would then be used to disqualify people from work would be unjustified. To insure fully voluntary consent we might also require that employees be given prior notification before any of these methods are used. There is no reason that employees should not be fully informed of the uses for such things as blood or urine samples. Random or blanket use of such methods typically would be unjustified, and they should be used only when a reasonable just cause is established. For example, drug testing only employees involved in accidents is preferable to mandating that all employees submit to random testing. The guiding question for such an exercise should be, Has the employee given her fully informed and voluntary consent to the loss of personal information? Finally, such intrusive information-gathering methods as secret surveillance, and blood, urine, or genetic sampling should be used only as a last resort and all other less-intrusive techniques have been used or been rejected.

REFLECTIONS ON THE CHAPTER DISCUSSION CASES

The first example comes from the legal case *Fortune v. National Cash Register*. Fortune was employed as a salesman by National Cash Register Co. with a contract that was terminable at will and without cause. In addition to his weekly salary, Fortune earned commissions based on the amount of sales made within his sales territory. He was to be paid 75 percent of his earned commission on the date on which the order was placed, and the remaining 25 percent when the order was delivered. In November 1968, a $5 million order was placed from within Fortune's sales area, with delivery scheduled over a four-year period. In the following January, after the first shipment was made, Fortune was terminated and as a result of his termination, he was not paid either the remaining commissions due him on the cash registers already shipped or any additional commissions on the cash registers scheduled to be subsequently shipped. Despite finding that NCR had breached no express term of its contract with Fortune by terminating him and depriving him of the additional commissions that he otherwise would be due, the Massachusetts Supreme Judicial Court held NCR violated the implied covenant of good faith and fair dealing by terminating him for the purpose of paying Fortune "as little of the bonus credit as it could."

The second example is from *Bone v. Ford Meter Box* (1991). In response to this lawsuit, the Indiana Legislature passed a law in 1991 that forbids employers from discriminating against employees based on their use of tobacco products. The law allows workers to sue their employer for damages if they have been discriminated against because they smoke. Janice Bone had worked at Ford two years when the company introduced a no-smoking policy for new hires and began a drug-testing program. The company fired Bone after a drug test revealed nicotine in her urine.

The third example is based on *Turic v. Holland Hospitality Inc.* Kim Turic, a 17-year-old mother of one, was employed at a Holiday Inn to bus tables in the restaurant and as a member of the room service staff. Upon learning she was pregnant, Turic informed her supervisor that she was considering an abortion and word spread throughout the workplace. A Michigan court ruled in favor of Turic's lawsuit on grounds that the dismissal violated her legal rights under the Pregnancy Discrimination Act and equal opportunity protection against sex discrimination.

The fourth example is from *Andersen v. Gus Mayer.* In this case, the courts ruled that Gus Mayer's denial of health insurance on the basis of Mr. Anderson's HIV status was a violation of the Americans with Disabilities Act.

The fifth example is taken from *Smyth v. Pillsbury.* Michael Smyth used his home computer to access his work e-mail account and communicate with his supervisor. Smyth's e-mails were highly critical of Pillsbury management, and included apparent threats. A Pennsylvania court ruled that, despite assurances to the contrary, Pillsbury had no obligation to treat e-mails as confidential. The court ruling claimed that the "company's interest in preventing inappropriate and unprofessional comments or even illegal activity over its e-mail system outweighs any privacy interest the employee may have in those comments."

The sixth example is based on *Soroka v. Target Stores.* Target Stores identified a set of emotional characteristics that they believed were problematic in security guards and hired psychological consultants to develop and administer pre-employment psychological screening tests. Target received reports on the evaluation from the consultants but did not receive the candidate's responses to specific questions. A group of job applicants sued Target claiming that the tests violated their privacy rights under California law. The California Court of Appeals struck down the individual questions as violating privacy rights. The case was settled prior to a final appeal when Target agreed to end the use of these tests.

The final example is from *Oil, Chemical, and Atomic Workers Union v. American Cyanamid* and *Automobile Workers Union v. Johnson Controls.* In January 1978 American Cyanamid notified its employees that it would institute a policy banning all women between the ages of 16 and 50 from working in departments where contact with chemicals was hazardous to the fetus, claiming that the plant contained "hundreds" of such chemicals. Only women who could provide medical documentation that they had been sterilized could remain in these units. OSHA issued a citation against Cyanamid in 1979, charging that it had violated the law's general duty clause, which provides that an employer must "furnish to his employees employment and a place of employment which are free from recognized hazards that are causing or are likely to cause death or serious physical harm." That decision was later overturned on the grounds that neither the exclusionary policy nor sterilization was a workplace "hazard" as defined by law. In the *Johnson Controls* case, the U.S. Supreme Court ruled that exclusionary policies violate equal opportunity laws.

REVIEW QUESTIONS

1. Explain the difference between an employee's legal rights and moral rights.
2. Explain three different meanings of a *right to work*. Which, if any, do you think should be among the moral rights of employees?
3. What is the legal doctrine of *employment at will*? Explain three different legislative or judicial limitations on this doctrine. Do you think any are unreasonable?
4. What is the definition of *due process*? How does this relate to the concept of *just cause*?
5. Explain and evaluate four major counterarguments to due process rights in the workplace.
6. Explain what you take to be the strongest argument in defense of an employee's right to participate in managerial decision making. Explain what you take to be the strongest argument against such a right.
7. Explain how individual bargaining between employer and employee would be the preferred method of the classical model of corporate social responsibility for establishing a healthy and safe workplace. Describe at least two objections to this approach.
8. Explain how the nature of the employer–employee relationship helps to determine the extent of privacy in the workplace.

ENDNOTES

[1] See *Fortune v. National Cash Register, Bone v. Ford Meter Box, Flanigan v. Davidson, Andersen v. Gus Mayer, Soroka v. Target Store,* and *Oil, Chemical, and Atomic Workers Union v. American Cyanamid.*

[2] For an early version of this conception of employee rights, see "A Defense of Employee Rights" by Joseph DesJardins and John McCall, *Journal of Business Ethics* 4, 1985, pp. 367–376.

[3] For example, Article 23 of the U.N. Universal Declaration of Human Rights states: "Everyone has the right to work, to free choice of employment, to just and favourable conditions of work and to protection against unemployment." The right to work in the tradition of Catholic social teaching is discussed in *Economic Justice for All: Pastoral Letter on Catholic Social Teaching and the U.S. Economy,* U.S. Catholic Bishops, 1986; and *Pacem in Terris* (Peace on Earth), Pope John XXIII, 1963. The right to a job has always been more controversial within the United States. The closest this issue ever got to becoming policy was the Full Employment and Balanced Growth Act of 1978 (usually referred to as the Humphrey-Hawkins Act after its sponsors Senator Hubert Humphrey and Representative Augustus Hawkins), which directed that federal monetary and economic policy take full employment as one of its major objectives.

[4] Norman Bowie, "A Kantian Theory of Meaningful Work," *Journal of Business Ethics* 17, 1998, p. 1083.

[5] Bowie, p. 1083.

⁶*Payne v. Western & A.A.R. Co.,* 81 Tenn. 507 (1884).

⁷Patricia Werhane, "Individual Rights in Business," in *Just Business: New Essays in Business Ethics,* ed. Tom Regan (New York: Random House, 1984), pp. 107–126.

⁸John McCall, "An Ethical Basis for Employee Participation," in *Contemporary Issues in Business Ethics,* 4th ed., eds. DesJardins and McCall (Belmont, CA: Wadsworth Publishing, 1996), pp. 199–206.

⁹McCall, p. 200.

¹⁰For example, McCall cites the cases of Volvo and Donnelly Mirrors, and the legally mandated co-determination practices in Germany, as evidence that employee participation can increase a business's competitiveness.

¹¹Mark Sagoff, "At the Shrine of Our Lady of Fatima or Why Political Questions Are Not All Economic," *Arizona Law Review* 23, 1981, p. 1283.

¹²*Griswold v. Connecticut* (1965) found privacy within the "penumbra" of rights established by the First, Third, Fourth, and Fifth Amendments. Criticism of this decision as a vague, judicially created right was a major factor in the U.S. Senate's rejection of the nomination of Robert Bork to the Supreme Court. Only eight years later the Supreme Court relied on this same understanding of privacy rights in reaching the still-controversial abortion decision in *Roe v. Wade.*

7 CHAPTER

Employee Responsibilities

E-mail and Internet policy

Important warnings for use of e-mail

...arnings listed below are of critical importance and no...
...rtain circumstances constitute a serious disciplinary...

...y in e-mail messages. Improper statements can give...
...y liability. Work on the assumptions that...
...ssages that are abusive, sexist,...
...dential mes...

L E A R N I N G   O B J E C T I V E S

After reading this chapter, you will be able to:

• Explain the nature and range of employee responsibilities;

• Explain the agency view of employee responsibilities;

• Understand the role of business professionals as gatekeepers;

• Explain managerial responsibilities;

• Explain and examine the concept of conflicts of interest;

- Analyze the responsibilities of trust and loyalty in the workplace;

- Analyze responsibilities for honesty in business;

- Analyze the ethical responsibilities concerning whistleblowing and insider trading.

DISCUSSION CASE: Professional and Managerial Responsibility at Enron and Arthur Andersen

On December 2, 2001, with its stock valued at just pennies per share, Enron Corporation declared bankruptcy and laid off over 4,000 employees. For a corporation once ranked the seventh largest of the Fortune 500 and whose stock's value had hovered around $90 per share only a year earlier, bankruptcy represented an amazing downfall. As information concerning the collapse became known over the following weeks and months, the truth about Enron and its accounting firm Arthur Andersen tells a shameful story of greed, dishonesty, and corruption that is perhaps unmatched in corporate history.

Enron was created in July 1985 through the merger of Houston Natural Gas and InterNorth, a natural gas pipeline company. Under the direction of CEO and Chairman Kenneth Lay, Enron evolved from a gas and energy supplier to an energy-trading company. Energy producers and suppliers commonly buy and sell futures as a management strategy aimed at securing future supplies and profiting from excess capacity. But Enron came to see energy as just another commodity that could be bought and sold on the open market. By the end of the 1990s, over 80 percent of Enron's reported earnings were from energy trading rather than from its gas supply and pipeline divisions. This transition was helped significantly by general movement towards deregulation of public utility industries, a political change for which Enron lobbied strongly. At its peak in late 2000, Enron was expanding its trading activities into many other areas, including broadband cable capacity and advertising space.

Energy markets have a well-deserved reputation for volatility. As every consumer realizes, the price of gasoline, natural gas, oil, and electricity can fluctuate wildly over a short period of time. This was one of the major reasons (the other being the monopolistic nature of utilities) for the traditional heavy regulation of the energy industry. Government regulation was seen as a means for providing price stability for business and price control for consumers.

To minimize these risks in an era of deregulation, it is common for traders to hedge their positions, effectively entering into futures contracts that balance present risks. Senior management at Enron chose to balance their risks by entering into agreements with companies that its own executives created for that very purpose. Enron's relationships with these *special purpose entities* (SPEs) were at the heart of the company's corruption and collapse.

Enron executives, particularly Chief Financial Officer Andrew Fastow, pioneered in the development of these SPEs what critics call "off-balance sheet" partnerships. Using its stock as collateral, Enron would create a partnership with a small number of outside investors. Accounting regulations allow anyone with a minimum of 3 percent equity share to be identified as the SPE's owner. These regulations also hold that as long as Enron owned less than 50 percent of the SPE's voting stock, its debts did not have to be accounted for on Enron's books. As a result of these two accounting regulations, these SPEs were technically separate business entities. With capital raised by these partnerships, again using Enron stock as collateral, the partnership then enters into a joint venture with Enron. The SPE supplies capital, Enron supplies assets, and, at least in theory, the joint venture proceeds. In the meantime, the money raised for the joint venture is used to pay off debt on Enron's assets. Thus, the entire process allowed Enron to record a lowering of its liabilities (as its debts were paid off) without also record-ing the corresponding increased liability (which had been shifted to the SPE). But because the SPE's debt was itself secured by Enron using Enron stock, the entire process is, while perhaps technically legal, nonetheless deceptive.

Three aspects of these relationships are particularly egregious. First, Enron's SPEs had little use other than to shift debt and risks off Enron's financial bal-ance sheets. Other business and financial institutions use SPEs when they seek to minimize risks of legitimate joint ventures. Enron seemed to have no reason for forming SPEs other than to create the deceptive impression it was financially in much better shape than it actually was. There were few legitimate joint ven-tures that were anything other than a façade for accounting deceits. Hedging its risks by entering into contracts with independent third parties, as is commonly done by many business institutions, does lower risk; hedging risks by entering into agreements with oneself does not. By financing these partnerships mostly with its own stock, Enron effectively was underwriting its own risks, which, of course, is not to underwrite them at all. Its relationships with these partnerships were being financed by Enron stock, and this provided a very strong incentive for Enron management to keep its stock value high. (The fact that senior man-agement also were being granted significant stock options was another reason.) Further, the entire financial stability of the corporation was like a house of cards, supported only by its continuing ability to shift debt onto these SPEs.

Second, the person managing these partnerships (and reaping signifi-cant personal profits from them as one of the "outside" limited partners) was Enron's Chief Financial Officer, Andrew Fastow. Thus, Fastow was negotiat-ing with himself (or his subordinates) in forming the deals between Enron and these SPEs. One such SPE alone, called LJM Cayman L.P. (limited partnership), reportedly earned its managing director—Andrew Fastow—millions of dol-lars. Later company investigations revealed that Fastow made $30 million from these partnerships. As an eventual result of its deals with just LJM, Enron had to take a billion-dollar writedown in its equity value.

Third, Enron was supported through all of this by its accounting firm, Arthur Andersen. Andersen was responsible for auditing Enron—that is, pro-viding allegedly unbiased and accurate financial reports. Such audit reports pro-vide the information that investors and creditors rely on when making decisions about investing in or extending credit to a corporation. But Arthur Andersen was also earning millions of dollars a year from Enron for consulting and advising work. Thus, the very professionals who had responsibility for providing unbiased and accurate audit information to Enron's board, its investors, its creditors, and its employees were also involved in advising Enron's management on how to keep legitimate debts off its balance sheets.

The collapse of Enron began slowly at first. In early 2001 a few stock analysts, most notably Jim Chanos of Kynikos Associates, began to raise questions about Enron's financial stability. A story by Bethany McLean in *Fortune* magazine also raised questions about Enron's valuation. Such skepticism was met with a combination of arrogance and condescension by Enron executives. Jeffrey Skilling, who replaced Kenneth Lay as CEO in February of 2001, told McLean that her questioning was "unethical," that Enron's business was simple to understand, and only people who wanted to "throw rocks" at Enron failed to acknowledge that.[1] At about the same time Skilling was publicly claiming that Enron's stock value should be worth $126 a share, more than 50 percent higher than its actual value.

Evidence suggests that these outsiders were not the only people to have doubts. Skilling and Lay sold over a million shares of Enron stock between November 2000 and September 2001, hardly the acts of people who believed that the stock price would increase by 50 percent. Numerous other high-level insiders, including board members and Enron's General Counsel, also sold hundreds of thousands of shares during this period. Further, internal Arthur Andersen documents show that its executives also had real doubts about Enron's finances. An Andersen memo from February 2001 discussed the possibility of dropping Enron as a client. Andersen executives chose not to do this, acknowledging the multimillion dollar annual fees it received from Enron. For advice concerning just two of the hundreds of the SPEs it helped establish (LJM and Chewco), Andersen billed Enron $5.7 million above its annual auditing fees.

Other insiders also called attention to Enron's shaky finances. In May 2001, Vice-Chair Clifford Baxter warned that the SPE partnerships were "inappropriate." Baxter, who resigned later that year, also made over $35 million selling more than one-half million shares of Enron stock. Former company treasurer Jeff McMahon was transferred after complaining to CEO Skilling about the secrecy that surrounded the partnerships. Finally, Vice-President Sherron Watkins, herself a former Andersen employee, warned Lay and other Enron executives about "serious accounting improprieties" beginning in the summer of 2001. In one letter to Lay, she claimed, "I am incredibly nervous that we will implode in a wave of accounting scandals."

As the financial news grew worse, the ethical picture continued to deteriorate. Jeffrey Skilling resigned on August 14, 2001, citing personal reasons. When he testified under oath before Congress in early 2002, Skilling repeatedly claimed that he believed that Enron was in solid financial shape at the time of his resignation and that his resignation had nothing to do with increasing financial difficulties. Within days of Skilling's resignation and of receiving Watkins's letter, Lay (who had returned as president and CEO after Skilling's resignation) exercised options on thousands of shares of Enron stock, making almost $2 million. By the end of August, Lay had sold over $16 million worth of Enron stock and Skilling had sold an additional $15 million. At this same time, Lay was assuring employees and the public that the company was in good financial shape. In late September, Lay urged employees to continue buying Enron stock, which was then selling at only $25 per share. Starting in late October, ostensibly as a result of a change in plan administrators, employee 401(k) retirement plans, over 60 percent of which was in Enron stock, were frozen, prohibiting employees from selling Enron stock. By the time the plan was reopened, the stock's value was only $9 a share.

By late September 2001, Andersen's auditors had decided that previous accounting decisions concerning the SPE partnerships were incorrect and over $1 billion would have to be reduced from Enron's valuation. On October 12, an Andersen lawyer instructed employees to destroy all but the most essential documents concerning the Enron audit. This shredding of documents would continue for months, well after Enron was subject to numerous legal investigations.

On October 16 Enron issued its third-quarter financial report and acknowledged a quarterly loss of $618 million. The following day it announced the results of Andersen's accounting decision and the resulting $1 billion reduction in asset value as a result of losses from SPEs. Because the financing for these SPEs was based on Enron stock, the more the stock price fell the faster the overall financial crisis accelerated. From October 16 until October 26, Enron stock fell from $33 a share to $15 a share. On October 22 the Securities and Exchange Commission announced that it had begun an inquiry of Enron that CEO Lay said he "welcomes." The next day Lay publicly insisted that Enron was "performing very well" and that criticisms of CFO Fastow were unfair. The following day Andrew Fastow was granted a "leave of absence" from which he never returned.

On November 8, 2001, Enron acknowledged that widespread accounting errors in four previous years had overinflated Enron's worth by $600 million and admitted that additional information might still be forthcoming. The following day Dynegy, Inc., a smaller competitor, announced that they had reached a tentative agreement to purchase Enron for $10 billion. Three weeks later, Dynegy backed out of the deal claiming that they, too, had been misled about Enron's financial status. In the following days, Enron's stock continued to fall and its credit rating was lowered to junk bond status, thereby causing more of the debt that financed LPEs to come due. On December 2, Enron filed for bankruptcy.

Throughout all of this, Enron's board of directors, and in particular the board's audit committee, should have been fulfilling their fiduciary roles as stewards of stockholder interest. While many on the board claim that they were uninformed about these dealings, the evidence suggests otherwise. It was the board itself that had given Andrew Fastow permission to ignore the corporate prohibition against conflicts of interest when he negotiated contracts between Enron and the SPEs in which he held positions. Board members were also among the insiders selling large quantities of stock throughout 2001. But, like so many corporate boards, Enron's board was made up of many individuals appointed by the CEO more for status and prestige than for business or financial acumen. Among the members of Enron's board audit committee were Wendy Gramm, former chairwoman, U.S. commodity futures trading commission, and John

Wakeham, former UK secretary of state for energy and member of the House of Lords. While working for the U.S. government during the first Bush administration, Gramm was a leading advocate for deregulation of the energy industry, a decision made late in the Bush administration that greatly benefited Enron. Gramm was appointed to Enron's board soon after leaving government service. She is the wife of Senator Phill Gramm from Texas, a member of the Senate banking, finance, and budget committees, who received $100,000 in campaign contributions from Enron for his last two campaigns.

DISCUSSION QUESTIONS

1. What were the responsibilities of the accountants at Arthur Andersen? To whom did they owe these responsibilities?
2. Who was harmed by the insider trading of Enron executives? What harm, if any, was done to employees who were prevented from selling Enron stock in their 401(k) accounts?
3. Should insiders, either at Enron or at Arthur Andersen, have blown the whistle on unethical activities sooner?
4. Who, if anyone, was harmed by Andrew Fastow's dual roles as Enron's CFO and as managing partner of Enron's SPEs?
5. What laws or policies would you recommend to prevent future Enrons?

7.1 INTRODUCTION

Chapter 6 considered a range of potential rights that employees might claim within the workplace. Rights can be seen as claims that individuals have against others to be treated in certain ways or to receive specific goods. My rights determine what is owed to me by others. We now turn to the question of responsibilities, or what I owe to other people.

What do I owe to other people? A moment's reflection suggests that this question is too broad. The most reasonable answer would be that it depends; it depends on who the other person is. The responsibilities that I owe to my children are different than what I owe to strangers. My responsibilities to my mortgage company differ from my responsibilities to my employer. (This observation raises similar issues to the discussion of privacy in chapter 6.) In this way, we can think of responsibilities as involving three factors: (1) a person A, (2) another person or institution B, and (3) a relationship R that exists between A and B. The responsibilities that A has to B are a function of that relationship R, and therefore before we can determine A's responsibilities we must examine the nature of that relationship. For example, the contractual relationship that I have with my mortgage company determines to a fairly exact degree what I owe to that company. The relationship of love and dependency between children and parents determines what parents owe to children. So what, then, are the relationships found in business?

At first glance the answer might seem simple. Workers are employees and the employment relationship establishes a variety of responsibilities that employees owe to their employers. We can reflect back on an earlier quotation from Milton Friedman to see this view most clearly:

> In a free-enterprise, private property system a corporate executive is an employee of the owners of the business. He has direct responsibility to his employers. That responsibility is to conduct the business in accordance with their desires, which generally will be to make as much money as possible while conforming to the basic rules of society, both those embodied in law and those embodied in ethical custom. . . . [T]he key point is that, in his capacity as a corporate executive, the manager is the agent of the individuals who own the corporation . . . and his primary responsibility is to them.[2]

But as the Enron case demonstrates, this view is too simplistic. A business manager certainly is an agent of the corporation and therefore does have specific responsibilities to the stockholders. But a manager may also be a professional (e.g., an engineer, a lawyer, a physician, or an accountant) who has professional responsibilities as well. Sherron Watkins was not only an Enron vice president, she was also an accountant. Her letter to Kenneth Lay recognized the possibility that managerial responsibilities may sometimes conflict with professional responsibilities. The Enron case also demonstrates the reality that employees also have a personal life outside of the workplace and within that context they have responsibilities as citizens as well as having responsibilities to their family and friends. This chapter considers a range of responsibilities that an individual might encounter in the workplace.

7.2 THE NARROW VIEW OF EMPLOYEE RESPONSIBILITIES: EMPLOYEES AS AGENTS

If our responsibilities are a function of the nature of relationship we have with others, we need to consider the employee–employer relationship. The quotation from Milton Friedman used in Section 7.1 is an example of what I will call the narrow view of employee responsibilities. Within the United States, the employee–employer relationship that underlies this perspective has roots in the common law concept of agent-principal and this legal concept can guide our analysis of an employee's ethical responsibilities.

In general, an agent is a person who acts on behalf of another person. Not all agents are employees. For example, your real estate agent or investment advisor is your agent but not your employee. Accountants employed by Arthur Andersen were nonetheless the agents of Enron. However, the common law tradition within the United States has historically treated all employees as agents of employers (the "principal"). As an agent, the employee is hired to perform certain tasks and has a duty to act on behalf of the principal. While this "fiduciary" relationship creates responsibilities on both sides, the primary responsibilities lie with the employee who owes to the employer duties of loyalty, obedience, and confidentiality among others.

Agency relationships vary in the amount of latitude an agent possesses in decision making. The common law tradition views nonmanagerial employees as having very little discretion in the workplace. In fact, the law has traditionally described the normal employee–employer connection as a *master–servant* relationship. In such a relationship, the employer exercises a great deal of control over the nature and terms of employment. The servant is understood as lacking any special expertise and, thus, needs direct and constant supervision. For example, a secretary or factory worker is hired to perform specific tasks within regular hours for specified wages and under close supervision. The "servant's" responsibility is to obey the employer's direction and the employer's responsibility is to pay the agreed-upon wages.

Managerial employees have greater discretion and a greater responsibility to act on the best interests of the employer. Managers are understood to have special expertise that owners must rely on and this expertise justifies greater responsibility. Thus, a manager has the legal authority to act on behalf of the corporation—to spend its money, commit it to contracts, hire and fire its employees—and has greater autonomy in making such decisions. In general, managers are understood to have a strong fiduciary duty to act in the best financial interests of the owners. However, along with this increased responsibility, managers are free from close day-to-day oversight by owners.

The implications of this model of employer–employee relations are significant for the range of employee responsibilities. The law holds that employee-agents owe legal duties of loyalty, trust, obedience, and confidentiality to the employer-principal. These responsibilities override the personal interests that an employee might bring to the workplace. This seems to be what Friedman has in mind when he says that a manager's "primary" responsibility is to the owners of the business. Thus, for example, this model suggests that Sherron Watkins's responsibility to her employer would preclude her whistleblowing to the Security and Exchange Commission. Obeying and trusting the decisions of Enron management, she had a duty to be a loyal employee and hold in confidence the information she learned in her work.

Of course, no one would argue that an employee's legal responsibility to obey an employer overrides all other ethical and legal responsibilities. Even Friedman acknowledges responsibilities to obey the law and conform to other ethical custom. So the real issue is to determine the extent that competing responsibilities limit the duty to employers. On this narrow view there are very few such responsibilities to trump the primary duty to follow the desires of the business owner. Even managers who have greater freedom from the day-to-day supervision by owners have a primary responsibility always to act in accord with their desires.

But is this narrow view ethically defensible? Perhaps the most basic question to ask concerns the ethical foundations for the narrow view. Why would anyone think that an employee should have an overriding responsibility to obey the desires of an employer? Two answers, reminiscent of the discussions in chapters 2 and 3, suggest themselves. First, because employees, especially perhaps managerial employees, play a particular role within the economic system, and because that economic system works to everyone's benefit, the special role-specific responsibilities that employees take on within that system override other ethical considerations. This is a version of the utilitarian argument reviewed previously. The second defense appeals to the property rights of owners and prevention of the economic harms they might suffer at the hand of employees. But as we also saw in chapters 2 and 3, these two ethical approaches face serious challenges. To consider this issue further, let us approach this question by considering nonmanagerial and managerial employees separately.

As applied to nonmanagerial employees the narrow view would require that an individual's normal responsibilities be left at the door of the workplace. Not the least of which is what I would call the responsibility to be responsible. We normally wouldn't excuse someone from responsibility just because they were obeying the commands of someone else. (Think of the case of war-crime trials as the most dramatic example where this defense is universally rejected.) Defense of the narrow view will need to identify something distinctive about the employee–employer relationship that justifies this unusual workplace requirement.

At first glance, the narrow view would seem to have a ready rationale. Employees consent to obeying employers when they take a job. Since they agree to this condition when they come to work, they are not truly abandoning their own responsibility when they follow the commands of employers. But this response is not persuasive. First, consent alone is not sufficient to excuse someone from other responsibilities. For example, as the war-crime case demonstrates, volunteering for military service doesn't mean that one must blindly obey every order. A blanket obligation for all employees to obey their employers come what may is an unreasonable abdication of personal responsibility. It makes little sense to claim that an employee has an ethical responsibility to obey an unethical directive issued by an employer, for example.

The unreasonableness of this response is only increased by the fact that most employees are in a vulnerable position when dealing with employers. Even if voluntarily taking a job would create some responsibility to obey one's employer, we would still need to examine the question of how free employees are in this relationship. The choice of obeying someone's command or jeopardizing one's job is a fundamentally coercive situation and thus the consent involved is not fully free. Under the direction of Jeffrey Skilling, for example, Enron had the reputation as a place where "uncooperative" employees were quickly demoted, transferred, or fired. Because employers have the authority to fire employees, and because such authority makes employees vulnerable to the acts of employers, employees deserve protection from arbitrary use of that authority. This is a point made previously in our discussion of employment at will and employee rights to due process. The discussion of due process in chapter 6 gave us one way to think about nonarbitrary uses of employer authority.

A more reasonable conclusion for nonmanagerial employees is that they have a responsibility to obey the directives of an employer when those directives are job-related, reasonable, and when they do not violate legal or ethical duties. To claim that they must be job-related prevents employers from turning employees into personal servants. An employer's authority exists only within the employment relationship and thus only extends to work-related issues. This condition would mean, for example, that employees have no responsibility to run personal errands for employers. The condition that employer directives be reasonable means, among other things, that an employee be capable of carrying out the directive ("ought implies can" in the language of ethics), that the directive be within the normal job responsibilities of the employee, and that it doesn't place the employee at risk. Finally, the third condition means that an employer cannot require that an employee violate the law, cause harm to anyone, or commit any act that violates the employee's own ethical integrity. It is surely unreasonable to hold that an employee has an ethical responsibility to act unethically.

Finally, against this background, we should consider what a nonmanagerial employee owes the employer in terms of work effort. Do employees have a responsibility to work as hard and as much as an employer desires? Are employers free to establish any standards for the amount and quality of work? Do I violate my responsibility as an employee when I put forth something less than full effort full-time?[3]

Certainly employers desire that employees perform at an optimal level at every moment at work. But just as certainly this expectation is unreasonable, particularly for those who would otherwise cite the market as the final arbitrator of social policy. The labor market, to the degree that it is efficient, would do a good job of establishing acceptable work effort levels. If my employer can get another employee to work harder and longer than me for my wages, I will lose my job in a competitive labor market. In general, employees have the responsibility only to put forth a fair day's effort for a fair day's pay.

The narrow view of employee responsibilities is more plausible when the employees hold positions of managerial authority. In this case managers have the legal authority to act on behalf of employers (often, but not always, corporations). This authority is justified by the fact that managers possess an expertise that the employer lacks. The inequality of expertise, and the corresponding responsibility to act on behalf of the employer, is the crucial idea that lies at the heart of agency theory. In general, one hires an agent (e.g., a real estate agent or a lawyer) when you need a special expertise to accomplish your goals. Since you lack and your agent possesses the requisite knowledge, you are in a vulnerable position. This is the reverse of the nonmanagerial employee where employers have greater authority over employees. As suggested in chapter 6, in that case employees deserve protection offered by employee rights and employers have specific responsibilities to employees. The principle in both cases is the same: to protect vulnerable parties from potential harm by those who can exercise some control over them; the party with greater power and authority has greater responsibility to the vulnerable party. In the case of managerial employees, to protect the employer-principal from potential harm that this vulnerability might cause, the law creates responsibilities for the agent to act on the employer's behalf.

This model makes ethical sense in many situations. If I grant someone the power of attorney to enter contracts in my name, I am made vulnerable by that relinquished authority. If I open my financial records to an outside accountant, I am at risk that this information might be used against me. From this, it follows that these individuals do have a strong obligation to act on my best interests and not use that authority for their own interest at my expense. Their expertise is, after all, what they bring to the contract and what I have agreed to purchase. In general, business managers do have an ethical responsibility to act in the best interests of their employer. But, as even Friedman admits, this responsibility to act on behalf of the employer-principal is not unlimited. Once again, the real question focuses on the limits of this responsibility. When and under what conditions do the responsibilities of managers as business agents trump their other ethical responsibilities?

There are cases in which normal ethical responsibilities are trumped by role-specific duties. Physicians and lawyers, for example, have specific professional responsibilities of confidentiality and loyalty that override their personal interests and may sometimes override such normal ethical considerations as honesty and truthfulness. It would be unethical for an attorney to divulge details of her client's defense strategy, and it would be unethical for a physician to sell patients' medical records to a pharmaceutical company. Similarly, auditors have explicit legal responsibilities that override, at least in theory, the responsibilities they have to clients. But should business management be considered as having similar professional role-specific responsibilities? Does the role of a business manager, like the role of a physician or lawyer or auditor, for example, serve social ends important enough that people in those roles can sometimes be exempt from normal ethical responsibilities? Rather than try to answer this question in general, it is advisable to consider this question in more specific terms. What specific responsibilities do business managers have to their employers? What happens when these responsibilities conflict with other interests and responsibilities?

One important area of conflicting managerial responsibilities occurs when a manager is also a professional. Lawyers and auditors, for example, have specific professional responsibilities that can trump both their own personal interests and the interests of their business employers. Perhaps the Arthur Andersen case illustrates this point most famously. Andersen's auditors were paid by Enron, but their responsibilities conflicted with the interests of Enron's executive management and stockholders. This issue parallels another conflict between professional and managerial responsibilities that made headlines in 1986.

In January 1986 the space shuttle *Challenger* exploded just after takeoff, killing all seven crew members. In the aftermath of this disaster, public attention focused on decisions made in the hours before launch. Later evidence showed that both the rocket manufacturer, Morton Thiokol, and NASA were concerned about the reliability of O-rings used to seal various rocket stages. Engineers at Morton Thiokol had found evidence that these O-rings failed to seal properly at low temperatures. For both financial and public relations reasons, both Thiokol and NASA faced pressure to launch on schedule, but as the launch date approached the weather forecast called for unusually low temperatures. At a prelaunch meeting on the evening before, Thiokol engineers renewed their recommendation to delay the launch. According to Roger Boisjoly, a Thiokol engineer responsible for the O-rings, senior Thiokol executives asked those present in the meeting to "make a management decision" and "take off your engineering hat and put on your management hat." Those present then voted to change the engineers' recommendation and advise NASA to proceed with the launch. The next morning, minutes after launch, the *Challenger* exploded as a result of O-ring failures.

Before turning to the question of whether or not business managers might have professional responsibilities that override the financial interests of their employers, we turn to an examination of the role of professionals and professional responsibility in business.

7.3 PROFESSIONAL ETHICS AND THE GATEKEEPER FUNCTION

There are many cases in which a person's professional duties override what are normally considered to be one's ethical responsibilities. As the executives at Thiokol implicitly recognized, professional responsibilities can sometimes conflict with the interests of other people. Lawyers, for example, have a duty to hold in confidence information about their client, even if doing so allows other people to be misled or deceived. An attorney may know that her client actually did commit a crime, but she has a professional duty not to reveal that information to the police. A journalist knows who leaked confidential government information to the press, but he has a professional duty not to reveal the name of the whistle-blower. A family member might want to know the nature of a patient's illness, but a physician has a professional duty to hold such information in confidence. As an employee of a hospital, a nurse has a responsibility to follow management directives, but as professionals, nurses have a responsibility to advocate for patients' interests even at the expense of the hospital's financial interests.

The discussion that opened this chapter pointed out that our responsibilities are a function of the relationships that we have with others. In general, these relationships can be understood in terms of the roles that we play: as parent, spouse, friend, teacher, and so forth. One's social role is determined by the web of relationships we have with others, and, thus, some responsibilities are role-specific. Within contemporary societies, many such roles are associated with certain professions. Typically, one thinks of doctors, nurses, engineers, and lawyers as professionals. Within business contexts, auditors, accountants, financial analysts, and insurance brokers are often considered professionals.

Professions are distinguished from other jobs in that a profession involves some very specialized knowledge or expertise (e.g., the law, medicine, engineering). Typically this is knowledge that serves the public good, and as a rule work as a professional must be certified by some public agency. Professionals may enjoy certain legal or social privileges (e.g., only doctors can write prescriptions, only lawyers can practice law, only engineers can certify building plans), and often, but not always, they are well compensated for their work. Importantly, for our purposes, professions have particular duties and responsibilities.

In general, we can think of professional duties as flowing from the special knowledge or expertise that professions have. Because this special expertise serves the public interest and because, lacking this expertise, others are made vulnerable by this disparity, society imposes special responsibilities on the professional. For example, as an engineer, Roger Boisjoly had a responsibility to ignore the recommendation of his supervisor and insist on a decision that would have hurt his employer financially. Ordinarily, an employee has a responsibility not to harm the employer's financial interests.

Within the business and economic context, some professions have evolved to serve very important functions within the economic system itself. Remember that even such a staunch defender of free market economics as Milton Friedman believes that markets can function only when certain conditions are met. It is universally recognized that markets must function within the law, they must assume full information, and they must be free from fraud and deception. Insuring that these conditions are met is an important internal function for market-based economic systems. Several important business professions, for example, attorneys, auditors, accountants, and financial analysts, function in just this way. Such professions can be thought of as "gatekeepers" or "watchdogs" in that their role is to insure that those who enter into the marketplace are playing by the rules and conforming to the very conditions that insure the market functions as it ought. These professions can be understood as intermediaries, functioning between the various parties in the market. Auditors verify a company's financial statements so that investors' decisions are free from fraud and deception. Analysts evaluate a company's financial prospects or creditworthiness so that banks and investors can make informed decisions. Attorneys function to insure that decisions and transactions conform to the law. Indeed, even boards of directors can be understood in this way. Boards function as intermediaries between a company's stockholders and its executives, and they should insure that executives act on behalf of the stockholders' interests.

Unfortunately, and awkwardly, many of these professional intermediaries are paid by the business that they watch over. As the Arthur Andersen case so clearly demonstrated, this can create real conflicts between a professional's responsibility and his or her financial interests. Certified *public* accountants have a professional responsibility to the public. But, they work for clients whose financial interests are not always served by full, accurate, and independent disclosure of financial information. Thus, real conflicts exist between professional duties and a professional's self-interest.

In one sense, the ethical issues regarding such professional responsibilities are clear. Because professional gatekeeper duties are necessary conditions for economic legitimacy, they should trump whatever responsibilities an employee might otherwise have. David Duncan's responsibilities as an auditor should have overridden the *prima facie* responsibility that he had to follow the directive of Enron's management and Arthur Andersen's financial interests in consulting for Enron. But knowing what one's duties are and fulfilling those duties are two separate issues.

In explaining this point, philosophers sometimes distinguish between two different meanings of having a *reason* to do something. In one sense, a reason refers to the legitimacy or justification for acting in a certain way. On this account, having a reason means to be justified in doing what one does. As an auditor, David Duncan had a good reason, i.e., he was justified, to blow the whistle on Enron's deceptive accounting practices. But in another sense, having a reason means something more like being motivated to act in a certain way. Reason in this sense is less a logical or cognitive issue than it is a psychological one. While Duncan had a reason to act, there were many reasons why he did not.

Much of philosophical ethics is concerned with the justificatory sense of reason. But we still want to ask why, given that there was an ethical justification for doing so, didn't Duncan do as he ought to have done? Answering this question returns us to the previous discussion in chapter 1 of personal morality and social ethics.

As a matter of personal morality, we must recognize that acting on principle sometimes can require real courage, or discipline, or willpower. It is exactly for this reason that virtue ethics encourages the development of personal habits and character that will make it easier to act in ways that we know are ethically right. Perhaps David Duncan lacked the courage of his convictions, perhaps he feared for his job, or perhaps he simply didn't care about his responsibilities. Courage, fear, caring are all matters of character. It would seem that our ethical judgment about David Duncan and other auditors involved in Enron is less a matter of what they knew or didn't know than it is a matter of their character. It was not as if auditors don't know that fraud is wrong. They knew it was wrong, but lacked the motivation and character to act accordingly.

While each of us individually is responsible for our own character, virtue ethics also emphasizes the importance of moral development and moral education. Our habits are developed over time and they are greatly influenced by our surroundings. Thus, one lesson to be drawn from such consideration is that businesses must be conscious of the culture and surroundings in which employees work. Had Arthur Andersen or Enron a different corporate culture, a culture in which principles were respected and individuals encouraged to act ethically, perhaps auditors such as David Duncan would have been more likely to act according to their professional duties.

There are also implications of this for social ethics. If we recognize that the gatekeeper function is necessary for the very functioning of economic markets, and if we also recognize that it can be difficult for individuals to fulfill their gatekeeper duties, then society has a responsibility to make changes. For example, as long as auditors are paid by the clients on whom they report, there will always be an apparent conflict of interest between their duties as auditors and their own financial interests. This is a good reason to make structural changes in how public accounting operates. Perhaps it ought to be boards rather than management who hire and work with auditors. Perhaps public accounting ought to be paid for by public fees. Perhaps legal protection or sanctions ought to be created to shield professionals from conflicts of interest. Perhaps the law should prohibit audit firms from working as consultants to the very firm they audit. From the perspective of social ethics rather than personal morality, certain structural changes would be the more appropriate response to the accounting scandals of recent years.

This discussion has emphasized the professions as conventionally understood to point out that business managers often have conflicting responsibilities. We turn now to the more general ethical responsibilities that a person, in his or her role as professional manager, might have.

7.4 MANAGERIAL RESPONSIBILITY AND CONFLICTS OF INTERESTS

What specific responsibilities do business managers have to their employers? To answer this question we first need to consider the interests of the business principal, described variously as the owner, the employer, the investor, the stockholder, or the firm itself. These diverse terms suggest that this issue may not be as simple as it at first appears. Surely there are some clear cases in which the interests of the principal determine the agent's responsibility unambiguously. If I hire a real estate agent, my interest is in having my property sold to a qualified buyer at the highest price in the shortest time. But what interests should be served by a corporate manager? The answer suggested by the narrow view of managerial responsibility (as represented by Milton Friedman) is to conduct the business in accordance with the "desires of the owners" which is "to make as much money as possible."

This apparently simple answer disguises a variety of issues. In a corporate setting, the "owners" range from institutional investors representing thousands of individuals and institutions to day traders seeking a fast profit from slight changes (up or down) in stock price. Consider who you would identify as the owners of Enron Corporation. Besides thousands of individual investors, Enron stock was owned by employees through their 401(k) retirement plans, senior executives, mutual funds, retirement plans from many states and institutions, and numerous other institutional investors such as banks and insurance companies. As we have seen, the stock was also used as collateral for loans and joint ventures involving various partnerships. These diverse owners have equally diverse desires. Some individual investors buy stock because they believe in the company and its products; some are playing the stock for short-term gain. Some see their stock ownership as an investment in a company and its technology; some see it as a long-term investment for personal retirement and security; some see it as a game for short-term profit. Given this variety, it is clear that the desires of owners can and do conflict. Most obviously, long-term fiscal stability for a business can be attained only when managers wisely reinvest in the corporation itself. But reinvesting in capital, labor, and research and development comes at a price: lower returns, at least in the short term, for stockholders. On the other hand, managing a business solely with an eye towards increasing share price can undermine the stability and security of the firm. This is what *Fortune* magazine called the "cult of the shareholder" and identifies as the "single biggest reason" behind such recent accounting scandals as Enron and Arthur Andersen.[4]

For a more adequate model of the owner-manager relationship, we can return to the discussion of stakeholder theory from chapter 3. That discussion distinguished between owners and investors and concluded that managers have a responsibility to a variety of stakeholders. The corporation is not simply the personal property of private stockholders to do with as they choose. It is a social institution that serves a variety of individual and institutional stakeholders. On this view, business managers have a responsibility to represent the best interests of the company, not just the financial desires of investors. In general, the interest of the company is to survive as a fiscally stable enterprise providing goods and services to consumers, wages and benefits to employees, and a competitive rate of return on investment to stockholders.

As a contrast to this model, consider the transition of Enron from an energy company to a trading company. As a gas pipeline company, Enron supplied consumers with needed goods and services. Under an earlier era of government regulation, Enron could have continued doing this with a guaranteed reasonable rate of return for investors and a stable workplace for employees. But by succumbing to "the cult of the shareholder," Enron management ignored the interests of all but a few stakeholders and the tragic result was that nearly everyone lost.

But if the varied interests of various stakeholders are the interests that a business manager ought to serve, what interests might inappropriately conflict with these? As a first answer we can say which interests do *not* constitute an unethical conflict for managers. Those would be all those interests that stem from the professional responsibilities of managers. Since managers are hired exactly for their professional competence, exercising that competence even at the expense of stockholder profit does not unethically conflict with the manager's responsibility to the "owners" of business. Consider, for example, when Sherron Watkins complained to senior executives about Enron's accounting practices. Apparently, from the perspective of Lay and Skilling, her acts appeared disloyal. But since Watkins's managerial authority stemmed from her professional competence as an accountant, her responsibility to the business enterprise itself was to exercise that professional competence and not sacrifice it for short-term financial gain.

We can consider this issue in slightly different terms. Every decision that a business manager makes imposes costs on someone. As any standard economic textbook suggests, *costs* are understood as opportunities forgone, things given up. Any decision, by definition, involves giving up some alternatives in favor of others, that is, involves imposing costs. An ethical and competent manager will impose costs—make decisions—that serve the end of maintaining a fiscally stable enterprise. A responsible manager will do this by balancing the competing demands of various stakeholders. This is the expertise that managers bring to business and this is the expertise that should not be sacrificed for the narrow interests of only one group of stakeholders. Managerial decisions will sometimes impose undesired costs on stockholder/investors, as they sometimes will for employees, consumers, and other stakeholders. Such decisions are ethically responsible, contrary to what the narrow view of managerial responsibility would hold, when they are done for the best interests of the firm itself.

Of course, there can be cases in which managers impose costs upon stockholders (and other stakeholders) unethically. Conflicts of interest occur when the personal interest of managers interfere with the professional judgments of managers. When Andrew Fastow represented Enron as its chief financial officer in negotiations with firms in which he held a position of managing partner, and from which he would eventually "earn" $30 million, he was involved in a straightforward conflict of interest. Since the primary responsibility of a manager is to exercise that professional judgment conscientiously, an unethical conflict of interest occurs when personal interests hinder that judgment. In effect, the vulnerability that characterizes the principal-agent relationship is exploited for the personal benefit of the agent. It is difficult to believe that Fastow was representing the best interests of Enron stakeholders in these negotiations.

Another clear case of an unethical conflict of interest occurs with the case of kickbacks. A *kickback* is an illegal payment that occurs when a portion of some payment is paid back—kicked back—to the payer as an incentive to make the original payment. So, for example, a manager who awards a contract to a construction company might receive money or other benefits back from that company as a condition of receiving, and an incentive for awarding, the contract. Since this personal benefit interferes with the professional judgment of the manager by improperly influencing the decision, kickbacks are unethical conflicts of interest.

Consider, as an example, what is referred to as *soft money* within the securities industry. According to critics, a widespread practice in the securities industry amounts to little more than institutionalized kickbacks. Soft money payments occur when financial advisors receive payments from a brokerage firm to pay for research and analyst services that, in theory, should be used to benefit the clients of those advisors. Such payments can benefit clients if they are used by the advisor to improve the advice offered to the client. The practice gets abused, becomes an unethical conflict of interest, when the money is used for the personal benefit of the advisor. In 1998 the Securities and Exchange Commission released a report that showed extensive abuse of soft money. Examples included payments used for office rent and equipment, personal travel and vacations, memberships at private clubs, and automobile expenses. In such cases, the client could no longer trust the integrity of the professional judgment of their financial advisor.

This example points to the importance of trust in the relationships of business manager to various stakeholders. While trust is an important aspect of any contractual relationship (I trust that you will deliver the product I purchased from you), it is particularly important in situations such as the principal-agent relation when one party is vulnerable to the acts of the other. If a manager can legally commit a business to innumerable obligations, the stakeholders of that business must be able to trust the judgment of that manager. The general category of trust will be a helpful way to introduce our discussion of specific employee responsibilities within business.

7.5 TRUST AND LOYALTY IN THE WORKPLACE

Because managers have authority over corporate resources and because all other stakeholders depend on the manager's decisions on how to use those resources, it is essential that stakeholders be able to trust managers. To trust someone is to be confident in and rely upon their judgment when one is vulnerable to their decisions. With Enron's stock price falling, CEO Lay advised employees to trust him and the company. While he continued to sell his own shares, many employees lost the bulk of their retirement accounts. But what makes a manager worthy of trust? What character traits, which virtues, makes someone trustworthy?

The first responsibility of a trustworthy manager is to develop and maintain professional competence and expertise. In general employees hired for a professional competence, whether this is competence as an engineer, accountant, lawyer, financial analyst, programmer, and the like, have a responsibility to ensure that their judgments are informed by the best professional standards available. When investors trusted Arthur Andersen's audit of Enron, they assumed (mistakenly) that the auditors were exercising due diligence in their accounting practices.

Beyond competence other responsibilities are often attributed to business managers. Among the most common and controversial is an alleged duty of loyalty. Loyalty is understood as a willingness to make personal sacrifices in the interest of the firm and, following the model of agency law in which agents have a legal duty of loyalty, it is often claimed the employees have an ethical responsibility to be loyal employees.

To what degree do any employees have a responsibility to make personal sacrifices for the firm? Consider the following case as a means to understand loyalty, and disloyalty, in the workplace. Early each summer a large bank hires a dozen recent college graduates for credit analyst positions. As often happens in corporate hiring, these new employees go through several months of intense training. In the case with which I am familiar, the bank hired several finance and accounting professors from a distinguished university to teach specialized and advanced courses to these trainees. In effect, the bank pays these new employees a salary while they receive state-of-the-art training in finance and banking. When these employees completed this training they became highly marketable in the local banking community. Several of these employees were soon offered jobs at competing banks at salaries well above what they were earning at the original bank. Would these employees be disloyal if they resigned to take a position at a competing bank?

Philosopher Ronald Duska argues that employees have no responsibility of loyalty to their employers.[5] Duska characterizes loyalty as a willingness to sacrifice that is based in relationships of mutual enrichment. One can be loyal only to those persons and institutions with whom one is engaged in a project of common benefit. On Duska's view, the employment relationship is simply a contractual arrangement that serves the individual self-interests of the parties. Because the overriding goal of business is profit, "companies are not the kind of things that are properly the objects of loyalty." It follows that employees have the responsibility only to uphold their end of the contract and have no responsibility to make sacrifices beyond that. If, in the banking case, the employees had no contractual commitment to the original bank, they would be free to leave their position and work for a competing bank. Loyalty or disloyalty is simply irrelevant to situations in which both parties seek their own self-interest.

Duska is particularly concerned that loyalty in business too often is a one-way street. "Loyal" employees are expected to sacrifice for the firm, but seldom is business willing to sacrifice for employees. Just as the bank would be willing to fire those trainees who performed poorly, employees should be free to leave a job to improve their salary. The case of Enron employees who blindly remained loyal to Kenneth Lay, while he sold millions of dollars of Enron stock, is an excellent example of what concerns Duska. The lack of reciprocity between employers and their employees is what underlies Duska's claim that a company is an inappropriate object of loyalty.

One can quibble with Duska's definition of loyalty. Perhaps he makes too much of the notion of sacrifice. While a willingness to sacrifice might be a part of loyalty, it would seem the devotion and faithfulness to a common goal is both more essential to loyalty and what explains the willingness to sacrifice. Perhaps Duska also underestimates the possibility that some businesses are committed to the benefit of their employees. One thinks of Aaron Feuerstein and Malden Mills as described in chapter 1 as an example of reciprocal loyalty. Finally, Duska may also underestimate the willingness of business to sacrifice for employees. One could also point out the sacrifice that the bank made in paying for the training that its employees were now selling to competitors.[6] Nevertheless, Duska's general point is well taken. Claims for loyalty can sometimes be little more than a disguised way to exploit employees' willingness to make sacrifices for the firm. As the Enron case showed all too clearly, there are few things more tragic in business than long-term loyal and devoted employees losing their jobs when managerial decisions go awry. Loyalty can be a risky thing for nonmanagerial employees. Unless and until the firm has demonstrated a willingness to sacrifice on behalf of employees, those employees have little reason to demonstrate loyalty to the firm.

But once again, the case may be different for managerial employees. The firm, after all, has placed trust in managerial decisions and as a manager the employee has assumed the firm's interests as his or her own. The firm and all its stakeholders rely on the manager to protect their interests. Thus, being faithful to those interests and being willing to sacrifice personal interests for that goal does seem more appropriate than in the case of nonmanagerial employees. This is not to say, however, that managers have a duty to be totally devoted to the firm. The firm's interests themselves, even the wide interests implied by a stakeholder model, must always be balanced against other ethical concerns.

Consider two potential cases of managerial disloyalty. In Sherron Watkins's case, some Enron management thought her to be a disloyal employee. But surely charges of disloyalty here are little more than criticism aimed at protecting the self-interests of both Enron itself and individuals within it. If this was a case of disloyalty, it was a case in which there was no ethical responsibility to remain loyal. This suggests that loyalty is not always a good thing.

A second case involves a CEO who is in the midst of negotiating a major contract for her firm and is offered a more attractive position elsewhere. Assume the contract can secure the business's financial stability for many years and depends a great deal on both the negotiating skills of this CEO and her abilities and reputation as an effective manager. If she were to walk away now, there is a likelihood that the deal would fall through and the firm be considerably harmed. Does she have a responsibility to remain loyal to the firm and pass up the alternative position? (Did Andrew Fastow have a responsibility to forgo $30 million in personal profit by remaining loyal to his duty as Enron's CFO?)

On Duska's view, she does not. This would simply be a case of the self-interest of the employee conflicting with the self-interest of the firm. Because the firm would never be willing to sacrifice its self-interest (profitability) out of loyalty to the CEO, the CEO has no responsibility to sacrifice her self-interest for the firm. Yet, there is something ethically troubling with that option. The firm, and its many stakeholders, is relying on the actions of its CEO and is vulnerable to harm that only the CEO can prevent. Unlike the Enron case, this is a harm that is undeserved and that the firm can rightfully expect the CEO to minimize, if not prevent. It can rightfully expect that because, at least implicitly, the CEO has made a commitment to do so.

This suggests a reasonable conclusion regarding employee loyalty. If loyalty means a willingness to sacrifice one's own interests by going above and beyond ordinary employee responsibilities, then, as Duska suggests, we ought to be suspicious of calls for employee loyalty. Yet we also must recognize that some employees commit themselves to make such sacrifices when they agree to act as the legal agents of business. On this perspective, perhaps workplace loyalty is better understood as a willingness to remain faithful to one's commitments even at the cost of lost personal benefits. A business firm ought to be able to trust that employees will keep their commitments, but it has no ethical basis to expect employees to go beyond this and sacrifice for the firm.

7.6 RESPONSIBILITIES TO THIRD PARTIES: HONESTY, WHISTLEBLOWING, AND INSIDER TRADING

The focus of this chapter so far has been on the responsibilities that employees have to the firm. But this does not exhaust the range of employee responsibilities. Beyond the normal responsibilities that all people have and the responsibilities that we have as employees, employees can also have responsibilities to third parties outside of the workplace. We will look at three topics that involve employee responsibilities to parties other than their employers.

Honesty

It might seem obvious to claim that employees have an ethical responsibility to be honest. Nevertheless, there are some who think that business has many occasions in which something less than full honesty is, if not required, at least tolerated. One such occasion, in advertising and marketing, will be examined in greater detail in a following chapter. But there are many other occasions in which a person working in business has an incentive to be dishonest to co-workers, to customers, to competitors, and to employers. At this point we will consider a more general claim that bluffing in business is ethically permissible.

In an essay that has become a classic within business ethics, Albert Carr argued that deception and bluffing are acceptable strategies within business.[7] Carr argued that business has the impersonal character of a game and, like such games as poker, business has its own rules and standards. Bluffing, lying, deception, and manipulation are all, on Carr's view, part of successful business strategy and are perfectly permissible within business. Carr's argument is an argument from analogy; business is relevantly like poker and just as the game of poker is exempt from the ordinary requirements of morality so, too, is business:

> Poker's own brand of ethics is different from the ethical ideals of civilized human relationships. The game calls for distrust of the other fellow. It ignores the claim of friendship. Cunning deception and concealment of one's strength and intentions, not kindness and openheartedness, are vital in poker. No one thinks any the worse of poker on that account. And no one should think any the worse of the game of business because its standards of right and wrong differ from the prevailing traditions of morality in our society.[8]

Significant and persuasive challenges can be raised against Carr's argument. He overestimates the prevalence and acceptability of dishonesty within business, for example. There are also major disanalogies between business and games such as poker that weaken the conclusions drawn from that analogy. Finally, even if business did have its own set of ethical conventions, that fact alone would not exempt business from ordinary ethical evaluations. Nevertheless, there can be some business situations in which dishonesty is common and apparently acceptable. Consider the case of bluffing during contract negotiations.

Several years ago Kirby Puckett, the popular star centerfielder for the Minnesota Twins baseball team, was negotiating a new contract with the team. During this time he made a very well-publicized trip to Boston where he visited the Boston Red Sox, toured their baseball park, and had contract discussions with their management. Minnesota fans and sportswriters reacted quickly to put pressure on the team to re-sign Puckett to a long-term and very lucrative contract. After re-signing with the Twins, Puckett admitted that he always intended to re-sign with the Twins and had used the trip to Boston as a negotiating tool to get the Twins to increase their offer.

This type of bluffing is not uncommon in contract negotiation. One party leads the other to believe something that is not true (i.e., I will take another job if you don't improve the offer, we will go on strike unless our wages are increased, we will sell this product to another customer if you don't agree to the sale today). Is such bluffing unethical?

Three general reasons are typically cited to explain the ethical responsibility to be honest. A utilitarian rationale concludes that dishonesty undermines the ability of people to communicate and thus will have adverse social consequences. Honesty and the trust that it creates are essential preconditions for all cooperative social activities. The Kantian tradition in ethics argues that dishonesty treats others as a means to our own ends and thus disrespects the dignity of other persons. A third ethical perspective looks not to dishonesty's effect on others, but to what dishonesty does to the dishonest person. A dishonest person must maintain two identities: (1) the one shown to the "victim" of the dishonesty and (2) the one hidden from the victim who carries out the deception. But this practice, especially if practiced habitually, undermines a person's own integrity. Integrity involves a moral wholeness, authenticity, and coherence. Integrity plays an important role in establishing one's own identity and self-worth. The dishonest person, by necessarily maintaining two *personas,* lacks moral integrity.[9]

If these are the three major explanations of the value of honesty, dishonesty and bluffing in business can be ethical only if they adequately respond to these concerns. In general, it is plausible to claim that some dishonest acts can have beneficial social consequences that do not threaten the stability of underlying social practices. It would be harder to claim, however, that routine dishonesty would not erode the trust that does seem essential to social cooperation. A view such as Carr's might also be able to respond to some of the Kantian concern. Carr's suggests that "a falsehood ceases to be a falsehood when everyone involved know about it" and this implies that some dishonest acts would not manipulate others and treat persons as mere means. But this assumes that the victims know that they are being bluffed and that they consent to participating in the practice. While both assumptions might sometimes be true in some business situations, it is unlikely that they commonly occur. A bluff can work as a bluff only if the person being bluffed believes that it is true, that is, only if he or she is deceived (e.g., if the Twins really believed that Puckett was bluffing, they would have had no incentive to increase their offer). Furthermore, unlike poker games, individuals often have no choice but to participate in business practices. Finally, while perhaps an occasional dishonest act doesn't threaten one's own integrity, a social practice that encourages and endorses dishonesty certainly would.

Consider the continuous public reassurances made by Kenneth Lay during the time Enron's stock was falling. It would be easy to interpret his actions as a strategy aimed at bluffing investors. If enough people *believed* Enron's stock was stable and stopped their selling, the stock price would stabilize whether or not the company itself was financially stable. Was this bluff justified?

No doubt Lay would argue that it was. Because the collapse of Enron would harm many people, a bluff aimed at keeping the company afloat would serve the "greater good." However, this would be a disingenuous application of the utilitarian principle of attaining the greatest good for the greatest number. Anyone who bought or held on to Enron stock as a result of Lay's bluff would, at the very least, be taking a much greater risk than they believed. A successful bluff on this occasion would have achieved the greater good of some (i.e., those, like Lay himself, who were looking to continue selling the stock) at the expense of many others.

Whistleblowing

A whistleblower is an employee or other insider who informs the public or a government agency of an illegal, harmful, or unethical activity done by their business or institution. Had Sherron Watkins informed the Securities and

Exchange Commission, rather than Kenneth Lay, of Enron's accounting irregularities, she would have been performing an act of whistleblowing. The language of "blowing the whistle" comes from sports where a referee or umpire
blows a whistle to stop play and call attention to illegal or improper conduct.
Whistleblowing raises ethical concerns because, unlike the neutral umpire in
sports, employees are considered by some people to be team members whose
loyalty to the team should preclude blowing the whistle. Thus whistleblowing pits responsibilities to third parties (those potentially harmed by the business's activities) against employees' responsibility to their employer. Because
whistleblowing puts the whistleblower at risk, it also raises concerns about
the employee's responsibility to self and to one's dependents. Balancing these
three types of responsibilities—to the public, to one's employer, and to one's
own commitments—sets the ethical context for whistleblowing. The ethical
issue of whistleblowing thus involves both its permissibility and its obligatori-
ness. Is it permissible to blow the whistle on one's employer? Is it ever ethically
obligatory to do so?

Philosopher Richard DeGeorge has developed a persuasive analysis of the
ethics of whistleblowing.[10] DeGeorge argues that three conditions must be met
before whistleblowing can be ethically permissible. First, there must be a real
threat of serious harm that the whistleblowing seeks to address. Since the act of
whistleblowing itself can cause harm to the firm and its other employees, the
harm that whistleblowing seeks to prevent must override the harm that it does.
Second, the whistleblower should first seek to prevent the harm more immediately through channels internal to the firm. This condition seeks the most efficient means to prevent harm while minimizing the other harms that it can cause.
Third, if possible, the whistleblower should exhaust all internal procedures for
preventing the harm. DeGeorge recognizes that there can be occasions when
internal mechanisms are inappropriate, but in general potential whistleblowers
should make good-faith efforts to work within the firm. When such efforts are
made and the potential harm is real, whistleblowing is ethically permissible.

DeGeorge argues that whistleblowing becomes ethically obligatory when
two further conditions are met. First, the whistleblower must have documented
evidence to convince impartial observers of the firm's role in causing the harm.
Without such evidence an employee has no obligation to take the risks inherent in blowing the whistle. Finally, the whistleblower must have good reason
to believe that blowing the whistle will prevent the harm. One cannot have an
ethical obligation to take significant risks in order to achieve doubtful benefits.

Insider Trading

Insider trading generally refers to the practice of buying or selling securities
(stocks and bonds) on the basis of nonpublic information that one has obtained
as an "insider." The clearest example would be a case in which a business manager or director buys (or sells depending on the likely effect of the information)
a large quantity of the firm's stock based on inside information just before that

information is made public. By buying (or selling) the stock at a price below (or above) what the market will demand when the information is made public, the insider seemingly has benefited inappropriately from inside information. That insider has profited personally from inside information in a way that the law says is illegal and most people think to be unethical. Insider trading raises interesting ethical questions concerning one's responsibilities to the firm, to stockholders, and to financial markets.

One of the most egregious aspects of the Enron case was the insider trading that occurred throughout 2001. Virtually every top executive sold significant amounts of Enron stock at a time when they had reason to believe, or should have had reason to believe, that Enron was in serious trouble. While maintaining a public façade with assurances that Enron was in good financial health, which helped keep investors willing to buy the stock at inflated prices, these executives reaped personal fortunes selling the stock to unsuspecting investors. Despite appearances that insider trading is unethical, some observers argue that it is ethically appropriate. Such arguments are usually market-based and contend that inside trading is an efficient means to disseminate accurate information that, in turn, moves stock prices closer to the point that reflects their true value. Large purchases (or sales) of stock efficiently provide information to financial markets that will react quickly in the direction of equilibrium. The sales of insider stock sent the correct message to the market: The price quickly sought the equilibrium that accurately reflected Enron's worth. Others argue that allowing insider trading would provide strong incentives for insiders to work to benefit the firm.[11]

But neither of these arguments is ethically persuasive. Critics charge that even if insider trading moved financial markets towards efficiency, it would do so only by unfair and unethical means. Anyone who bought the stock sold by Kenneth Lay and his associates, especially if they did so on the basis of his reassurances, were straightforwardly defrauded. Critics also point out that an insider can benefit by trading on bad news as well as good news and thus might well have an incentive to work against the firm's best interests. Again, as the Enron case so clearly demonstrated, employees can use inside information to sell a stock before bad news becomes public.

Three arguments, each relying on a particular understanding of employee responsibilities, are cited in ethical criticisms of insider trading. Some argue that insider trading is unfair to other security traders since those outsiders lack the same information and thus are unfairly disadvantaged in the marketplace. A second critique claims that the information used in insider trading is the property of the firm. Thus, when insiders use it without permission and in ways that harm other stockholders, they have done something unethical. A third argument claims that insider trading violates the trust implied by the fiduciary relationship between a firm and its employees.

The unfairness argument may not be as convincing as it first appears. As an individual investor I would certainly feel mistreated if I bought/sold stock at a high (or low) price to someone who knew in advance that the price was about to fall (or rise). But have I been treated unfairly? Does the other party have a responsibility to me to disclose the information it possesses? It would seem not. Unequal information is not, in itself, unfair. Suppose another person had simply conducted more diligent and extensive research than I and as a result was able to benefit at my expense. There seems no ethical problem if he or she uses that unequal information to his or her advantage (and my disadvantage) in a stock transaction. The unfairness claim is more persuasive when I am disadvantaged by inside information to which I lack equal and fair access. What seems unfair is the advantage that one gets by virtue of being an insider. It is not just unequal information, but it is unequal in a way that even due diligence cannot equalize. But, do insiders have a responsibility to provide other traders with equal access to inside information? To whom do insiders owe responsibility?

When an insider trades on inside information there are two other types of investors who might claim to be harmed. One is the person, let's call him the potential investor, who claims that, had he had the inside information, he could have benefited as much as the inside trader. Thus, he was harmed in the sense of being denied a possible windfall. But this person has little legitimate ethical claim on what could have been. Consider the complaints of Enron employees who were prevented from selling their 401(k) stock during Enron's collapse. If their complaint is that they, too, should have been able to sell Enron stock at artificially inflated prices, they would have little ethical support. If they knew what Lay and others knew and sold on that basis, they would have been just as guilty of unfair insider trading as the others.

A second type of investor, let's call her an actual investor, is the person who sells her stock to the insider (or purchases it from, in the case of future detrimental information) without knowing what the insider knows. In this case, the stock transaction is a zero-sum game where one person's gain is another's loss. This transaction is more troubling and begins to looks a lot more like a case of fraud.

Again, consider the Enron case of insider trading. Senior managers knew that accounting irregularities were likely to become public, and in anticipation of this news, they began selling large amounts of stock (or exercising options). In the following weeks, the stock price did collapse and they benefited accordingly. Potential investors (or sellers) who did not have an equal opportunity to reap similar windfalls cannot claim to have had any legitimate right violated. It does not seem that the insider has harmed this potential investor in any ethically relevant way. But the actual investor, the person who bought her stock from the insiders, suffers a harm that is more real. Specifically, this harm stems in large part from the fact that the stockholder was harmed by someone—company insiders—who had a responsibility to act on her behalf.

Thus, insider trading violates responsibilities that corporate agents have to their principals, and this suggests that the ethical criticisms of insider trading based on property rights and fiduciary duties are connected to the unfairness claim. The inside information is not, by definition, public. It is private information that rightfully belongs to the firm. Managers have a fiduciary responsibility to the firm that prohibits benefiting personally at the expense of the firm. Trading on inside information involves misappropriating private resources for personal gain in a way that harms the firm's investors. Because investors rely on managers to represent their interests, insiders who trade on inside information violate that trust and defraud the very people they have a responsibility to represent. While some unspecified future investors may benefit from more efficient and accurate stock prices as a result of insider trading, actual investors are denied benefits that they had legitimate ethical claims to.

REFLECTIONS ON THE CHAPTER DISCUSSION CASE

Enron and Arthur Andersen have become synonyms for corporate greed and corruption, but as it turned out this case was only the start of a wave of corporate and accounting scandals. The list of companies and people implicated in ethical or legal scandals since 2001 is extensive: WorldCom, Global Crossing, Adelphia Communications, Sunbeam, Tyco, ImClone, Tenet Healthcare, HealthSouth, Rite Aid, Merrill Lynch, J.P. Morgan, Citigroup, Marsh & McLennan, Al Dunlap, Martha Stewart, Dennis Kozlowski, even Richard Grasso and the New York Stock Exchange itself.

It can be tempting to look for a single cause when reflecting on these scandals. Was it individual greed? Did people just not understand what they were doing? Did they not know right from wrong? Was it a matter of lack of government oversight? Lack of managerial leadership? The hope is that if the cause can be identified, changes can be made to prevent such things from occurring again.

Identifying the causes of corporate scandals and creating strategies to prevent them are an important part of business ethics. As described in chapter 1, philosophical ethics involves issues both of personal morality and social ethics. Using this framework, we can assess corporate scandals at three levels: in terms of individuals, in terms of corporate structure and practices, and in terms of governmental and social institutions.

Examining this case from the point of view of an individual raises a number of questions. Some questions involve ethical justifications: What would you have done if you were Sherron Watkins or David Duncan? What should they have done differently? The individual perspective also challenges us to think about personal motivation: Why did these people act as they did? How could they have acted differently? How do we explain the difference between people who succumb to temptation of riches and those who resist it?

From an institutional perspective, these scandals have given rise to significant activity within corporations. Human resource departments now take ethics training seriously in a way they never did previously. Many businesses now have ethics officers and ombudsmen on staff to encourage employees to act responsibly and to provide them with opportunities to report unethical activities. The topic of corporate culture has drawn significant attention from managers seeking to encourage ethical behavior by setting high ethical expectations. Enron and Arthur Andersen provide excellent case studies for organizational behavior. What did they do wrong as an organization? What structural changes could have been made that might have prevented the implosion of Enron? How do employees learn a company's norms and values? How can high ethical standards be transmitted from theory to practice?

Finally, from a governmental perspective the recent scandals have already resulted in significant legal action. The U.S. Congress passed the Sarbanes-Oxley Act in 2002. Major provisions of that law include a requirement that financial reports be certified by a company's CEO and CFO; a ban on personal loans to executive officers and directors; faster reporting of trades by insiders; prohibition on insider trades during pension fund blackout periods; and criminal and civil penalties for securities violations, including significantly longer jail sentences and larger fines for corporate executives who misstate financial statements. In addition to this new law, prosecuters throughout the country, and New York State Attorney General Elliot Spitzer most famously, are more regularly investigating and prosecuting corporate crime. Neither the Congress nor the Securities and Exchange Commission has banned the dual audit and consulting role for accounting firms that many believe played a major role in these scandals.

REVIEW QUESTIONS

1. Explain how responsibilities can depend upon the relationships one has with other people.
2. How is the relationship between a person and her real estate agent or lawyer similar to the relationship between an employer and employee? How are they different?
3. How might the narrow view of employee responsibilities be defended ethically? What are its shortcomings?
4. What is a conflict of interest and when and under what conditions are they unethical? Do the dual roles of auditor and consultant, as played by Arthur Andersen and other major accounting firms, constitute an unethical conflict of interest?
5. Define *trust* and *loyalty*. Do all employees have a responsibility to be trustworthy? To be loyal? Why does Duska believe that loyalty is inappropriate in the workplace?
6. In what way is business like poker? In what ways is it different?
7. What conditions does DeGeorge suggest are necessary to make whistleblowing ethically permissible? When is it ethically required? On DeGeorge's grounds, would Sherron Watkins have been justified in blowing the whistle to the Securities and Exchange Commission?
8. Explain at least two ethical objections to insider trading. What, exactly, was wrong (if anything) with insiders selling Enron's stock throughout 2001?

ENDNOTES

[1]See "The Enron Disaster: Lies. Arrogance. Betrayal" by Bethany McLean, *Fortune,* December 24, 2001.

[2]Milton Friedman, "The Social Responsibility of Business Is to Increase Its Profits," The *New York Times Magazine,* September 13, 1970.

[3]Such a view is used by those who claim, for example, that employers have a right to test employees for drug use. Drug use presumably prevents an employee from performing at an optimal level. Because, from this perspective, employers have a legitimate expectation that employees do perform at such levels, they have a legitimate claim to know about and prevent employee drug use. See Joseph DesJardins and Ronald Duska, "Drug Testing in Employment," *Business and Professional Ethics Journal,* for a refutation of this claim.

[4]Readers should review the discussion of the classical model of corporate social responsibility from chapter 3 for a fuller analysis of this issue. The perspective emerging from this chapter parallels the emergence of stakeholder theory described in chapter 3. See also, "Dirty Numbers," *Fortune,* February 18, 2002, pp. 75–84.

[5]Ronald Duska, "Whistleblowing and Employee Loyalty," originally published in Joseph DesJardins and John McCall, eds., *Contemporary Issues in Business Ethics,* 2nd ed. (Belmont, CA: Wadsworth, 1990), pp. 142–146.

[6]This banking case is based on a situation with which I was personally familiar. Interestingly, a bank manager explained that the bank saw the training simply as an investment. They knew in advance that only a certain percentage of the trainees would remain with the bank long term and that these losses were already built into the salaries and training expenses. He didn't see the training expenses as a sacrifice and was unwilling to characterize those who left as disloyal.

[7]Albert Z. Carr, "Is Business Bluffing Ethical?" *Harvard Business Review* 46 (January–February, 1968).

[8]Ibid., p. 9.

[9]See Joseph Kupfer, "The Moral Presumption against Lying," *Review of Metaphysics,* vol. 36 (1982), for an insightful discussion of the harmful effects lying has on the liar's own character.

[10]Richard DeGeorge, *Business Ethics,* 5th ed. (Upper Saddle River, NJ: Prentice Hall, 151999), ch. 10.

[11]For good summaries of the arguments for and against insider trading, see Jennifer Moore, "What Is Really Unethical about Insider Trading?" *Journal of Business Ethics* 9, 1990, pp. 171–182; and Patricia Werhane, "The Ethics of Insider Trading," *Journal of Business Ethics* 8, 1989, pp. 841–845.

Marketing Ethics: Product Safety and Pricing

...ny sink. Brush cooking racks with a stiff wire brush to remove any remaining food... pointed away from face and spray from a distance of 9-12 inches. Allow foam to work for 20 minutes or longer. 3) Wipe rack with wet cloth or sponge, rinsing frequently. **4)** Follow Step 7 above.

KEEP OUT OF REACH OF CHILDREN.

DANGER: Contains sodium hydroxide **(LYE).**
WILL BURN SKIN AND EYES. Avoid contact with skin, eyes, mucous membranes and clothing.
HARMFUL IF SWALLOWED. Do not ingest. **AVOID BREATHING SPRAY MIST. WEAR LONG RUBBER GLOVES WHEN USING.**
FIRST AID: SKIN - rinse immediately and remove contaminated clothing, wash thoroughly with soap and water and continue flushing with water for at least 10 minutes. If discomfort persists, call a physician immediately.
EYES - rinse immediately, remove any contact lenses and continue flushing with water for at least 15 minutes. If discomfort persists, call a physician immediately.
IF SWALLOWED DO NOT INDUCE VOMITING - rinse mouth thoroughly with water, drink water or milk. Call a physician immediately.

Important Facts:
Encourage your local authorities to establish a program to recycle this can. This can is made from an average of 25% recycled steel (10% post-consumer).

Questions? Comments? Call 1-800-228-4722
Reckitt Benckiser...

L E A R N I N G   O B J E C T I V E S

After reading this chapter, you will be able to:

- Understand a range of ethical issues that arise in marketing;

- Apply an ethical framework for evaluating marketing ethics;

- Explain the ethical dimensions of products liability law ranging from caveat emptor to strict products liability;

- Explain the ethical issues surrounding the concept of negligence;

- Provide an ethical analysis of strict products liability;

- Explain the ethical issues involved in product pricing.

DISCUSSION CASE: Safety and Pricing in the Pharmaceutical Industry

B oth prescription and over-the-counter drugs have been at the center of some landmark ethical cases in marketing. One classic liability case involved the synthetic estrogen hormone DES (diethylstilbestrol). DES was prescribed beginning in 1940 to help women with some complications of pregnancy. The drug had been widely tested in clinical trials and initially proved successful in reducing the number of miscarriages. However, in the early 1970s a connection was discovered between the use of DES during pregnancy and clear cell cancer (adenocarcinoma) in a small number of daughters of women who had used DES during pregnancy. These cancers did not typically appear until more than a decade after the drug was used, with most appearing when the daughters were between 14 and 20 years old. In 1972 the FDA prohibited all marketing of the drug for use during pregnancy. DES became a classic case of strict products liability in which manufacturers were held liable for damages caused by the drug, despite the fact that they were not negligent in its design, manufacture, or marketing.

In recent years it has been alleged that antidepressant drugs such as Prozac and Zoloft are linked with an increased risk of suicide and violence. More than 50 million people worldwide, many of them young adults and children, have used these drugs to counter depression and anxiety. In the mid-1990s, the families of the victims of a multiple murder suicide sued Eli Lilly, maker of Prozac, alleging that Lilly withheld data critical of the drug's safety from the FDA. Lilly was acquitted at trial, but the verdict was later invalidated when it was disclosed that Lilly had secretly reached a financial settlement with the families.

More recently, the arthritis drug Vioxx was withdrawn from the market when studies suggested an increased risk of blood clots that could lead to strokes or heart attacks. On September 30, 2004, Vioxx's manufacturer Merck & Company announced a voluntary recall of the drug that was first introduced in 1999 as a pain reliever for arthritis. This was the largest recall of a prescription drug in history. Celebrex, a similar drug manufactured by Merck's rival Pfizer, had not been withdrawn as of January 2005. By all indications, both Vioxx and Celebrex had been effective in relieving the pain associated with arthritis. Both drugs had been heavily marketed by their manufacturers, and each was very profitable, reportedly earning more than $2 billion annually for Merck and Pfizer. In November 2004, the Food and Drug Administration, the federal regulatory body that oversees prescription drugs, announced that Vioxx may have contributed to as many as 27,000 heart attacks and cardiac deaths since it was introduced in 1999. The FDA did not order the recall, explaining that they had not yet had the opportunity to study the data related to the dangerous side effects. During the fall of 2004, allegations surfaced that Merck had received information about the greater risks associated with Vioxx a year prior to the recall. Critics charged that Merck continued to market the drug aggressively even after being advised of such risks and even advised their sales representatives on how to avoid answering questions relating to side effects.

Such allegations concerning Merck's actions regarding Vioxx stand in stark contrast to Merck's reputation that resulted from its actions with another of its drugs. Mectizan is a Merck drug that prevents river blindness, a disease prevalent in tropical nations. Caused by parasitic worms spread by insects living along tropical rivers, river blindness infects millions of people annually, causing severe rashes, itching, and loss of sight. A single tablet of Mectizan administered once a year can relieve the symptoms and prevent the disease from progressing.

On the surface, Mectizan would not be a very profitable drug to bring to market. The once-a-year dosage limits the demand for the drug among those people who require it. Further, the individuals most at risk for this disease are among the poorest people living in the poorest regions of Africa, Asia, Central America, and South America. In 1987 Merck began a program that provides Mectizan free of charge to people at risk for river blindness. Cooperating with the World Heath Organization, UNICEF, and the World Bank, Merck's program has donated more than 700 million tablets of Mectizan distributed to 40 million people each year since 1987. The program has also resulted in the development of a health care system, necessary to support and administer the program, in some of the poorest regions of the world. In 1998 Merck expanded the program to include people at risk for lymphatic filariasis (commonly known as elephantiasis). By 2004 Merck estimated that this program reached an additional 20 million people. By all accounts, Merck's Mectizan Donation Program has significantly improved the lives of tens of millions of the most vulnerable people on earth. Merck's actions were explained by reference to part of its corporate identity statement: "We are in the business of preserving and improving human life."

Merck is not the only pharmaceutical company with a reputation for taking very costly action to protect public health. In 1982 Johnson & Johnson voluntarily recalled its best-selling Tylenol® product when seven people died after consuming cyanide-laced packages of Tylenol®. While the evidence was soon clear that the packages had been tampered with after the product left Johnson & Johnson facilities, and while no packages outside of the Chicago area were involved, the company quickly and voluntarily issued a nationwide recall for all Tylenol® products. Some 31 million bottles of Tylenol®, valued at $100 million, were taken off the market. Beyond this cost, immediately after the recall Johnson & Johnson's stock price fell by 15 percent and Tylenol® lost significant market share to its competitors in the very competitive over-the-counter pain reliever market. Johnson & Johnson executives, including CEO James Burke, cited the company's credo in defending their action. That credo rank-orders Johnson & Johnson's responsibilities to customers first, followed by employees, management, local and world communities, and, only then, to stockholders. Johnson & Johnson's stock soon recovered, as did Tylenol®'s place as the leading brand of analgesic medication. Many observers believed that the quick and impressive response to this crisis played a role in this financial recovery.

As Merck and Johnson & Johnson discovered, exemplary actions within the competitive pharmaceutical industry can be very costly. Of course, not all companies are as willing to take such actions. In 2000 it was estimated that more than 25 million people living in sub-Saharan Africa are infected with the AIDS virus, a number that represents an increase of almost 4 million people over 1999. More than 2.5 million died of AIDS in the year 2000. It is estimated that over 16 million have already died of AIDS since this contemporary plague began in the early 1980s. Thirty-five percent of Botswana's population is reportedly infected with AIDS.

While there are no available cures for this disease, there are drugs available that can combat the disease and prolong the life of infected people. A year's supply of generic versions of these drugs can be manufactured for as little as $350 per person. Unfortunately, these drugs are protected by patents that are owned by major pharmaceutical companies. Patents and the corresponding property rights they create make the manufacture of generic versions of these drugs, without permission of and payment to the pharmaceutical companies, illegal. Even at the generic prices the drugs would be difficult for most infected people to afford. At the prices charged by the pharmaceutical companies, these drugs were impossible for them to obtain.

In December 1997 South Africa passed legislation that sought to remedy this situation. This law allowed South Africa to license the manufacture of generic versions of AIDS drugs without permission of the pharmaceutical companies that owned the patents. It also allowed the importation of these drugs from other countries where they are sold at lower prices, again without permission of the patent owners.

Before the law was passed, the pharmaceutical companies lobbied hard against it. Both the United States and the European Union, on behalf of the companies, also lobbied against the law. After it was passed, threatened legal action prevented South Africa from implementing the law. In early 2001, 39 of the world's largest pharmaceutical companies filed suit to overturn the South African law. The pharmaceutical companies offered several arguments to support their claim. They argued that the law violated the property rights created by their patents, that they deserved profits to pay for previous research, that they needed future profits to fund further research, and that without an adequate health care infrastructure to follow up and care for patients, the drugs would make little difference in the fight against AIDS. A few months later, in April 2001 the companies withdrew the lawsuit and agreed to negotiate with the South African government to find ways to make the drugs available at an affordable price. Some companies admitted that the lawsuit was a bad idea from the start and acknowledged that they should be working to help people with AIDS. Other companies conceded that they were influenced by strong international public opinion against the suit. By all accounts, the lawsuit was a public relations disaster. Critics further charged that the companies abandoned the suit only to avoid divulging information that they would have preferred to keep secret, including the amount of governmental support they receive for research, pricing policies, and the actual manufacturing costs of the drugs.

DISCUSSION QUESTIONS

1. Is it safe to assume that when you purchase a drug you will be safe from harm as long as you use the drug as it was prescribed?
2. Is it fair to hold companies liable for damages caused by their products when they were not negligent in manufacturing or marketing the product?
3. Assuming that neither were negligent, what ethical differences exist between the responsibility of the manufacturers of DES for the harms it caused and the responsibility of Johnson & Johnson for the harms caused by cyanide-laced Tylenol®?
4. In light of the Vioxx recall, what responsibilities does Pfizer have regarding its comparable drug Celebrex?
5. Many drugs, such as Mectizan, are effective yet not very profitable. Such drugs are often referred to as "orphan drugs" because, while worthy, no one is willing to step forward to be responsible for producing and marketing them. What responsibilities should pharmaceutical companies have for these orphan drugs?
6. Do you agree with Johnson & Johnson's credo that puts stockholders last in line of corporate responsibility?
7. Should lifesaving drugs be protected by patents? If so, for how long should a single company be allowed to control that drug's manufacture? If not, what incentives exist for a private company to research and develop lifesaving drugs?
8. Economists tells us that there are no free lunches. Making AIDS drugs available at low cost in Africa or making Mectizan available for free will mean that consumers elsewhere pay higher prices for their drugs. Should lifesaving pharmaceuticals be priced according to the user's ability to pay? Should, for example, AIDS patients in the United States subsidize AIDS patients in Africa? Should the consumers of Merck's other drugs subsidize the Mectizan program? Should Merck's stockholders?
9. When deciding on the price to charge for lifesaving drugs, should executives of pharmaceutical companies follow Milton Friedman's advice to "make as much money as possible for stockholders"? What might Friedman say about Merck's Mectizan program and Johnson & Johnson's Tylenol® decision?

8.1 INTRODUCTION: MARKETING AND ETHICS

Despite the fact that marketing is one of the core disciplines of business, marketing ethics as a field of study has only recently become a focus within business ethics. While product safety and advertising, admittedly two central parts of marketing, have received a good deal of attention, areas such as pricing, market research, sales, target marketing, and social marketing have received much less.[1]

The essence of marketing is frequently explained in terms of the Four P's: *product, pricing, promotion,* and *placement.* Since this framework will be used to organize chapters 8 and 9, it is worth considering this characterization in some detail. Marketing involves all aspects of creating a product or service and bringing it to market where an exchange can take place. The concept of an exchange between a seller and a buyer is central to the "market" and is the core idea behind marketing. But this simple model of a seller bringing a product to the marketplace gets complicated fairly quickly.

Even before a product is created, a producer might first consider who, if anyone, is interested in purchasing it. The product might then be redesigned or changed in light of what is learned about potential buyers. Once the product is ready for market, the producer must decide on a price that will be mutually acceptable. At first glance, the minimal asking price should be the production cost plus some reasonable profit. But the producer might also consider who the buyers are and what they can afford, how price might influence future purchases, how the price might affect distributors and retailers, and what competitors are charging before settling on a price. The producer might also consider advertising the product to attract new potential purchasers and offer incentives to promote the product among buyers. The producer might consider the lost production that results from the trip to the market and therefore consider hiring someone else, a salesperson, or delegating someone, a "retailer," to handle the actual exchange itself. They might be more concerned with cash flow than profit and therefore be willing to ask a price that is below production costs. Producers might consider where and under what conditions the product is sold, and might decide that the best chance for a sale will occur only among certain people. The producer might also consider issues of volume, and price the product in such a way to ensure profit only after certain sales targets are met. Finally, throughout this entire process the producer might conduct market research to gather information and use that information in production, pricing, promotion, and placement decisions.

All of the factors considered and each decision made throughout this process is an element of marketing. What, how, why, and under what conditions is something *produced?* What *price* is acceptable, reasonable, fair? How can the product be *promoted* to support and enhance sales? Where, when, and under what conditions should the product be *placed* in the marketplace?[2]

Each of the Four P's also raises important ethical questions. What responsibilities do producers have for the quality and safety of their products? Who is responsible for harms caused by a product? Are there some products that should not be produced, or does consumer demand decide all production questions? Is the consumer's willingness to pay the only ethical constraint on fair pricing? Should the ability to pay be a factor in setting price? Do all customers deserve the same price, or can producers discriminate in favor of, or against, some consumers? What effects will price have on competitors? On retailers? Are deceptive or misleading ads ethical? What ethical constraints should be placed on sales promotions? Is the information gathered in market research the property of the business that conducts the research? What privacy protections should be offered for marketing data? Is it ethical to target vulnerable populations such as children or the elderly? What responsibilities does a producer have when marketing in foreign countries? What responsibilities do producers have to retailers? To competitors? To suppliers?

The present chapter will examine a variety of ethical issues having to do with production and pricing. We'll pay particular attention to questions of product safety and products liability. Chapter 9 will examine ethical issues in advertising, sales, and product placement.

8.2 ETHICAL ISSUES IN MARKETING: AN OVERVIEW

We can take the simple model of a single exchange between two individuals as a useful way to introduce an ethical framework for marketing ethics. This simple situation in which two parties freely agree to the exchange is *prima facie* ethically legitimate. The Kantian tradition in ethics would see it as upholding respect for individuals by treating them as autonomous agents capable of pursuing their own ends. The utilitarian tradition would take their agreement as evidence that each is better off then they were prior to the exchange and thus conclude that overall happiness has been increased.

This assessment is only *prima facie* because, like all agreements, certain conditions must be met before we can conclude in fact that autonomy has been respected and mutual benefit achieved. Thus, for example, we would need to establish that the agreement resulted from an informed and voluntary consent, and that there was no fraud, deception, or coercion involved. When these conditions are violated, autonomy is not respected and mutual benefit not attained. Furthermore, even when such conditions are met, other values may override the freedom of individuals to contract for mutually beneficial purposes. Thus, for example, the freedom of drug dealers to pursue mutually agreeable ends is overridden by society's concern to maintain law and order.

In general, therefore, it will be helpful to keep three concerns in mind as we approach any ethical issue in marketing: To what degree are the participants respected as free and autonomous agents rather than being treated simply as means to the end of making a sale? To what degree does the transaction provide actual as opposed to merely apparent benefits? What other values might be at stake in the transaction? Let us consider these three issues in more detail.

It is not always easy to determine if someone is being treated with respect in marketing situations. As a first approximation we might suggest two conditions. First, the person must freely consent to the transaction. But how free is "free"? Surely transactions completed under the threat of force are not voluntary and therefore are unethical. But there are many degrees of voluntariness. For example, a consumer facing a life-threatening illness may choose to take drugs with serious side effects that a healthier person would find unacceptable. A patient receiving a prescription from her physician may not be in a position to request a generic version of that drug. From this perspective, the more a consumer needs a product, the less free he or she is to choose and therefore the more protection he or she deserves from unsafe products or unscrupulous manufacturers. The history of prescription drug regulation is witness to this fact. Or consider the anxiety and stress that accompany any illness or medical condition. When marketing practices exploit that anxiety to sell unnecessary drugs or to downplay the potential side effects, it is not at all clear that the consumer has made a fully voluntary choice. More dramatic cases of price gouging, price-fixing, and monopolistic pricing clearly raise the issue of freedom in marketing. Practices aimed at vulnerable populations such as children and the elderly also raise questions of voluntariness. Thus, an adequate analysis of marketing ethics challenges us to be sensitive to the many ways in which consumer choice can be less than fully voluntary.

A second condition for respect requires that the consent be not only voluntary, but also informed. Informed consent has received a great deal of attention in the medical ethics literature where it is shown that patients are at a distinct informational disadvantage in situations dealing with health care professionals. Similar disadvantages can occur in marketing situations. Outright deception and fraud clearly violate this condition and are unethical. But there can also be many more nuanced cases of deception and misleading marketing practices. The complexity of many consumer products and services can also mean that consumers may not understand fully what they are purchasing. Consider as an example all that would be involved for a consumer to determine which arthritis drug offers the best treatment, or whether a generic version of a widely marketed drug is safe and effective. Consider also the many people who have very weak mathematical skills. Imagine such a person trying to decide on the economic benefits of whole life versus term insurance, or a 48-month auto lease versus a five-year purchase loan at 2.9 percent financing. In general, while some businesses claim that an "informed consumer is our best customer," many others recognize that an uninformed consumer can be an easy target for quick profits.[3] Serious ethical questions should be raised whenever marketing practices either deny consumers full information or rely on the fact that they lack relevant information or understanding.

The second ethical concern looks to the alleged benefits obtained through market exchanges. It is common to find economics textbooks assuming that consumers are benefited, almost by definition, whenever their preferences are satisfied in the market. But this assumption won't bear up under close scrutiny. There are many purchases that do not result in actual benefit. For example, impulse buying, and the many marketing techniques used to promote such consumer behavior, cannot be justified by appeal to satisfying consumer interests. The ever-increasing number of individual bankruptcies suggests that consumers cannot purchase happiness. Empirical studies provide evidence that suggest that greater consumption can lead to unhappiness, a condition called by some "affluenza."[4] So, if simple consumer satisfaction is not a conclusive measure of the benefits of market exchanges, one must always ask about the ends of marketing. What goods are attained by successfully marketing this product or service? How and in what ways are individuals and society benefited from the product?

The third set of factors that must be considered in any ethical analysis of marketing is values other than those served by the exchange itself. Such primary social values as fairness, justice, health, and safety are just some of the values that can be jeopardized by some marketing practices. For example, a bank that offers lower mortgage rates in affluent neighborhoods than it does in inner-city neighborhoods might be involved only in deals that are mutually beneficial since they do not, in fact, sell mortgages in the inner city. But such contracts would violate important social norms of equal treatment and fairness. There may be a very strong market for such things as certain body parts of endangered species. There is also, unfortunately, a market for children. But just because someone wants to buy something and someone else is willing to sell it does not mean that that transaction is ethically legitimate. An adequate ethical analysis of marketing must ask who else might be affected by the transaction. How, if at all, are their interests represented? What social goods are promoted, and which are threatened, by marketing this product?

One must also ask what are the true costs of production. An adequate ethical analysis of marketing must consider externalities, those costs that are not integrated within the exchange between buyer and seller. Externalities show that even if both parties to the exchange receive actual benefits from the exchange, other parties external to the exchange might be adversely affected. One thinks of the environmental or health impact of marketing products such as SUVs, pesticides, and tobacco as examples in which significant social costs would be ignored by a simple model of individual consumer exchange. With these issues in mind, we can now turn to a closer examination of two major aspects of marketing ethics: responsibility for product safety and pricing.

8.3 ETHICAL RESPONSIBILITY FOR PRODUCTS: FROM CAVEAT EMPTOR TO NEGLIGENCE

As we saw in chapter 7, although the concept of responsibility plays a major role in ethical discussions, it is not a clear and unambiguous notion. There are at least three common uses of responsibility that are relevant to an examination of business's responsibility for its products. Consider what one might be asking by the question: "Who is responsible for this?"

Imagine you come upon a traffic accident in which an SUV has rolled over into a ditch. You ask a group of people standing to the side: "What happened? What is responsible for this?" In the first sense of responsibility, you would be asking about the *cause* of what you see: who, or what, caused this accident to happen? Imagine the driver answering, "I did it, but it wasn't my fault. I was driving when the tire blew out and turned sharply to the left which caused the car to roll over." A second sense of responsibility involves assigning blame or fault. To ask "Who is responsible?" in this sense is to inquire about who is to be held liable for the harm. The driver's answer shows that one can be responsible in the first sense but not in the second. One might cause some wrong but not be liable or at fault for it. On the other hand, had the accident resulted from the driver reaching to dial a cell phone and taking his eyes off the road, you would hold him liable for acting irresponsibly.

There is a third sense of being responsible that involves neither the cause nor liability but means something closer to "taking care of" or being accountable. Thus we speak of being responsible for a child's school expenses or assuming responsibility for an elderly parent's bills. One might be assigned responsibility for certain chores or be described as a responsible person. For group projects in class, one student is responsible for research, another for typing, another for presenting to the class. This sense of responsibility shows that one can be accountable without any suggestion of culpability, fault, or blame.

Each of these senses of responsibility is relevant to issues of product safety and marketing ethics. One of the first, and often most difficult, questions of product safety concerns determining the cause of any harms. What caused the Ford Explorers to crash during blowouts of their Firestone tires? Was it the design, the manufacturing process, or some component of the tire? Was it the design and stability of the Explorer? Was it the driver's own behavior? Was it some combination of all these factors? The concept of negligence, a central notion in product liability law, is one way in which fault is assigned (intentionally or recklessly causing harm would be other ways of causing harms). Thus, manufacturers who fail to inspect their products before sending them to the market, or who rush them to market without adequate testing, can be held culpable (at fault) for harms caused by this negligence. The legal doctrine of strict products liability is more a doctrine of no-fault accountability. If a product defect has caused a harm, the manufacturer is held accountable even though not at fault. Finally, some argue that manufacturers should be accountable for the entire life cycle of the products they bring to the market, including recycling the product back into the production stream.

The focus for much of the discussion of business's responsibility for product safety is on assigning liability (fault) for harms caused by unsafe products. The legal doctrine of strict products liability is ethically controversial exactly because it holds a business accountable for paying damages in cases where it was not at fault. We will consider the case of strict products liability in more detail in the following section. For the present, let us examine the various standards for holding business liable for its products.

The caveat emptor approach understands marketing on a simple model of a contractual exchange between a buyer and seller. From this perspective, business has only the responsibility to uphold its end of the bargain by providing a good or service at an agreed-upon price. Unless a seller explicitly warrants a product as safe—unless, in other words, the seller promises otherwise—buyers are liable for any harms they suffer. Every purchase was assumed to involve the informed consent of the buyer and was therefore assumed to be ethically legitimate.

As the case of prescription drugs suggests, however, there were problems with this approach. In part, it assumes that consumers do adequately understand and judge products so that they can reasonably be expected to protect themselves. But consumers don't always understand products fully and they are not always free to choose not to purchase some things. Starting in the 1960s, a number of important legal cases shifted the burden from consumers to producers by allowing consumers to assume that products were safe for ordinary use. By bringing goods and services to the market, producers were implicitly promising that their products were safe under normal use. The ethical basis for this decision is the assumption that consumers would not give their consent to a purchase if they had reason to believe that they would be harmed by it when used in a normal way.

But as long as the marketing relationship was understood on the contract model, there was an easy way for manufacturers to escape responsibility. If courts were going to assume that consumers had been given an implied warranty of safety, manufacturers could avoid responsibility by expressly limiting or denying any warranty. Thus, limited or expressed warranties could shelter manufacturers from legal responsibility for their products. Consumers could only recover damages as outlined by the producer. All too often, such limitations are explained in small print at the bottom of a sale agreement and typically in language that only lawyers can understand. Thus, despite appearances that consumers were consenting to such limitations, a more fair and accurate interpretation is that such one-sided agreements fail to meet the standards of truly informed consent.

Negligence, a concept from the area of law known as torts, provides a second avenue for consumers to hold producers responsible for their products. The distinction between contract law and tort law also calls attention to two different ways to understand ethical duties. Under a contract model, the only duties that a person owes are those that have been explicitly promised to another party. I have duties to the mortgage company, for example, because I have agreed or promised to do certain things. On a narrow contractarian view of ethics, our only duties are those that have been taken on explicitly and voluntarily. Otherwise, I owe nothing to anyone. The ethical perspective that underlies tort law holds that we all owe other people certain general duties, even if we have not explicitly and voluntarily assumed them. Specifically, I owe other people a general duty not to put them at unnecessary and avoidable risk. Thus, although I have never explicitly promised anyone that I will drive carefully, I have an ethical duty not to drive recklessly down the street.

Negligence is a central component of tort law. As the word suggests, negligence involves a type of ethical neglect, specifically neglecting one's duty to exercise reasonable care not to harm other people. One can understand many of the ethical and legal issues surrounding manufacturers' responsibility for products as the attempt to specify what constitutes negligence in their design, production, and sale. What duties, exactly, do producers owe to consumers?

One can think of possible answers to this question as falling along a continuum. On one extreme is the contractarian answer: Producers owe only those things promised to consumers in the sales agreement. At the other extreme is something closer to strict liability: Producers owe compensation to consumers for any harms caused by their products. In between these extremes is a range of answers that vary with different interpretations of negligence. We have already suggested why the strict contractarian approach is not convincing. In the next section we shall examine the pros and cons of strict products liability. The remainder of this section will examine the important concept of negligence.

Negligence can be characterized as a failure to exercise reasonable care or ordinary vigilance that results in an injury to another. In many ways, negligence simply codifies two fundamental ethical precepts: "ought implies can" (we cannot reasonably oblige someone to do what they cannot do) and "one ought not harm others." People have done an ethical wrong when they cause harm to others in ways that they can reasonably be expected to have avoided. Negligence includes acts of both commission and omission. One can be negligent by doing something that one ought not (e.g., speeding in a school zone) or by failing to do something that one ought to have done (e.g., neglecting to inspect a product before sending it to market).

Consider a case that received a good deal of media attention a few years ago. In 1992 a 70-year-old woman was severely burned when a cup of coffee she had just purchased at a McDonald's drive-through window spilled on her lap. She apparently held the cup between her legs and tried to pry off the lid as she drove away. The coffee was hot enough (185 degrees) to cause third-degree burns which required skin grafts and long-term medical care. A jury awarded this woman $2.86 million, $160,000 for compensatory damages and $2.7 million in punitive damages. Should McDonald's be held liable for these injuries? Were they negligent in serving such hot coffee at a drive-through window? Was the consumer negligent in her own actions?

Negligence involves the ability to foresee the consequences of our acts and failing to take steps to avoid the likely harmful consequences. The standards of forseeability, however, raise interesting challenges. One standard would hold people liable for only those harms that they actually foresaw occurring (actual forseeability). Thus, for example, someone would be acting negligently if, on the basis of engineering tests, they concluded that a fuel tank placed behind the rear axle would puncture and explode during crashes at speeds below 30 miles per hour, yet still brought the car to market. But this standard of actual forseeability is too restricted. If someone actually thinks that harms are likely to result from their acts and proceeds nonetheless, they have committed a serious wrong and deserve harsh punishment. Such a case seems more akin to recklessness or even intentional harm, than negligence. But this standard would also imply that unthoughtful people cannot be negligent, since one escapes liability by not actually thinking about the consequences of one's acts. "I never thought about that" would be an adequate defense if we used this standard of negligence. Yet this surely is part of what we are after with the concept of negligence. We want to encourage people to be thoughtful and hold them liable when they are not.

A preferable standard would require people to avoid harms that, even if they haven't actually thought about, they should have thought about had they been reasonable. For example, presumably McDonald's did not actually think that their customers would be severely burned by coffee. But had they thought about what people who are driving cars when served coffee might do to hold their cups when they drove away from the window, they could have foreseen the likelihood of spills. The fact that McDonald's had received over seven hundred prior burn claims about their coffee suggests that a reasonable person would have concluded that this was a dangerous practice. This "reasonable person" standard is the one most often used in legal cases and seems to better capture the ethical goals of the very concept of negligence. People are expected to act reasonably and are held liable when they do not.

But even the reasonable person standard can be interpreted in various ways. On one hand, we expect people will act in ways that would be normal or average. A "reasonable" person does what we could expect the ordinary, average person to do. There are problems using this standard for both consumer and producer behavior. It may turn out that the ordinary average consumer is not as smart as we might hope. The average person doesn't always read, or understand, warning labels, for example. The ordinary and average person may thoughtlessly place a cup of very hot coffee between her legs as she drives out of a parking lot and into traffic. The average person standard, when applied to consumers, risks exempting many consumers from taking responsibility for their own acts. When applied to producers, the average person standard sets the bar too low. We can expect more from a person who designs, manufactures, and sells a product than average and ordinary vigilance.

Reasons such as these can lead us to interpret the reasonable person standard more normatively than descriptively. In this sense, a "reasonable" person assumes a standard of thoughtful, reflective, and judicious decision making. The problem with this, of course, is that we might be asking more of the average consumers than they are capable of giving. Particularly if we think that the disadvantaged and vulnerable deserve greater protection from harm, we might conclude that this is too stringent a standard to apply to consumer behavior. On the other hand, given the fact that producers do have more expertise than the average person, this stronger standard seems more appropriate when applied to producers than to consumers.

8.4 STRICT PRODUCTS LIABILITY

As described previously, the negligence standard focuses on the actions of the people involved. Specifically, either or both the consumer or producer can be held responsible when they have acted negligently. In the McDonald's coffee case, for example, the jury concluded that the consumer should also be held partially liable for her own injuries since she did not exercise reasonable care when she held hot coffee in her lap while driving. McDonald's itself was also negligent because they should have taken steps to prevent the sort of accident that was easily foreseeable.

Strict products liability, on the other hand, focuses not on the actions of the people involved but rather on the performance of the product itself. Some harms occur in ways that can only be described as an accident. That is, there was nothing anyone could have done otherwise that could have prevented the harm. Neither the producer nor the consumer acts negligently, but the consumer gets injured nonetheless. The question then arises: In the absence of fault who should bear responsibility, who should be accountable, for paying damages? The strict products liability standard assigns this responsibility to producers.

Consider the drug DES described in the Discussion Case that opened this chapter. In this case, a product proved defective during normal use. Hundreds of women got cancer because of a drug that their mothers took and which may have actually facilitated their own birth. Given all that was known about the drug, it would be unreasonable to accuse either the manufacturers who made the drug, the physicians who prescribed it, the pharmacists who sold it, or the women who used it of negligence. No one could have reasonably foreseen the harm that was being caused by this drug. Nevertheless, as in all strict products liability cases, there were victims in this case and someone must be accountable for these harms.

It is crucial to understand that despite the language of "products *liability*" these cases do not involve assigning blame or fault. If someone was at fault, this would be a case of negligence and that standard would be applied. But in these cases, no one was at fault, no one could have reasonably been expected to have acted differently. Yet harms have occurred and someone must assume responsibility (in the sense of accountability) for these damages. Minimally, someone must pay the health care costs for the women who have cancer as a result of this drug. In this sense, perhaps the legal language of "products liability" should be replaced with the language of "products accountability."

There are really only three options in this case. The consumers can be made accountable for their own harms. Society can be held accountable. The product manufacturers can be held accountable. Holding the consumer accountable, what is sometimes called the *tough luck* standard, seems overly severe. Not only would the consumers suffer the injury itself, but they would also bear the financial costs as well. Making the consumer suffer in both ways seems cruel, especially since in these cases we know what caused the injury and we know that others have benefited from the fact that the consumer bought the product that caused their injury. Holding society in general accountable is an option, but would seem to commit us to a socialized insurance system. If we hold society accountable for injuries and disease caused by consumer products, we would be hard pressed to deny social accountability for all injuries and disease (why favor only those caused by products?).

Considerations such as these leave as the only option producer accountability, which is the strict liability standard in place within the United States at present. But critics charge that this system is unfair, costly, and socially unwise. It is unfair because it holds producers responsible for things over which they had no control (since there was no negligence involved, there was nothing they could have done otherwise). It is costly because it adds significant hidden costs to every consumer product and places domestic producers at a competitive disadvantage with foreign businesses. It is socially unwise because it discourages product innovation and encourages frivolous and expensive lawsuits.[5]

But these criticisms are not persuasive. Philosopher John McCall argues that strict liability is no more unfair than it would be to hold the injured consumers accountable.[6] If business should not be penalized for harms that were beyond their control to prevent, neither should consumers be penalized for harms that they could not prevent. Thus, it cannot be argued that strict liability should be rejected as unfair if the alternative of consumer liability is equally unfair for the same reasons. McCall also argues that empirical evidence suggests that the strict liability standard is not as costly, nor as likely to generate frivolous lawsuits, as critics suggest.[7]

Nevertheless, some of the standard arguments used to justify the strict liability standard are not without problems themselves. George Brenkert points out that juries typically offer two justifications for holding manufacturers strictly liable. Manufacturers are best able to pay for the damages caused by their products, and strict liability creates an added incentive for producing safe products. But, as Brenkert argues, neither of these arguments is fully convincing. Holding manufacturers liable because they are best able to pay may, in fact, be false. Some manufacturers may be unable to pay liability for their products. For example, the Johns Manville company faced bankruptcy due in large part to its liability for the asbestos products it manufactured. But even if manufacturers could afford payment, this fact alone does not justify making them pay. My neighbor is better able to pay my bills than I, but this fact would not justify sending him those bills. The incentive argument is also unpersuasive. It assumes that strict liability would motivate manufacturers to do something differently to avoid accidents when they design, test, and market their products. But this confuses the negligence case with the strict liability situation. With strict liability there was nothing the manufacturer could have done differently.

So, two common arguments used to criticize strict liability—unfairness and cost—seem unconvincing. Likewise, two common arguments used to justify this standard seem unconvincing. Both McCall and Brenkert argue, however, that fairness does count in favor of the strict liability standard. Brenkert argues that the exchange between seller and buyer should be understood on the model of a competition in which each party competes with the other to optimally satisfy their own interests. Central to the idea of fair competition is an element of equal opportunity. Brenkert argues that when a consumer is injured by a product, that consumer is unfairly disadvantaged in the economic competition and is denied an equal opportunity to compete in the marketplace. Fairness demands that the party that benefits from the unfair advantage, the manufacturer whose product caused the injury, compensate the injured party. Compensation returns the parties to equal standing and the economic competition can therefore continue.[8] Compensatory justice requires that people be compensated for undeserved harms by the party that has caused, or has benefited from, that harm.

McCall's fairness argument is slightly different. He argues that assigning the costs for injuries caused by defective products to other consumers of the product and to the shareholders of the company is more appropriate than assigning the costs to the injured consumer or to society at large. By holding the manufacturer liable, the costs are passed on, ordinarily through increased liability insurance costs, to those who stand to benefit from the product (i.e., product users and stockholders). This is only fair because it means that the full costs of the product (every opportunity forgone in the production and sale of the product) is paid by those parties involved. Injured consumers have not voluntarily accepted the injury as part of the cost they are paying for the product. These injuries are externalities that fairness requires to be internalized into the exchange. That is, the injuries should be paid for by those who benefit from the exchange, other users of the product, and stockholders in the company. Both McCall and Brenkert understand strict liability more as a process of compensation for undeserved harms, than liability in the sense of assigning fault or blame. Parties that benefit from an exchange in which one party is undeservedly injured owe compensation to the injured party.

Before moving from strict liability issues, two further points should be noted. First, the strict liability standard does not entail that producers are accountable for every injury caused by their products. Manufacturers are not liable when consumer negligence causes the injury. Manufacturers are also exempt if the product cannot be proven to be defective. "Defective" is understood as unreasonably dangerous in normal use. This brings us to a second concluding point. Some products are inherently dangerous and thus might reasonably be expected to cause injury. In such a case, inherently dangerous products are not defective and thus manufacturers cannot be held liable for injuries they cause. Something like this argument has, so far, exempted most cigarette and handgun manufacturers from strict liability for the harms regularly caused by their products. Of course, these manufacturers can still be held liable for any negligence in the design or marketing of their products. The major settlements between tobacco companies and individual states in recent years, for example, has focused mostly on the actions of the companies in marketing their products. We will look at these issues in more detail in chapter 9.

8.5 ETHICS AND PRICING

What values should determine an ethically legitimate price? In this chapter's overview of ethical issues in marketing, I suggested three general ethical concerns as guiding principles: respect for individual autonomy, provision of actual benefits to the parties involved, and values other than those served by the exchange itself. These three concerns also provide a focus for ethics and pricing. On the surface, a fair price is a price that both parties to an exchange agree upon. Thus the values of autonomy and mutual benefit to the parties involved underlie an ethics of pricing. But a product's price also affects third parties, including competitors who might be priced out of the competition and retailers who must live with manufacturers' corporate pricing policies. Thus, values such as fairness and equal opportunity also are relevant to pricing ethics.

Let's start with a simple case of one buyer and one seller. A fair price would be a price that both agree to, with the consent of each party establishing the limits of what the other can expect. In a competitive market, both buyer and seller are protected by the availability of other buyers and sellers who move the price towards an equilibrium that seems fair to both sides. A seller cannot raise the price too high if there are competitors willing to sell lower, and the buyer can't drive the price too low if there are other buyers willing to pay a higher price.

But the real world seldom matches this idealized marketplace and the ways in which actual markets fall short of this ideal provide a helpful way to think about fair pricing. Consumers, of course, are not always fully informed nor fully free in the marketplace. Thus informed consent, a necessary condition for respecting autonomy, can be missing in some pricing situations. Pricing for such things as prescription drugs and other health care products are seldom things that consumers fully understand or for which they have alternatives available. The AIDS drugs in Africa case described in this chapter's discussion case provides a good example of such situations on a global scale. Among the millions of people in Africa who have AIDS, few have the education, understanding, and income sufficient to negotiate a price for AIDS drugs in an informed and free way. Patents for the drugs prevent competitors from entering this market and lowering prices through competition.

Three major ethical issues in pricing involve situations in which markets fail to ensure a fair price in this way. Price gouging, monopolistic pricing, and price-fixing are all cases in which consumers lack the freedom to negotiate what is required to ensure fair market pricing. Price gouging occurs when the buyer, at least temporarily, has few purchase options for a needed product and the seller uses this situation to raise prices significantly. Energy companies, for example, have been accused of price gouging during the period of rolling blackouts in California during the summer of 2001. A local hardware store that doubles the price of a portable generator after a hurricane has taken unfair advantage of consumer needs. The night of the tragic attacks at the World Trade Center and the Pentagon, there were numerous reported cases in which gasoline stations doubled and tripled their prices when some consumers rushed to buy gas in near panic. In such cases, the seller exploits a lack of freedom on the buyer's part to extract extraordinarily high prices. Such practices are unethical because the transaction is fundamentally unfree and the seller exploits the buyer's limitations.

Monopolistic pricing and price-fixing are similar unethical practices. In these cases, either individual companies or a group of conspiring companies use their market power to force consumers to pay a higher price than they would have if there were real competition in the marketplace. Microsoft's Windows operating system, gasoline, airline travel, and credit card interest rates have all been alleged to be guilty of monopolistic pricing or price-fixing. In general, two factors must be considered when judging whether a price is fair to consumers: consumer freedom and available competition. The greater freedom a consumer has to walk away from a product, the less likely it is that the seller can set an unfair price. Second, the greater the competition within a market, the less likely that unfair pricing can occur. If consumers have alternatives available, unfair pricing is less likely. Of course, the more one finds uniformity of prices within an industry—and credit card interest rates, prescription drugs, and air travel come immediately to mind—the less likely it is that real competition exists.

These pricing issues have all involved the value of respect for the autonomy of consumers and their relative freedom in accepting a price. But a second, more utilitarian, value involved in pricing concerns the actual benefits that consumers obtain through pricing. It may seem surprising to suggest that there are any ethical issues involved in this aspect. After all, it would seem that consumers are benefited from low prices so that the only ethical issue from this more utilitarian perspective is balancing the benefits to buyers from low prices with the benefits to sellers of high prices. Thus, as the market would hold, any pricing that is mutually agreed on can be considered a price that optimally satisfies all parties.

But could consumers ever be benefited from higher prices than they could otherwise pay? Consider what can happen when a large national chain begins to operate in a small community. Such companies as Wal-Mart, Home Depot, and online automobile brokers are well-known examples, but restaurant chains, grocery stores, clothing stores, and fast-food stores provide similar situations. In many cases, the immediate benefit to consumers is lower prices. For all the obvious reasons (and some not so obvious), larger national chains can often sell the same products at lower prices than local smaller firms. Some critics of the market consolidation that occurs in these situations argue that consumers are not benefited from the lower prices provided by these businesses.

Some economic evidence suggests that money spent with local businesses remains in the community to create more economic growth than money spent with national retailers. Locally owned businesses are more likely to reinvest in their community, hire locally, rely on local suppliers, and use such local professional services as banking, legal advice, accounting firms, and advertising agencies. Local businesses are more likely to offer personalized service and make greater contributions to local charities and community events than are national firms. Locally owned firms are more likely to remain loyal to the local community. As a consumer, one might benefit from slightly lower prices for a gallon of milk at Wal-Mart than the local family-owned grocery store. But as a citizen, one might receive greater benefits by paying more for some consumer products and supporting local businesses. The economic model that suggests that individuals are better off whenever they pay lower prices may be too simplistic on both economic and ethical grounds.

An ethical analysis of pricing should also move beyond the two parties involved in the exchange. Ethical issues can also arise in respect to parties that are external to the exchange, particularly as they affect competitors, partners in the distribution channel such as suppliers and retailers, and potential consumers who can be priced out of the market. Especially important in these cases are the values of fairness and equal opportunity.

Firms compete in many ways, of course, including competition through price, quality, and service. More importantly, they can compete fairly or unfairly. Unfair price competition can occur in several ways. Predatory pricing occurs when a product is temporarily priced below the actual costs as a means of driving competitors out of business. So, if a large national chain can sell a gallon of milk at below costs for a long enough period, it can drive smaller family-run grocery stores out of business. The size of the chain store allows it to absorb the losses, perhaps even indefinitely, in a way that is unavailable to the smaller store. Consumers may benefit from lower prices, but the larger community may suffer from fewer choices and lost competition.

There are difficult ethical questions raised by this practice. On one hand, some will claim that there is nothing unfair about this competition. If a large store can sell some products below cost, so much the better for consumers. All the efficiency benefits of large retailers should be passed on to consumers and there is nothing unethical if smaller store cannot compete. After all, a competitive market should drive out uncompetitive firms by driving prices down. On the other hand, we need to recognize that competition is ethically legitimate only as long as it is fair and as long as it does not cause undeserved harms. We also need to recognize that values other than economic efficiency and consumer preferences can be at stake. The "price" of economic efficiency may involve social and political "costs" to the wider community.

One concern with this is the utilitarian and economic one mentioned above. Lower prices might be a tactic employed to drive out competition and, over the long term, will only result in higher prices. Thus, the (long-term) consumer interests are best served by restricting (short-term) low prices. But even if the long-term price can be held low and consumers therefore benefit long term, low prices can be part of a more general unfair competition. Society generally benefits economically by price competition. But it can be the case that some parties to the competition are unfairly denied an equal opportunity to compete. Consider two examples.

Some automobile manufacturers have long desired to consolidate the automobile distribution system, in some cases even seeking to own and operate retail stores themselves. Most automobile dealerships are privately owned businesses that operate as a franchise of the manufacturer. Most automobile manufacturers also consistently use price incentives and other rebates to stimulate sales. It is not unusual for these rebates to be tied to certain sales targets. For example, in what are called *stair-step* programs the dealer may receive a $200 rebate per car sold for the first 10 units sold, $500 per car for the next 10, and so forth. The result of this is that larger retailers effectively pay a lower price per unit than smaller retailers. Perhaps not coincidentally, smaller dealers therefore face greater competition and are driven from the market, which results in the consolidation of distribution points that many manufacturers seek. A real ethical question must be raised. Does such price discrimination constitute unfair competition among retailers? Even if consumers benefit from lower prices, the benefit may be achieved by causing undeserved harm to small businesses.

Consider also cases in which government subsidies affect price. The U.S. federal government grants huge subsidies to the nuclear power industry, for example, by limiting the liability that the industry would face in the event of an accident. The federal government also subsidizes the coal, natural gas, and oil industries by granting below-market prices for access to federal lands, tax support for building pipelines, and by paying for the military protection to secure access to foreign oil supplies. One result of this is that consumers pay much lower energy prices in the United States than they would if the price were set by a fully free and competitive market. Another result is that the alternative energy industry is unable to compete on price.

The crucial lesson to be drawn from this example is not one of assigning blame or praise. We should recognize that whichever side one supports, one is acknowledging that the lowest, mutually acceptable, price alone is an insufficient basis for determining the ethical legitimacy of pricing policies. If you support alternative energy industries, you would say that even though consumers pay a low price for energy, the competition that establishes that price is unfair. If you support subsidies for the nuclear and fossil fuel industries, you would likely claim that other social values (e.g., economic growth, energy independence, and so forth) are so important that the price of some goods should not be left to the free market to establish.

A second and final concern picks up from this point. Low, mutually acceptable prices play a role in an economic system. But, as we have seen several times throughout this text, that economic system is itself a part of a broader social and political system. Values more at home in that social and political system can sometimes lead to an ethical rejection of low prices. Consider an example mentioned previously. A lending institution might make a decision to offer lower mortgage rates in a high-income, predominately white neighborhood than it offers in a lower-income, predominately African American neighborhood. Given the inequality of wealth, one could make the case that this is a prudent decision on financial grounds. But such discriminatory pricing would also be judged ethically unacceptable. Or consider pricing for such public goods as public lands, national parks, and wildlife. A true market price, based on the willingness of consumers to pay, might well see national parks sold to development companies, and endangered species sold to big-game hunters. Market price, alone, would not adequately reflect the true value of such things. When there are social costs involved in a transaction, costs not reflected in the price agreed upon by the two parties to the transaction, then the price agreed to would be neither fair nor socially beneficial.

This chapter has examined a variety of ethical concerns raised by product safety and pricing. Chapter 9 will examine the two remaining core topics of marketing ethics: advertising and target marketing.

REFLECTIONS ON THE CHAPTER DISCUSSION CASE

The idea that individual consumers are in the best position to protect themselves from dangerous products is an attractive notion for several reasons. This approach seems to treat each individual with the respect they deserve as autonomous beings. Individuals are left alone to sort through their own preferences and decide for themselves the level of risk they are willing to take in order to attain whatever benefits the product provides. This caveat emptor approach is also thought to be the most efficient means for attaining optimal consumer satisfaction. Placing responsibility on individual consumers might also provide an incentive for people to develop important virtues such as diligence, caution, discipline, and thoughtfulness.

But, as the model introduced early in this chapter suggests, such an approach must assume that consumers are making a fully informed and voluntary decision when purchasing a product. Pharmaceuticals, both prescription and over-the-counter, provide a good test case for such assumptions. Warnings of side effects appear on product labels and accompany most drug advertisements. Yet real questions arise concerning the percentage of consumers who both read and understand such warnings. Further, the anxiety and fear that can accompany medical conditions, not to mention the real threat to life and health, challenge the notion that consumer choice for drugs is fully voluntary.

Other social values are also at stake in debates concerning drug safety and pricing. The rising cost of health care, fueled to a large extent by prescription drug prices, is among the most serious financial challenges facing not only consumers, but private businesses and government. Pharmaceutical companies point to the great expense involved in research, development, and product testing. Yet real competition is constrained by patents and other barriers to entry faced by generic drugs. Reports that large pharmaceutical companies spend more on marketing than on research also casts doubts on the fairness of drug pricing. We consider some ethical issues concerning marketing of drugs in the discussion case in the next chapter.

Finally, long-term risks associated with highly complex chemicals will never be eliminated. As the DES case demonstrated, drugs can cause harms a generation in the future. This means that the evidence provided by clinical trials will always be incomplete and, therefore, that risks will always be present. Thus, as a society, we must decide who should bear the costs of those unavoidable risks: the consumers who get harmed by the drug, the pharmaceutical companies who profit from them, or the wider society through tax policy or government programs.

REVIEW QUESTIONS

1. Explain three general ethical concerns that should be raised in marketing ethics.
2. Describe several ways in which consumers are less than free in making choices about which products to purchase.
3. Explain why caveat emptor would be the ethically preferred product safety approach of the free market economic theory.
4. Explain the concept of negligence and offer an ethical defense of the claim that drug manufacturers should be held liable for negligent testing or production of their products.
5. To what extent should manufacturers be held liable for harms caused by their products?
6. Evaluate three different ethical arguments used to justify the policy of strict products liability.
7. Explain three ways in which the lowest price might not be the ethically best price.

ENDNOTES

[1]A helpful review of the present state of marketing ethics can be found in Patrick E. Murphy, "Marketing Ethics at the Millennium: Review, Reflections, and Recommendations" in *The Blackwell Guide to Business Ethics,* edited by Norman Bowie (Malden, MA: 2002), pp. 165–185. See also Gene Laczniak and Patrick Murphy, *Marketing Ethics: Guidelines for Managers* (Lexington, MA: Lexington Books, 1985), and Gene Laczniak and Patrick Murphy, *Ethical Marketing Decisions: The Higher Road* (Upper Saddle River, NJ: Prentice Hall, 1993). An insightful introduction to the philosophical issues can be found in George Brenkert, "Marketing Ethics," in *A Companion to Business Ethics,* edited by Robert Frederick (Malden, MA: Blackwell Publishing, 1999), pp. 178–193.

[2]Product "placement" is sometimes used in a narrower sense than I will use it. In that narrow sense, a marketing agent arranges to have the product appear in a movie or television segment thereby achieving subtle promotion for the product. I use the term more broadly to refer to any marketing activity that promotes the product to a targeted market segment.

[3]An informal Internet search found over a hundred companies advertising with this slogan. They ranged from real estate companies to antique dealers, and from long-distance phone providers to water filtration systems dealers. Presumably those who disagree do not advertise that fact.

[4]See, for example, *Affluenza: The All-Consuming Epidemic* by John de Graaf, David Wann, and Thomas Naylor (San Francisco: Berrett-Koehler Publishers, 2001). A 1997 PBS television show of the same title, produced by KTCS Television and Oregon Public Television, is a useful classroom tool and is available in video tape format from Bullfrog Films.

[5]For a detailed development of these and other criticisms of the strict products liability standard, see Peter W. Huber, *Liability: The Legal Revolution and Its Consequences* (New York: Basic Books, 1988).

[6]John McCall, "Fairness, Strict Liability, and Public Policy," in *Contemporary Issues in Business Ethics,* 4th ed., edited by Joseph DesJardins and John McCall (Belmont, CA: Wadsworth Publishing, 2000), pp. 328–329.

[7]See "Assessing Product Liability Alternatives," Introduction to Chapter 10 in *Contemporary Issues in Business Ethics,* pp. 308–310.

[8]George Brenkert, "Strict Products Liability and Compensatory Justice," originally published in *Business Ethics: Readings and Cases in Corporate Morality,* edited by W. Michael Hoffman and Jennifer Mills Moore (New York: McGraw-Hill, 1984).

9 CHAPTER

Marketing Ethics: Advertising and Target Marketing

After reading this chapter, you will be able to:

- Analyze the ethics of manipulation and deception in marketing and sales;
- Explain the regulatory standards governing advertising;
- Analyze the arguments concerning marketing that violates consumer autonomy;

- Explain the ethics of target marketing;

- Analyze the ethics of marketing to vulnerable people and populations.

DISCUSSION CASE: Advertising and Marketing in the Pharmaceutical Industry

"Last year hospitals dispensed ten times as much Tylenol® as the next four brands combined." "Hospitals recommended acetaminophen, the aspirin-free pain reliever in Anacin-3, more than any other pain reliever." "Three out of four doctors recommend the active ingredient of Anacin, the greatest pain fighter ever discovered." "One awkward moment with my doctor ended two awkward years with my wife. With Viagra, she and I have a lot of catching up to do." "Your dad wants you to have things he never had. Like hair." "Zocor. It's your future. Be there."

Each of these statements has been used in advertisements that are part of the multibillion dollar industry of marketing pharmaceuticals. In 2004 estimates were that pharmaceutical companies spent $3.5 billion on direct-to-consumer (DTC) advertising. For example, Merck spent $161 million advertising in 2000, $79 million on Vioxx in 2003, and $71 million advertising Vioxx in the nine months of 2004 leading up to the drug's withdrawal from the market in September 2004. Pfizer spent $87 million advertising Celebrex in 2003. Total marketing expenditures for all pharmaceuticals in 2000 was estimated at $15 billion, the majority of this money spent advertising in medical journals, on promotional materials supplied to health care professionals, and for free samples provided to doctors and hospitals.

Health care costs have skyrocketed for both individuals and for business. In 2004 the total spending on health care in the United States was $1.7 trillion, or 15 percent of the gross domestic product. Between 1980 and 2000, sales of prescription drugs in the United States tripled. In 2003 prescription drugs sold directly to consumers (as distinct from drugs dispersed in hospitals and other medical settings) totaled $200 billion. Sales of over-the-counter medications are a smaller percentage of GDP but still represent annual sales of tens of billions of dollars. Sixty percent of Americans receive their health care through employer-sponsored insurance programs. From 2001 to 2003, monthly premiums for employer-supplied health care experienced three straight years of double-digit increases. One estimate suggests that, by 2006, employer-supplied health care benefits will cost $10,000 per employee.

In light of escalating health care costs and increased company expenditures on marketing, pharmaceutical advertising has come under increased scrutiny. The United States is one of only two industrialized countries (New Zealand is the other) that allow DTC advertising of prescription drugs. A change in Food and Drug Administration (FDA) regulation in 1997 allowed companies to advertise prescription drugs directly to consumers without providing the detailed risk information that was previously required. That change resulted in an explosion in DTC drug advertisements.

The FDA has always had the authority to regulate advertising judged to be deceptive to consumers or unfair to competitors. In fact, some classic cases of deceptive and unfair advertising involved over-the-counter pain medications. That multibillion dollar market is dominated by three pain relievers—aspirin, acetaminophen, and ibuprofen—and four major pharmaceutical companies: Sterling Drug (maker of Bayer aspirin), Johnson & Johnson (Tylenol® and Medipren), American Home Products (Anacin), and Bristol-Meyers (Bufferin, Excedrin, Datril, Nuprin).

Because the drugs themselves are chemically and therapeutically identical, and because they are not protected by patents, the products can be differentiated in the marketplace either through pricing or through advertising and branding. The major pharmaceutical companies face price competition from generic versions of aspirin, acetaminophen, and ibuprofen packaged under supermarket, drugstore, and discount chain brand names. These companies compete among themselves through marketing, of which some has been very misleading.

Early aspirin advertisements emphasized the speed at which the particular brand worked, despite the fact that the active ingredient, aspirin, was identical in all brands. Anacin was described as offering "fast, fast, relief." Bufferin was "twice as fast as aspirin," despite the fact that its only active ingredient was aspirin. Bayer aspirin offered the "fastest relief of pain" and St. Joseph's aspirin was described as "faster than other leading pain relief tablets." American Home Products promoted its aspirin by claiming that "three out of four doctors recommend the ingredient in Anacin," the "greatest pain fighter ever discovered."

When Johnson & Johnson claimed truthfully that "last year hospitals dispensed ten times as much Tylenol® as the next four brands combined," they did not disclose that the hospitals were given free samples or highly discounted supplies of Tylenol®. When American Home Products claimed that "hospitals recommended acetaminophen, the aspirin-free pain reliever in Anacin-3, more than any other pain reliever," they did not disclose the fact that the acetaminophen recommended was Tylenol®.

Advertisements promoting prescription drugs have increased significantly since the FDA changes in 1997. Arguments in support of this type of marketing are that it provides information to consumers, respects consumer choice, encourages those who are reluctant to seek medical care to do so, gets more people into the health care system, addresses real public health issues, and increases competition and efficiency in the pharmaceutical industry. Opponents claim that these ads increase the unnecessary use of drugs; that because all drugs have harmful side effects, the ads increase public harms; that the ads increase reliance on pharmaceutical health care treatments and discourage alternative therapies and treatments, many of which have fewer side effects; that these ads manipulate and exploit vulnerable consumers; that they often provide misleading and incomplete information; that they alienate patients from physicians by bypassing the gatekeeper function of medical professionals; and that they treat social and behavior problems with medical and chemical solutions.

Among the most widely marketed drugs since the FDA changes are Lipitor, Zocor, Prilosec, Prevacid, Nexium, Celebrex, Vioxx, Zoloft, Paxil, Prozac, Viagra, Cialis, Levitra, Propecia, and Zyban. These drug names, most of which are literally household words today, were unheard of or nonexistent merely ten years ago. Together, they accounted for more than $21 billion in sales in 2002.

These drugs treat the following conditions: ulcers and acid-reflux (Prilosec, Prevacid, Nexium); high cholesterol (Lipitor, Zocor); arthritis pain (Celebrex, Vioxx); depression, panic attacks, anxiety (Zoloft, Paxil, Prozac); "erectile dysfunction" (Viagra, Cialis, Levitra); hair loss (Propecia); and cigarette and nicotine withdrawal (Zyban).

Ads for these drugs often appeal to such emotional considerations as shame, fear, embarrassment, social, sexual, and romantic inferiority, vanity, helplessness, and vulnerability. Many of these drugs are heavily advertised in women's magazines and during television sporting events.

Perhaps no marketing campaign has received as much critical attention as has the combined effort of the Viagra, Cialis, and Levitra campaigns to counteract erectile dysfunction. Much of the criticism has focused on the ad placements, particularly places where young children would see them such as during prime-time television and during high-profile sporting events. Other criticisms suggest that, although these drugs can be used to treat real medical conditions, they are being marketed as little more than sex toys. Erectile dysfunction can be a problem for older men and especially for men recovering from such medical treatments as prostate surgery. But for younger and otherwise healthy men, the primary causes of erectile dysfunction are alcohol consumption, obesity, lack of exercise, smoking, and the use of other prescription drugs. All of these causes are either easily addressed without reliance on pharmaceuticals or, like alcohol abuse, potentially unsafe with the use of these drugs.

One controversial attempt to market pharmaceuticals was reported by the *Boston Globe* in 2002. The *Globe* reported that sales representatives for TAP Pharmaceuticals, makers of Lupron Depot, an analgesic for treating pain associated with prostate cancer, were instructed to attend meetings of a prostate cancer support group to promote the drug directly to cancer patients. While pharmaceutical companies often provide support groups with financial assistance and informational materials, many critics believed that this action crossed the line of acceptable marketing. Evidence of this activity came to light during a wider federal investigation of TAP's marketing practices.

In 2001 TAP pleaded guilty of participating in a criminal conspiracy with doctors by providing them with free samples of Lupron which the doctors later billed to Medicare and patients. Federal prosecutors also charged TAP executives and mid-level managers with fraud, alleging that TAP employees bribed doctors and hospitals with cash, free vacations, and free samples as incentives for them to prescribe Lupron. Defendants argued that the samples and gifts were standard industry practice and did not amount to a bribe. In December 2004 a jury acquitted the individuals involved. TAP itself settled its case with the government by agreeing to pay $150 million restitution to consumers and insurance companies for what the government charged were artificially inflated drug prices. The prices were inflated because of the alleged bribes paid to doctors. TAP did not admit to any wrongdoing, claiming that it settled to avoid further legal costs.

A final case of marketing drugs to targeted populations involves the drug Strattera, Eli Lilly's prescription medication that controls attention deficit disorder and hyperactivity (ADHD) in children. This ad ran in magazines such as *Family Circle* (September 2003) under the simple title "Welcome to Ordinary." The ad pictures two boys holding up a model airplane that they have finished building, a challenging task for a child with ADHD. The ad reads: "4:30 p.m. Tuesday. He started something you never thought he'd finish. 5:20 p.m. Thursday. He's proved you wrong." The ad suggests that if a child with ADHD is not "ordinary," it is the parents who are "wrong" because all it would take would be Strattera to solve their problem. The same issue of *Family Circle* contained ads for McNeil Pharmaceutical's Concerta and Shire Pharmaceutical's Adderall, the two major competitors to Strattera.[1]

In October 2003 the President's Council on Bioethics issued a report titled "Beyond Therapy: Biotechnology and the Pursuit of Perfection." In this report they wrote, "In a major and worrisome change from previous practice, drug companies have taken to marketing drugs directly to parents, with spot ads depicting miraculous transformations of anxious, lonely, or troublesome children into very confident, honor-roll students." Do you think that such ads directed at parents are worrisome?

DISCUSSION QUESTIONS

1. Should prescription drugs be marketed directly to consumers?
2. What do you think is the most effective means to market a drug that is chemically and therapeutically identical to its competitors? What do you think is the most ethical way to market such drugs?
3. In what ways might a consumer suffering from a medical condition be less than fully free in making choices about medications? What psychological conditions undermine consumer autonomy?
4. How would you distinguish between sales representatives offering free samples and offering a bribe?
5. What ethical difference, if any, exists between a sales representative providing cancer support groups with financial assistance and informational materials versus attending support group meetings to promote a drug directly to patients?
6. What are your opinions of the Viagra, Cialis, and Levitra marketing campaigns? Would you describe them as tasteful? Offensive? Informative? Ethical?
7. Should there be special regulations governing the marketing of drugs to the elderly/to children? To medical patients? Should the FDA return to stricter regulation of drug advertisements?

9.1 INTRODUCTION: ETHICS OF SALES, ADVERTISING, AND PRODUCT PLACEMENT

Chapter 8 examined ethical issues surrounding the first two P's of marketing: products and pricing. In this chapter we examine the ethics of the final two P's of marketing: promotion and placement of products. Specifically, we shall focus on the ethics of advertising and sales and ethical issues of target marketing. There are overlaps, of course, among all four P's. For example, one major way to promote a product is through price incentives and sales. There will also be overlaps between product promotion and target marketing. How one chooses to promote a product will depend to a large extent on the target audience. Ethically, marketing promotions that are acceptable when targeted to some consumers may be less than acceptable when targeted to others. One of the themes of this chapter examines the issue of consumer autonomy and how it may be influenced by sales and advertising practices and how some targeted consumer groups might be more vulnerable to manipulation than others.

The goal of all marketing is the sale, the eventual exchange between marketer and consumer. A major element of marketing is sales promotion, the attempt to influence the buyer to complete a purchase. Target marketing and marketing research are two important elements of product placement, seeking to determine which audience is most likely to buy, and which audience is most likely to be influenced by product promotion.

There are, of course, ethically good and bad ways for influencing others. Among the ethically commendable ways to influence another are persuading, asking, informing, and advising. Unethical means of influence would include threats, coercion, deception, manipulation, and lying. Unfortunately, sometimes sales and advertising practices employ deceptive or manipulative means of influence or are aimed at audiences that are susceptible to manipulation or deception. Perhaps the most infamous and maligned of all marketing fields is automotive sales, especially in used car markets. The concept of manipulation, and its subset of deception, is central to the ethical issues explored in this chapter and can help organize the following sections.

To manipulate something is to guide or direct its behavior. Manipulation need not involve total control, and in fact it more likely suggests a process of subtle direction or management. Manipulating people implies working behind the scenes, guiding their behavior without their explicit consent or conscious understanding. In this way, manipulation is contrasted with persuasion and other forms of rational influence. When I manipulate people, I explicitly do not rely on their own reasoned judgment to direct their behavior. Instead, I seek to bypass their autonomy (although successful manipulation can be reinforced when the persons manipulated *believe* that they have acted of their own accord).

One of the ways in which we can manipulate someone is through deception, one form of which is an outright lie. I need not deceive you to manipulate you, although I would be happy if you falsely believed that you were not being manipulated. We can manipulate someone without deception, as when I get my sons to mow the lawn by making them feel guilty about not carrying their share of family responsibilities. Or I might manipulate my students into studying more diligently by hinting that there may be a quiz during the next class. These examples raise a very crucial point because they suggest that the more I know about your psychology—your motivations, interests, desires, beliefs, dispositions, and so forth—the better able I will be to manipulate your behavior. Guilt, pity, a desire to please, anxiety, fear, low self-esteem, pride, and conformity can all be powerful motivators. Marketers for prescription and over-the-counter medications rely on many of these factors to promote their products. Knowing such things about another person provides effective tools for manipulating his or her behavior.

We can see how this is relevant to marketing ethics. Critics charge that many marketing practices manipulate consumers. Clearly, many advertisements are deceptive, and some are outright lies. We can also see how marketing research plays into this. The more one learns about customer psychology, the better able one will be to satisfy their desires, but the better able one will also be to manipulate their behavior. Critics charge that some marketing practices target populations that are particularly susceptible to manipulation and deception. Consumers suffering from medical conditions may be especially vulnerable to advertisements that suggest cures, pain relief, or other therapeutic benefits.

But the ethics of these issues is not without controversy. While a strong ethical case can be made against lying and deception, it is less clear that all cases of manipulation are unethical. Is it unethical for me to exploit my sons' guilt in order to get them to mow the lawn? Do I manipulate someone whenever I appeal to their own motivations? Is it manipulation when I appeal to a male's ego to sell a product that slows hair loss? Further, deciding on the boundaries of manipulation is quite a challenge. Have I manipulated students when I hint that a reading assignment might appear on the exam? Have I manipulated consumers when I promote Anacin-3 as the pain-relieving medication most recommended by hospitals? When, and under what conditions, is manipulation unethical? What, exactly, is the difference between persuading people by appealing to their interests (e.g., "You should study if you want to receive a high grade") and manipulating them?

We will examine many of these questions in the sections that follow. For the present, it will help to return to some of the ethical themes introduced previously. The Kantian tradition in ethics would have the strongest objections to manipulation. When I manipulate someone I treat him or her as a means to my own ends, as an object to be used rather than as an autonomous person in his or her own right. Manipulation is a paradigm example of disrespect for persons since it bypasses their own rational decision making. Because the evil rests with the intention to use another as a means, even unsuccessful manipulations are guilty of this ethical wrong.

As we might expect, the utilitarian tradition would offer a more conditional critique of manipulation, depending on the consequences. There surely can be cases of paternalistic manipulation, in which someone is manipulated for his or her own good. But even in such cases, unforeseen harms can occur. Manipulation tends to erode bonds of trust and respect between persons. It can erode one's self-confidence and hinder the development of responsible choice among those manipulated. In general, because most manipulation is done to further the manipulator's own ends at the expense of the manipulated, utilitarians would be inclined to think that manipulation lessens overall happiness. A general practice of manipulation, as critics would charge occurs in many sales practices, can undermine the very social practices (e.g., sales) that it is thought to promote as the reputation of sales is lowered. Used car sales, once again, is a good example of such a situation.

A particularly egregious form of manipulation occurs when vulnerable people are targeted for abuse. Cigarette advertising aimed at children is one example that has received major criticism in recent years. Marketing practices targeted at elderly populations for goods and services, such as insurance (particularly Medicare supplemental insurance), casinos and gambling, nursing homes, and funerals, have been subjected to similar criticisms. Pharmaceutical marketing that targets people who are suffering from disease or chronic pain, or that targets parents of children suffering from ADHD, also seems particularly troubling.

We can suggest the following general guidelines. Marketing practices that seek to discover which consumers might already and independently be predisposed to purchasing a product are ethically legitimate. So, for example, an automobile dealership learns from its manufacturer's marketing department that the typical buyer of their car is a college educated female who enjoys outdoor activities and earns more than $40,000. Sending a targeted direct mail piece to everyone within an area who matches these criteria seems an ethically legitimate marketing practice. Marketing practices that seek to identify populations that can be easily influenced and manipulated are not. Sales and marketing that appeal to fear, anxiety, or other nonrational motivations are ethically improper. For example, an automobile dealer who knows that an unmarried or widowed woman is anxious about the purchase and who uses this anxiety as a way to sell extended warranty insurance, disability insurance, theft protection products, and the like, is unethical.

Marketing research seeks to learn something about the psychology of potential customers. But not all psychological categories are alike. Some are more cognitive and rational than others. Targeting the considered and rational desires of consumers is one thing; targeting their fears, anxiety, and whims is another.

9.2 REGULATING DECEPTIVE AND UNFAIR SALES AND ADVERTISING

"Last year hospitals dispensed 10 times as much Tylenol® as the next four brands combined." "Hospitals recommend acetaminophen, the aspirin-free pain reliever in Anacin-3, more than any other pain reliever." Both of these statements were true when they were widely used in marketing campaigns for Tylenol® and Anacin-3. But were they deceptive? What is not said in the Tylenol® advertisement is the fact that Johnson & Johnson, the manufacturer of Tylenol®, supplied Tylenol® to hospitals at either greatly reduced costs or as free samples to physicians. American Home Products, the manufacturer of Anacin-3, did not disclose in their ads the fact that the particular brand of acetaminophen that hospitals recommended more than any other was, of course, Tylenol®.

The U.S. Federal Trade Commission (FTC) is charged with regulating deceptive and unfair marketing practices. As long ago as 1944, the FTC was investigating manufacturers of aspirin products for deceptive sales practices. Because there are no chemical and therefore no medicinal differences between various brands of aspirin, acetaminophen, and ibuprofen (the three major non-prescription analgesic drugs), manufacturers can compete either through price or through marketing. The widespread availability of generic brands of these products shows how cheaply they can be sold. But the unwillingness of many consumers to purchase generic brands, and the high relative costs of name brands, shows the effectiveness of advertising.

Critics charge that the history of the marketing campaigns for these products is filled with manipulative and deceptive practices. The "combination of highly proven and active ingredients" of Anacin was simply aspirin and caffeine, and no evidence supported such claims. Anacin was claimed to offer "fast, fast relief," Bufferin was "twice as fast as aspirin," St. Joseph's aspirin was "faster than other leading pain relief tablets," and Bayer offered the "fastest relief of pain." The only active ingredient in each of these products was aspirin, and there was no chemical difference between the brands of aspirin. Thus, the claims of increased effectiveness or speed were simply false.

The FTC's mandate is to regulate marketing practices that are deceptive or unfair. This regulatory stance is helpful because it shows how these two standards are connected. Consider why Tylenol® would make the claim about the disproportionate amount of Tylenol® dispensed by hospitals. What could their intention be? One could say that it is simply a truthful claim about Tylenol®. Yet there are hundreds of other truthful things they could have said about their product, but they chose only this one. They certainly didn't do it in order to call attention to the fact that hospitals were receiving the drug at deep discounts. The only possible explanation for this marketing campaign is that Tylenol® intended consumers to be influenced by the appearance of an endorsement by hospitals. They wanted consumers to believe that hospitals were dispensing Tylenol® in such large numbers because the medical profession believed that Tylenol® (and not other brands of acetaminophen) was the best treatment for pain. That is, they hoped, intended, and took steps to ensure that consumers would believe something that was not true. They intended to deceive consumers, and through this deception Johnson & Johnson sought to manipulate consumers.

Consumers get harmed by such deception when they end up purchasing a product that they might not otherwise have bought, and often at a price higher than they might have otherwise paid. (Since the producer has chosen to compete through marketing rather than through price, we have some indication that consumers pay higher prices than they otherwise would have.[2]) These commercial and economic harms are the result of the ethical harm of being manipulated and used as a means to another's end. But, when a consumer gets deceived, competitors get cheated out of the chance to compete fairly in the marketplace. A competitor loses because the deceptive practice has succeeded. Any marketing practice that is deceptive to a consumer is, by that very fact, unfair to competitors. The FTC standards of deception and unfairness are two sides of the same unethical coin.

Society, through its legal and ethical standards, has very good reasons to ban deceptive and unfair marketing practices. Protecting consumers from being cheated out of their money and protecting the integrity of fair competition in the marketplace are strong incentives for social sanctions against deception. But while there is near universal agreement that deceptive marketing practices are wrong, determining precise standards for what constitutes deception, and for how best to regulate it, is more challenging.

Our ethical analysis of deceptive practices located a primary ethical wrong with deception in the intent of the deceiver. Intending to deceive people in order to manipulate their buying behavior is to treat them as a mere means to one's own ends. As a consequence of this, one approach to regulating deception would target those marketing practices that are intended to deceive. Our ethical analysis also suggested that the ethical wrong caused by deceptive practices lies in the harmful consequences to consumers, competitors, and overall market efficiency. Thus, a second approach to regulation emphasizes marketing practices that actually deceive consumers, thereby focusing on the effect rather than intent of the practice.

There are strengths and weaknesses to both approaches. To regulate intended deception, the FTC would need to determine the state of mind of the marketers. In practice, this has the FTC evaluating the marketing practice in terms of *expected* deception, that is, determining the intent by judging what can be reasonably expected to result from the practice. So, for example, one would conclude that Johnson & Johnson intended to deceive consumers by judging that the Tylenol ad could reasonably be expected to deceive consumers. Critics charge that this approach has the undesirable consequence of allowing government regulators to punish businesses not on the basis of what they have actually done, but on the basis of what bureaucratic judgment thinks might happen.[3] Defenders argue that it is preferable for government to prevent deceptive practices than to regulate only after the harms have been done.

On the other hand, regulating marketing practices that actually do, in fact, deceive people may be both too strong and too weak a standard. It might be too strong in the sense that it may well turn out that consumers are deceived by many relatively trivial marketing practices. Marketing scholar Ivan Preston tells the story of a consumer who threatened a lawsuit over a beer ad that the consumer found deceptive.[4] The ad, for a holiday beer named Old Frothingslosh, identified the beer as "the pale stale ale for the pale stale male," and described it as the only beer with foam on the bottom. The consumer was surprised to discover that this claim was untrue and the beer's foam rose to the top! Recently, an elderly man flew across the country, not once but twice, when he received a magazine sweepstakes mailing informing him that he had "already won $1 million" (in large print), *if* "his numbers matched the winning numbers" (in small print). It may turn out that more consumers are deceived than one would think. The actual deception standard may be too weak in the sense that it places the burden on consumers to take the initiative and come forth to prove the deception. Of course, there are many reasons for thinking that this is unlikely, not the least of which is the fact that a successful deception will not be revealed to the consumer. Many consumers may never know that they have been deceived since a necessary condition for being deceived is that, at least at one time, one doesn't know that one is being deceived.

In addition to these two interpretations of the deception standard, there is another controversy concerning regulatory standards. As suggested above, the capacity to be manipulated or deceived is a function of one's own psychology: one's desires, motivations, thoughtfulness, beliefs, and so forth. This implies that some people are more easily manipulated and deceived than others. The Old Frothingslosh example cited above shows that some people can be deceived by some fairly trivial information. On the other hand, avoiding deception in financing or insurance for complex products such as cars and homes can require some pretty sophisticated analysis. Regulating deceptive practices will depend on whether we assume consumers are reasonable or relatively ignorant.

Once again, there are strengths and weaknesses to either alternative. Adopting a "reasonable" consumer standard seems most fair and, well, reasonable. It assumes the best about consumers and doesn't hold marketers to extreme and difficult standards. The cost of this approach is that it does abandon protection to those consumers who may well deserve the greatest protection, namely, those most vulnerable and susceptible to deception.

Combining these alternatives creates a range of possible standards, from cases in which ignorant consumers might be expected to be deceived (the most stringent standard on marketing but offering the greatest protection) to cases in which only proved deceptions of reasonable consumers are regulated (the most loose standard). It might well be most reasonable to apply different standards to different products, marketing practices, and/or targeted markets.

9.3 MARKETING ETHICS AND CONSUMER AUTONOMY

Defenders of advertising argue that despite cases of deceptive practices, overall advertising contributes much to the economy. The majority of advertisements provide information to consumers, information that contributes to an efficient function of economic markets. These defenders argue that over time, market forces will weed out deceptive ads and practices. They point out that the most effective counter to a deceptive ad is a competitor's ad calling attention to the deception.[5]

Beyond this question of what advertising does *for* people, a second important ethical question asks what advertising, specifically, and marketing in general, does *to* people.[6] People may well benefit from business's marketing of its products. People learn about products that they may need or want, get the information that helps them make responsible choices, and even sometimes are entertained. But marketing also helps shape culture, some would say dramatically so, and the individuals who develop and are socialized within that culture. Marketing can have direct and indirect influence on the very persons we become. How it does that, and the kind of people we become as a result, is of fundamental ethical importance. Critics of such claims either deny that marketing can have such influence or maintain that marketing is only a mirror of the culture of which it is a part.

The initial proposal in this debate was offered by economist John Kenneth Galbraith in his 1958 book, *The Affluent Society*. Galbraith claimed that advertising and marketing were creating the very consumer demand that production then aimed to satisfy. Dubbed the dependence effect, this assertion held that consumer demand depended upon what producers had to sell. This fact had three major and unwelcome implications. First, by creating wants advertising was standing the law of supply and demand on its head. Rather than supply being a function of demand, demand turns out to be a function of supply. Second, advertising and marketing tend to create irrational and trivial consumer wants and this distorts the entire economy. The "affluent" society of consumer products and creature comforts is in many ways worse off than so-called undeveloped economies because resources devoted to contrived, private consumer goods were therefore denied to more important public goods and consumer needs. Taxpayers deny school districts small tax increases to provide essential funding while parents drop their children off at school in $40,000 SUVs. A society that cannot guarantee vaccinations and minimal health care to poor children spends millions annually for cosmetic surgery to keep its youthful appearance, and billions of dollars each year on drugs to slow hair loss, to counteract erectile dysfunction, to lose weight, to ease heartburn caused by overeating, or to help stop smoking. Finally, by creating consumer wants, advertising and other marketing practices were violating consumer autonomy. Consumers who thought themselves free because they were able to purchase what they want are not in fact free if those wants are created by marketing. In short, consumers are being manipulated by advertising.

Such a claim, if true, would have overwhelming ethical implications. Individual autonomy, the central element of Kantian respect for persons, would be violated by the creation of wants. If consumers are manipulated to pursue trivial and contrived products, then market exchanges only appear to, but do not actually, increase overall satisfaction. If the law of supply and demand were reversed, then the democratic nature of markets, and the ability of consumer demand to limit the power of the owners of capital, would be a façade. The claim that supply follows demand is used by defenders of capitalist economies to explain the democratic nature of markets (they are only giving consumers "what they want"). It also is used to explain why the consolidation of wealth in the hands of a few is not dangerous, since if the owners of productive capital do not conform to consumer demand, they will lose their investment. But if Galbraith is correct, these two major political rationales are proven unsound. The "dependence effect" is a major issue indeed.

Ethically, the crucial point was the assertion that advertising violated consumer autonomy. The law of supply and demand is reversed, and the economy of the affluent society is contrived and distorted, only if consumer autonomy can be violated, and consumers manipulated, by advertising's ability to create wants. But can advertising violate consumer autonomy and, if it can, does this occur? What does advertising do *to* people and to society?

An initial thesis in this debate claims that advertising controls consumer *behavior*. Autonomy involves making reasoned and voluntary choices, and the claim that advertising violates autonomy might mean that advertising controls consumer choice. Psychological behaviorists and critics of subliminal advertising, for example, would claim that advertising can control consumer behavior in this way.[7] But this seems to be an empirical claim and the evidence suggests that it is false. For example, some studies show that more than half of all new products introduced in the market fail, a fact that should not be true if consumer behavior could be controlled by marketing. Consumers certainly don't seem controlled by advertising in any obvious sense of that word.

But there is a more subtle way in which consumer autonomy might be violated. Rather than thinking that advertising controls behavior, perhaps advertising creates the wants and desires on the basis of which consumers act. The focus here becomes the concept of *autonomous desires* rather than *autonomous behavior*. This is much closer to the original assertion by Galbraith and other critics of advertising. Consumer autonomy is violated by advertising's ability to create nonautonomous desires.

A helpful exercise to understand how desires might be nonautonomous is to think of the many reasons people buy the things they buy, consume the things they do, and why, in general, people go shopping. These questions are reminiscent of some issues introduced in the discussion case for chapter 5 concerning why people work. After certain basic needs are met, there is a real question of why people consume the way they do. People buy things for many reasons, including the desire to appear fashionable, for status, to feel good, because everyone else is buying something, and so forth. The interesting philosophical question at this point is where did *these* desires originate and how much has marketing influenced these nonnecessity purchases.

Surely there can be such things as nonautonomous desires. These would be desires that are not voluntary, desires that we do not freely choose. A drug addict who desires more heroin would be a paradigmatic example of someone with a nonautonomous desire. Some might think that a nonautonomous desire is any desire that can be traced to or originate from advertising. But surely this interpretation is too open-ended. Advertising provides information from which I can learn and on the basis of which I can autonomously choose to desire something. The fact that I attained the information from advertising counts no more against the autonomy of that desire than does the fact that I learned about democracy in school counts against the autonomy of my desire to support democratic governments.[8]

The clearest examples of nonautonomous desires are found in addictions, as when an alcoholic "wants" another drink. This is something he or she desires, but the desire is not freely and rationally chosen. We can understand this point better by introducing the notion of *first-order* and *second-order* desires. My first-order desires are those wants that I just happen to have at any given time. But rational and conscious human beings are also able to step back from their desires and reflect rationally back upon them. By stepping back in this way we can ask such second-order questions as "Why do I want what I want? Do I really want this?" This ability to step back (what Socrates would have called leading an examined life) is a central component of autonomy because it is an essential part of rational decision making. It may turn out that, upon reflection, I do not want (second-order want) what I in fact want (first-order want). The alcoholic wants another drink in one sense, but would renounce that desire were it not for his or her addiction.

As a first approximation, we can say that an autonomous desire is one that is not rejected or repudiated upon rational reflection. Autonomous wants are first-order wants that are consistent with, and not denied by, second-order wants. Does advertising violate consumer autonomy by creating nonautonomous first-order wants? Robert Arrington argues that it does not.[9] While he admits that there might be individual cases in which advertising might control behavior or produce compulsive behavior, Arrington argues that marketing influences us by appealing to pre-existing and independent desires. Since marketing does not prevent consumers from renouncing those desires, we must assume that those desires are autonomous and conclude that advertising does not violate autonomy.

A closer examination suggests that this issue is more complicated. Arrington suggests that our desires are autonomous as long as we don't renounce them the way that an addict might try to renounce or repudiate the desire. Several critics point out that the failure to renounce a desire is not, alone, sufficient to demonstrate that that desire is autonomous. A fuller account of autonomous desires is offered by the philosopher Gerald Dworkin.[10] Dworkin suggests two conditions for autonomy. The first, similar to Arrington's discussion of renouncing one's desires, is what Dworkin calls *authenticity*. A desire is autonomous if it is authentic in the sense that it is not renounced or rejected by the person who has it. So, for example, I may desire revenge on someone out of a motivation of jealousy. This desire for revenge is authentic so long as I do not desire that I not be so jealous. That is, a first-order desire is authentic as long as there is no second-order desire that repudiates it. But Dworkin argues that authenticity is not sufficient. In order for a desire to be autonomous, it must also be independently accepted by the individual. If an individual does not or cannot rationally reflect upon the first-order desires, then the fact that he or she doesn't renounce it is not conclusive evidence that it is an autonomous desire. For example, the fact that I have no second-order desire to reject my strong motivation by jealousy might be due to the fact that I have never thought about

my jealous personality in a calm and thoughtful manner. To be fully autonomous, I need to critically reflect on my first-order desires. In Dworkin's terms:

> Autonomy is conceived of as a second-order capacity of persons to reflect
> critically on their first-order preferences, desires, wishes, and so forth, and the
> capacity to accept or attempt to change these in light of higher-order prefer-
> ences and values.[11]

Philosopher Roger Crisp makes a similar point in a response to Arrington.[12]
The fact that consumers do not renounce the choices they make is not conclusive
evidence that those choices are autonomous. The failure to renounce a desire
(or, expressed positively, the fact that we accept a desire) makes it an authentic
desire, in Dworkin's terms. But we still need to know if it can be, or why it is
not, renounced. We still need to know why the first-order desire is accepted. We
would need to know, in Dworkin's terms, if it is independent. It might be the
case that consumers do not renounce their marketplace choices because of the
very effectiveness of advertising.

Let us apply this analysis more directly to marketing. Both Dworkin and
Crisp would hold that for a first-order consumer desire to be autonomous,
two conditions must be met. First, the consumer does not, in fact, renounce or
repudiate the purchase. Such a condition explains the rationale behind many
state laws that allow consumers a two- or three-day cooling off period in which
they can unilaterally repudiate a sales agreement. Recognizing that consumers can be pressured or manipulated into a purchase agreement, many states
allow consumers to back out of the agreement if, upon reflection, they choose to
renounce the desire expressed in the agreement. A second condition on autonomous desires would require that consumers have the capacity to critically
reflect on the desire and to accept it as their own.

Consider the phenomena that we might describe as therapeutic shopping
in which people go shopping to feel better or as a response to depression, or
simply as entertainment. On such occasions consumers purchase something
because it makes them feel good, or they like it. Of course, marketing plays a
major role in designating shopping as entertainment or therapy. On Arrington's
view, the desire to feel good is autonomous as long as the consumer does not
(soon?) come to regret the purchase and repudiate it much the way an alcoholic
might wake up with a hangover and pledge "never again." But Dworkin and
Crisp would argue that the desire is not fully autonomous unless the consumer
critically reflects on that desire. A fully autonomous consumer would ask such
questions as: "Why do I shop to feel good? Is another consumer purchase really
going to make me happy?" Without asking such questions, the first-order desire
to buy something is not fully one's own and not fully autonomous.

Of course, defenders of advertising and marketing will point out that even
if this analysis is correct and some consumer choices are not fully autonomous,
nothing in any of this has shown that advertising and marketing are responsible for violating autonomy. All that has been shown is that some consumers
do not always act in a fully self-conscious and reflective way. What does this
have to do with marketing ethics?

Two things: First, some critics have charged that marketing is partially responsible for the inability of some consumers to step back and critically reflect on these desires. Second, some marketing practices seem to target and exploit those consumers who lack the capacity, or who have a diminished capacity, for making fully autonomous choices. Let us consider the first of these issues before turning to the second in the following section.

Richard Lippke offers a more subtle critique of the role of advertising and marketing in failing to respect consumer autonomy.[13] Relying on the work of Dworkin and others, Lippke points out that autonomy should be understood as a long-term capacity, more a matter of degree than something that characterizes any specific act or desire. Autonomy is not something that one has at one moment and not at the next. Autonomous people live their lives in a self-reflective manner and have the habit, the disposition, and the capacity to deliberate about their lives. By doing this, autonomous individuals shape the entire course of their own lives. Understood in this way, we can recognize that certain conditions are necessary to support the development of these capacities and dispositions. Autonomy requires a variety of intellectual skills, discipline, attitudes, and motivations. But, according to Lippke, it is exactly these capacities and skills that get undermined and weakened by mass marketing and persuasive advertising. All persuasive (as opposed to informative) advertising carry what Lippke calls *meta-messages,* which explicitly oppose the development of the intellectual virtues that are necessary for leading an autonomous life:

> Ads subtly encourage the propensity to accept emotional appeals, oversimplification, superficiality, and shoddy standards of proof for claims. Evidence and arguments of the most ridiculous sorts are offered in support of advertising claims. Information about products is presented selectively (i.e., bad or questionable features are ignored), the virtues of products are exaggerated, and deception and misinformation are commonplace. The meanings of words are routinely twisted so that they are either deceptive or wholly lost."[14]

On Lippke's view, advertising undermines consumer autonomy in an indirect, but still very powerful way. The cumulative effect of mass advertising impedes the development of those intellectual capacities necessary for leading an autonomous life. In this way, advertising subverts the social conditions of autonomy.

9.4 TARGETING THE VULNERABLE: MARKETING AND SALES

The opening section of this chapter spoke in general terms of ethical and unethical ways of influencing people. Unethical modes of influence seek to bypass the agent's rational and voluntary decision-making process. One way to bypass an agent's rational ability is to appeal to psychological motivations such as fear and guilt. That section also spoke of ethical and unethical ways of target marketing. A marketing practice that targets pre-existing and considered desires was judged ethically appropriate. A marketing practice that targets potential customers on the basis of their fears, anxieties, or whims was attempting to manipulate the consumer and therefore was not ethical. This section will examine in more detail marketing practices that target vulnerable populations.

Consider two examples of target marketing. In one case, based on market research supplied by the manufacturer, an automobile dealer learns that the typical customer for a particular model is a single woman, under 35 years old, college educated, has annual income in the $30,000–40,000 range, and enjoys outdoor sports and recreation. Knowing this information, the dealer targets advertising and direct mail to this audience. Ads depict attractive and active young people driving the car brand and enjoying outdoors activities. A second targeted campaign is aimed at selling an emergency call device to elderly widows who live alone. This marketing campaign depicts an elderly woman at the bottom of a stairway crying out, "I've fallen and can't get up!" These ads are placed in media likely to be seen or heard by elderly women. Are these marketing campaigns on an equal ethical footing?

The first marketing strategy appeals to the considered judgments which consumers, presumably, have settled on over the course of their lives. People with similar backgrounds tend to have similar beliefs, desires, and values, and often make similar judgments about consumer purchases. We have no reason to believe that their consumer purchases are motivated by anything other than their considered judgments about their own interests. Target marketing in this sense is simply a means for identifying likely customers based on common beliefs and values. On the other hand, there does seem to be something ethically offensive about the second case. While there may well be a legitimate market for such devices and marketing directed to elderly women is not unethical in itself, this campaign aims to sell the product by exploiting the real fear and anxiety that many older people experience. This marketing strategy clearly tries to manipulate people by appealing to nonrational factors such as fear or anxiety rather than relying on straightforward informative ads.

Yet it could be pointed out that no particular consumer is being exploited or manipulated since each individual consumer is free to ignore the ads and not purchase the product. Further, defenders of this type of marketing might claim that the fear of falling while living alone is no more irrational than the desire of young women to drive sleek and sporty automobiles. Is there anything to the claim that elderly women living alone are more vulnerable than younger women and that this vulnerability creates greater responsibility to marketers? In general, do marketers have special responsibility to the vulnerable?

To answer these questions we need first to consider the concept of vulnerability. To be vulnerable is to be susceptible to some harm. People can be vulnerable in many ways. High blood pressure or a genetic predisposition can make someone vulnerable to a heart attack or stroke. Leaving the keys in one's car makes you vulnerable to car thieves. In general, a person is vulnerable if there is some factor that predisposes that person to a greater risk of harm than what is faced by others. Deciding which factors makes one vulnerable is both an empirical and a conceptual question. For example, to discover which members of a population are most vulnerable to heart attacks, one might conduct an empirical study to find those factors most highly correlated with heart attacks. But beyond these empirical questions, we also need to determine what we mean by identifying someone as particularly susceptible to harm.

Returning to our question, are elderly people living alone particularly vulnerable? The answer to this depends on what we mean by particularly vulnerable. There are two general senses of vulnerability that are relevant for the discussion of target marketing. In one sense, a person is vulnerable as a consumer by being unable in some way to participate as a fully informed and voluntary participant in the market exchange. Valid market exchanges make several assumptions about the participants: They understand what they are doing, they have considered their choice, they are free to decide, and so forth. What we can call *consumer vulnerability* occurs when a person has an impaired ability to make an informed consent to the market exchange. A vulnerable consumer lacks the intellectual capacities, psychological ability, or maturity to make informed and considered consumer judgments. Children would be the paradigmatic example of consumer vulnerability. The harm to which such people are susceptible is the harm of not satisfying one's consumer desires and/or suffering the financial harm of losing one's money. Elderly people living alone are not necessarily vulnerable in this sense.

There is a second sense of vulnerability in which the harm is other than the financial harm of an unsatisfactory market exchange. Elderly people living alone are susceptible to injuries from falls, from medical emergencies, from expensive health care bills, from loneliness. Alcoholics are susceptible to alcohol abuse, the poor are susceptible to bankruptcy, single women walking alone at night are vulnerable to sexual assault, accident victims are susceptible to high medical expenses and loss of income, and so forth. What we can call *general vulnerability* occurs when someone is susceptible to some specific physical, psychological, or financial harm. Pharmaceutical marketing, almost by definition, involves promoting drugs to people who are vulnerable in this sense.

From this we can see that there can be two types of marketing that target vulnerable populations. Some marketing practices might target those consumers who are likely to be uninformed and vulnerable as consumers. Marketing aimed at children, for example, aims to sell products to customers who are unable to make thoughtful and informed consumer decisions. Other marketing practices might target populations that are vulnerable in the general sense as when, for example, an insurance company markets flood protection insurance to home owners living in a river's floodplain. Are either, or both, of such targeting examples ethically legitimate?

As an initial judgment, we must say that marketing that is targeted at those individuals who are vulnerable-as-consumers is unethical. This is a case of taking advantage of someone's frailty and manipulating that for one's own advantage. Clearly a portion of marketing and sales targets people who are vulnerable as consumers. Just as clearly such practices are wrong.

Of course, there are difficulties in deciding who is vulnerable in this sense. Marketing activities target populations, not individuals, and other than children there is perhaps no population that we can identify as essentially vulnerable. Suggestions that the poor or a particular ethnic group, for example, are vulnerable as consumers because they are poor, or Hispanic, or African American, can be insulting, patronizing, and empirically false on the face of it. Nevertheless, targeting certain groups when one has reason to believe that a percentage of that group is particularly vulnerable as consumers is ethically dubious at best. Good test questions to ask include: "Why target this group? What about them makes one think that they are likely consumers for this product?" High potency malt liquor and other alcoholic beverages marketed in the inner city is a good test case. Why might inner-city residents, people who tend (on average) to be poor and disenfranchised from most positions of social influence and power, be a good market for high potency alcoholic drinks? It is difficult to imagine an answer other than the fact that marketers recognize that many people in such a situation seek to deaden their despair with alcohol.[15]

One way that this issue plays out involves groups who are vulnerable in both senses. Often times a person can become vulnerable as a consumer *because* they are vulnerable in some more general sense. The vulnerability that many elderly have in respect to injuries and illness might cause them to make consumer choices based on fear or guilt. A family member grieving over the death of a loved one might make choices in purchasing funeral services based on guilt or sorrow, rather than on a considered judgment. A person with a medical condition or disease is vulnerable and the anxiety or fear associated with this vulnerability can lead to uninformed consumer choices. An inner-city resident who is poor, uneducated, and chronically unemployed is unlikely to weigh the full consequences of the choice of alcoholic beverage.

A number of marketing campaigns seem to fit this model. The most abhorrent (and stereotypical) example is the ambulance-chasing attorney seeking a client for a personal-injury lawsuit. An accident victim is vulnerable to many harms and while experiencing the stress of this situation is unlikely to make a fully informed choice about legal representation. Marketing campaigns that target the elderly for such products as supplemental medical insurance, life insurance, emergency call devices, funeral services, and insurance often target the fears, anxiety, and guilt that many elderly people experience.

But just as there can be people who are made vulnerable as consumers because they are vulnerable to other harms, there can also be cases in which people become vulnerable to other harms because they are vulnerable as consumers. Perhaps this is the most abhorrent case of unethical marketing. Certain products—tobacco and alcohol are the most obvious examples—can make an individual vulnerable to a wide range of health risks. Marketing campaigns for these products that target people who are vulnerable as consumers seem ethically repugnant. This explains the particular public outrage directed at tobacco companies who target young people. It may also characterize marketing of alcoholic beverages in poor inner-city neighborhoods. Marketing malt beverages, fortified wines, and other alcoholic drinks to poor inner-city residents must acknowledge that many people in such situations are not fully autonomous consumers. (One might also think of marketing alcohol to young people in general and on college campuses in particular.) Many people in such situations drink to get drunk. They drink to escape; they drink because they are alcoholics.

The discussion so far has concerned marketing practices in general. Defenders of marketing might point out that marketing targets populations and not individuals. This means that marketers cannot be held liable for decisions that any individual makes because any individual may choose not to buy the marketed product. Defenders would point out that it is difficult to attribute any direct causal connection between a marketing campaign and an individual consumer's choice to buy a product. One cannot hold marketing liable because one cannot "prove" that it caused the purchase.

Surely such a claim would be disingenuous. If marketers really believed that marketing was causally ineffective in influencing consumer choice, they would undercut their own careers. If they truly believed this, then selling their services to businesses would be a straightforward case of fraud. The service that marketers sell to business either works or it does not. If it does work, if marketing can and does influence consumer choice, then marketing cannot disavow ethical responsibility for the consequences of those choices. If it does not work, and if marketers know that, then marketing professionals perpetrate a fraud on anyone who purchases their services. But even if there is some truth to the claim that marketers cannot be liable for individual choices that consumers make because they never target any individual consumer, a similar defense is unavailable in sales.

In a sales situation, an individual salesperson deals not with a general population but with individual customers. Thus, the causal connection between the customer's choice and the sales activity can be evaluated much more directly than in mass marketing cases. If we discover a situation in which a salesperson relies on appeals to fear or anxiety, for example, then we can only assume that this is intended to manipulate the person into a purchase. Because a salesperson has a range of sales tactics and strategies available, and because they usually deal directly with individual customers, we can assume that the choice of sales strategy is based on the salesperson's judgment about what will likely prove influential with this particular customer.

Unlike general marketing activities, sales occur in what we might call a feedback situation. In dealing with an individual, a salesperson (like anyone involved in an interpersonal exchange) continuously receives direct and tacit feedback from the potential customer. In light of that feedback, the salesperson can (and does if they are skilled in sales) adjust the sales pitch accordingly. Salespeople are explicitly trained to do this.

The point of this is that a defense against unethical manipulation that might be used in marketing is unavailable in sales. The marketer might claim that any deception that occurs is unintentional; marketing aims at general populations and any deception that occurs was an unintended (although perhaps foreseeable) consequence. But sales practices that rely on deception, or that appeal to the nonrational fears, desires, and dispositions of customers, cannot make even this claim. Salespersons have a choice to stop the sales pitch if they reasonably believe that the customer is not fully autonomous in making the decision. They are better positioned to avoid manipulation and deception, and if they fail to do so they should be accountable for that decision.

REFLECTIONS ON THE CHAPTER DISCUSSION CASE

Pharmaceuticals are a socially very valuable product, saving countless lives and improving the quality of life for millions of people. As the discussion case of the previous chapter suggests they can also be very dangerous products. Health care costs, led by escalating costs of prescription drugs, impact all of society, and especially employers and employees. How such drugs are marketed, therefore, is a concern not only for potential consumers, but for everyone.

Deception depends, in part, on the deceived person's cognitive and emotional capacities. It is easier to deceive a child than an adult, a careless person than a thoughtful one, an anxious and frightened person than a relaxed and alert one. It is easier for anyone to be deceived about complicated information than it is about simple and obvious facts. It is worth considering at length how vulnerable to deception and manipulation about complex pharmaceuticals are people who are ill or face other medical concerns.

It is also worth speculating about how much of a market there would be for Viagra, Cialis, and Levitra had the FDA not loosened its regulations on drug advertisements. The same question can be asked about other drugs that aim to treat what are called "lifestyle" conditions such as obesity, smoking, high cholestorol, heartburn, and even such problems as allergies, hair loss, anxiety, and depression. This is not to suggest that these conditions are not real or serious, but it is to suggest that they might not best be treated with pharmaceuticals. These products are a useful test case for the analysis of consumer autonomy examined in this chapter.

The complexity of pharmaceuticals also raises important questions about the role of government regulation. Regulating the pharmaceutical industry for both safety and truthfulness requires that the regulators have accurate and timely information about the drugs. Yet, government regulators must rely primarily on the industry itself to provide that information.

REVIEW QUESTIONS

1. Distinguish between manipulation, deception, and a lie. Does the ethical wrong with these practices depend most directly on the consequences or on the intent?
2. Distinguish between ethically acceptable means of influencing another and ethically improper means to influence another. Apply your answer to the case of pharmaceutical ads.
3. Explain how the FDA's standards of deception and unfairness are related. How might an advertisement be both deceptive and unfair?

4. What things does advertising do *for* consumers? What does advertising do *to* consumers? In what ways has advertising done anything to you?
5. Distinguish between autonomous and nonautonomous behavior. Explain the difference between autonomous and nonautonomous desires. Do you have any desires that you would characterize as nonautonomous? What is the difference between first-order and second-order desires?
6. To what degree do you think that modern marketing has created a dysfunctional affluent economy in which irrational and trivial consumer demand has replaced personal and social needs?
7. Explain two ways in which a consumer could be described as vulnerable. What factors might make a person vulnerable in each sense? What are the ethics of marketing to the vulnerable?

ENDNOTES

[1] This discussion case was developed from numerous sources, including the following: *The Truth about Drug Companies,* by Marcia Angell, M.D. (N.Y.: Random House, 2004); "New Study Criticizes Marketing of Prescription Arthritis Drugs," by Marc Kaufman, *The Seattle Times,* January 25, 2005; "Truth in Advertising: Rx Drug Ads Come of Age," by Carol Rados, *FDA Consumer,* 03621332, July/August 2004, Vol. 38, Issue 4; "Cancer Drug Pitched in Support Groups: Effort Highlights an Ethical Debate," by Thanassis Cambanis, *The Boston Globe,* November 12, 2002; "The Pharmaceutical Industry—To Whom Is It Accountable?" by Marcia Angell, *The New England Journal of Medicine,* vol. 342, no. 25, June 22, 2000, pp. 1902–4; U.S. General Accounting Office, "Prescription Drugs: FDA Oversight of Direct-to-Consumer Advertising Has Limitations," October 2002; "All Gifts Large and Small: Toward an Understanding of the Ethics of Pharmaceutical Industry Gift-Giving," by Dana Katz, Arthur Caplan, and Jon Merz, *American Journal of Bioethics,* Summer 2003.

[2] For a more detailed discussion of the relationship between advertising and price, see "Consumer Prices and Advertising," by Paul Farris and David Reibstein, in *Encyclopedic Dictionary of Business Ethics,* edited by Patricia Werhane and R. Edward Freeman (Malden, MA: Blackwell Publishing, 1997).

[3] See, for example, James Miller, one-time FTC Commissioner, "Why FTC Curbs Are Needed" in *Advertising Age,* March, 1982.

[4] See Ivan Preston, *The Great American Blow-Up* (Madison, WI: The University of Wisconsin Press, 1975).

[5] For a well-known statement of this view, see Theodore Levitt, "The Morality (?) of Advertising," *Harvard Business Review* 48, 1970, 84–92.

[6] I adopt here the phrase used by the United States Catholic Bishops in their pastoral letter on the American economy, *Economic Justice for All* (Washington, DC: 1986). "Every perspective on economic life that is human, moral, and Christian must be shaped by three questions: What does the economy do *for* people? What does it do *to* people? And how do people *participate* in it?" p. 1.

[7] See, for example, Vance Packard, *The Hidden Persuaders* (New York: Pocket Books, 1958), and B.F. Skinner, *Beyond Freedom and Dignity* (New York: Alfred Knopf, 1971).

[8] For a critique of the claim that any desire originating in advertising is nonautonomous, see F. A. von Hayek, "The *Non Sequitur* of the Dependence Effect," *Southern*

Economic Journal, 1961, and reprinted in Beauchamp and Bowie, *Ethical Theory and Business* (Englewood Cliffs, NJ: Prentice Hall, 1979), pp. 496–501.

[9] Robert Arrington, "Advertising and Behavior Control," *Journal of Business Ethics* I, 1982, pp. 3–12.

[10] Gerald Dworkin, "Autonomy and Behavior Control," in DesJardins and McCall, *Contemporary Issues in Business Ethics*, 1st ed. (Belmont, CA: Wadsworth Publishing, 1985), pp. 159–166. Dworkin's views are developed more fully in his *The Theory and Practice of Autonomy* (Cambridge: Cambridge University Press, 1988).

[11] Dworkin, *Theory and Practice of Autonomy*, p. 20.

[12] Roger Crisp, "Persuasive Advertising, Autonomy, and the Creation of Desire," *Journal of Business Ethics* 6, 1987, pp. 413–418.

[13] Richard Lippke, "Advertising and the Social Conditions of Autonomy," *Business and Professional Ethics Journal* 8, no. 4 (1988), 35–58, and his *Radical Business Ethics* (Lanham, MD: Rowman and Littlefield, 1995).

[14] *Radical Business Ethics*, pp. 108–109.

[15] This account of vulnerability differs from, but owes much to, George Brenkert's analysis in "Marketing and the Vulnerable," *Business Ethics Quarterly*: The Ruffin Series Special Issue No. 1, 1998, pp. 7–20. For an insightful analysis of marketing alcohol in the inner city, see George Brenkert, "Marketing to Inner-City Blacks: Powermaster and Moral Responsibility," *Business Ethics Quarterly* 8, No. 1, pp. 1–18. Readers familiar with Brenkert's writings will recognize how much of the present chapter has benefited from his work.

10 CHAPTER

Business's Environmental Responsibilities

L E A R N I N G   O B J E C T I V E S

After reading this chapter, you will be able to:

- Describe standard understandings of corporate environmental responsibility;
- Explain the concepts of sustainable economics and sustainable development;
- Compare and contrast standard economic models with sustainable economics;
- Provide an analysis of market-based solutions to environmental challenges;
- Analyze arguments supporting a model for sustainable business;

- Describe the business model of Natural Capitalism;
- Describe the implications of Natural Capitalism for contemporary business.

DISCUSSION CASE: Interface Corporation and Sustainable Business

Carpet manufacturing would not normally be thought of as an environmentally praiseworthy industry. Many carpet fibers are derived from petroleum, a nonrenewable resource, and synthesized with fiberglass and PVC—two known carcinogens—to create the fibers used to manufacture carpeting. The carpeting is then dyed, and the waste produced from this process contains various toxins and heavy metals. Carpet manufacturing factories are heavy industrial producers of CO_2 emissions. Used carpet, especially nylon-based products, are not recycled and therefore end up in landfills. This carpet waste is often toxic and nonbiodegradable.

Reflecting on the environmental record of the carpeting industry, Ray Anderson, the founder, CEO, and chairman of Interface, a $1 billion-a-year carpeting and floor-covering corporation, suggested that "in the future, people like me will go to jail."[1] That now seems unlikely given recent changes at Interface. Over the last decade under Anderson's leadership, Interface has become a leader in the movement to make business environmentally sustainable.

"Sustainability" and "sustainable development" have become something of a mantra among many in the environmental community. The concept of sustainable business can be traced to a UN report authored by then-Prime Minister Gro Bruntland of Norway in which sustainability was defined as the ability "to meet the needs of the present without compromising the ability of future generations to meet their own needs." Since the mid-1990s, Anderson has moved to make Interface a model of sustainable business practices.

Perhaps the most significant change at Interface involves a redefinition of their business. Interface is making a transition from selling carpeting to leasing floor-covering services. On a traditional business model, carpet is sold to consumers who, once they become dissatisfied with the color or style or once the carpeting becomes worn, dispose of the carpet in landfills. There is little incentive here to produce long-lasting or easily recyclable carpeting. Once Interface shifted to leasing floor-covering services, incentives are created to produce long-lasting, easily replaceable and recyclable carpets. Interface thereby accepts responsibility for the entire life cycle of the product it markets. Because they retain ownership and are responsible for maintenance, Interface strives to produce carpeting that can be easily replaced in sections rather than in its entirety, that is more durable, and that can eventually be remanufactured. Redesigning their carpets and shifting to a service lease has also improved production efficiencies and reduced material and energy costs significantly. Consumers benefit by getting what they truly desire at lower costs and fewer burdens.

But Interface has also committed itself to wider-ranging changes. Interface has set seven distinct corporate goals on its road to sustainability. One goal is to continue to redesign their business to focus on delivering services rather than material. This produces incentives to create products that are long-lasting and recyclable rather than products with "planned obsolescence." A second goal is to eliminate, and not simply reduce, all forms of waste. A third goal is to make any and all products that are emitted from the production process nontoxic. Fourth, Interface seeks to reduce energy use and move to renewable and nonpollution sources of energy. Their fifth goal is to "close the loop" of the production process, so that everything that comes out of the process can be recycled back into productive uses. Sixth, Interface strives for resource efficiencies, seeking to transport information rather than products and people. This goal encourages plants to be located near suppliers and retailers and supports information technology, video-conferencing, e-mail, and telecommuting. Finally, Interface is committed to raising community awareness of natural systems and our impact upon them.

DISCUSSION QUESTIONS

1. Interface shifted from a product-based to a service-based company. The growing popularity of leasing in the automotive and computer business suggests that paying for services rather than products might be an innovation that others can adopt. Can you think of other industries and businesses that might make a similar shift? As a consumer, which would you prefer?
2. Some critics argue that sustainability is popular only because it allows industrialized countries to believe, falsely, that consumer-driven lifestyles can continue indefinitely. In what ways do you believe your own lifestyle is sustainable? Unsustainable?
3. Should manufacturers be legally liable for "cradle to grave" responsibility for their products? Should manufacturers be responsible to recycle their products after consumers are finished with them? Who should pay for disposal of consumer goods at the end of their product life?
4. What government policies might encourage other businesses to follow Interface's lead? What government policies hinder such activities?
5. What responsibilities, if any, do we have to future generations? How might these responsibilities change contemporary business?

10.1 CORPORATE SOCIAL RESPONSIBILITY AND THE ENVIRONMENT

A helpful way to begin our analysis of business's environmental responsibilities is to return to the models of corporate social responsibility described in chapter 3. Consider how the classical model of corporate social responsibility would account for business's environmental responsibilities. On the classical model, business's only responsibility is to maximize profit within the law. By doing this, business fills its role within a market system which, in turn, serves the greater overall (utilitarian) good of optimally satisfying consumer preferences (i.e., more people will get more of what they want). Let us examine the implications of this model for the four central environmental issues of pollution and waste, resource conservation, preservation, and biological diversity.

In a well-known book, William Baxter argued that there is an optimal level of pollution that would best serve society's interests. This optimal level is best attained, according to Baxter, by leaving it to the workings of a competitive market.[2] (The reasoning here is identical to what we saw with the market's account of caveat emptor for protecting consumer safety and individual bargaining for protecting employee health and safety.) Denying that there is any "natural" or objective standard for clean air or water (as this view would deny there is an objective state of perfect health), Baxter begins with a goal of "safe" air and water quality, and translates this goal to a matter of balancing risks and benefits. Society *could* strive for pure air and water, but the costs (lost opportunities) that this would entail would be too high. A more reasonable approach is to aim for air and water quality that is safe enough to breathe and drink without costing too much. This balance, the "optimal level of pollution," can be achieved through competitive markets. Society, through the activities of individuals, will be willing to pay for pollution reduction as long as the perceived benefits outweigh the costs.

The free market also provides an answer for resource conservation. From a strict market economic perspective, resources are "infinite."[3] Julian Simon, for example, has argued that resources should not be viewed as material objects but simply as any means to our ends. History has shown that human ingenuity and incentive have always found substitutes for any shortages. As the supply of any resource decreases, the price increases, thereby providing a strong incentive to supply more or provide a less costly substitute. In economic terms, all resources are fungible. They can be replaced by substitutes and in this sense resources are infinite. Resources that are not being used to satisfy consumer demand are being wasted.

A similar case can be made for the preservation of environmentally sensitive areas. Preservation for preservation's sake would, in Baxter's phrase, be a "waste" since it would represent resources that are "employed so as to yield less than they might yield in human satisfactions."[4] Natural objects have no value in their own right and have value only to the degree that humans place value upon them. Again, in Baxter's words:

> I reject the proposition that we *ought* to respect the "balance of nature" or to "preserve the environment" unless the reason for doing so, express or implied, is the benefit of man. I reject the idea that there is a "right" or "morally correct" state of nature to which we should return. The word "nature" has no normative connotation."[5]

Thus, for example, preserving a natural wilderness area rather than developing it as a ski resort should be done only if people are willing to pay more for open space than for skiing. The land itself or the wildlife living on it have no worth independent of what humans desire to use it for. (An interesting philosophical question for defenders of the market at this point is: "Why not?" Assuming that they have no independent worth because market economics has no theoretical place for them begs the question against those who defend the claim that they do have independent value.)

Finally, on a strict free market view, preserving biological diversity is an appropriate policy goal only if doing so satisfies more consumer preferences than the alternative. If people are willing to pay to preserve species, then doing so is a legitimate business goal. Again, Baxter says it best:

> My criteria are oriented towards people, not penguins. Damage to penguins, or sugar pines, or geological marvels is, without more, simply irrelevant. . . . Penguins are important because people enjoy seeing them . . . . I have no interest in preserving penguins for their own sake. . . . [T]his attitude does not portend any massive destruction of nonhuman flora and fauna, for people depend on them in many obvious ways, and they will be preserved because and to the degree that humans do depend on them.[6]

Note that from this perspective, defenders of the market would claim that they are serving the four environmental policy goals outlined previously. While they may not share the values of many environmentalists on such topics as the intrinsic value of animals and other natural objects, they are committed to responsible goals for reducing pollution and waste, conserving resources, and preserving natural areas and biological diversity. Of course, they argue that the best means for determining exactly what those goals entail and how best to achieve them is through the workings of a competitive market. Business need only fulfill its responsibility within the market by pursuing profit within the law.

Challenges to this narrow view of corporate social responsibility are familiar by this point. A variety of market failures, many of the best known of which involve environmental issues, point to the inadequacy of market solutions. One example is the existence of externalities, the textbook example of which is environmental pollution. Since the "costs" of such things as air pollution, groundwater contamination and depletion, soil erosion, and nuclear waste disposal are typically borne by parties "external" to the economic exchange (e.g., people downwind, neighbors, future generations), free market exchanges cannot guarantee optimal results.

A second type of market failure occurs when no markets exist to create a price for important social goods. Endangered species, scenic vistas, rare plants and animals, and biodiversity are just some environmental goods that typically are not traded on open markets (when they are, it often is in ways that seriously threaten their viability as when rhinoceros horns, tiger claws, elephant tusks, and mahogany trees are sold on the black market). Public goods such as clean air and ocean fisheries also have no established market price. With no established exchange value, the market approach cannot even pretend to achieve its own goals of adequately meeting consumer demand. Markets alone fail to guarantee that such important public goods are preserved and protected.

A third way in which market failures can lead to serious environmental harm involves a distinction between individual decisions and group consequences. Important ethical and policy questions can be missed if we leave policy decisions solely to the outcome of individual decisions. Chapter 3 presented the case of individual choice and SUV purchasing as a classic example of such a market failure. (A similar challenge was raised against market solutions to such health concerns as exposure to workplace chemicals.) The example demonstrated that the overall social result of individual calculations might be significant increases in pollution and such pollution-related diseases as asthma and allergies. A number of alternative policies (e.g., restricting SUV sales, increasing taxes on gasoline, treating SUVs as cars instead of light trucks in calculating CAFE standards) that could address pollution and pollution-related disease would never be considered if we relied only on market solutions. Because these are important ethical questions, and because they remain unasked from within market transactions, we must conclude that markets are incomplete (at best) in their approach to the overall social good. In other words, what is good and rational for a collection of individuals is not necessarily what is good and rational for a society.

Such market failures raise serious concerns for the ability of economic markets to achieve a sound environmental policy. Defenders of the narrow view of corporate social responsibility and their economic theory have responses to these challenges, of course. Internalizing external costs and assigning property rights to unowned goods such as wild species are two responses to market failures. But there are good reasons for thinking that such ad hoc attempts to repair market failures are environmentally inadequate. One important reason is what was earlier called the first-generation problem. Markets can work to prevent harm only through information supplied by the existence of market failures. Only when fish populations in the North Atlantic collapsed, for example, did we learn that free and open competition among the world's fishing industry for unowned public goods failed to prevent the decimation of cod, swordfish, Atlantic salmon, and lobster populations. That is, we learn about market failures and thereby prevent harms in the future only by sacrificing the first generation as a means for gaining this information. When public policy involves irreplaceable public goods such as endangered species, rare wilderness areas, and public health and safety, such a reactionary strategy is ill-advised.

But more important than these problems from within the economic approach is the criticism that denies that environmental problems are economic concerns at all. This criticism would reject leaving business's environmental responsibilities to the workings of a competitive market because environmental issues are not economic issues at all. In a series of articles culminating in the book *The Economy of the Earth,* Mark Sagoff develops an insightful and convincing case against the use of economic analysis as the dominant tool of environmental policy makers.[7] Sagoff's analysis is worth reviewing here.

Sagoff argues that economic recommendations concerning the environment rest upon a serious confusion between wants or preferences on one hand, and beliefs and values on the other. Economics deals only with wants and preferences because these are what get expressed in an economic market. The market can measure the intensity of our wants by our willingness to pay (by price), measure and compare individual wants (through cost-benefit analysis), and determine efficient means for optimally fulfilling wants. But markets cannot measure or quantify our beliefs or values. Because many environmental issues involve our beliefs and our values, economic analysis is beside the point. When economics is involved in environmental policy, it treats our beliefs as if they were mere wants and thereby seriously distorts the issue.

What exactly is the distinction between wants and beliefs, and why is it important? When individuals express a want or personal preference, they are stating something that is purely personal and subjective. Another person has no grounds to challenge, rebut, or support my wants. Wants are neither true nor false. If I express my preference for chocolate ice cream, someone cannot challenge that and claim, "No, you don't." I have a privileged status with regard to my wants. In the public sphere, they are taken as a given. Thus do economists treat human interests. Willingness to pay measures the intensity with which I hold my wants (I won't pay more than a few dollars for a dish of chocolate ice cream), but willingness to pay says nothing about the legitimacy or validity of that want.

Beliefs, on the other hand, are subject to rational evaluation. They are objective in the sense that reasons are summoned to support them. Beliefs can be true or false. It would be a serious mistake (a "category mistake" in Sagoff's terms) to judge the validity of a belief by a person's willingness to pay for it. Putting a price on beliefs misunderstands seriously the nature of belief.

Sagoff reminds us that when environmentalists argue that we ought to preserve a national forest for its aesthetic or symbolic meaning, they are not merely expressing a personal want. They are stating a *conviction* about a public good that should be accepted or rejected by others on the basis of reasons, not on the basis of who is most willing to pay for it. Because economics has no way to factor them into its analysis, beliefs and convictions are either ignored or treated as if they were mere wants.

This tendency to reduce all beliefs and values to wants and preferences also seriously distorts the nature of the human being. This distortion treats people at all times as *consumers*. People, at least in so far as the economist or policy maker is concerned, are simply the locations of a given collection of wants. People care only about satisfying their personal wants, and the role of the economist or public official is to determine how to maximally attain this end and not to judge its worthiness. A view such as this was no doubt involved when Vice President Cheney introduced the administration's energy plan by acknowledging that while conservation might be an admirable personal virtue, it was an insufficient basis for sound public policy.

This leads to a second major challenge to economic analysis. By ignoring the distinction between wants and beliefs, market analysis threatens our democratic political process. By treating us as always and only *consumers,* market analysis ignores our lives as *citizens.* As consumers, we may seek to satisfy personal wants; as citizens, we may have goals and aspirations that give meaning to our lives, that determine our nature as a people and culture, that define what we stand for as a people. The market leaves no room for debate, discussion, or dialogue in which we can defend our beliefs with reasons. It ignores the fact that people are active thinkers, not merely passive "want-ers." Most importantly, by ignoring the distinction between wants and beliefs, economic analysis reduces the most meaningful elements of human life—our beliefs and values—to matters of mere personal taste or opinion. Ours is a liberal democratic society— liberal in the sense that we value personal liberty to pursue our individual goals, but democratic in the sense that collectively we seek agreement about public goods and shared goals. Thus, our political system leaves room for both personal *and* public interests. We are all, at one and the same time, both private individuals and public citizens. Market analysis ignores this public realm and thereby undermines our democratic political institutions. According to Sagoff,

> Our environmental goals—cleaner air and water, the preservation of the wilderness and wildlife, and the like—are not to be construed, then, simply as personal wants or preferences; they are not interests to be "priced" by markets or by cost-benefit analysis, but are views or beliefs that may find their way, as public values, into legislation. These goals stem from our character as a people, which is not something we choose, as we might choose a necktie or a cigarette, but something we recognize, something we are. These goals presuppose the reality of public or shared values that we recognize together, values that are discussed and criticized on their merits and are not to be confused with preferences that are appropriately priced in markets. Our democratic political processes allow us to argue our beliefs on their merits.[8]

10.2 BUSINESS'S RESPONSIBILITY AS ENVIRONMENTAL REGULATION

Considerations such as these should lead us to conclude that business has wider environmental responsibilities than those required under a narrow free market approach. A common alternative argues that some goods are so important that they should be exempt from the preference optimizing trade-offs that occur within markets. We've seen this approach before, for example, in our discussions of employee rights and consumer safety. This alternative would support limits, typically in the form of government regulation, on business's economic goals. Such laws as the Clean Air Act, the Clean Water Act, and the Endangered Species Act function in this way by establishing minimal standards for protecting air, water, and species. Once these minimum standards are met, business is then free to pursue its economic goals within the market.

Norman Bowie, for example, has defended a modified version of this narrow view of corporate social responsibility which, in chapter 3, we called the Moral Minimum. On this model, business's economic goals are constrained by an obligation to obey a "moral minimum." Business must first meet certain moral obligations which, once met, then free business to pursue profits. Within this context, Bowie considers if business has any special environmental obligations.[9] Bowie argues that apart from the duties to cause no avoidable harm to humans, to obey the law, and to refrain from unduly influencing environmental legislation, business has no special environmental responsibility. Business may choose, as a matter of supererogation, to do environmental good, but it is otherwise free to pursue profits by responding to the demands of the economic marketplace without any particular regard to environmental responsibilities. In so far as society desires environmental goods (e.g., lowering pollution by increasing the fuel efficiency of automobiles), it is free to express those desires through legislation or within the marketplace. Absent those demands, business has no special environmental responsibilities.

This approach is an improvement over the narrow view in that it acknowledges the legitimacy of exempting some environmental goals from market trade-offs. Thus, this view is consistent with Sagoff's analysis of environmental issues. As citizens, we are free to create laws that regulate and restrict what we, as consumers, desire. Our beliefs and values, expressed through law as well as through consumer choices, establish an ethical context in which we can then pursue our economic ends.

Thus, this Sagoff-Bowie approach would argue that citizens should rely on democratic processes to establish environmental goals. Citizens are also free to use their power as consumers to demand that business provide environmentally sound goods and services. But absent law or consumer demand, business has no particular environmental responsibility.

Several problems suggest that this approach will prove inadequate over the long term. First, it underestimates the influence that business can have in establishing the law. The Corporate Automotive Fuel Efficiency (CAFE) standards is a good example of how this can occur. A reasonable account of this law suggests that the public very clearly expressed a political goal of improving air quality by improving automobile fuel efficiency goals (and thereby reducing automobile emissions). However, the automobile industry was able to use its lobbying influence to exempt light trucks and SUVs from these standards. It should be no surprise that light trucks and SUVs represent the largest selling, and most profitable, segment of the auto industry. To his credit, Norman Bowie recognizes this and argues that business has an obligation to refrain from using its influence to shape environmental regulation. Unfortunately, this seems as praiseworthy a proposal as it is unlikely to have any practical political effect.

Second, this approach also underestimates the ability of business to influence consumer choice. To conclude that business fulfills its environmental responsibility when it responds to the environmental demands of consumers is to underestimate the role that business can play in shaping public opinion. Advertising is a $200 billion a year industry in the United States alone. It is surely disingenuous to claim that business passively responds to consumer desires and that consumers are unaffected by the messages that business conveys. Assuming that business is not going to stop advertising its products or lobbying government, the market-based approach to environmental responsibility that is implicit within this model of corporate social responsibility is inadequate.

Further, there are good reasons to minimize the range of ethical responsibilities enforced by law. The law functions best when it provides general targets for, and side constraints upon, managerial discretion. The law is a crude tool to use to micromanage managerial decisions. It is preferable, on both economic and moral grounds, to expect business to meet its ethical responsibilities without having these mandated by law.

Finally, standard models of corporate social responsibility also underestimate the range of managerial discretion once the duties of law and the moral minimum are met. What can be lost in these discussions is the very important fact that there are many ways to pursue profits within the side constraints of law and morality. Such views also assume that economic growth is environmentally and ethically benign. In the remainder of this chapter, I will argue that it is decidedly not. Business's environmental responsibilities cannot be met without a conscious restructuring of business operations.

10.3 BUSINESS'S ETHICS AND SUSTAINABLE ECONOMICS

A more comprehensive challenge to the ability of markets to set reasonable environmental policy has been raised in the work of Herman Daly and other economists working on sustainable development and ecological economics. Daly makes a convincing case for an understanding of economic *development* that transcends the more common standard of economic *growth*.[10] There are, Daly argues, biological, physical, and ethical limits to growth, many of which the present world economy is already approaching, if not overshooting. Unless we make significant changes in our understanding of economic activity, unless quite literally we change the way we do business, we will fail to meet some very basic ethical and environmental obligations. According to Daly, we need a major paradigm shift in how we understand economic activity.

We can begin with the standard understanding of economic activity and economic growth found in almost every economics textbook. What is sometimes called the *circular flow model* (Figure 10-1) explains the nature of economic transactions in terms of a flow of resources from businesses to households. Business produces goods and services in response to the market demands of households. These goods and services are shipped to households in exchange for payments back to business. These payments are in turn sent back to households in the form of wages, salaries, rents, profits, and interests. These payments are received by households in exchange for the labor, land, capital, and entrepreneurial skills used by business to produce goods and services.

Two items are worth noting. First, natural resources are undifferentiated from the other factors of production. On this model, the origin of resources is never explained. They are simply owned by households from which they, like labor, capital, and entrepreneurial skill, can be sold to business. In the words of Julian Simon, "As economists or consumers, we are interested in the particular services that resources yield, not in the resources themselves."[11] Those services

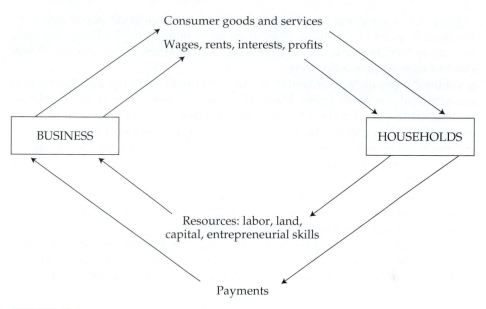

Consumer goods and services

Wages, rents, interests, profits

BUSINESS

HOUSEHOLDS

Resources: labor, land,
capital, entrepreneurial skills

Payments

FIGURE 10-1

can be provided in many ways and by substituting different factors of production. In Simon's terms, resources can therefore be treated as "infinite."

A second observation is that this model treats economic growth as not only the solution to all social ills, but also as boundless. To keep up with population growth, the economy must grow. To provide for a higher standard of living, the economy must grow. To alleviate poverty, hunger, and disease, the economy must grow. The possibility that the economy cannot grow indefinitely is simply not part of this model.

Three points summarize the challenges this model faces into the near future. First, a large percentage of the world population today lives in total privation. One estimate has 1.2 billion people, almost 20 percent of the world's population, living in abject poverty. Eight hundred million people suffer from malnutrition.[12] Obviously, current economic arrangements do not provide for the basic needs of hundreds of millions of people. One reasonable estimate is that the 25 percent of the world's population living in industrialized countries consume 80 percent of the world's resources. The current economic paradigm addresses this problem by promoting further economic growth in the developing world. Yet the world would require significant economic growth during the next few decades just to meet the basic needs of the other 75 percent of the planet's population. According to some estimates, it would need to grow by a factor of five- to tenfold over the next 50 years in order to bring the standard of living of present populations in the developing world in line with the standard of living in the industrialized world.

Second, the world's population during this period will continue to increase significantly, particularly in the most impoverished and already highly populated regions. Even assuming a reduced rate of growth, worldwide population over the next 50 years likely will double, to about 11 billion people. Thus, economic activity to meet the basic needs of the world's population in the near future will need to increase proportionately.

Finally, the only sources for all this economic activity are the natural resources of the earth itself. Many of these resources—clean air, drinkable water, fertile soil, and food—cannot be replaced by the remaining factors of production. We cannot breathe, drink, eat, or grow food on labor, capital, or entrepreneurial skill alone. Because the world's environment is already under stress from current economic activity, the future looks bleak unless major changes take place. Given these realities, we must create an economic system that can provide for the needs of the world's population without destroying the environment in the process. This, according to some, is the role of sustainable economics and sustainable development.

Daly argues that neoclassical economics, with its emphasis on economic growth as the goal of economic policy, will inevitably fail to meet these challenges unless it recognizes that the economy is but a subsystem within Earth's biosphere. Economic activity takes place within this biosphere and cannot expand beyond its capacity to sustain life. All the factors that go into production—natural resources, capital, entrepreneurial skill, and labor—ultimately originate in the productive capacity of the earth. In light of this, the entire classical model will prove unstable if resources move through this system at a rate that outpaces the productive capacity of the earth or of the earth's capacity to absorb the wastes and by-products of this production. Thus, we need to develop an economic system that uses resources only at a rate that can be sustained over the long term and that recycles or reuses both the by-products of the production process and the products themselves. A model of such a system, based on the work of Daly, is printed as Figure 10-2.

Figure 10-2 differs from Figure 10-1 in several important ways. First, there is a recognition that the economy exists within a finite biosphere that encompasses little more than a few miles'-wide band surrounding the earth's surface. From the first law of thermodynamics (the conservation of matter/energy), we recognize that neither matter nor energy can truly be created; it can only be transferred from one form to another. Second, energy is lost at every stage of economic activity. Consistent with the second law of thermodynamics (entropy increases within a closed system), the amount of usable energy decreases over time. "Waste energy" leaves the economic system continuously and thus new low entropy energy must constantly flow into the system. Ultimately, the only source for low-entropy energy is the Sun. Third, natural resources are no longer treated as an undifferentiated and unexplained factor of production emerging from households. Natural resources come from the biosphere and cannot be created ex nihilo. Finally, wastes are produced at each stage of economic activity and these wastes are dumped back into the biosphere.

The conclusion that should be drawn from this new model is relatively simple. Over the long term, resources and energy cannot be used, nor wastes produced, at rates at which the biosphere cannot replace or absorb them without

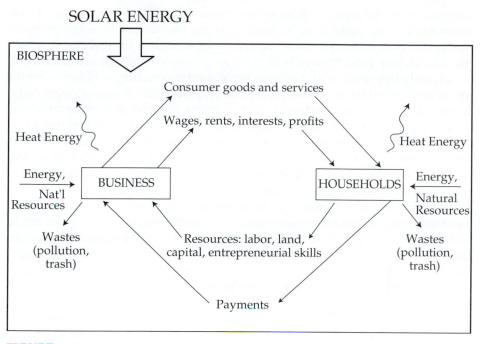

SOLAR ENERGY

BIOSPHERE

Consumer goods and services

Wages, rents, interests, profits

Heat Energy

Heat Energy

Energy,
Nat'l
Resources

BUSINESS

HOUSEHOLDS

Energy,
Natural
Resources

Wastes
(pollution,
trash)

Resources: labor, land,
capital, entrepreneurial skills

Wastes
(pollution,
trash)

Payments

FIGURE 10-2

jeopardizing its ability to sustain (human) life. These are what Daly calls the "biophysical limits to growth."[13] The biosphere can produce resources indefinitely, and it can absorb wastes indefinitely, but only at a certain rate and with a certain type of economic activity. This is the goal of sustainable development. Finding this rate and type of economic activity, creating a sustainable business practice, is the ultimate environmental responsibility of business.

Figure 10-2 also provides us with a model for interpreting the four policy areas of environmental consensus presented previously. The consensus for eliminating pollution and wastes, for prudent use of resources, for preserving environmentally sensitive areas, and for biodiversity can be understood as requiring economic institutions to operate in a sustainable manner within the biosphere.

10.4 BUSINESS ETHICS IN THE AGE OF SUSTAINABLE DEVELOPMENT

Three criteria—the three pillars of sustainability—are often used to judge sustainable practices. Sustainable development must be economically, environmentally, and socially satisfactory. Economically, sustainable practices must be able, in the words of the World Commission on Environment and Development (an agency of the United Nations), to meet the "needs of the present without compromising the ability of future generations to meet their own needs." Environmentally, they must do so without harming the ability of the biosphere to sustain life over the long term. Socially, they must address the real needs of people, particularly those hundreds of millions of people who lack adequate food, water, and other necessities. I suggest three similar criteria by which we should judge models of business's environmental responsibility. Business ought to be arranged in such a way that it adequately meets the economic expectations of society (i.e., jobs, income, and goods and services) in an efficient manner. Business ought also to be arranged in a way that supports, rather than degrades, the ability of the biosphere to sustain life, especially but not exclusively human life, over the long term. Business also ought to be arranged in a way that addresses minimum demands of social justice.

As we begin to consider how business should be restructured in order to meet its environmental responsibilities, it is worth emphasizing a point made previously. We should not underestimate the range of managerial discretion. Business managers, rightfully, enjoy a wide range of decision-making discretion. As Ray Anderson and Interface Corporation demonstrate, there are many ways to pursue and attain profitability. We must move away from the view of environmental responsibilities as side constraints on *the* pursuit of profit, as if there is only one way to pursue profits, and ethical responsibilities are a barrier to that. Rather, we must recognize that some avenues to profitability are environmentally risky, and others environmentally prudent and sensible. Fortunately, we have some good models for environmentally sustainable business practices.

In *Natural Capitalism*, authors Paul Hawken, Amory Lovins, and Hunter Lovins provide a conceptual model for, and numerous examples of, sustainable business practices.[14] I will follow their work in sketching some specifics of an environmentally responsible business model.

Natural Capitalism offers four guiding principles for the redesign of business. First, the productivity of natural resources must and can be dramatically increased. This constitutes a further development of what is sometimes called *ecoefficiency.* A second principle, called *biomimicry* or *closed-loop design,* requires that business be redesigned to model biological processes. By-products formerly lost as waste and pollution must be eliminated, reintegrated into the production process, or returned as a benign or beneficial product to the biosphere. Third, traditional models of business as producer of goods should be replaced with a model of business as provider of services. The old economy focuses on producing goods (e.g., light bulbs and carpets), when consumer demand really focuses on services (e.g., illumination and floor-covering). This shift can provide significant incentives for accomplishing the first two goals. Finally, business must reinvest in natural capital. As any introductory textbook in economics or finance teaches, responsible business management requires a reinvestment in productive capital. Because traditional economic models have ignored the origin of natural capital, they have neglected to include reinvestment in natural capital as part of prudent business practice. An environmentally responsible business must address this shortcoming.

Both ecoefficiency and biomimicry can be understood in terms of Figure 10-2. Ecoefficient management would discover ways to reduce the rate at which natural resources flow through the economic system. *Natural Capitalism* contains numerous examples in which managerial decisions regarding the design of both products and production methods have increased resources efficiency by a factor of 5, 10, and in some cases even 100. The standard growth model of economic development tells us that we can meet the needs of the poorest 75 percent of the world's population by increasing economic growth by a factor of 5–10. Ecoeffcient business practices aim for the same end by increasing efficiency, and therefore decreasing resource use, by a factor of 5–10.

Examples of ecoefficiency can be found in many areas of business operations. Business managers must find ways to meet consumer demand with fewer resources. A simple example would be a housing developer who designs a neighborhood with cluster housing, green spaces, habitat corridors, and biking trails instead of the traditional "cookie-cutter" development pattern. Each development pattern can be profitable, but one is more environmentally destructive than the other. Energy demand is another particularly apt example for this responsibility. *Natural Capitalism* describes the redesign of an industrial pumping system at Interface Corporation. With an eye towards reducing energy demand, the redesign with larger and straighter pipes resulted in a 92 percent, or twelve-fold, energy savings. Energy efficient windows, lighting, motors, and insulation in the design and upgrade of every building would greatly reduce overall energy use while still meeting present production targets.

Ecoefficiency alone is only part of the solution. The principle of biomimicry attempts to eliminate the wastes produced by even ecoeffcient production processes. Business managers have a responsibility to seek ways to integrate former wastes back into the production system, transform wastes into biologically beneficial elements, or, minimally, produce wastes at rates no faster than the biosphere can absorb them.

The ultimate goal of biomimicry is to eliminate wastes altogether rather than reducing them. If we truly mimic biological processes, the end result of one process (e.g., leaves and oxygen produced by photosynthesis) is ultimately reused as the productive resources (e.g., soil and water) of another process (plant growth) with only solar energy added.

The evolution of business strategy toward biomimicry can be understood along a continuum. The earliest phase has been described as "take-make-waste." Business takes resources, makes products out of them, and discards whatever is left over. A second phase envisions business taking responsibility for its products from the "cradle to grave." Sometimes referred to as "life cycle" responsibility, this approach has already found its way into both industrial and regulatory thinking. Cradle to grave, or life cycle responsibility, holds that business is responsible for the entire life of its products, including the ultimate disposal even after the sale. Thus, for example, the cradle to grave model would hold business liable for groundwater contamination caused by its products even years after they had been buried in a landfill.

Cradle to cradle responsibility extends this idea even further and holds that business should be responsible for incorporating the end results of its products back into the productive cycle. This responsibility, in turn, would create incentives to redesign products so that they could, efficiently and easily, be recycled.

The environmental design company McDonough and Braungart, founded by architect William McDonough and chemist Michael Braungart, has been a leader in helping businesses reconceptualize and redesign business practice to achieve sustainability. Their book, *Cradle to Cradle,* traces the life cycle of several products, providing case studies of economic and environmental benefits attainable when business takes responsibility for the entire life cycle of products. Among their projects is the redesign of Ford Motor Company's Rouge River manufacturing plant. This $2 billion redesign will introduce sustainable principles to one of the world's largest industrial complexes. Reinvestment in productive capital is a basic economic responsibility for every business manager. Doing so in the way that Ford intends, in a way that addresses environmental and social concerns as well as economic ones, should be among the ethical responsibilities of every business manager.

The third principle of sustainable business practice may require a greater paradigm shift in business management. Traditional manufacturing aims to produce goods; this new model shifts to providing services. This shift, according to *Natural Capitalism,* will reinforce principles of both ecoefficiency and biomimicry. Traditional economic and managerial models interpret consumer demand as the demand for products (e.g., washing machines, carpets, lights, consumer electronics, air conditioners, cars, computers). A service-based economy interprets consumer demand as a demand for services (e.g., clothes cleaning, floor-covering, illumination, entertainment, cool air, transportation, word processing). *Natural Capitalism* provides examples of businesses that have made such a shift in each of these industries. This change produces incentives for product redesigns that create more durable and more easily recyclable products.

Interface Corporation, described in the discussion case that opened this chapter, is a well-known innovator in this area. Interface has made a transition from selling carpeting to leasing floor-covering services. On the traditional model, carpet is sold to consumers who, once they become dissatisfied with the color or style or once the carpeting becomes worn, dispose of the carpet in landfills. There is little incentive here to produce long-lasting or easily recyclable carpeting. Once Interface shifted to leasing floor-covering services, incentives were created to produce long-lasting, easily replaceable, and recyclable carpets. Interface thereby accepts responsibility for the entire life cycle of the product it markets. Because it retains ownership and is responsible for maintenance, Interface now produces carpeting that can be easily replaced in sections rather than in its entirety, that is more durable, and that can eventually be remanufactured. Redesigning its carpets and shifting to a service lease has also improved production efficiencies and reduced material and energy costs significantly. Consumers benefit by getting what they truly desire at lower costs and fewer burdens.

Finally, business managers have a responsibility to reinvest in natural capital, the one factor of production traditionally ignored in economic and financial analysis. The principle involved in this is simple, but its implementation is a challenge. The principle is that business has a responsibility not to use resources at rates faster than what can be replenished by the biosphere, and especially ought not to destroy the productive capacity of the biosphere itself. The financial analogue is a business that liquidates capital for operating expenses or the household that spends savings as income. The prudential and responsible decision is to use the income generated by capital for living expenses while reserving the capital itself for long-term viability. So, too, with natural capital. We ought to use this capital only at the rate at which it can renew itself.

Because the productive capacity of the biosphere is a true public good and because of the many market failures and incentives for individuals to act irresponsibly in such cases, reinvestment in natural capital is perhaps one business responsibility that should be especially subject to government regulation. Business managers ought to do so, but as individuals operating within competitive markets they cannot be expected to do so. Tax incentives to encourage such investment, and tax penalties for uncompensated resource extraction, are one option.

The roof of the Ford Rouge factory is one simple example of reinvesting in nature. This roof will be covered with ivylike sedum plants that will not only reduce water runoff and add insulation value but, like all plants, they will also convert carbon dioxide (a major auto-emission pollutant) to oxygen. Tax subsidies for such decisions, especially if there are short-term economic disincentives for doing this, seem a reasonable policy. We already have a model for this in gasoline taxes that are earmarked for highway construction and repair. There is no reason why similar taxes could not be targeted at other industries that treat nature's capital as income and the monies devoted to a reinvestment in nature's capital.

10.5 CONCLUSIONS

This chapter has provided a blueprint for how we ought to think about business's environmental responsibilities. I have argued for an approach that balances economic considerations with environmental responsibilities. I suggested that competitive markets, even those constrained by law and moral obligation, are unlikely to allow business to meet reasonable environmental responsibilities. Yet strong market conditions are necessary if business is to meet our legitimate economic expectations as well. Reconceiving business's ethical responsibilities in light of the economics of sustainable development provides a model for how business institutions might meet both our environmental and economic expectations.

REFLECTIONS ON THE CHAPTER DISCUSSION CASE

Interface encountered significant business challenges and disappointments in 2000–2003. A national and international economic downturn resulted in a substantial decrease in office and commercial construction, which represents over

80 percent of Interface's business. Sales of its broadloom carpet declined by one-third. As a result of this lost business, Interface had to reduce its worldwide staff by 30 percent. By 2004 business improved and Interface returned to profitability, in part due to the increased efficiencies created during the economic downturn.

But Interface's modular carpeting business remained strong, accounting for more than 50 percent of their 2003 sales, and its sustainability initiatives continued. The company estimates that the total savings of its sustainability initiatives during the years 1995 to 2003 were over $230 million. Obviously, these savings were another factor in the company's ability to weather the economic storm. Part of these savings were due to a decrease of more than 30 percent in total energy consumption in its manufacturing processes. The company also reported that manufacturing processes realized significant and measurable decreases in greenhouse gas emissions and water usage. It reduced its reliance on petroleum-based materials by 28 percent since the sustainability initiatives began in 1994.

Interface refers to environmental challenges as "Mount Sustainability," and it admits that even after ten years it still has a long way to go to the summit. Clearly, even with strong and widespread support from its CEO and throughout the rest of the corporation, sustainability is not something easily achieved.

Three questions are worth considering at this point. First, are there other manufacturers that could follow the Interface example, particularly in the shift from a product-based to a service-based business model? Second, how dependent is this shift upon strong leadership? Some suggest that the Interface story is unique because of the values and personality of Ray Anderson. Is it possible to achieve a major shift in corporate culture without leadership from the highest corporate levels? Third, which ethical categories are best applied to Interface? For example, as described previously, Norman Bowie distinguished between acts that cause harm, acts that prevent harm, and acts that accomplish good. Bowie argues that moral obligations, the "moral minimum," involve only the duty to cause no harm. Is the shift towards sustainability something that, like corporate philanthropy, is to be praised as doing good but is not something ethically obligatory? Are the sustainability initiatives at Interface doing good, preventing harm, or not causing harm? Do all companies have an ethical duty to follow Interface's lead?

REVIEW QUESTIONS

1. How would you define a *sustainable* business? What are the three pillars of sustainability?
2. Give examples of at least two market failures and explain how they represent challenges to the free market understanding of business's environmental responsibilities.
3. What is the difference between *consumer desires* and *citizen beliefs?* How is this distinction relevant to business's environmental responsibility?

4. What is the *circular flow model* of economic transactions? Explain how this model differs from the sustainable economics of Herman Daly.
5. Explain the four guiding principles of *natural capitalism* as developed by Lovins, Lovins, and Hawken.

ENDNOTES

[1]The Anderson quote is from "In the Future, People Like Me Will Go to Jail," in *Fortune*, May 24, 1999, pp. 190–200. Information of the Interface Corporation can be found on the company website, www.interfaceinc.com.

[2]William Baxter, *People or Penguins: The Case for Optimal Pollution* (New York: Columbia University Press, 1974).

[3]Julian Simon, *The Ultimate Resource* (Princeton, NJ: Princeton University Press, 1981).

[4]Baxter, op. cit., p. 5.

[5]Baxter, p. 8.

[6]Baxter, p. 5.

[7]Mark Sagoff, *The Economy of the Earth* (New York: Cambridge University Press, 1990).

[8]Ibid., pp. 28–29.

[9]Norman Bowie, "Money, Morality, and Motor Cars," In W. Michael Hoffman, Robert Frederick, and Edward Petry (eds.), *Business, Ethics, and the Environment* (New York: Quorum Books, 1990), pp. 89–97.

[10]Herman Daly, *Beyond Growth* (Boston: Beacon Press, 1996).

[11]Simon, op. cit., p. 12.

[12]See, for example, John Bongaarts, "Population: Ignoring its Impact," in *Scientific American*, January 2002, pp. 67–69. Bongaarts's essay is one of four critical responses to Bjorn Lomborg, *The Skeptical Environmentalist* (Cambridge University Press, 2001) published by Scientific American. Lomborg's is only the most recent attempt to downplay the reality of any worldwide environmental crisis. The four reviews in *Scientific American* raise significant and insurmountable challenges to Lomborg's methodology and data.

[13]Daly, op. cit., pp. 33–35.

[14]Hawken, Paul, Lovins, Amory, and Lovins, Hunter, *Natural Capitalism* (Boston: Little, Brown and Company, 1999).

11 CHAPTER

Diversity and Discrimination

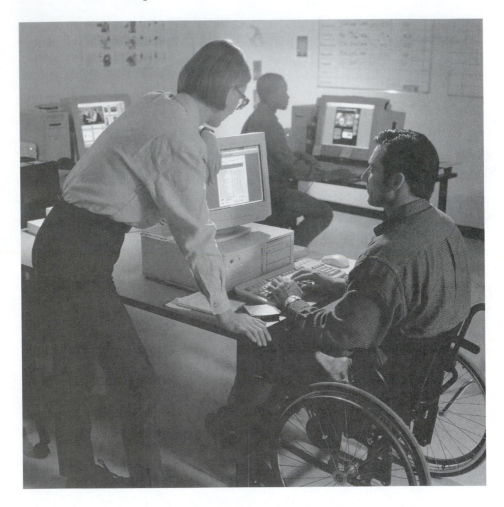

LEARNING OBJECTIVES

After reading this chapter, you will be able to:

- Describe a range of ethical issues raised by a diverse workforce;
- Explain workplace discrimination;

232

- Distinguish between equal opportunity, affirmative action, and preferential treatment;

- Explain the ethical basis of equal opportunity and affirmative action;

- Analyze the ethical arguments for and against preferential treatment in the workplace;

- Describe the issue of workplace sexual harassment.

DISCUSSION CASE: Female Foreman and the Brotherhood

Margaret Reynolds was hired as an electrician at the Atlantic City Convention Center in 1985. Two years later she was appointed as a "subforeman" for the West Hall section of the Convention Center. In late September of 1987, shortly after the 1987 Miss America pageant closed, Ms. Reynolds and 16 other electricians were discharged by the Convention Center. The next day, 7 electricians were rehired and within three days 12 electricians were back working at the center. Ms. Reynolds was not among the 12. Ms. Reynolds sued both the Convention Center and her local union of the International Brotherhood of Electrical Workers claiming that she was a victim of sexual harassment while working at the Convention Center and that she was fired because she was a woman.

The United States legal system recognizes two forms of sexual harassment. Quid pro quo (Latin for "this for that") harassment occurs when granting sexual favors is made a condition of employment, as when a manager threatens an employee with dismissal unless she agrees to a sexual relationship with him or promises workplace benefits to an employee who does submit to his sexual offer. Hostile work environment occurs when a pattern of sexual harassment within the workplace prevents a woman from doing her job. Both forms of sexual harassment are understood to be forms of employment discrimination on the basis of sex, an activity prohibited by the Civil Rights Act of 1964. That law makes it illegal to deny anyone equal employment opportunities on the basis of sex.

In defining sexual harassment, the Equal Employment Opportunities Commission (EEOC) guidelines describe the kinds of workplace conduct that may be actionable under the law. These include "[u]nwelcome sexual advances, requests for sexual favors, and other verbal or physical conduct of a sexual nature." These guidelines provide that such sexual misconduct constitutes prohibited "sexual harassment," whether or not it is directly linked to the grant or denial of an economic quid pro quo, where "such conduct has the purpose or effect of unreasonably interfering with an individual's work performance or creating an intimidating, hostile, or offensive working environment." In concluding that "hostile environment" (i.e., non quid pro quo) harassment violates the law, the EEOC relied upon legal precedents developed in cases of racial and ethnic discrimination. Those precedents gave employees the right to work in an environment free from discriminatory intimidation, ridicule, and insult. If such an environment existed and interfered with the terms, conditions, and privileges of employment, courts held that unlawful discrimination had occurred. In the words of one court, "[T]he phrase 'terms, conditions or privileges of employment' in [Title VII] is an expansive concept which sweeps within its protective ambit the practice of creating a working environment heavily charged with ethnic or racial discrimination. . . . One can readily envision working environments so heavily polluted with discrimination as to destroy completely the emotional and psychological stability of minority group workers. . . ." In applying these standards to a case of alleged sexual harassment, another court concluded that "sexual harassment which creates a hostile or offensive environment for members of one sex is every bit the arbitrary barrier to sexual equality at the workplace that racial harassment is to racial equality. Surely, a requirement that a man or woman run a gauntlet of sexual abuse in return for the privilege of being allowed to work and make a living can be as demeaning and disconcerting as the harshest of racial epithets." [Court of Appeals for the Eleventh Circuit, in *Henson v. Dundee*, 682 F.2d 897, 902 (1982).]

Of course, not all harassment sufficiently affects the "terms, conditions and privileges of employment." For sexual harassment to be actionable, it must be sufficiently severe or pervasive "to alter the conditions of [the victim's] employment and create an abusive working environment."

Margaret Reynolds claimed that the work environment among the electricians at the Atlantic City Convention Center was both severe and pervasive enough to create an unjust barrier to her employment. According to the United States Department of Labor, women constituted just 2.3 percent of all workers in the construction trades in the year 2000. Women also held about the same percentage of supervisory positions within construction trades. Only 1 of the other 17 electricians employed by the Convention Center was a woman.

By all accounts, this workplace was normally characterized by obscene, vulgar, and crude comments and behavior. The court acknowledged that the workplace environment was "pervaded by a lexicon of obscenity" and "permeated by profanity." It was apparently normal for workers to refer to each other by obscene names and to regularly use vulgar and crude language and gestures. On only several occasions, however, was Ms. Reynolds specifically and directly targeted by such behavior and language, being called a "cunt" and "douche-bag cunt" on two occasions by co-workers. On several occasions, other co-workers would grab their crotch as they walked by her. On several other occasions some male workers refused to work with or for Ms. Reynolds. There was also some evidence that her supervisors received complaints during the Miss America pageant that pageant organizers felt uncomfortable having female construction workers present during the pageant.

In deciding the Reynolds case, a United States District Court considered whether this workplace environment was so hostile and offensive that it constituted sexual harassment. The court acknowledged that it was common for male electricians to call each other obscene names and make obscene, crude, and sexual gestures to other males. Ms. Reynolds admitted that while some of these comments seemed intended to offend her, most of the time it was just the way the male workers behaved. She also admitted that she herself had used obscene language at work and had also called male workers obscene names under her breath.

In *Margaret Reynolds v. Atlantic City Convention Center,* the District Court ruled that "in an atmosphere otherwise permeated by obscenity," the few occasions when harassment was targeted at Ms. Reynolds were not "sufficiently severe and persistent to affect seriously the psychological well-being of a reasonable employee." The court ruled that the harassment aimed at Ms. Reynolds was "isolated" rather than "pervasive" and that "these gestures and remarks were not made in church." Given the "totality of the circumstances," the harassment experienced by Ms. Reynolds did not alter the conditions of her work sufficiently to constitute an unjust denial of equal employment opportunity. It would appear, from the court's perspective, that part of the normal terms and conditions of construction work is an atmosphere of obscene and crude language and behavior. Since it was not specifically targeted at a woman and since it was not explicitly nor exclusively sexual, this normal standard of behavior did not discriminate and therefore was not illegal.

DISCUSSION QUESTIONS

1. Are there some jobs that are inappropriate for women to hold?
2. Does workplace vulgarity and obscenity represent a particular barrier to women?
3. Was there anything particularly "sexual" about the harassment aimed at Ms. Reynolds? Would the same language and behavior aimed at a man mean the same?
4. Construct a parallel case involving racial or ethnic workplace harassment. Do the conclusions you reach concerning racial or ethnic harassment match the conclusions you reach concerning sexual harassment?
5. Is there a difference between harassment based on sex and harassment based on gender? Should both be covered by equal opportunity laws?
6. Did Ms. Reynolds have as equal an opportunity to succeed in her job as a man?

11.1 INTRODUCTION: DIVERSITY AND EQUALITY

Data from the 2000 U.S. census confirm the common observation that the American workforce is becoming increasingly diverse. Within the civilian labor force, the percentage of male workers is projected to increase by less than 10 percent between the years 1998 and 2008, while the number of women workers is projected to increase by more than 15 percent. During the same period, the percentage of African American workers will increase by almost 20 percent, the Hispanic workers by 36 percent, and Asian American workers by over 40 percent.[1]

These figures from the workforce parallel general population data. Between 1990 and 1999, the U.S. white population increased just over 7 percent. During the same period, the African American population increased 14 percent, Hispanic population increased 40 percent, and the population of Asian American and Pacific Islanders increased 44 percent.[2] White males have not comprised the majority of the U.S. workforce since the 1970s.

Managing this changing and diverse workforce presents business management with both opportunities and challenges. Greater diversity within labor pools provides management with the opportunity to find employees with a wider range of talents, experiences, and abilities. Companies that find, recruit, hire, and retain such workers can achieve many competitive advantages in the marketplace.

Nevertheless, an increasingly diverse population in and out of the workforce creates challenges to business as well. As the Reynolds case demonstrated, what is acceptable and normal behavior with one type of worker can be offensive and a barrier to others. A diverse workforce will very likely experience similar situations in which differences among genders, ethnic groups, and cultures can create significant barriers to an efficient and peaceful workplace. Further, the workplace is but a subset of the wider society, and social concerns of equality and discrimination can be expected to appear within the workplace.

Despite decades of legal and political initiatives to bring equal opportunities to women and minorities, significant economic and social inequalities remain in the wider society. Business institutions are a prime resource for addressing these inequalities. An increasingly diverse workforce also has not yet translated into increased diversity in positions of authority, in equality of wages and benefits, and in positions of power and prestige. Evidence suggests that true equal opportunity does not yet flourish within business institutions.

Consider the mixed record on workplace equality for women. Women have made significant gains in many professional careers, for example. Between 1970 and 1990, the percentage of women physicians more than doubled from 7.6 to 16.9 percent. Between 1973 and 1993, the percentage of women lawyers and judges increased from 5.8 to 22.7 percent, and women in engineering increased from 1.3 to 8 percent.[3] Yet women remain clustered in lower-paid and lower-status jobs, are relatively absent from higher-paying blue-collar and management positions, and continue to be paid lower wages than men. Forty percent of native-born working women fill positions classified as "administrative support" and "service" by the U.S. Bureau of Labor Statistics, while fewer than 16 percent of male workers fill such jobs. In private industry, white men comprise 65 percent of managerial positions, white women hold 25 percent, minority men 6.5 percent, and minority women less than 4 percent. Women in general hold less than 5 percent of all senior-level positions in major corporations.[4]

Significant wage gaps correlated with gender and race also persist. Overall women still make only 75 cents to a man's dollar (up from 63 cents in 1979). White women in 1993 earned 70.8 percent of the salary of white men, while black women and Hispanic women were paid 63.7 percent and 53.9 percent, respectively. Across the board, women with the same training and educational credentials are paid less than their male counterparts. According to data from the 2000 U.S. census, native-born women with college degrees earn 74 cents for every dollar an equally educated native-born man earns, and the percentage remains very constant for all educational levels. Even the most highly educated women soon fall behind equally educated men. For example, a study of the Class of 1982 Stanford MBAs found that by 1992 the men in the class were far more likely than the women to work as CEOs, vice presidents, or directors, and, as a result, received more pay. Sixteen percent of men from this class at Stanford held CEO job titles, while only 2 percent of women were CEOs. Twenty-three percent of male 1982 Stanford MBA graduates worked as corporate vice presidents and 15 percent served as directors, compared with 10 percent of women who were vice presidents and 8 percent of women who held director positions. On average, the women Stanford MBA graduates from the Class of 1982 made 73.1 percent of the salaries of men graduates. Holding age constant also does little to eliminate the wage gap. The AMA found in 1989 that women physicians under age 40 made 66.6 percent of male salaries, women between 40 and 49 years earned 58.4 percent, and women 50 and over were paid 66.4 percent of a male physician's salary.[5]

The situation for minority workers is at least as bleak. In 1940 black men earned on average only 40 cents for every dollar earned by white men. By 1990 black men's wages had climbed to about 75 percent of white men's, and, by 1998, to 76 percent. Real wages (wages adjusted for inflation) of black men overall have stagnated or even declined since 1975. Further, the unemployment rate of black men remains twice that of white men, and their labor force participation rate lags behind that of whites. While these rates improved dramatically with the strong economy in the period 1993 to 1999, the unemployment rate of adult black men is still in the range of 6 to 7 percent and that of black teens in the range of 25 to 30 percent.[6] Comparable unemployment for white men was about half that for black males.

In this chapter, we shall consider what ethical responsibilities business has for addressing these challenges. We shall be guided at the start by a brief review of the early development of equal opportunity law. Before we start, perhaps a reminder about the importance of shifting perspectives within ethical controversies is worthwhile.

The majority of people reading this book will be college students, and approximately half will be male. The natural inclination will be to approach this issue as soon-to-be job applicants who will either benefit from, or be hindered by, policies of affirmative action and preferential hiring. I am willing to predict that the majority of college-aged white males will oppose preferential hiring policies, not surprising perhaps. My advice to all readers is that you try to take the point of view of different parties to these debates. Consider the legitimacy of affirmative action and preferential policies from the point of view of various job applicants, as well as business managers and democratic citizens. Consider not only how you might be affected by such policies, but also how they might contribute to, or hinder, the development of a just society.

11.2 DISCRIMINATION, EQUAL OPPORTUNITY,
AND AFFIRMATIVE ACTION

An increasingly diverse workplace does present business with many challenges. Some, such as attracting and retaining skilled workers, are managerial. Others, such as insuring that workers of diverse backgrounds and expectations are treated fairly, are ethical. The following sections will examine the ethical questions raised by affirmative action and preferential hiring policies that are aimed at alleviating the racial, sexual, and ethnic inequalities sketched above.

Some might think that it is unfair or unreasonable to hold business responsible for such an intractable social problem as racial, sexual, or ethnic discrimination. From this perspective, business only has a responsibility to obey the law that prohibits discrimination in employment, but anything beyond that is asking too much of what are, after all, economic institutions. Accordingly, as long as business does not deny equal treatment and equal opportunity, it has fulfilled its legal and ethical responsibility concerning discrimination in work and commerce. This common view is worth considering at some length.

The first thing to note is that this view rests upon the assumed value of equality. This in itself is testimony to how far this legal and ethical debate has advanced in just a few decades. As recently as the 1960s, many state laws not only allowed but actually required racial segregation in public places and in schools. Women were also excluded from many jobs, many professions, and many schools for decades after they received the right to vote in 1920. It is easy to forget (if in fact students of the twenty-first century ever even knew) that the Civil Rights Act of 1965 was politically a very controversial measure that required significant changes throughout American society, not the least of which was in the workplace and in commerce. (It would be interesting in this regard to consider if Margaret Reynolds's co-workers really were committed to giving women an equal opportunity to work as electricians.)

But if twentieth century history is mixed on discrimination, surely the twenty-first century is not. A commitment to equal treatment for each individual, providing each person with equal economic opportunity, is about as strong an ethical consensus as exists, at least in North America, Europe, and throughout much of the rest of the world. The ethical basis for this consensus can be found as a fundamental tenet of all major ethical theories, if not a fundamental assumption of morality itself. All individuals deserve equal moral standing. As a first approximation of business's ethical responsibility concerning discrimination, then, we can say that the commitment to equal opportunity requires business not to discriminate in any of its activities. This responsibility is sometimes referred to as requiring a policy of *passive nondiscrimination*. Business fulfills this responsibility as long as it does not do what is wrong—that is, as long as it does not discriminate. The remaining question is whether business has the further responsibility to take some positive, or "affirmative," action to counter the effects of discrimination. The question becomes, Is legal access, what is often called formal equal opportunity, a sufficient public policy for addressing the problem of discrimination? To answer this question, we need to consider in more detail exactly what this problem is.

Let us first note that discrimination itself is not necessarily a bad thing. *Discrimination* most generally refers to the ability to make distinctions, as when we describe someone as having discriminating tastes in food or music. In the workplace, we reasonably expect employers to make discrimination between employees by making distinctions between those who are hired and those who are not, between those who are promoted and those who are not, and so forth. Ethical problems arise only when the criteria used in making such discrimination are unethical or unfair.

For example, suppose I am hiring someone for a position to create and maintain a Web site for my business. It makes perfect sense to discriminate between job candidates on the basis of computer literacy and experience in working on Web sites. If I discriminate on the basis of job-relevant criteria, it would seem that I have acted in an ethically responsible way. All candidates have an equal opportunity to apply for the job, but only the person best qualified gets to be hired.

Consider a slightly different example. Suppose I have a pool of qualified candidates for this position and must discriminate between equally qualified people. Suppose also that one of the candidates graduated from my alma mater, Southern Connecticut State University. Suppose, as a loyal alumni, I like to support my school and I therefore offer the job to that candidate. I do not claim that this candidate is better qualified than others, only that I have a personal preference for SCSU graduates. Have I done anything wrong by discriminating on the basis of personal preference rather than job-relevant criterion?

Let us now change this example somewhat. Imagine that my preference was not for hiring Southern Connecticut graduates, but for hiring white males. One could imagine such a preference among Margaret Reynolds's co-workers, for example. What, if anything, is the difference between hiring preferences that favor one's alma mater and those that favor white males? Or suppose, as is often done, a company gives hiring preference to family members of present employees? Is this company's desire to reward loyal employees a violation of equal opportunity?

Reflecting back on discussions in earlier chapters, we can review several general ethical perspectives on this issue. A utilitarian concern for economic efficiency would be inclined to support a narrow view of employment qualifications. Managers should make hiring decisions based primarily on the ability of the candidate to perform the job efficiently and skillfully. But as in all utilitarian calculations, other consequences (e.g., the goodwill of long-term employees whose family is given preference in hiring) must also be considered. A more libertarian approach that emphasizes property rights and managerial prerogatives would support greater latitude for managerial discretion in hiring. A general concern for justice, however, would constrain both approaches to ensure that all individuals are treated with fairness and equal respect.

Acknowledging that decisions such as the Southern Connecticut hire are often made, we might say that when all other qualifications are equal, employers should enjoy wide latitude in making hiring decisions. Of course, the degree of managerial prerogative might depend on whether or not the business was privately owned by the person making that decision or a human resource manager making the decision within a publicly traded corporation. This discretion should also depend on how the position is advertised and described. Job openings that acknowledge a preference for families of present employers won't create misleading expectations among candidates. Nevertheless, as long as the other candidates have an equal chance of being in a similar position (they could have attended Southern Connecticut, or they could just as likely have applied for a position with someone from their alma mater), and as long as they were not misled in the application process, nothing obviously unfair was done to them.

On the other hand, those candidates from other colleges might claim that there is something unfair about hiring someone based on unadvertised personal preferences rather than job-relevant qualifications. They might claim that there was something deceptive about what amounts to a hidden agenda in the process, and they might claim that while they were given legal equal opportunity, they really weren't given a fair chance at the position. To overcome the hidden advantage of a Southern Connecticut graduate, other candidates would have had to have been more qualified than the person who received the job. Thus, in effect, they were being held to higher standards and therefore, despite the appearance of a formal equal opportunity, they were not in fact being treated equally.

If it truly were a matter of random chance that they were competing with a Southern Connecticut graduate for a position being controlled by a Southern Connecticut graduate, and if they just happened to choose another school that had an equal chance of having its own active alumni hiring, then perhaps no serious unfairness has occurred. That is, if they had an equal opportunity to obtain the deciding criteria, or if there were truly other and equal opportunities open for them, then the decision might not be unfair. Given these conditions, the decision between equally qualified candidates was, in effect, made on random grounds (like flipping a coin) and thus was not unfair.

But are women and people of color in the same position as the candidates from nonfavored colleges? It seems clear that they are not. Obviously, one doesn't choose one's race, gender, or ethnic background. In this sense, individuals do not deserve whatever benefits or burdens get attached to those characteristics by society. Like the candidate from Southern Connecticut, any advantage in the job market enjoyed by white males is undeserved. Also, given the systematic inequality across society, women and people of color are less likely to have similar opportunities of being favored by someone in a position of hiring authority.

As suggested by the Margaret Reynolds case, legal access alone may not be enough to give a woman or a person of color a really fair chance to succeed in a predominately white, or predominately male, workplace. This is not to say that decisions that favor white males are the result of conscious and intentional bias. But seemingly benign factors, such as personal preference (such as the preference for certain school graduates) or criteria such as "collegiality" or whether or not someone will "fit in," can result in a hidden bias in favor of what is already established as "normal." What is often referred to as the old boys' network is a good example of such a situation. Such seemingly neutral factors in getting jobs such as having connections with someone within the company, recommendations from family friends, and having attended the right schools can turn out to have a very conservative bias, reinforcing the status quo, which turns out to be disadvantageous to women and people of color.

Consider another case in which disparate treatment can result from seemingly normal and equal treatment. Some evidence suggests that women will tend to have lower salary expectations than men. (Given the facts of wage differentials, this is not surprising perhaps.) Imagine two equally qualified candidates, one man and one woman, have been offered an entry-level position with a major corporation. Put yourself in the position of the human resource manager who will be negotiating the starting salary. You are committed to hiring both candidates and, as normal in such cases, you have a salary range within which you can operate. As a manager, your strategy is to offer the lowest starting salary that you think will get them to accept the job offer (too low and you may not get them to accept, too high and you are not doing your job to control labor costs). As often happens, you separately ask the two candidates for their salary expectations and discover that the woman is willing to accept a lower salary than the man.

Even assuming that the manager is a person of goodwill with no bias against women, there are strong institutional incentives to offer the woman a lower salary. Assume further that, as time goes on, both employees receive evaluations as having done equally good work and each gets an equal percentage pay raise. The result is an ever-widening salary gap. Occasions when disparate treatment occurs from such implicit and subtle factors (rather than from intentional bias) are sometimes referred to as institutional discrimination. To the degree that such discrimination does occur, simple legal access and passive nondiscrimination on behalf of employers will not address unequal treatment in the workplace.

Perhaps the most obvious reason why simple legal access and passive nondiscrimination are thought inadequate is the fact that, four decades after the Civil Rights Act, there remains widespread unequal treatment throughout the economy. It is fair to say that equal opportunity alone has not solved many of the problems it was designed to address. Given the facts of inequality outlined above, there seem only two options available. Either society and business can continue to rely on equal opportunity and nondiscrimination, which implies that women and people of color must continue to wait for full equality, or society and business can take more active steps to address social and economic inequality.

What I will call affirmative action refers to any policy or action, aimed at securing a more equal workplace, that goes beyond simple legal access or passive nondiscrimination, but that does not alter the standards or qualifications for employment. Affirmative actions policies, therefore, do provide some positive (affirmative) benefit for a previously disadvantaged group, but do so in ways that do not change or lower qualifications.

Before developing this topic, it is important to reflect on the language used in these debates. The concepts of *equal opportunity, affirmative action, preferential treatment,* and *reverse discrimination* are used very ambiguously in social debates and discussions. Those who defend policies of preference tend to identify them simply as equal opportunity of affirmative action and thus benefit from the relatively benign meaning of those terms. Critics of preferential policies will tend to call them reverse discrimination and treat them as indistinguishable from affirmative action polices, thus equating anything other than equal opportunity as unethical discrimination. For the sake of clarity, at least, I think we can offer some definitions that will not prejudge the issue rhetorically.

Equal opportunity—the opposite of segregation—refers to the commitment to legal access regardless of gender, race, or ethnic background. This is what we have called *passive nondiscrimination*. Policies described as color blind or gender blind are classic examples of equal opportunity policies. There is universal support for equal opportunity within all major ethical traditions and contemporary political philosophies.

Affirmative action refers to any positive steps taken to alleviate unequal treatment that move beyond passive nondiscrimination. For clarity's sake, we will limit affirmative action policies to those that do not change the previously existing standards or qualifications. So, for example, a human resources office that recruits women and minority candidates, encourages them to apply, advertises in media that appeal to women or minorities, and provides support for women or people of color who are hired is engaged in affirmative action. Margaret Reynolds's employer, for example, did not provide locks on the women's bathroom or shower. Because the men's bathrooms and showers did not have locks, such a decision might be consistent with a gender-blind equal opportunity. Taking such steps to provide greater security for women than what is offered to men would have been a simple example of affirmative action. Perhaps the most common example of affirmative action is the widespread practice of recruiting qualified women and minority candidates. Since this is a positive step taken to benefit women and minority candidates that is not taken for white males, this goes beyond simple equal opportunity.

Note that, in one sense, such actions do put the white male at a relatively disadvantageous position compared to where he would have been had the employer not done it. The candidate pool is larger and therefore his chances of getting the job are lowered. But few would think that the white male has been harmed in an ethically relevant sense because he has not been denied anything to which he had a legitimate ethical claim. No one's rights are violated when an employer seeks to increase the applicant pool for its positions.

Other affirmative action policies might involve hiring a minority affairs officer, or a diversity coordinator whose job is to help manage an increasingly diverse workplace by troubleshooting problems, providing support for new hires, advising and mediating disputes, and generally trying to support and retain new employees. Again, these represent affirmative steps taken to support women and minority employees, but since it does not deny white male employees anything to which they have a right, such policies are generally uncontroversial. It is very common, in fact, to find employers describing themselves as an "equal opportunity/affirmative action" employer in job postings and advertisements. The frequency of such notices testifies to the overall social consensus surrounding affirmative action policies.

More controversial, both ethically and politically, are policies that grant preference to women or people of color by affecting the qualifications for a job in a way that benefits these previously disadvantaged groups. We will reserve the phrase preferential treatment for policies that go beyond affirmative action by seemingly changing the job standards in an effort to hire more women and people of color. Critics of such programs tend to call them *reverse discrimination,* and since it is in dispute if such is the case, we shall avoid that phrase in favor of the more neutral preferential treatment. Defenders of these policies tend to identify them as affirmative action, perhaps more specifically as strong affirmative action to distinguish them from the "weaker" version described above. We turn now to a closer examination of these more controversial policies.

11.3 PREFERENTIAL TREATMENT IN EMPLOYMENT

On the face of it, giving "preferences" to any job applicant appears to violate the ethical commitment to equal treatment. But as the Southern Connecticut graduate example showed, not every preference in hiring is unethical. Further, if the preference is given as a means for fulfilling other ethical responsibilities, it may turn out to be ethically praiseworthy if not required. Before considering the arguments for and against preference in hiring, let us first distinguish various forms that preferential hiring might take.

Perhaps the preferential policy closest to affirmative action would, in the case of otherwise equally qualified candidates, give preference to the previously disadvantaged candidate. This is similar to how we described the case of giving preference to a graduate from your college alma mater. In such a situation, rather than rely on some personal preference or random procedure, the decision between equally qualified candidates is made in a way that addresses the social inequality. Affirmative action policies seek to increase the pool of qualified candidates, and then assume that those women and people of color who are most qualified will be hired. This initial type of preferential treatment policy goes one step further and hires those women and people of color who are equally, but not necessarily more, qualified.

A second type of preferential policy would identify members of previously disadvantaged groups in the pool of qualified applicants and give them preference in the hiring decision, even if there is another candidate, typically a white male, who is more qualified. This situation treats membership in a disadvantaged group as itself a qualification for the job.

A third type of preferential policy would simply require that members of disadvantaged groups be hired with only minimal consideration given to qualifications. Effectively, this would be the policy of those who favor hiring quotas for women and people of color. A human resources department with a quota for hiring women, for example, would be committed to hiring a certain percentage regardless of the number or qualifications of male candidates.

The first of these policies seems to raise the least serious ethical challenges. As in the college graduate case, the candidate denied a job by the first policy might claim that he was implicitly being held to higher standards than the person given preference. Like that case, there is some legitimate concern with unfairness here. Note also that such policies are least likely to effectively address the unequal treatment that women and people of color receive in the workplace. Since these policies only go slightly further than affirmative action, and since affirmative action has not advanced equality significantly over the last four decades, these policies are not likely to alter social and economic inequality noticeably.

The second and third types of preferential policy are more likely to have noticeable effects on inequalities. A quota system, in fact, would have an immediate impact by mandating equality in hiring results. One would immediately bring about equality in employment if every employer were required to meet a quota for women and minority hiring that matched the percentage of women and minorities in the general population. But these types of policies also raise the most serious ethical questions. Both policies seem to violate the white male's right to equal treatment and equal opportunity. Two fundamental ethical questions must therefore be addressed in our analysis of preferential treatment: Do preferential policies in fact violate the rights of white males, and are there other ethical considerations that would override this violation if in fact it did occur?

In July 2003 the United States Supreme Court announced a decision that addressed many of these issues. Examining a situation involving admissions policies at universities, this case established precedents for affirmative action and preferential policies in business as well. The Court's decision seems to allow the first and second types of preferential policies. The decision held that race, ethnicity, or gender can be treated as a qualification and therefore can, when all other factors are equal, determine the outcome.

The case before the Court involved the University of Michigan Law School, which relied on an admissions policy that took into account the ability of each applicant to contribute to the school's social and intellectual life. As part of this criterion, the school considered the applicant's race, on the assumption that a diverse student body would contribute to the goals of the law school, and a critical mass of minority students was required to accomplish that goal. Thus, although scores from LSAT tests, undergraduate college grades, letters of recommendation, and other traditional factors were primarily used to grant admission, an applicant's race was also a factor. Two white females who were denied admission brought the law suit, arguing that admission of minority students with lower grades and test scores violated their rights to equal treatment.

The case attracted significant attention in the corporate sector as well as in higher education. General Motors Corporation filed an *Amicus Curiae* ("friend of the court") brief in support of the law school's admission policy. By doing this

GM went out of its way, and at great expense to itself, to be identified as a stakeholder and to argue publicly in support of affirmative action. In its brief, GM claimed that the need to insure a racially and ethnically diverse student body was a compelling reason to support affirmative action policies. GM claimed that "the future of American business and, in some measure, of the American economy depends on it."

GM claimed that in its own business experience "only a well educated, diverse workforce, comprising people who have learned to work productively and creatively with individuals from a multitude of races and ethnic, religious, and cultural backgrounds, can maintain America's competitiveness in the increasingly diverse and interconnected world economy." Prohibiting affirmative action "likely would reduce racial and ethnic diversity in the pool of employment candidates from which the nation's businesses' own efforts to obtain the manifold benefits of diversity in the managerial levels of their work forces."[7]

The Supreme Court ruled that diversity can be a compelling state interest in admissions to state educational institutions. Because private sector business faces a less strict standard than state institutions in this regard, this decision sets a precedent for hiring policies in the private sector as well. However, the Court offered a more ambiguous judgment on the particular admissions policies aimed at achieving this goal. By a 5–4 vote, the Court approved the Michigan Law School's policy that gave each individual candidate consideration and that would stray from race-neutral grounds only when evidence existed to show that diversity is not being produced. However, at the same time the Court also voted 5–4 against the admission policy of the undergraduate program at Michigan. That policy granted admission based on a point system in which membership in an underrepresented class received 20 out of a maximum 150 points. For comparison, academic factors counted up to 100 points, being a Michigan resident counted for 10 points, alumni children received 4 points, and notable personal achievement received 5 points. The court ruled that 20 points almost guaranteed admission and that this therefore violated the rights to equal treatment of nonminority candidates.

Thus in the Michigan case, the Supreme Court allows, but does not require, affirmative action programs that aim at creating a more diverse student body. The Court did not explicitly address the question of whether or not private employers could use similar programs. It would seem that if a private employer would connect workplace diversity to important social goals of the employer, the Court would allow these as well. GM's claims regarding the value of a diverse workforce would presumably be just this sort of connection.

A variety of philosophical arguments have been offered to support or refute the ethical legitimacy of preferential hiring. Some appeal to deontological concepts such as rights, duties, justice, and fairness. For example, some argue that preferential policies are unjust because they violate the rights of white males. Others argue that preferential policies are obligatory means for compensating people for harms they have suffered. Other arguments are more consequentialist and utilitarian, arguing that, on balance, preferential policies produce either beneficial or detrimental consequences. For example, some defend preferential hiring as a means of providing more role models for young women and people of color. Others reject these policies as likely to create more discrimination as a backlash against gender or racial preferences. For convenience sake, the following sections will examine only deontological arguments for or against. If any of these arguments are sound, if they violate rights or are required by compensatory justice, for example, then either the beneficial or detrimental consequences can legitimately be discounted.

There seem to be two general deontological arguments that the white male could make to support the claim that his rights have been violated. The first, what we shall call the merit argument, claims that by ignoring or overriding qualifications, preferential policies violate the white male's right to have hiring decisions based on merit. According to this view, the most qualified person has earned the right to the job and a denial of this is to violate a principle of merit. The second argument more simply claims that preferential treatment violates the white male's right to be treated with equal respect and given equal opportunity. From this perspective, preferential policies are a straightforward case of reverse discrimination.

Likewise there are two major deontological arguments in support of preferential policies. One claims that preference is due to women and people of color as a means for compensating them for past harms. Allowing past discrimination to go uncompensated is unfair and unjust. The second major argument claims that, properly understood, the commitment to equality and equal treatment requires that presently disadvantaged people be granted preference as a means for securing real equality in the workplace.

11.4 ARGUMENTS AGAINST PREFERENTIAL HIRING

The merit argument claims that something unjust occurs when hiring decisions are based on factors other than qualifications for a job. From this perspective, the most qualified candidate has earned or deserves the job and denial of this desert is unjust. Since preferential hiring policies violate this merit principle, they are unjust.

Four issues need to be examined in order to determine if this argument is sound. First, we need to decide if in fact such a merit principle seems a reasonable requirement of justice. Second, the qualifications used to establish merit must themselves be fair and open to all. Third, as a practical matter, we would need to have some reasonable way to determine and measure qualifications so that we have a way to decide who is most qualified. Finally, we need to consider if diverse ethnic or gender background might itself serve as a job qualification.

For the first issue, let us assume that a fair and objective determination of qualifications can be made so that we have a clear identification of "the most qualified" person for the job. Can we say that this person has earned the job, or deserves it in such a way that if they are denied the job, an injustice has been done? It would seem that, without some qualifications, we cannot. Does every candidate for every job have a legitimate expectation that the decisions will be based solely on qualifications? The answer to this might depend on where such an expectation arose. A position that is publicly advertised with stated qualifications would seem more bound to the merit principle than one not so advertised. As mentioned previously, we also might want to distinguish privately owned businesses and publicly traded corporations. A private business owner who hires a son or daughter, for example, seems justified in ignoring a more qualified candidate. But what about our example of hiring a candidate from one's alma mater? The merit principle would suggest that such a decision is unjust and we would therefore have to conclude that injustice is widespread throughout the economy.

To conclude that the most qualified candidate has a legitimate ethical claim upon a job is to treat jobs more as social goods that should be distributed on fairness grounds rather than as the private property of business owners that can be distributed as they see fit. Our discussions in chapters 5 and 6 might lead us to conclude that this is a reasonable conclusion, albeit one that more libertarian versions of corporate social responsibility would be loath to accept. More utilitarian versions of markets and economic responsibilities would tend to favor a merit principle, although other social consequences would also have to be calculated.

These considerations suggest that, from the perspective of the job applicant, qualifications are more backward-looking accomplishments (e.g., education and grades) by which the job has been earned. From the business perspective, qualifications are more forward-looking indicators of how likely it is that the candidate will do well in the job. The first option seems to give job applicants too much control over the conditions of employment. Absent an explicit promise that certain accomplishment will lead to jobs (did anyone ever promise you that the person with the highest grades will get the best jobs?), the prior expectations of job applicants cannot determine who should get jobs. The second option suggests that business has greater latitude in determining qualifications by determining what they hope to accomplish with the position. In general, we can conclude that the most qualified candidate has a *prima facie* legitimate claim to be hired only for positions for which the qualifications are publicly and previously advertised, assuming that the qualifications themselves are fair and objective.

But to what degree are the qualifications for positions fair and open to all? Here the answer is ambiguous. It is easy to generate quite a diverse list of factors that function as qualifications for a job. Depending on the particular job, they can range from very minimal qualifications (e.g., a temporary agricultural laborer) to quite extensive qualifications (e.g., a chief financial officer for a major corporation). A useful exercise would be to pick a variety of jobs and generate a list of relevant factors that would qualify one for the job. For each factor, ask whether every candidate has an equal and fair chance to attain the relevant qualification. How many of these qualifications have been "earned" and how many are a matter of luck or random chance? We have already discussed numerous characteristics that function as qualifications but that might be suspect. Graduating from the "right" school, having the right "connections," having a helpful letter of introduction or recommendation, being able to "fit in" with present workers and be a good colleague. These considerations suggest that we must be careful with the concept of qualifications.

This brings us to the third issue. Is there a fair and reasonably objective way to determine qualifications? If you generate a list of relevant factors, you are likely to find that they fall into several general categories. Some factors that we think of as qualifications, such as experience or seniority within a firm, are more a matter of past accomplishments that have "earned" the position. Many other factors are more forward-looking predictors of future success. Still others, such as being related to a present employee, may have little to do with the specific candidate or job and more to do with other goals and purposes of the business. In this case, a firm is using its jobs as a means to reward loyalty of present workers. This suggests that for any given job there will unlikely be any strict algorithmic method for determining the "most" qualified candidate.

Consider a case of hiring someone for a position in the information technology and computer department of a business. It turns out that men outnumber women in computer science majors and training programs by about 2 to 1. Thus, in general, there more likely will be more men than women applying for such jobs, and men will tend to have more experience working in computer technology. It also turns out to be the case that in this fast-changing field, a great deal of on-the-job training occurs over the course of an employee's career. What counts as qualifications in this case? From one perspective, past experience in classes and programming "qualifies" a person for the job. Thus, in one sense, men are generally "more qualified" for the job than women since there are more men with experience and training in this field. From the business perspective, however, past experience is less relevant than flexibility and the ability to learn quickly and easily. Suppose the business manager believes that people with prior training are more likely to be tied to a peculiar approach to information technology and therefore are less likely to be flexible and less willing to learn new approaches. Who is the most qualified person in such a case?

This leads us to the final issue: Might a job candidate's gender or ethnic background itself function as a qualification for a job? For example, I teach at a Catholic all-women's college. Might it be legitimate for this school to give hiring preference to Catholics and women? Is it legitimate for a medical practice to give preference to female gynecologists? Might a company seeking to attract new minority business give preference to hiring minority employees? More generally, given the beneficial opportunities that are provided by a diverse workforce, could a business claim that gender and ethnic diversity are themselves qualifications in that they make positive contributions to the workplace?

These are difficult questions to answer. In the first major U.S. Supreme Court case dealing with preferential treatment, *Bakke v. Regents of the University of California*, the Supreme Court ruled that race may be used as one among many qualifications for admission to universities. The court accepted the University of California claim that diversity among the student body contributes to the overall academic mission of the school. Yet, presumably, we wouldn't accept a claim made by the Atlantic City Convention Center that being a male makes one more qualified to work in the vulgar construction environment. Nor would we accept the claim that being a white male makes one more qualified to work in an all-male law firm because it makes it more likely that one would fit in and succeed in that setting.

A reasonable conclusion would seem to acknowledge the possibility that being a woman or a person of color can make positive workplace contributions, but that the burden of proof rests with those who make such claims. That is, the presumption should favor equal, gender-blind, and color-blind policies. Given the unequal economic status that whites and males already enjoy, any hiring decision that favors white and male candidates should receive especially close scrutiny. If employers have good reasons to prefer women or candidates of color (and the arguments examined in the following section claim that they do), then perhaps a job candidate's gender or ethnic background might count as a qualification for a job.

The second major argument against policies that grant preference to women or people of color appeals to the principle of equal treatment. As we said previously, discriminating between job candidates is not itself unjust. Discrimination is only unjust when it is made on the basis of criteria that are not job-relevant and that deny disfavored candidates equal consideration and respect. According to this argument, preferential treatment policies deny white males the equal respect and consideration that is their due. This argument is at the heart of the reverse discrimination characterization of preferential hiring policies.

Do policies that give preference to hiring women and people of color violate the right to equal treatment of white males who are competing for the same position? I think an honest answer to this question is that it depends. First, hiring policies that prefer women and people of color—that discriminate on the basis of gender, race, or ethnic background—are ethically different from similar policies that gave preference to whites and males. Past discrimination against women and people of color was part of a systematic denial of equal treatment that was also accompanied by both explicit and implicit attitudes of inferiority and antagonism. The *reason* why women and people of color were denied equal opportunity is that they were considered inferior and unworthy. Unequal treatment in the workplace was part of a systematic denigration of women and racial or ethnic minorities. Whatever else might be true of preferential policies favoring women and people of color, white males are not now, and will not soon be, victims of similar systematic mistreatment. It is unlikely within the foreseeable future than men will make only 76 cents for every dollar earned by a woman, or that white unemployment will be twice as high as black unemployment. The *reason* for denying equal opportunity to white men is ethically different from the reasons for past discrimination.

Nevertheless, individuals are denied an equal opportunity on the basis of factors—gender, race, ethnicity—that seem irrelevant and over which the job candidate has no control. *Prima facie* this is a violation of a right to equal treatment and ethically is highly suspect. However, two qualifications of this seem advisable. First, as mentioned previously, there may be some cases in which gender, race, or ethnic diversity might contribute to job performance and thus would be a job-relevant characteristic. In such a case, discrimination against a white male—on a par with discrimination against anyone lacking all of the relevant qualifications—would not be unjust. Second, the force of this objection might vary with the type of preferential policy in place. Hiring to fulfill a quota, in which white males are given no consideration at all, may be more unfair than programs that give preference only when all other qualifications are judged equal.

A final consideration of the argument from equality will provide a transition into the next section in which we examine arguments in support of preferential hiring. Some defenders of preferential policies acknowledge the fact that these policies do deny white males equal treatment. However, they usually make a distinction between *violating* someone's rights and *overriding* those rights for a more pressing ethical goal. Thus, even if a white male's right to equal consideration for a job were denied, the denial might not be ethically objectionable if it came about as the means for addressing other ethical obligations. The next section examines the ethical reasons supporting preferential policies and considers if such goals justifiably override equal opportunity for white males.

11.5 ARGUMENTS IN SUPPORT OF PREFERENTIAL HIRING

One of the major arguments to support preferential hiring claims that these policies are an ethically legitimate means for compensating people for the harms that they have suffered. Just as compensatory justice requires that consumers injured by a negligently designed product deserve to be compensated, a similar principle requires that individuals harmed by discriminatory hiring processes receive compensation for that harm. Failure to compensate continues a practice of undeserved disadvantages (for victims of discrimination) and undeserved advantages (of white males having to compete within an unfairly restricted job pool).

Three issues need to be resolved to adequately assess this argument. Compensatory justice requires that the compensation be proportionate to the harms done, that the party paying the compensation be responsible for the harm, and that the party receiving compensation be the party harmed. The ethical status of the compensatory argument depends on how these three requirements are met by preferential hiring policies.

At first glance, compensatory hiring practices do seem to compensate for harms done in a relatively straightforward and proportionate way. Women and people of color have been denied equal opportunity in the workplace (refer to the census data described in the opening sections of this chapter), so repaying that harm with preferential treatment in hiring and promotion seems reasonable. The "preference" in hiring is only an appearance that results from considering the issue only after the fact of the initial harm. Viewed for a longer range perspective, the preference only equalizes the situation and returns it to the point that it would have been had the original discrimination not occurred.

Consider, by analogy, a situation in which someone is defrauded of one thousand dollars. Compensatory justice would require that the person be repaid the one thousand dollars (other aspects of justice might require further payment as punishment, of course). If we only consider the situation at the point of (re-)payment, it has the appearance of a one-sided benefit to the injured party. But when we consider the situation within the context of the original fraud, compensation is a repayment that brings the scales of justice back into balance. Of course, preferential hiring does not compensate women and people of color for other harms they might have suffered (e.g., it doesn't compensate for slavery). It does, however, reasonably compensate for unjust harms done in the workplace.

The second condition on compensatory justice is more controversial. It appears, especially to young white males who are denied equal access, that the people paying the compensation are not responsible for causing the harms. It was not, after all, present generation young white males who discriminated against women and people of color in the workplace. Since they are not responsible for the harm, it would be unfair to cause them harm in return.

Defenders of the compensatory argument respond by denying that young white males are making the repayment. The compensation is being repaid either by the private business or by society, either or both of which do bear some of the ethical culpability for past discrimination. In making this compensatory payment, young white males are denied the competitive advantage they previously enjoyed and appear to be harmed. However, they are only being denied something which they did not deserve (i.e., an unfair competitive advantage).

Critics reply that young white males would lose this undeserved competitive advantage if society adopted equal opportunity policies. Actual preferences go further and deny them something more serious, namely, equal employment opportunities. In response to this, defenders point out that while young white males may not be responsible for past harms, they have benefited from those harms. Thus, while they are not culpable for causing the harms, neither can they expect to receive benefits derived from them. In response, critics charge that if anyone has derived undeserved benefits from past discrimination, it is older white males who are already employed and promoted. True compensatory justice would seem to require that these individuals repay the harms done.

The final aspect of compensatory justice requires that those who receive compensatory payment are the same party that has been injured. It makes no sense, for example, to pay compensation for injuries received in a traffic accident to an uninjured bystander. Critics charge that preferences granted as a means for compensation do not compensate injured parties. This challenge is made in three ways. First, critics charge that the true victims of discrimination are past generations of women and people of color. Since present policies of preference benefit present generations, they fail to compensate those truly injured by discrimination. Second, they claim that to the degree that discrimination continues to harm present generations, preferential hiring policies benefit the least deserving members of those groups. The individual most suffering from past and present discrimination is the poor, uneducated, disenfranchised woman or person of color. The individual most likely to receive preferential treatment in the job market is the person already well positioned to compete for jobs—the educated, trained, and intelligent individual. Finally, critics explain that gender, race, or ethnicity may be inappropriate criteria to use in deciding preferences. Economic and social class is, on this view, a more appropriate criterion. Consider the following. Who is most deserving of preferential hiring to compensate for past injustice, a young Hispanic woman from a wealthy and educated family, or a young white male who was raised by a single mother in a poor inner-city neighborhood? Granting preferences to every woman and person of color is empirically misguided (because not every individual has been adversely affected by discrimination) and ethically misguided (because it treats people as a member of a group rather than as a unique individual).

Defenders of the compensatory argument typically will concede that the harms to be compensated are those done to present generation job candidates, rather than the harms done to past generations. Again, as the census data indicate, discriminatory treatment continues to be widespread across the economy. They also point out that the fact that greater injury is suffered by others does not mean that the preferential hiring granted to some is unjust. It only means that other forms of compensatory justice (perhaps reparations?) are also needed. Finally, they argue that the only means available to compensate for overall discrimination (e.g., the fact that women overall earn only 76 cents for every dollar earned by men) is to grant individual women preferential consideration in hiring and promotions.

This speaks to a more general concern with the compensatory argument. Defenders are challenged to specify if compensation is owed to groups or to individuals. The continuing harms of discrimination seem to fall on individuals *because* they are members of a particular group (i.e., because she is a woman, an African American, and so forth). Not every individual member of the group has suffered an equal harm (e.g., many women have enjoyed lives of wealth, status, and authority). Critics charge that if compensation in the form of preferences is paid to every group member regardless of whether or not they have been harmed, undeserved benefits will be given out at the expense of the equal opportunity of others. If, on the other hand, criteria other than group membership are used to allocate compensatory preferences, then there will be some equally deserving white males who will be unfairly ignored by compensatory preferences.

The second argument offered in support of preferential treatment appeals to a proper understanding of equality to claim that, in fact, the principle of equal treatment requires, rather than prohibits, preferences. What, exactly, is required by the right to equal treatment? As we have seen in the previous discussion of discrimination, equality does not commit us to identical treatment. I have still given you equal treatment when I discriminate against you by hiring a more qualified candidate. The crucial point here seems to be that you deserve equal consideration and respect, but that relevant differences can justify different and nonidentical treatment. Equality, in its most basic sense, requires us to treat likes alike. So what does equal consideration and respect imply for hiring policies?

This equality argument would claim that real or fair equal opportunity demands that individuals not suffer the effects of undeserved and unfair disadvantages. Ignoring such disadvantages for the sake of some formal principle of equal or identical treatment is to treat unlikes alike. That is, it is to violate equality. This argument is sometimes made as an argument from analogy. Imagine we are committed to a fair and equal race between two runners. One, through no fault of her own, is required to carry extra weight throughout the race. Despite a formal commitment to remove such unfair burdens, the fact remains that the weight is still there at present. Suppose also that we have studied the effects of extra weight and we learn that this extra weight means, on average, that the runner who carries it will finish only 75 percent of the race when the competition has finished. On this argument, giving the unfairly burdened runner a 25 percent lead at the start of the race is only to respect fair equal opportunity.[8] Ignoring the unfair disadvantage and requiring both runners to start at the identical place and time is only to perpetuate inequalities.

So it would be in hiring and promotion policies. Through no fault of their own, women and people of color suffer from an unfair disadvantage in the workplace. Hiring and promotion policies that, in the name of gender and color-blind equality, ignore such disadvantages only continue the practice of unequal opportunity. Granting preferences at each stage of the process makes the competition for jobs and all those goods that come with employment truly fair and equal.

11.6 SEXUAL HARASSMENT IN THE WORKPLACE

The Civil Rights Act of 1964 addressed the most severe forms of unjust discrimination in the workplace. The law made it unlawful for any employer:

> (1) to fail or refuse to hire or to discharge any individual, or otherwise to discriminate against any individual with respect to compensation, terms, conditions or privileges of employment because of such individual's race, color, religion, sex, or national origin or (2) to limit, segregate or classify his employees or applicants for employment in any way which would deprive or tend to deprive any individual of employment opportunities or otherwise adversely affect his status as an employee because of such individual's race, color, religion, sex, or national origin.

In some ways this law offered a very explicit statement of the employment implications of the ethical principle of equality. Individuals ought not to be denied equal employment opportunities based on such irrelevant factors as race, color, religion, sex, or national origin. Within a few years of passage, a type of behavior identified as sexual harassment began to be understood, legally and philosophically, as a type of sexual discrimination. By 1980, the

Equal Employment Opportunity Commission (EEOC) had established guidelines that defined illegal sexual harassment:

> Unwelcome sexual advances, requests for sexual favors, and other verbal or
> physical conduct of a sexual nature constitute sexual harassment when (1)
> submission to such conduct is made either explicitly or implicitly a term or
> condition of an individual's employment, (2) submission or rejection of such
> conduct by an individual is used as a basis for employment decisions affecting
> such individual, or (3) such conduct has the purpose or effect of unreasonably
> interfering with an individual's work performance or creating an intimidating,
> hostile, or offensive work environment.

These EEOC guidelines codify the two types of sexual harassment that many
legal scholars and observers had previously described. *Quid pro quo* harassment
occurs when submission to sexual favors is made a condition for employment.
Hostile work environment occurs when the overall workplace environment is so
pervaded with sexual harassment and intimidation that it creates an unfair barrier for women in the workplace.

From the earliest cases, sexual harassment was understood as a form of
sexual discrimination. On the surface, this seems reasonable and appropriate.
If a woman is harassed in the workplace because she is a woman, and if this
harassment reaches the point where it interferes with her ability to work, sexual
harassment is a case of unjust sexual discrimination. Beneath the surface, however, lie a number of difficult ethical and conceptual issues.

Quid pro quo harassment can take the form of threats ("have sex with me
or I won't give you a promotion") or offers ("if you have sex with me I can help
your career"). Both are forms of coercion or extortion. The clearest examples
involve an individual exploiting his position of workplace authority to obtain
sexual favors from an unwilling co-worker. But threats and offers occur very
often throughout the workplace. Managers often direct co-workers through the
use of threats ("do as I say or you'll get fired") or offers ("get this job done
and I'll promise you a promotion"). As witnessed in many of the cases discussed in chapter 6, some of these can become so severe and coercive that they
deserve to be protected by ethical or legal rights. But why does sexual harassment deserve any closer scrutiny? What makes sexual harassment an instance
of sexual discrimination?

Courts wrestled with this question through the 1970s and 1980s. Quid pro
quo sexual harassment becomes sexual discrimination when, and if, the harassment occurs (in the words of one court) "because of sex." Thus, in an early
case, the court in *Barnes v. Train* concluded unequal and harmful treatment was
not unlawful discrimination because it was based on her refusal to engage in
a sexual relationship with a supervisor, rather than because of her sex.[9] This
female employee wasn't mistreated "because she was a woman," but because
she refused the sexual advances of her supervisor. The court found such behavior "inexcusable," but not the type of unlawful discrimination prohibited by the
Civil Rights Act.

This case points to an ambiguity in such a phrase as "because of sex." In
one sense, "sex" refers to *gender,* in another it refers to *sexuality.* The court in the

Barnes case apparently interpreted "because of sex" to mean gender discrimination, wherein a woman is discriminated against because she is a woman. Surely
sex discrimination should concern unequal treatment on the basis of gender;
women should not receive unequal treatment in the workplace simply because
they are women. But the *kind* of unequal treatment women receive in quid pro
quo is of a sexual nature. The court in *Barnes v. Train* failed to see that the two
senses are related and concluded that because this treatment involved sexuality,
it didn't involve gender discrimination. The EEOC likewise seems to confuse
the issue when it characterizes the unlawful behavior as being only of a "sexual
nature." On the other hand, as the Margaret Reynolds case shows, gender discrimination need not involve harassment that is overtly sexual.

As a result of this ambiguity, both courts and employers faced several difficult challenges. If not false, it is at least an open question that every case of
harassment of a sexual nature is unjust discrimination. Innocent sexual banter
or flirtation, while sometimes unwelcome or crude, need not be discriminatory. Or, in the case of a bisexual manager who harasses a male employee, we
could have a case of harassment that is sexual but not gender-based. Serious
coercion or extortion is unethical and sometimes illegal, but it also need not
be discriminatory. On the other hand, there can be serious barriers to women
in the workplace, as the Margaret Reynolds case indicates, that do not involve
sexuality. Discriminatory treatment that is based on animosity towards women
rather than sexual desire should be the paradigmatic case of unjust discrimination, yet it does not fall within the quid pro quo "sexual nature" model.

In part as a response to such shortcomings of the quid pro quo model, but
also to account for another range of discriminatory cases, scholars and courts
also recognize the hostile work environment model. A careful reading of the
EEOC guidelines suggests that hostile work environment is little more than a
generalized version of quid pro quo harassment.

> Unwelcome sexual advances, requests for sexual favors, and other verbal or
> physical conduct of *a sexual nature* constitute sexual harassment when . . . such
> conduct has the purpose or effect of unreasonably interfering with an individ-
> ual's work performance or creating an intimidating, hostile, or offensive work
> environment. [emphasis added].

Thus certain "verbal or physical conduct of a sexual nature" can, even if not
in the form of an overt sexual offer or threat, so interfere with a woman's ability to work that it rises to the level of workplace discrimination. Unfortunately,
this is not a very clear guideline, ethically or legally. It seems to allow both too
many and too few cases into the category of unjust sexual discrimination.

This guideline seems to allow too many cases because it can treat relatively
innocent and benign banter or flirtation as unjust and illegal discrimination. To
be illegal, the conduct need not have the "purpose" of interfering with a woman's ability to work, only the actual effect. But this means that the illegal behavior can be determined not according to some public and objective standard, but
according to the subjective perception of the alleged victim. Thus, a relatively
prudish older woman might be terribly offended by language or conduct that

younger men and women find benign. In such a case, the guidelines could be read as holding that as long as a woman finds a coworker's conduct offensive enough to interfere with her work, it is harassment whether or not it was intended to be so. Such a standard surely would be unfair to employers if they were held legally liable every time a female employee *felt* harassed.

To address this issue, courts have relied on a concept traditionally called the *reasonable man* standard. According to this standard, the guidelines' language of "reasonableness" must be emphasized so that the conduct must have the effect of *"unreasonably* interfering" with work. This standard prevents allowing the victim's perceptions to be the sole determination of harassment. On this standard, illegal harassment occurs only if a reasonable man would find the conduct severe enough to interfere with work. Of course, the legal community has moved away from the language of reasonable *man* in recent decades, instead preferring to use a reasonable person standard. But herein lies a challenge. Do men and women differ over what constitutes unreasonable conduct of a sexual nature? Might a reasonable *woman* standard differ from a reasonable man on these cases and, if so, which should be used to determine the seriousness of the harassment?

Further, as we discussed in chapter 10, the *reasonable person* standard itself is ambiguous. Sometimes it is interpreted as an *ideal* standard that establishes a norm or objective criterion which people would adopt if they were to be reasonable (i.e., if they had the relevant facts, considered the issues objectively and carefully, and so forth). At other times, it is interpreted as an *average* or normal person standard, with the recognition that in fact and on average, people do not always act in thoughtful, informed, and reasonable ways. Thus, we can envision four separate categories for interpreting this reasonable standard: the ideally reasonable person, the average reasonable person, the ideally reasonable women, and the average reasonable women. Which standard ought to be used when judging the severity of workplace harassment?

There are two good reasons for making the shift from *person* to *women*. First, as might be suggested by the fact that the "person" standard has until only recently been the "man" standard, we should be alert to the possibility that "person" is simply a disguised version of "man."[10] In a society, and especially in the workplace that remains very male oriented, the reasonable person standard can have the effect of simply maintaining the status quo. What, for example, would a reasonable person expect of the workplace at a construction site except the sort of rough and crude behavior experienced by Margaret Reynolds? If such behavior is normal, then a reasonable person who accepts a job there should not expect anything different.

This view was adopted by Judge Keith in a dissenting opinion in the case of *Rabidue v. Osceola Refining Co.* Judge Keith argued that "unless the outlook of the reasonable women is adopted, the defendant as well as the courts are permitted to sustain ingrained notions of reasonable behavior fashioned by the offenders, in this case, men." In a situation in which the norm is one of prejudice or discrimination, adopting a "normal" standard for judging behavior is unlikely to adequately address injustice.

Of course, this concern is more telling against the "average" interpretation of reasonableness than it is against the "ideal" interpretation. A second concern seems to count against both, however. A second reason for adopting this standard appeals to what seems to be true in fact. When it comes to sexuality and sexual relationships, women and men do seem to perceive sexual experiences differently. Just as racial or ethnic epithets are perceived differently by different races and ethnic groups, so, it seems, is verbal and physical conduct of a sexual nature. If this is so, then society can address discriminatory harassment only by acknowledging that disenfranchised groups can be harmed by conduct that the "average" person thinks is "normal." (Consider, for example, how the "reasonable man" standard as applied in the Deep South in 1950 might have perceived the offensiveness of referring to an African American man as "boy.") If "reasonable" is interpreted as the ideal rather than average model, then we could hold persons responsible for what they should have, although perhaps have not in fact, known about how their conduct would be interpreted by others.

But there are also reasons to hesitate about a shift to a reasonable women standard. First, it can reinforce the kind of sexual stereotyping and paternalism that we should be rejecting. Women can be perceived as more sensitive, fragile, and delicate than men and thus they deserve extra protection from the rough and tough workplace. This can also create a dilemma for women in the workplace. On one hand they are perceived as delicate creatures who need protection, and thus in some ways don't belong in tough masculine workplaces such as construction sites or corporate board rooms. On the other hand, as Margaret Reynolds discovered, if they do take a job and try to fit in, they are perceived as "one of the guys" who don't qualify for protection from harassment.

A second reason to hesitate about a shift to a reasonable woman standard is that it may create an unfair situation for men. If women and men do perceive sexual situations differently, and if the average man truly does not perceive harassing situations as harassment, then it would appear unfair to hold men responsible for conduct that is unintended and misunderstood. If the gap between different perspectives is unbridgeable—if men not only do not but cannot understand from a women's perspective—then it would surely be unfair to hold men and their employer responsible for conduct that they could not understand to be harassment. If, as seems more reasonable, the gap can be bridged, then it seems more reasonable to hold men and employers responsible. But, once again, this means that this criticism is more telling against the average or normal standard than it is against the ideal, normative standard of reasonableness. On the ideal standard, even if men do not fully understand that they conduct harassment, one would hold them responsible because, if they were thoughtful and reflective, they should have known.

These considerations suggest that at least one version of the reasonable person standard might be defensible. Interpreted as an ideal of how any person, male or female, should think and reason before acting, the reasonable person standard would seem adequate.

REFLECTIONS ON THE CHAPTER DISCUSSION CASE

The Civil Rights Act of 1964 bars workplace discrimination on the basis of "race, color, religion, sex, or national origin." One of the important lessons of the Margaret Reynolds case concerns the distinction between sex and gender. Workplace discrimination can deny women an equal opportunity not only because of her sexuality but also because of what is understood as the proper social roles for men and women. These social roles are products of historical, psychological, political, philosophical, and cultural factors that are not easily understood, changed, or overcome by individuals or businesses.

A shift to gender as a protected category would also raise questions about discrimination against gays and lesbians. There is a long history of workplace discrimination against gays and lesbians, and, it is fair to say, U.S. society seems not to have reached a clear consensus on this topic. Many states have laws prohibiting workplace discrimination against gays and lesbians, and many companies provide equal employment benefits to their gay and lesbian employees, including family health coverage for partners.

A helpful exercise for examining these issues is to imagine a parallel case to Margaret Reynolds that involves another protected category. Imagine a devout and pious religious employee who faced a workplace environment that was hostile to religion. One could easily imagine such a situation for Muslim workers in the United States since September 11, 2001. Imagine a worker who, like Margaret Reynolds, faced daily hostile and offensive comments aimed at her religion. Imagine, too, that the workplace atmosphere was "permeated" by an anti-Muslim sentiment, although not particularly targeted at this worker. Could such a situation rise to the level of unlawful workplace discrimination on the basis of religion? How would this case be like the Margaret Reynolds case? How might it be different? Would the situation change if the person were a devout evangelical Christian rather than a Muslim and was offended by obscene and blasphemous statements of her co-workers?

The opening discussion case raised the question: Are there some jobs that are inappropriate for women to hold? We might want to ask a similar question: Are there some jobs that are inappropriate for a gay or lesbian person to hold? For Muslims? For devout Christians?

REVIEW QUESTIONS

1. What reasons, other than intentional discrimination, might explain the inequality of wages, employment, and positions of status?
2. Distinguish among *equal opportunity, affirmative action,* and *preferential treatment.*
3. When might discrimination in the workplace be justified? Might discrimination on the basis of gender or race ever be justified?
4. How would you distinguish between *gender harassment* and *sexual harassment?*

5. Should the severity of workplace harassment be determined solely from the point of view of the victim? Is this fair to the accused harasser?
6. Is there a difference between a *reasonable woman* and a *reasonable man?*

ENDNOTES

[1] All labor figures are from "Report on the American Workforce 2001," published by the Bureau of Labor Statistics, U.S. Department of Labor.

[2] Population data is from "Statistical Abstract of the United States, 2000: The National Data Book" (Census Bureau, 2000).

[3] See "Women in Medicine," American Medical Association 1993, and Bureau of Labor Statistics, "Current Population Survey—1963–1993."

[4] Report on "the American Workforce 2001," published by the Bureau of Labor Statistics, U.S. Department of Labor; Equal Employment Opportunity Commission, "Job Patterns for Minorities and Women in Private Industry," 1991; Glass Ceiling Commission, "Good Business: Making Full Use of the Nation's Capital," March 1995.

[5] For the overall wage gap figures, see "The Wage Gap," National Committee on Pay Equity, and Bureau of Labor Statistics, "Current Population Survey," 2000. The Stanford study can be found in Bette Woody and Carol Weiss, "Barriers to Workplace Advancement," Report to the Department of Labor, Glass Ceiling Commission, December 20, 1993. The AMA data is from American Medical Association, "Women in Medicine in America," 1991.

[6] See "Futurework: Trends and Challenges for Work in the Twenty-first Century," U.S. Department of Labor, 1999.

[7] "*Amicus Curiae* Brief in Support of the University of Michigan," General Motors Corporation, July 17, 2000, in *Grutter/Gratz v. The Regents of University of Michigan.*

[8] Something very close to this, in fact, occurs in automotive drag racing. Based on past performances and ability, one car is given a head start in the race. Thus, to make the race fair, an initial disadvantage is offset by granting one an extra advantage. What appears to be an unfair head start is, in actuality, a requirement of equal opportunity.

[9] In one of the very first cases of sexual harassment, *Barnes v. Train* (1974), the courts ruled against the woman because the workplace mistreatment was not "based on the plaintiff's sex" but on the fact that she refused to engage in a sexual relationship with her supervisor. While such behavior was inexcusable, it was not sexual discrimination.

[10] A version of this argument can be found in Debra A. DeBruin, "Identifying Sexual Harassment: The Reasonable Women Standard," in *Violence Against Women: Philosophical Perspectives*, edited by Stanley French, Wanda Teays, and Laura Purdy (Ithaca, NY: Cornell University Press, 1998), pp. 107–122.

12 CHAPTER

International Business and Globalization

After reading this chapter, you will be able to:

- Describe the range of ethical issues arising in a global business context;
- Analyze the issue of ethical relativism in a global setting;
- Describe the application of human rights to international business;

- Explain the ethical issues involved in globalization;
- Describe business's role and ethical responsibilities in an increasingly global economy;
- Analyze the ethical arguments concerning international sweatshops.

DISCUSSION CASE: Sweatshops

The list of companies that have been accused of profiting from sweatshop labor includes some of the best-known corporations in the global retail apparel industry: Nike, Wal-Mart, the Gap, Levi Strauss, Target, Donna Karan, New Balance, Guess?, Disney, Reebok, Adidas, Phillips-Van Heusen, Liz Claiborne, and Ralph Lauren. While other industries, including electronics, toys, and agriculture, have been linked to sweatshop conditions, the apparel industry has been at the center of many recent global controversies.

Public attention was focused on the sweatshop issue in 1995 with two events, one within the United States and the other in Honduras. In August 1995 police raided apartments in the Los Angeles suburb of El Monte and arrested the operators of a sweatshop in which more than 70 illegal Thai immigrants were held in virtual slavery. The workers were paid substantially less than the minimum wage and were kept in an apartment complex under armed guards and behind barbedwire fences. Their status as illegal immigrants was used as a threat to prevent them from escaping or demanding better wages and work conditions. The workers were sewing name-brand clothing that sold at such well-known retailers as Mervyn's and Montgomery Ward. That same year it was disclosed that young teen-aged girls, working 14-hour days in Honduran sweatshops, were producing clothing under the Kathie Lee Gifford label and sold at Wal-Mart.

These incidents received wide media coverage and launched global anti-sweatshop campaigns that continue to this day. Since that time news reports have described similar working conditions throughout the world: women and children held in near slavery conditions, working for pennies a day, subjected to physical and sexual abuse. The fashionable clothing marketed to consumers by some of the world's leading multinational corporations was being produced in some of the world's most notorious working conditions.

The apparel industry is very labor-intensive and seems particularly susceptible to a reliance on sweatshops. The industry has evolved a subcontracting system in which retailers such as Wal-Mart contract with the "name brand" suppliers like Kathie Lee Gifford. These suppliers typically do not manufacture the products themselves. Instead, they may design and market a product and subcontract production to outside and independent vendors. Very often, these vendors also subcontract the manufacturing to other companies who hire workers to assemble the product. Long practice within the industry has been to pay workers on the basis of each piece produced rather than a firm hourly wage.

Given a certain production target each day, as is often the case, workers are encouraged to put in long hours, and take-home work without overtime pay is common. The buying power of such large retailers as Wal-Mart and K-Mart or the market dominance of a Nike or Levi Strauss creates strong price pressure further down the supply chain as suppliers compete for vendor contracts, who compete for manufacturer contracts, who compete for business with large retailers.

Sweatshops have had a long history in the textile and apparel industries. In the United States, much textile manufacturing originated in New England mill towns, and clothing was manufactured in the garment districts of large cities such as New York. As workers became unionized and fought for higher wages and improved working conditions during the twentieth century, much of this industry moved from the industrial north to the nonunionized southern states. Now as global markets have opened up only a few decades after that migration, production continues to follow the lowest labor costs to countries such as Korea, China, Viet Nam, El Salvador, Honduras, and Indonesia.

Prior to the mid-1990s, name brand retailers could deny responsibility for the sweatshop conditions by claiming that they were not responsible for the actions of other companies far down their supply chain. The workers, after all, were not employed by Wal-Mart or Nike or K-Mart or Kathie Lee Gifford. As a result of public attention and consumer boycotts, few companies offer this defense today.

But there are various definitions of what constitutes a sweatshop. The United States Department of Labor, for example, defines a sweatshop as any factory that violates more than one of many central labor laws involving such things as overtime pay, minimum wage, safety and health regulations, and child labor laws. The United States General Accounting Office suggests that a sweatshop is any business that regularly violates both health or safety regulations and wage or child labor laws.

One problem with these definitions is that they connect sweatshops with the law. As the El Monte case demonstrates, sweatshops can continue to exist within the United States, but do so only illegally. Because sweatshops are defined in terms of violations of the law, any business that is a sweatshop is operating illegally. There are obvious benefits in this definition because of the clear consensus that business ought to obey the law. No business can object to government crackdowns on illegal operations. Problems arise, however, when similar working conditions exist in countries where there are few legal regulations of working conditions. This problem is particularly troubling because many of the countries involved are ruled by oppressive and corrupt governments. In these overseas sweatshops both local governments and some multinational corporations have defended, or at least denied liability for, sweatshop conditions.

Few companies have been more closely associated with the sweatshop issue than Nike, the world's largest athletic shoe and apparel maker. Nike was founded in 1964 by Phil Knight, who served as president and CEO until retiring at the end of 2004. Nike began as an importer and marketer of Japanese sports shoes, eventually designing their own brand of shoes that continued to be manufactured in Japan. When production and labor costs rose dramatically in the 1970s with an improving Japanese economy, Nike opened the first manufacturing plant of its own in the United States. Faced with increasing production and labor costs in the United States, Nike closed that plant a decade later. Today all of Nike's products are manufactured by subcontractors. In 1982 86 percent of Nike's shoes were manufactured in Korea and Taiwan; by 2001, over 90 percent of Nike's shoes were manufactured in China, Indonesia, Viet Nam, and Thailand. In 2004 Nike's supply chain employed more than 660,000 workers, predominantly women between the ages of 19 and 25, in more than 900 factories in more than 50 countries. Clearly, Nike has followed the historical pattern of the apparel industry and moved its production to follow the lowest labor costs. Due in part to its ability to keep production costs low, Nike's annual revenue averaged more than $10 billion between 2001 and 2003.

From the beginning, Nike's business model emphasized design and marketing rather than production. Nike's Web site describes it the following way: "Our business model in 1964 is essentially the same as our model today: We grow by investing our money in design, development, marketing and sales and then contract with other companies to manufacture our products." In response to some of the first criticisms raised against Nike's reliance on sweatshop workers, Nike vice president for Asia argued that Nike did not "know the first thing about manufacturing. We are marketers and designers."

Criticisms during the 1990s alleged that workers at manufacturing plants for Nike products were paid only pennies a day, subjected to harsh and appalling working conditions, prevented from organizing unions, and were physically and sexually harassed and abused. Most of the workers were young women, and many were children. Few of the countries in which Nike's products are manufactured had any labor laws protecting workers, and China and Viet Nam even had laws prohibiting independent trade unions. Local suppliers and Nike could truthfully claim that production conformed to local labor laws and Nike could deny responsibility for the local conditions workers faced in foreign lands.

Nike's corporate stance on these issues changed on May 12, 1998, when CEO Phil Knight delivered a speech to the National Press Club. Knight acknowledged that "the Nike product has become synonymous with slave wages, forced overtime, and arbitrary abuse." Knight committed Nike to improving the working conditions of all the people working in factories that produce Nike shoes and apparel. He announced a range of initiatives including establishing age limits to prevent child labor, increasing minimum wages, improving working conditions and prohibiting abuse, funding educational programs for workers, increasing microloan programs to support local economies, establishing public–private partnerships to encourage industrywide adoption of such standards, and establishing a monitoring program to report on the status and progress of such initiatives. Nike also engaged in a public relations campaign to defend itself against the criticisms.

By 1992 Nike had developed a Code of Conduct that requires all manufacturers in its supply chain to meet high standards of employment practices concerning wages, health and safety, child and forced labor, and environmental protection. Just a year earlier Levi Strauss had introduced the first ever such Code of Conduct in the textile and apparel industry. Before Nike enters into a contract with a foreign supplier, it requires that company, at its own expense, to have an internal audit conducted by an independent firm to determine the present level of compliance with these standards. Nike will enter into a contract with suppliers only if they are found to be in "substantial compliance" with the Code of Conduct. Ongoing supply chain relationships are subject to quarterly (for shoe suppliers) and biannual (for apparel and equipment suppliers) assessments to insure that this compliance is maintained.

While some critics believe that Nike has not gone far enough, clear progress has been made in improving the working conditions in several countries. Nike has been able to leverage its purchasing power in Viet Nam, where it accounts for virtually 100 percent of shoe exports, to significantly improve the working conditions in Vietnamese shoe factories. Wages for factory workers in Indonesia have risen 300 percent. Nike has established after-hours education programs for its workers in Viet Nam, Korea, Indonesia, Taiwan, China, and Thailand. Nike has also supported microlending programs, small low-interest loans especially targeted for poor women, in many communities surrounding its manufacturing plants.

Similarly, companies such as Levi Strauss, Motorola, Mattel, and Adidas have pursued aggressive programs to improve the lives, working conditions, and wages of workers in foreign factories that supply their products. Nevertheless, problems remain. Few companies have the purchasing power of these giant corporations that can be leveraged to convince local suppliers to change. Smaller firms simply do not have the clout to sway local suppliers. Also, some critics claim that resources spent on improving working conditions will be money not spent on wages for other workers, meaning that improved working conditions for some will result in fewer jobs for others.[1]

DISCUSSION QUESTIONS

1. What responsibilities do United States multinational corporations have for the working conditions in foreign plants? Do they have a strong obligation for improving working conditions, or are programs like Nike's more a matter of beneficence or charity?
2. Should the wages and working conditions of workers in less developed countries be left to the demands of the local labor market? Is it preferable for workers in foreign countries to have low-paid jobs and difficult working conditions, or no jobs?
3. Is compliance with local laws sufficient for corporate social responsibility?
4. What responsibilities, if any, do consumers have for products manufactured under sweatshop conditions?
5. Have companies such as Nike done enough to improve the lives of workers in foreign lands?

12.1 INTRODUCTION

Significant ethical issues are raised by an examination of the proper role of business in international settings. Beginning in the 1970s, a number of dramatic and well-publicized cases highlight these ethical issues. In the early 1970s, American-based International Telephone and Telegraph (ITT) was accused of widespread efforts to undermine the democratically elected Marxist government of Salvador Allende in Chile. In the 1970s Nestle faced worldwide boycotts over questionable marketing practices with infant formula in less-developed parts of the world. Throughout the 1970s and 1980s, Western, and particularly American, businesses came under pressure to withdraw from South Africa in protest of its racist apartheid government. In 1977 the United States federal government passed the Foreign Corrupt Practices Act which made it illegal for American multinational corporations to offer or pay bribes in order to do business in foreign countries. Widespread corruption and bribery scandals were the immediate cause of this law, and the continuation of such practices later led to the fall of governments in Japan and Italy. The 1990s witnessed extensive protests against international sweatshops and child labor used in the manufacture of clothing sold at K-Mart and shoes made by Nike. In 2001 worldwide protests against pharmaceutical companies changed the way AIDS drugs were sold and marketed in Africa. In the late 1990s and early 2000s, massive and violent street demonstrations in Seattle, Washington, D.C., Genoa, and Prague protested the economic polices of the World Bank, International Monetary Fund, and the G8 nations that, according to protesters, protect the profits of multinational corporations while exploiting the workers and environment of less developed countries.

This chapter will examine a range of ethical issues that confront international business. For simplicity's sake, these issues will be organized into two groups. Some ethical issues arise on the level of businesses and business managers who must decide on the applicability of their own ethical standards in foreign lands. These issues raise questions of ethical relativism and cross-cultural ethical values. A second set of ethical concerns involve the range of topics grouped under the term globalization. These more macrolevel concerns arise not just for individual businesses and managers, but quite literally for all citizens of every country in the world.

12.2 ETHICAL RELATIVISM AND CROSS-CULTURAL VALUES

Perhaps the most common issue faced by managers doing business in foreign lands stems from the realization that different cultures often have quite different value systems. When these value systems conflict, business must choose whether to obey the values of their "home" country, or conform to local values and practices. On issues as diverse as equality for women and ethnic or racial minorities, health and safety standards for workers, the acceptability of bribes and kickbacks, and environmental standards, some international standards

vary significantly from mainstream Western ethics. Given that significant financial benefits can result from following local ethical practices, it is tempting for
business to take the step from cultural relativism to ethical relativism. Because
cultures do differ in values, there is no reason for thinking that any one value
system is more legitimate than others. Thus, when in foreign lands one should
conform to local customs, even if that means accepting gender or racial apartheid, child labor, or bribery. The challenge of ethical relativism, it seems, arises
in very practical terms in international business.

But the challenge of ethical relativism, as described in chapter 2, does not
withstand careful analysis. The *fact* that cultures have different values (cultural
relativism) does not by itself imply that there are no objective standards for
deciding between conflicting values (ethical relativism). Several of the more
general objections to ethical relativism reviewed in chapter 2 can be brought to
bear on this issue.

First, we should be careful not to conclude too quickly that diverse cultures
do in fact hold diverse ethical values. Consider the case of doing business in
Indonesia during the regime of President Suharto. Until Suharto's regime was
overthrown in 1998, in order to do business in Indonesia one had to form a partnership with a local Indonesian business. Most of the Indonesian businesses that
formed such partnerships were owned or controlled by Suharto's close associates or family members. Bribes, kickbacks, and extortion were commonplace.
But now the question arises: In what sense were these practices "accepted"
in Indonesia? They were widespread and commonly known, but to call them
accepted is surely wrong. Indonesians who were not a part of the powerful elite
accepted this corruption only in the sense that dissent and opposition could be
met with violent and sometimes deadly reactions. The anticorruption reforms
that followed Suharto's overthrow are evidence that Indonesians share many
values with the West.

There are many other cases in which apparent diversity of values disappears upon closer examination. Corruption scandals that toppled governments
in Japan and Italy demonstrate that acceptance of bribery and kickbacks in
those countries was not as widespread as some would have thought. The fact
that political and economic elites tolerate corrupt and unethical conduct, especially in cases where they are the very ones to benefit from that conduct, is
hardly evidence to support the claim that what we take as unethical is ethically
acceptable in other countries.

A second issue calls attention to a distinction between ethical principles
and the application of those principles. Given different circumstances, conduct
that might be condemned or excused in one context might be excused or condemned in another. But this fact would no more count in favor of ethical relativism than the fact that we make distinctions between premeditated murder
and negligent homicide. Consider the different circumstances between a local
business owner operating in a corrupt regime, and an American-based multinational corporation doing business in the same place.

Suppose that, in order to do business with the state-controlled phone company, one had to pay bribes in order to have phones installed. Failure to pay

would result in long delays in getting phone service. For a local business, failure to pay bribes could literally mean the end of the business. Local firms typically have few other choices and thus it might make sense to excuse the payment of bribes in this circumstance. But note, excusing unethical behavior is not the same as justifying it. We do not say that bribery or extortion is justified or acceptable; only that, in such circumstances, payment of a bribe is understand- able and perhaps excusable. However, given that multinational corporations are not at all in similar circumstances, excusing their similar behavior is much less reasonable. Multinationals have many more choices available to them than are available to local businesses, not the least of which is to use their economic bargaining power to change the unethical practices.

A similar case might be made for low wages and unhealthy working condi- tions in sweatshops. There is an important difference between a local farmer, who may only be making subsistence wages himself, paying low wages to farm workers, and a multinational agricultural business paying similar wages. The fact that local populations tolerate working conditions that the industrialized world would judge unacceptable does not mean that such conditions are ethi- cally justified when doing business in that foreign land.

A third issue of international ethics concerns the virtue of integrity. Even in those cases in which a local culture holds values different from one's own, a per- son's own integrity would require that one's personal values not be abandoned.[2] Integrity is that virtue that maintains a person's own personal identity and char- acter. One's integrity preserves the very core of one's self. To abandon one's values in the face of disagreement or diversity is to undermine one's integrity.

Consider doing business in a culture that treats women as second-class citi- zens. Imagine that as a condition for doing business in this country, you will not be able to hire women for anything other than the most menial jobs, your own female employees will not be able to participate in negotiations with local firms, and they will not even be allowed out in public without a male escort and without their heads and faces covered. In these circumstances, one's options seem to be either to abandon one's own principles or stick to one's principles and walk away from business in this culture. A person's integrity surely counts against abandoning one's principles in such circumstances.

This is not to say that one should never compromise or tolerate diverse val- ues. But integrity does suggest that such questions are not to be decided solely on consequentialist, utilitarian, and economic grounds. Sometimes ethics asks that we act on principle. Such principles go a long way towards establishing who we are as a person.

A final observation calls attention to the fact that in many discussions of cultural relativism in international business, the values that are taken as unethi- cal are those of the "other" culture. The assumption seems to be that the ethics of the industrialized Western democracies are a given, and the only question remaining is whether or not those values should be compromised when they conflict with the values of a local culture. Let us now reverse this assumption and consider how local cultures might be expected to compromise when they conflict with the values brought in by multinational corporations.

We will examine this issue in more depth in a later section of this chapter. For now, consider only how this is related to the question of value relativism. How often does the question of abandoning one's own values to conform to local practices arise in situations where a multinational would be expected to abandon market and profit principles in order to conform? One could think of a number of circumstances where this could happen. The Mondragon region in Spain, as well as many other areas in Europe, have long traditions of worker ownership, worker co-ops, and workplace democracy. Many regions in Asia have traditions of lifelong employment. Many agricultural regions throughout the world have long practiced sustainable farming and forestry techniques. Many cultures throughout the world deeply value communitarian social welfare structures. Yet one seldom sees multinational corporations abandoning the profit motive so that they might better fit in with local cultural practices.

This suggests, at a minimum, a healthy dose of skepticism when one hears of a multinational business seeking to justify or excuse otherwise unethical conduct by appeal to local values and customs. When such appeals are advanced only when they contribute to the bottom line, we can take them for what they are: yet another instance where ethical responsibilities restrict self-interest. This fact alone is good reason not to abandon ethics in the face of a disagreement of values.

12.3 CROSS-CULTURAL VALUES AND INTERNATIONAL RIGHTS

If ethical relativism is not a coherent philosophical position, the question remains: Are there any values which can reasonably be applied across cultures? Nonrelativists answer yes. Philosopher Tom Donaldson, for example, describes both "minimalist" and "maximalist" answers to this question. We'll follow Donaldson's framework to investigate this issue.[3]

A minimalist approach, according to Donaldson, holds that business is free to pursue its economic interests as long as certain minimal moral rights are not violated in the process. Reminiscent of the moral minimum approach to corporate social responsibility described in chapter 3, the minimalist acknowledges only "negative duties" to cause no harm. Once these minimal conditions are met, corporations fulfill their ethical responsibilities by meeting their economic goals of producing goods, services, jobs, and profits for their consumers, employees, and shareholders. A maximalist approach believes that, given the influence, power, and resources that multinational corporations enjoy, they have a responsibility to provide positive benefits and support for the communities in which they operate. Both views agree that there are ethical standards that can be applied cross-culturally. Minimalists conclude that those values are minimal negative duties; maximalists argue for more extensive positive responsibilities.

In his own writings, Donaldson seems to provide a good example of the minimalist position. Donaldson argues that fundamental human rights can provide the basis for a list of international responsibilities for business. Citing such international documents as the United Nations's *Universal Declaration of Human Rights,* Donaldson suggests that there exists, in fact, a wide consensus on a variety of cross-cultural and universal values. Such universal rights provide the framework for the ethical responsibilities of international business. Among the rights that Donaldson describes are the following:

1. The right to freedom of physical movement.
2. The right to ownership of property.
3. The right to freedom from torture.
4. The right to a fair trial.
5. The right to nondiscriminatory treatment.
6. The right to physical security.
7. The right to freedom of speech and association.
8. The right to minimal education.
9. The right to political participation.
10. The right to subsistence.

Donaldson admits that there is room for dispute concerning the details of application or the range of such rights. Nevertheless, such rights would create duties for others—individuals, corporations, and governments—to respect those rights. A useful exercise would be to review some of the international ethical controversies mentioned at the start of this chapter and consider if recognizing such rights would help in the analysis of these problems. Would multinational businesses have acted differently if they were committed to such international human rights?

One of the major challenges to this minimalist approach is that it does not seem to explain why the responsibilities correlated with these rights should fall on the shoulders of multinational business. Many of these duties would seem more appropriately to belong to government and not private business. Further, given the fact that these rights are, in theory if not always in practice, already acknowledged cross-culturally, the minimalist approach does not seem to provide much help when cultural values conflict. International business ethics should provide guidance for business managers when their home country values come into conflict with those of the host country. For these and other reasons, some observers defend a more extensive and specific list of international business responsibilities.

Philosopher Richard DeGeorge has offered 10 such ethical guidelines that he believes can be applied cross-culturally.[4] According to DeGeorge's analysis, multinational corporations should

1. Do no intentional direct harm.
2. Produce more good than harm for the host country.
3. Contribute by their activity to the host country's development.
4. Respect the human rights of their employees.
5. Respect the local culture and work with and not against it.
6. Pay their fair share of taxes.
7. Cooperate with the local government in developing and enforcing just background institutions.

8. Recognize that majority control of a firm carries with it the ethical responsibility for the actions and failures of the firm.
9. Make sure that hazardous plants are safe and run safely.
10. When transferring hazardous technology to less-developed countries, be responsible for redesigning such technology so that it can be safely administered in the host country.

There seems to be two general ways to interpret and justify such a list of positive responsibilities to host countries. One could argue that such a list amounts simply to the application of more general minimalist duties. Thus, for example, the duty that stems from the right to physical security entails a responsibility for businesses that deal with hazardous materials or technology to take steps to ensure that people are protected from such hazards. From this perspective, the minimalist approach outlines general rights and responsibilities. The maximalist strategy is to specify in more detail the implications that these rights and duties have for businesses operating internationally. This approach seems to work for several more specific international responsibilities for business.

A second interpretation of these maximalist responsibilities understands them being derived from an implicit social contract between multinational businesses and the host countries. Such responsibilities arise as part of the implied contract. As in any contract, parties enter into them only if they can reasonably expect to benefit from the agreement. A multinational business enters a foreign country only if it believes that it will reap a net benefit from such a move and host countries are justified in similar expectations. Multinationals are allowed to operate in a country if and only if that host country can expect more good than harm from the arrangement. Once again, this interpretation seems to make sense of many of the maximalists' list of responsibilities.

12.4 GLOBALIZATION AND INTERNATIONAL BUSINESS

We shift now to a more macrolevel analysis of business's international responsibilities. Ethical issues surrounding globalization have taken center stage in discussions of international relations within just the last few years. What are these ethical issues and what role and responsibilities do multinational businesses have in these issues?

Even as recently as a decade ago, a discussion about globalization and international trade would have been unusual in a text on business ethics. International relations have traditionally been understood solely in terms of relations between states. These issues were more at home in political science and macroeconomics than in business management. Such an approach is no longer adequate in the opening years of the twenty-first century. Decisions made within businesses can have as great an influence on international affairs as those made within government. In fact, many of the criticisms of globalization cite this as one of the central problems of worldwide economic integration. In the view of some critics, decisions made by unelected corporate officials motivated by profit and self-interest have replaced the decisions made by political officials who, in democratic lands at least, should be motivated by the best interests of their citizens.

What is globalization? As street demonstrations from Seattle to Prague to Genoa have shown, this term carries powerful political and ethical connotations. In the most straightforward sense, *globalization* refers to a process of international economic integration. While international trade and cooperation have existed for as long as there have been nations, this process of international economic integration has become increasingly more common and has accelerated in just the last decade or two. International trade agreements such as the General Agreement on Tariffs and Trade (GATT) and the North American Free Trade Agreement (NAFTA) opened borders to freer trade. The continuing integration within the European Union, including the adoption of a single currency (the Euro) beginning in 2002, has turned Europe into what is essentially a single economy. International loans from the World Bank have supported major development projects throughout the world. Monetary policies established by the IMF have made it increasingly easy for capital to flow between countries. Perhaps less slowly, immigration policies are making the international flow of people and labor easier. Recent economic recessions in Japan and the United States, along with currency devaluations in Mexico and Argentina, testify how interdependent the world's economies truly are.

The ethical case for free trade and international economic cooperation has been widely accepted by governments, industry, and economists. The major argument in favor is a more generalized version of the market argument we examined in chapters 2 and 3. The pursuit of profit within social and economic arrangements that secure free and open competition will allocate resources to their most highly valued uses and distribute those resources in ways that will produce the greatest good for the greatest number of people. Globalization is the process of extending this free and open competition beyond national borders. International competition for labor, jobs, goods and services, natural resources, and capital will, over time, increase the overall well-being of everyone.

Two corollaries of this view are worth mentioning. First, the economic growth and development that flows from more free and open trade is thought to be the most effective way to improve the well-being of the most impoverished people in the world. International economic integration, according to defenders of globalization, is an essential step in worldwide economic growth and only this growth can adequately address worldwide poverty and deprivation. Second, defenders of this process argue that economic integration is a major impediment to conflict. The more countries cooperate economically, the less likely they will be to fight militarily. Thus, globalization is seen as a major step in reducing both poverty and the possibility of war.[5]

As we saw in the opening discussion case for this chapter, a variety of public interest groups so disagree with these arguments that they have been willing to take to the streets to demonstrate against globalization. Advocates from organized labor, environmentalism, human rights groups, and pro-democracy organizations reject the ethical legitimacy of continued international economic integration. To help analyze these arguments, we can organize them into three categories: globalization harms rather than benefits the poor; globalization encourages a "race to the bottom" of environmental, health, safety, and workplace regulation; globalization undermines rather than supports equal rights and self-determination.

12.5 GLOBALIZATION AND THE POOR

The general outlines of the market-based argument are familiar by now. A free, competitive, and open international market will lead to a more efficient and optimal distribution of economic goods and services. More people will get more of what they most desire and hence more people will be better off than otherwise. We have seen versions of this argument at several points throughout this text. Is it a sound argument?

Part of the difficulty analyzing this argument stems from the realization that it involves both empirical and conceptual/ethical questions. The empirical question asks whether or not living standards, particularly among the poor and less-developed nations, improve under conditions of international economic integration. The conceptual and ethical questions examine the sense in which people are thought to be "better off" with economic growth.

The answer to the empirical question is ambiguous. Consider what the theory predicts will happen in the labor market. Jobs should be exported to countries with less expensive labor. In industrialized countries, this will most likely mean that jobs of the lowest-paid workers will be lost (it would be unlikely that poor countries will have a surplus of skilled and professional workers looking for employment). In turn, this will tend to depress wages in the industrialized countries, again particularly among the lowest-paid workers. The theory suggests that, as consumers, these unemployed or underemployed workers will also benefit by lower costs for the goods and services imported from the country to which jobs have been exported. It would also predict that, over time, the increased economic growth of the poorer country will increase the demand for industrial goods and thus create jobs back in the industrialized countries. In the meantime, the displaced workers would surely be suffering.

As we have seen before, the market argument is utilitarian. The recipient of the beneficial consequences is the collective "greatest number of people" and this can disregard the harms done to individuals in the process. Even if the theoretical "overall" benefits will occur, many *actual* individuals and their families may be harmed in the process. Empirically, no doubt there are specific identifiable workers who have been hurt by the movement of jobs out of their home country. The theoretical question is whether or not other workers have been benefited by new jobs created elsewhere in the country. The ethical question is whether such benefits outweigh the harms.

It would be worthwhile at this point to reflect back upon the story of Malden Mills and Aaron Feuerstein. Exporting production and labor would have been the recommended action under free market theory. Many workers and communities in the region around Malden Mills had already been hurt by the export of textile jobs to other regions and other countries. Feuerstein chose not to do that because no amount of theoretical benefits could outweigh the actual obligations he owed to his long-term loyal employees and the community in which they all lived.

What about workers in the poorer country? Are they not benefited from the jobs created by free trade? The answer to this question is at least as much conceptual and ethical as it is empirical. Defenders of free trade argue that workers in poor countries are benefited because new jobs make them better off than they were previously. Critics charge that many exported jobs pay bare subsistence wages and create sweatshop conditions. This challenge raises conceptual questions on both individual and national levels.

Market theory tells us that these newly employed workers are better off because they have chosen to take these jobs, and individuals would not choose to do something if the harms are greater than the benefits. In a relative sense, this seems true. People whose options are utter poverty or long hours at subsistence wages under sweatshop conditions will likely choose to work. They are better off than they otherwise would have been. Critics respond that the choice to work under such conditions is little more than extortion and exploitation by business. "Your money or your life" is also a choice, but it is not one international business should aim to emulate. Someone who chooses to surrender her money to an armed robber is also relatively better off than she otherwise would have been, but this fact does not justify the actions of the robber.

What, then, are the ethical responsibilities of international business to their employees in both host countries? In general, we should conclude that they are similar to their responsibilities to employees in their home countries. Obviously, if wages and benefits are very similar in the host countries, there will be no incentive to export jobs in the first place. This not only defeats the purpose of free trade, it also means that workers in host countries receive no benefits at all. On the other hand, we need to recognize that human beings are not merely "factors of production" whose value is determined by labor markets. Wages and benefits somewhere between those paid in the home country and the minimal wages that will get people to work in the host country seem required. One proposal would be to pay wages at rates comparable, given the differing standards of living between home and host countries, to those paid in the home country. For example, independent economic indicators could be used to determine how minimum wage in the home country would translate into the economy of the host country. Fair wages would be determined comparably, rather than being left to labor markets alone to determine. If it takes two people earning minimum wages to support a family of four just above the poverty level in the United States, a minimum wage in the host country would be similarly determined. Such an approach would benefit the business by still attaining employees at lower costs but would pay those employees a fair wage.

In practice, many international businesses do not directly employ workers in the host countries. Many rely on local firms and independent contractors to supply workers. There are many reasons for doing this, some less ethical than others. Hiring individuals to sew clothing or shoes and paying them as "independent contractors" on a per-item basis may be little more than a smokescreen for avoiding responsibility for fair wages and benefits. As independent contractors they supposedly are responsible for the terms and conditions of their own employment. A reasonable principle is that if an international business wants to benefit from less costly local labor, they should take full and direct responsibility for how those workers are treated. The most obvious means for doing this is to hire these people directly.

Returning to the more general question, overall are local national economies in host countries harmed or benefited from the arrival of international business? Further, given the overwhelming poverty in many areas of the world, what alternative to freer trade and further economic integration is likely to be as effective in alleviating poverty and economic deprivation?

I do not think that specific and unqualified answers to these questions are possible or reasonable. The type of sustainable economic development as described in chapter 10's treatment of environmental responsibilities would be one place to start. Generally, market economies have the potential to create tremendous economic growth in poor countries; ethical responsibilities require that businesses which seek to benefit from that growth not do so by exploiting the human and natural resources of host countries.

But there is a major conceptual issue in the background to these questions. Even if it is true that freer trade and greater international economic integration can improve the economic well-being of *any* nation that adopts free trade and free market policies, it does not follow that these policies can improve the economic well-being of *all* countries. Logicians call the inference from what is true of parts to the conclusion that it is also true of the whole the fallacy of composition. It does not follow that if any poor country can improve its economy through exports, all poor countries can improve economically through exports. For example, if every poor country tried to import low-paying jobs and increase exports, the demand and price of both would be driven down. Policies that may benefit individual nations when adopted individually might have the effect of harming all nations that adopt them simultaneously.

12.6 "RACE TO THE BOTTOM"

A second set of ethical challenges to global economic activity is that freer trade and economic integration creates incentives to weaken or do away with environmental, labor, health, and safety regulations. Such regulations constitute "barriers to trade" and, given competition for economic growth, countries will have strong incentives to be the first to offer multinational corporations less regulation and restrictions. There will, in terms used often by critics, be a "race to the bottom" of regulation.

There are numerous examples of local environmental or labor standards being successfully challenged by competing countries as violations of free trade agreements such as GATT or NAFTA.[6] Consider, for example, the type of workplace health and safety regulations required by OSHA and examined in chapter 6. Such regulations raise the costs of doing business in the United States. This creates an incentive for a business to move jobs out of the United States to countries without such protections. Traditionally, a country in that situation might impose tariffs on imports from the other country as a means to offset higher local prices that result from regulations. Under free trade agreements enforced by the WTO, such tariffs are no longer permissible. The result is that the home country faces competitive pressures to eliminate health and safety regulations so that its industries can compete more effectively under the rules of free trade. Local regulations are a barrier to the ability of local businesses to compete in world trade. (Considerations such as these and the export of jobs as described in the previous section go a long way to explain why labor groups have been at the forefront of globalization protests.)

Consider also how environmental regulations create barriers to free trade. In 1992 the United States Congress passed a law that prohibited the sale of tuna that was not harvested by methods that protected dolphins. Dolphin-free tuna nets are an available, but costly, option. In 1999 the WTO prohibited the United States from enforcing this law because it created an unfair barrier to tuna imports. Another example involves the European Union's attempt to ban imports of hormone-treated beef. The United States appealed this decision to the WTO claiming it was an unfair barrier to free trade. The EU now faces the threat of trade sanctions if they refuse to abandon this ban.

The point is that regulation on economic activity for any ethical reason—to protect the environment, workers, family farms, domestic industries, or consumers—is likely to be judged a barrier to free trade. Given worldwide commitment to free trade agreements, there is a strong incentive to abandon these regulations. It is easy to understand how this would and should occur in theory. Well-publicized cases provide examples of how it occurs in fact. But the empirical evidence is less clear.[7] The trend over recent decades, admittedly the time at which globalization was just beginning to grow, is that environmental, workplace, and consumer regulation has been increasing rather than decreasing in both wealthy and poor countries.[8] A fair assessment seems to be that there are and will remain strong incentives working against local environmental, labor, and consumer regulation. Free trade agreement and the WTO will be the major engines for such deregulation. Nevertheless, strong worldwide political consensus on such values mitigates against them.

Perhaps the only responsible position to take on international free trade is one that parallels the familiar ethical restrictions placed upon markets within national borders. No economic market exists in a vacuum. Even in theory, markets require extensive background conditions (free and open competition, perfect information, legally enforceable and tradable property rights, rationally self-interested agents, and so forth) to function. In practice, of course, actual markets never attain the perfection described by theory. In recognition of this, nongovernmental agencies such as the World Bank, the WTO, and the IMF, and the governments that support them, must acknowledge that "free" markets and "free" trade must be regulated by considerations of fairness and social justice.

Environmental, labor, consumer, and other ethical regulations set the moral minimum from which market competition can then commence. Widespread international agreement on such regulation is possible, as the Montreal Protocol (limiting manufacture of CFCs to protect the atmospheric ozone layer) and the Kyoto Agreement (yet to be endorsed by the United States) have shown. Such regulations are not barriers to fair and open competition if they are accepted and endorsed universally. They establish the context in which markets can then be left to operate.

One ethical responsibility for business that follows from this echoes the environmental responsibility for business defended by Norman Bowie and discussed in chapter 10. If social regulation is to set the minimally acceptable conditions on market transactions, and if these regulations are accurately to reflect the ethical consensus of citizens, business ought to refrain from trying to influence such policies. Society, through its political institutions, should set the ethical and legal guidelines under which business is allowed to operate. This can occur internationally as well as nationally.

12.7 DEMOCRACY, CULTURAL INTEGRITY, AND HUMAN RIGHTS

Another set of criticisms is that increased global economic integration threatens deeply held noneconomic values. Critics charge that institutions such as the WTO, World Bank, and IMF are themselves undemocratic bureaucracies that threaten the political values of democracy and self-determination in both poor and industrialized countries. A corollary to this is often that private multinational corporations are replacing legitimate governments as the true international decision makers. Further, global market capitalism fueled by multinational corporations seeking to expand worldwide markets for their products creates a cultural homogenization that threatens local cultures and traditions.

Critics of the World Bank and the IMF often raise the challenge that their economic policies undermine self-determination in poorer countries seeking international financial help. Financial aid to poor countries is always made contingent upon those countries accepting a range of policies intended to promote economic stability and growth. Thomas Friedman, *New York Times* columnist and author of the best-selling book *The Lexus and the Olive Tree*, calls such policies the Golden Straitjacket.[9] According to Friedman, the policies required by the World Bank and the IMF are the very same policies that a country could choose to follow for itself if it "opts for prosperity." These policies include

> Making the private sector the primary engine of economic growth, ... shrinking the size of state bureaucracy, maintaining as close to a balanced budget as possible..., eliminating and lowering tariffs on imported goods, removing restrictions on foreign investment, getting rid of quotas and domestic monopolies, increasing exports, privatizing state-owned industries and utilities, ... making their currency convertible, [and] opening ... industries, stock, and bond markets to direct foreign ownership and investment.[10]

As a result, according to Friedman, two things happen:

> Your economy grows and your politics shrinks. . . . The Golden Straitjacket
> narrows the political and economic choices of those in power to relatively tight
> parameters. That is why it is increasingly difficult these days to find any real
> differences between ruling and opposition parties in those countries that have
> put on the Golden Straitjacket. Once your country puts on the Golden Strait-
> jacket, its political choices get reduced to Pepsi or Coke—to slight nuances of
> policy . . . , but never any major deviation from the core golden rules.[11]

Critics of the WTO often reach similar conclusions about the effects of international trade agreements on both poor and industrialized countries. As we saw
on the "race to the bottom" arguments, trade agreements seem to trump local
decision making and thereby undermine self-determination and democracy.

Critics also charge that such institutions as the World Bank, the IMF, and
the WTO are themselves undemocratic and secretive. Decisions are made by
unelected bureaucrats, typically economists, bankers, and former corporate
officials, whose discussions are not public and who answer to no public constituency. Because these decisions often have the effect of benefiting multinational
businesses, the inference is that multinational corporations are controlling these
decisions behind the scenes.

To the charge that Golden Straitjacket policies undermine local control and
self-determination, defenders such as Friedman argue that these policies are
simply rational requirements if a nation chooses prosperity over poverty. A
nation cannot expect foreign investment, from either the World Bank or private
investors, if it does not have in place policies that make this investment financially sound. On this view, financial and economic norms are analogous to scientific laws discovered by social scientists. *If* one chooses economic growth and
prosperity, *then* past practice advises that one should do such and such. The
Golden Straitjacket is no more than an outline of these "such and such" rules.
Poor nations are free to reject this straitjacket, but if they do so they cannot reasonably expect that economic prosperity will follow from alternative policies.

Defenders offer two responses to the charge that globalization undermines democracy within the industrialized countries. First, as suggested in the
analysis of the "race to the bottom" argument, the empirical evidence for this
claim is at least ambiguous. Political regulation for such goals as environmental, worker, and consumer protection seems to increase rather than decrease in
industrialized countries. If global institutions such as the World Bank, the IMF,
and the WTO were undermining national sovereignty, one would expect less
rather than greater regulation among industrialized countries.

As a case in point, defenders remind us that authoritarian governments
historically have been the most likely ones to shun free market policies. Only
by keeping their borders closed did countries like East Germany and the Soviet
Union in recent history, and North Korea presently, prevent their citizens from
choosing with their feet which political and economic arrangements they prefer. History suggests that democratic countries tend to favor freer markets and
freer trade.

The second response points out that all of these institutions (e.g., the World Bank, the IMF, the WTO) were created by, and owe their continued existence to, decisions by individual nations. These institutions exist and have authority only because nations have agreed to have them exist with authority. Given that politically legitimate governments have freely entered into the agreements that created and control these international financial institutions, it would seem more reasonable to accuse critics of supporting undemocratic policies. Defenders can argue that what environmental, labor, and other special interest groups could not win in their own national elections, they now seek to achieve through street protests and demonstrations. If there is a crisis of illegitimacy in these debates, it rests with the protestors and not with duly constituted institutions.

A final challenge is the claim that organizations such as the World Bank and WTO are secretive and undemocratic. Decisions are typically made behind closed doors, with the public learning about them only when policies are announced. Not only has no one elected the people serving in these positions, but the decisions are made without input from any outsiders who might disagree. A right to participate in these decisions for anyone affected by them (as was argued by John McCall in chapter 6) seems a fundamental requirement of fairness.

Defenders of these institutions argue that the proper model for these institutions is not a legislature but a judiciary. Most decisions involve conflict resolution, negotiation, and compromise. The WTO acts more like an arbitrator helping parties resolve disagreements than a legislator creating public policy. In such a setting, privacy and secrecy often make it easier to reach mutually acceptable decisions. Carrying on these discussions in the public spotlight can make it more difficult for countries and their leaders to float ideas, consider compromises, and change their mind.

There are, no doubt, many legitimate concerns over the influence and policies of such international institutions as the World Bank, the IMF, and the WTO. The Golden Straightjacket as described by Thomas Friedman does impose sometimes undesired restrictions on sovereign nations. These policies do seem to favor, at least in the short term, those people and businesses within a host country already in relatively secure financial positions and those outsiders who already possess most of the world's wealth. Market capitalism and consumerism seem to be the social structures being imposed by these groups and such changes surely threaten the integrity of many indigenous cultures and practices.

On the other hand, worldwide poverty, all of the social ills that follow from it, and a growing worldwide population upsurge call out for a strong response. When we recognize that much of the wealth of the industrialized world relies on the resources and markets in the developing world, we must acknowledge that taking steps to relieve poverty is more than an act of charity. It is the ethical duty of the citizens and businesses of the industrialized world to act.

If we believe that the industrialized and wealthy nations have a duty to help alleviate the effects of poverty, we must consider the appropriate means for doing this. Direct grants of financial aid and food and goods, while no doubt necessary in many cases in the short term, do not seem to be effective long-term strategies. Not the least of concerns is that such donations can undercut the local agricultural and industrial base by flooding the local market with competition.

The policies of the World Bank, the IMF, and the WTO assume that economic growth is the path to stable self-sufficiency. Their policies support foreign investment in local economies, free trade, and stable currencies. The implicit claim is that these policies are most likely to benefit local economies. The challenge to those who recognize the problems with this approach is to specify either an alternative that is as likely to benefit local societies, or to identify restrictions and regulations that prevent or minimize the harms created by the influx of foreign business and capital. For business involved in these events, these latter responsibilities seem most essential.

REFLECTIONS ON THE CHAPTER DISCUSSION CASE

Debates surrounding international sweatshops provide an opportunity to review many of the ethical issues introduced in this book. Questions concerning the nature and limits of corporate social responsibility, the adequacy of market mechanisms for addressing social problems, the rights of workers, the responsibilities of marketers for their supply chain, consumer responsibility for business, equal opportunity, sexual harassment, and even environmental protection all arise within the context of sweatshops and outsourced manufacturing facilities.

Market-based economic arguments concerning sweatshops should be familiar by now. Pursuing lowest labor and production costs, the so-called race to the bottom in labor and capital markets, insures that companies contribute to the well-being of both workers and less developed countries most efficiently. These low costs allow less developed countries to attract foreign investment which, in turn, raises the local standard of living. On the other hand, voluntarily paying wages higher than necessary to secure an adequate labor supply would result in fewer overall people being employed. Further, allowing individuals to decide for themselves whether or not to accept such jobs is the best means for respecting worker autonomy and avoiding unwarranted paternalism.

But there are overwhelming objections to this approach. First, the market approach tends to understand the issue of sweatshops exclusively as a wage issue. Wages are certainly a part of the problem and there are, of course, interesting economic arguments on both sides of that debate. But low wages are only one aspect of the ethical wrong of sweatshops, and the economic approach can encourage us to disregard other pressing ethical issues. Perhaps market-based solutions might have a role to play with regulating workplace health and safety, but few would suggest that there is, or should be, a market for such things as physical and sexual abuse and child labor. When such conditions exist, there is an ethical obligation for governments and companies to prevent them even if this results in inefficient overall economic distribution.

But even on its own grounds the economic argument has serious faults. First, the conditions necessary for an efficient exchange—free and open competition, adequate information, the availability of other options, free and voluntary choice—are seldom met in the case of international sweatshops. Further, it is also not the case that multinational companies face only two options: either increase wages for some or maintain employment levels. When one considers that Nike agreed to pay Tiger Woods $100 million over five years, LeBron James $90 million over seven years, Kobe Bryant $40 million over five years, and the Manchester United soccer team $500 million for endorsements, we can see that the business model might have alternatives available. Finally, increased costs for wages may not be a zero-sum game. Some economic evidence suggests that increased wages can result in increased productivity, as healthier and happier workers pay added dividends to business.[12]

This case also demonstrates that business ethics is not always and exclusively about ethical wrong-doing. Nike, Adidas, Levi Strauss, and Motorola are just some companies that have raised the bar for ethical business practice. High standards can be achieved—perhaps more easily for some successful companies than others, but perhaps some are more successful because of their higher standards.

REVIEW QUESTIONS

1. Can you identify any ethical values that legitimately can be applied cross-culturally?
2. How far should the principle "When in Rome, do as the Romans do" extend in international business?
3. Are there any conditions under which an American business could employ child labor in a developing country?
4. What are three arguments against the trend towards globalization? How would defenders of globalization respond to each?
5. What is meant by "the race to the bottom"?
6. Is it possible for the rest of the world to live a consumer lifestyle on a par with the United States? Would this be a good thing? Who should decide this?

ENDNOTES

[1]This case was developed from a variety of sources, including Nike's Web site (www.nike.com/nikebiz), which contains many documents and corporate statements concerning this issue. Phil Knight's 1998 statement is also available on that site: (www.nike.com/nikebiz/news/pressrelease.jhtml?year=2001& month=05&letter=g). An informative and substantive book on sweatshops that includes conceptual analyses, case studies, and descriptions of best practices is *Rising above Sweatshops*, edited by Laura Hartman, Denis Arnold, and

Richard Wokutch (Westport, CT: Praeger Publishing, 2003). Other sources included *Monitoring Sweatshops: Workers, Consumers, and the Global Apparel Industry* by Jill Esbenshade (Philadelphia: Temple University Press, 2004) and *Making Sweatshops: The Globalization of the US Apparel Industry* by E.I. Rosen (Berkeley: University of California Press, 2002).

[2]This point has been made by Richard DeGeorge among others. See his "International Business Ethics," in *A Companion to Business Ethics,* edited by Robert Frederick (Oxford: Blackwell Publishers, 1999), pp. 233–242, and his *Competing with Integrity in International Business* (New York: Oxford University Press, 1993). I owe much of my thinking on these issues to DeGeorge's work.

[3]Donaldson introduces this distinction most clearly in "International Business Ethics" in *Encyclopedic Dictionary of Business Ethics,* edited by Patricia Werhane and R. Edward Freeman (Oxford: Blackwell Publishers, 1997), pp. 346–348. But, see also his "Rights in the Global Market" in *Business Ethics: The State of the Art,* edited by R. Edward Freeman (New York: Oxford University Press, 1991), pp. 139–162, and *The Ethics of International Business* (New York: Oxford University Press, 1989).

[4]Richard DeGeorge, *Competing with Integrity in International Business* (New York: Oxford University Press, 1993).

[5]A very helpful review of many of the debates on globalization from a source generally sympathetic to it can be found in "Globalization and Its Critics," a special section of *The Economist,* September 29, 2001.

[6]See, for example, Hilary French, "GATT: Menace or Ally?" in *Worldwatch,* vol. 6, no. 5 (September/October 1993); David Korten, *When Corporations Rule the World* (West Hartford, CT: Kumarian Press, 1995); Frederick Frommer, "Caught in the Net," *Animal Watch* (Fall 1999); and *Public Citizen News,* vol. 19, no. 4 (January/February 1999).

[7]For a review of the research on this and other questions concerning justice and free trade from an economic scholar who has an admitted sympathy to the poor and for environmental protection, see Daniel Finn, *Just Trading* (Peabody, MA: Abington Press, 1996). Finn seems to conclude that regulated and well-monitored international trade remains an effective means for alleviating poverty and protecting the environment.

[8]See both "Globalization and Its Critics," op. cit., and *Just Trade,* ibid., for some evidence of this.

[9]Thomas Friedman, *The Lexus and the Olive Tree* (New York: Farrar, Straus, and Giroux, 1999).

[10]Ibid., pp. 86–87.

[11]Ibid., pp. 87–88.

[12]A defense of a market-based response to sweatshops can be found in Ian Maitland, "The Great Non-Debate over International Sweatshops," in Joseph DesJardins and John McCall, eds., *Contemporary Issues in Business Ethics* (Belmont, CA.: Wadsworth Publishing, 5th edition, 2005). Responses to Maitland can be found in Denis Arnold and Norman Bowie, "Sweatshops and Respects for Persons," *Business Ethics Quarterly* 13 (2), 221–42; and Denis Arnold and Laura Hartman, "Moral Imagination and the Future of Sweatshops," *Business and Society Review* 108 (4), 425–61. My own thinking on this issue has been greatly influenced by these authors.

Index

I1